T0392048

Unholy Sensations

Unholy Sensations

*A Story of Sex, Scandal, and California's
First Cult Scare*

JOSHUA PADDISON

OXFORD
UNIVERSITY PRESS

OXFORD
UNIVERSITY PRESS

Oxford University Press is a department of the University of Oxford.
It furthers the University's objective of excellence in research, scholarship,
and education by publishing worldwide. Oxford is a registered trade mark of
Oxford University Press in the UK and certain other countries.

Published in the United States of America by Oxford University Press
198 Madison Avenue, New York, NY 10016, United States of America.

© Oxford University Press 2025

Library of Congress Cataloging-in-Publication Data
Names: Paddison, Joshua, 1974– author.
Title: Unholy sensations : a story of sex, scandal, and California's first cult scare / Joshua Paddison.
Description: New York, NY, United States of America : Oxford University Press, [2025] |
Includes bibliographical references and index.
Identifiers: LCCN 2024051282 (print) | LCCN 2024051283 (ebook) |
ISBN 9780197775325 (hb) | ISBN 9780197775356 | ISBN 9780197775349 (epub)
Subjects: LCSH: Brotherhood of the New Life. | Harris, Thomas Lake, 1823–1906.
Classification: LCC BX9998 .P33 2025 (print) | LCC BX9998 (ebook) |
DDC 289.9—dc23/eng/20250110
LC record available at https://lccn.loc.gov/2024051282
LC ebook record available at https://lccn.loc.gov/2024051283

DOI: 10.1093/oso/9780197775325.001.0001

Printed by Marquis Book Printing, Canada

MIX
Paper | Supporting
responsible forestry
FSC® C103567

Contents

Introduction

Secrets of the Sonoma Eden Unveiled

On February 16, 1892, Alzire Chevaillier took the stage in San Francisco's Irving Hall to deliver what she promised would be "startling revelations." Chevaillier was an accomplished public speaker, reformer, magazine editor, and mental healer from Boston and, more recently, New York City. For two months, she had been at the center of a media firestorm of her own making. In the pages of the *San Francisco Chronicle*, *New York World*, and other publications, Chevaillier waged a campaign to destroy a spiritualist colony called Fountaingrove, located near Santa Rosa in northern California. She insisted that Fountaingrove's leader, the reclusive mystic, poet, and wine-grower Thomas Lake Harris, operated a secret "den of sensuality" that ensnared and corrupted unsuspecting women. Harris's occult powers were so great, she said, that he could hypnotize followers into turning over their life savings and spending their days toiling in physical labor while he dined on "oysters and champagne." He commanded men and women to bathe together and practice "free love," becoming his depraved "spiritual harem." Chevaillier said she could prove these accusations with a stack of affidavits and letters from ex-members of Fountaingrove, as well as by what she had seen with her own eyes—for she had spent the previous summer at the colony as Harris's guest.

Up to this point, Chevaillier had made all of her allegations in print; this night was the first time she spoke in public about Fountaingrove. An advertisement for the talk promised "Secrets of the Sonoma Eden Unveiled," and about two hundred San Franciscans paid the fifty cents admission price to hear her talk. Despite the moral indignation that fueled her campaign, she may have felt nervous when taking the stage. Women giving public lecturers were no longer rare by 1892, but a woman speaking on the explosive topic of sex—especially "unnatural" sex outside of Christian marriage—ran the risk of having her reputation tainted no matter how pure her motives. Yet Chevaillier delivered her lecture, a two-and-half-hour denunciation of Harris, whom she declared the "greatest black magician today."

Unholy Sensations. Joshua Paddison, Oxford University Press. © Oxford University Press 2025.
DOI: 10.1093/oso/9780197775325.001.0001

TO-NIGHT! TUESDAY

FEBRUARY 16th,

IRVING HALL

SECRETS OF THE SONOMA EDEN UNVEILED

STARTLING REVELATIONS BY

MISS A. A. CHEVAILLIER

T. L. HARRIS and his SPIRITUAL HAREM

The Governor appealed to to uproot this den of sensuality, and the Masons called upon to expel Harris from their order.

Miss Chevaillier is a brilliant woman and a fascinating speaker.   She has lectured to crowded audiences in Cooper Union Hall, New York and elsewhere.

Her analysis and description of Thomas Lake Harris the strange Primate, His Career, his Mysticism, his Religion and the gross immorality of his teachings will afford an intellectual treat and a story of intense interest.

Admission 50 Cents

Francis, Valentine & Co., Printers and Engravers, 517 Clay St.

Flyer for Alzire Chevaillier's talk, February 16, 1892. CMI box 22, Harris-Oliphant Papers, courtesy Rare Book and Manuscript Library, Columbia University Library.

The major San Francisco papers—the *Chronicle, Examiner, Call*, and *Bulletin*—all printed accounts of her lecture, as did the *Los Angeles Times* and other out-of-town papers, extending and expanding the ongoing scandal with a new cycle of press coverage.[1] As an experienced writer and editor, Chevaillier knew she was feeding the media outlets what they wanted, a juicy story that helped sell newspapers to urban readers. She did so for her own ends, to better apply public pressure on Harris to send him either to prison or at least into exile from Fountaingrove. But as a woman, she walked a risky path. Could she control the story? Or would Harris—a wealthy and powerfully connected man—seize control? How much of what Chevaillier said about Harris was actually true? And did it matter to the newspaper editors and wider public disturbed and fascinated by her accusations?

This book tells the story of Alzire Chevaillier, Thomas Lake Harris, and the scandal that threatened to wreck them both. From December 1891 to June 1892, the peak months of the scandal, newspapers from San Francisco to London published thousands of articles about Chevaillier, Harris, and the goings on at Fountaingrove. Though largely forgotten today, the scandal's twists and turns captivated readers with a volatile mix of sex, religion, and racial exoticism. Out of the scandal came a new kind of public menace—what newspapers called the "cult." Before Charles Manson, before Jim Jones, and before Father Yod, there was Thomas Lake Harris, California's first notorious "cult leader."

The English word "cult" is derived from the Latin *cultus* and originally referred simply to religious veneration. For most of the nineteenth century, those in the English-speaking world used "cult" infrequently as a neutral synonym for sect, denomination, or religion.[2] Also, certain prominent writers such as William Shakespeare, Charles Dickens, and Robert Browning were said to have cults—devoted followings.[3] It was not until the early 1890s that the word "cult" began to take on new, derogatory meanings. A designation always applied by outsiders, cults were groups or movements that violated religious, cultural, and sexual norms to such an extent that they seemed dangerous to the dominant moral order. Cults were said to be led by cult leaders, figures whose seeming authoritarian control over their followers troubled American values of independence, free will, and self-control. Cult leaders, by definition, deserved surveillance and suppression by authorities, the media, and the public.

"There is, to be clear, no such thing as a cult," writes religion scholar Richard Kent Evans. "It is a way of policing the boundaries of the category of religion, of deciding which beliefs and practices are legitimate and which are not."[4] Groups labeled cults seem to be too controlling, too violent, or too strange, making "real religions" seem voluntary, peaceful, and rational in contrast. To say that cults do not exist, other than as a pejorative term applied by outsiders to certain religions, is not a way of excusing or denying the authoritarian, manipulative, and downright abusive behavior that can occur within certain groups. Such behavior does occur, but it occurs within what we generally call "religions" too. Since the American cult scare of the 1970s, two generations of religion scholars and historians have interrogated the concept of the cult, demonstrating how the category has vilified certain minority religious movements.[5] Yet almost no scholar has looked into the origins of the category, why it emerged in the 1890s, and how it became established in the popular imagination.[6] Nor has any scholar examined how Chevaillier's campaign against Harris helped establish the emerging categories of the cult and the cult leader.[7]

Thomas Lake Harris was not the only religious figure labeled a cult leader during the early 1890s, but this book shows how the scandal surrounding him helped establish a set of signifiers that would come to define the term. These signifiers included important visual elements, notably Harris's long beard and intense, "hypnotic" gaze, as well as traits that would thereafter be associated with cult leaders: his California commune, his dangerous charisma, his "bizarre" religious beliefs, his "harem" made up of brainwashed followers, his willful disruption of traditional marriage and family, and the moral danger he supposedly posed to white women. Sometimes viewed as a calculating fraud, at other times a delusional lunatic, Harris seemed to twist notions of family, pervert notions of spirituality, and defile notions of community. Despite Harris's attempts to neutralize Chevaillier and her accusations, he emerged as the archetype for the modern cult leader.

A close-up look at the Fountaingrove scandal further reveals the potent racial dimensions of the term cult. Some of Harris's followers were Japanese immigrant men, a fact that loomed large in the early weeks of the scandal. The presence of Japanese men at Fountaingrove helped outsiders cast Harris and his movement as un-American, un-Christian, and racially Other. Media accounts racialized Harris and his followers in more subtle ways as well, often depicting them in Orientalist terms, such as referring to Harris's "harem" and calling him a "fakir," a term usually applied to Muslim or Hindu ascetics. The "deviant" sex that allegedly went on at Fountaingrove made them, like Mormon polygamists before them, racially suspect.[8] As with the term "heathen," the word "cult" has always been a marker of both religious and racial difference.[9]

This story also shows how the word "cult" has, from the beginning, carried scandalous connotations of sexual experimentation and impropriety. Harris claimed he and his followers practiced strict celibacy, a state of living that threatened American traditions of marriage and procreation. Outsiders mocked and doubted Harris's claims of celibacy, just as they did those of Shakers and Catholic clergy during the nineteenth century.[10] Chevaillier insisted instead that "vile" sex went on at Fountaingrove: sex between Harris and his female followers as well as extramarital sex between Fountaingrove colonists as commanded by Harris.

"Sex haunts new religions," writes scholar Megan Goodwin, pointing to the accusations of "bad" or nonnormative sexual practices that have dogged religious outsiders throughout U.S. history.[11] In fact, sexual experimentation has been a hallmark of new religions, from the celibacy of the Society of Universal Friends and the Shakers to the "complex marriage" practiced by the Oneida perfectionists, from the spouse-swapping of the Kingdom of Matthias to the polygamy of the Church of Jesus Christ of Latter-day Saints.[12] All of these groups encountered hostility, persecution, and outright violence from outsiders for violating dominant sexual norms. The new category of the cult drew on this tradition of demonizing the sexual practices of marginalized religious groups, to the point that the oft-used phrase "sex cult" would be redundant.

Chevaillier strove to save young women from the moral dangers of Fountaingrove, pointing to the gendered aspects of the term cult. Despite the existence of large numbers of new religious movements led by women, in the popular imagination the cult leader has usually been a male authority figure taking advantage of his feminized followers.[13] Chevaillier helped establish this pattern by arguing that Harris's "hypnotic" powers took away women's ability to refuse him, forcing them to relinquish control of their money, labor, and sex lives. According to Chevaillier, Harris robbed women of what we today call consent.[14] This accusation tapped into larger cultural anxieties about women's changing place in society as industrialization and urbanization unsettled dominant gender roles. Like emerging concerns about "white slavery," which centered on young women supposedly lured into prostitution, Chevaillier's campaign simultaneously insisted on women's right of spiritual, financial, and sexual self-determination—to be capable of consent—while nonetheless activating conservative ideas of innate female weakness and victimhood.[15] Chevaillier's portrayal of Harris as an old-fashioned patriarch with unholy control over his "family" drew on earlier models of corrupt slave owners, depraved Catholic priests, evil Mormon polygamists, and licentious mesmerists. In so doing, she helped establish the cult as a site of unchecked male supremacy and female victimhood out of step with modern gender roles.

From the Fountaingrove scandal onward, calling a group a cult was to mark it as outside religious, racial, sexual, and gender norms, all at the same time. The term, in its modern sense, arose in the early 1890s because of that powerful multivalency. Anti-cult activists, of whom Chevaillier was one of the first, played on prevailing cultural anxieties to attack cults, emphasizing their danger to Christianity, whiteness, marriage, and womanhood. At the same time, activists like Chevaillier drew on older prejudices, especially anti-Catholicism (she referred to Harris as "Primate," for example, a term used within the Catholic Church for certain archbishops), anti-Mormonism (she called Harris's movement "worse than Mormons"), and anti-Islam. The new term "cult" would prove immensely durable, gaining wider and wider use over the course of the twentieth century, but the central characteristics of the cult would be put in place during the Fountaingrove scandal and change surprisingly little in subsequent years.

The Fountaingrove scandal furthermore marked California as a special breeding ground for cults, establishing what writer Carey McWilliams would later call the state's "fabled addiction to cults and cultists."[16] Well before Harris moved with some of his followers from upstate New York to California in 1875, the so-called Golden State had a reputation for unorthodox thinking and heterogeneity despite the best efforts of Protestant missionaries and ministers.[17] Seeking a "way station" for the Church of Jesus Christ of Latter-day Saints on the Pacific coast, Brigham Young had authorized the formation of a Mormon colony at San Bernardino in 1851.[18] Spiritualism also flourished in California, taking advantage of what one spiritualist deemed the state's unique "spirit of universal freedom of thought, expression, and action."[19] By the late 1880s, dozens of spiritualists, Theosophists, Christian Scientists, and occultists were lecturing, offering classes, and founding associations in the state.[20] California also saw the emergence of numerous new religious movements that were not directly transplanted from other places, such as William Monéy's Reformed New Testament Church, founded in Los Angeles in 1855.[21] California's reputation for freedom, opportunity, and innovation attracted new religions like Harris's and placed the state at the center of emergent conceptions of cults and cult leaders.

Immigrants from China, and later from Japan, Korea, and India, brought with them to California a variety of Asian religions that added to the state's unique religious landscape. The arrival of "joss houses" and Buddhist temples sparked widespread concerns about religio-racial "pollution" among many white Christians, but others were intrigued.[22] A Swedish-born metaphysician named Herman Vetterling founded the nation's first Buddhist newspaper, *The Buddhist Ray,* in Santa Cruz in 1888, drawing in elements from Swedenborgianism, Theosophy, and spiritualism. In the early 1890s, Theosophists sponsored lectures on Buddhism in San Francisco and Los Angeles, prompting a Protestant backlash.[23]

With its strong Asian presence and history of religious hybridity and experimentation, California would be ground zero for battles over cults from the very start of the category's existence. California had been militarily conquered, Protestantized, and "tamed" during the mid-nineteenth century, but those processes remained ongoing in the 1890s as cults emerged as the state's newest threat to America's religious purity. Like the concept of the frontier—"the meeting point between savagery and civilization," according to historian Frederick Jackson Turner—the concept of the cult created a line between safe and dangerous, normative and deviant, and American and un-American.[24] In short, the Fountaingrove scandal provided all of the things newspaper editors knew would make a compelling story: unusual religious doctrines shrouded in secrecy, unsavory sexual practices featuring white women and Asian men, and an evil villain with mysterious mental powers in Harris, all located in a setting—California—already associated with Asian culture, unruly behavior, and frontiers of religion, race, gender, and sexuality.[25]

The media's role in creating and sustaining the category of cults cannot be overstated. Newspapers were undergoing rapid changes in the 1890s as more and more papers began emulating Joseph Pulitzer's *New York World,* which pioneered the use of the "scandal story" to boost circulation. All scandals were good, explained Pulitzer's top editor John Cockerill, but those involving a "fracture of the Vth, VIth, VIIth, VIIIth, or IXth Commandments" were best.[26] The combustible combination of "strange" religion and "bad" sex in cult scandals would prove to be an alluring one. Sociologist Ari Adut has defined scandals as "moral disturbances" that, through publicity, threaten to "contaminate" the wider public.[27] Cult scandals such as Chevaillier's exposé of Fountaingrove would become an increasingly popular subgenre of the scandal story because of their multiple forms of transgression and contaminating power. Even more than sex scandals involving politicians, cult scandals offered the public a titillating glimpse into an alternative way of living that anyone, theoretically, could fall into.

New printing technologies in the late nineteenth century allowed periodicals to utilize more and better quality photographs and illustrations, and these images would play a crucial role in defining cults. High-speed presses, cheap pulp-based paper, improvements in wood-engraving techniques, and new photographic processes, such as line-engraving and half-tone, ushered in a "golden age of illustration."[28] Cartoons and illustrations of Harris would help establish important visual aspects of what a cult leader looked like.

In addition to feeding this new, sensation-focused journalism, the Fountaingrove scandal also served the needs of certain onlookers. Surprisingly, it was Christian Scientists, Theosophists, spiritualists, Swedenborgians, and members of other minority religions, rather than Protestant or Catholic leaders, who most hotly debated the scandal, with some voices defending Harris but most hastening to explain why their group was immune to such vulgarities lest they be similarly labeled a dangerous cult. Historians have tended to study these movements in isolation or as part of a shared metaphysical tradition, but the story of Harris's scandalous career reveals deep divisions between and within new religions in the nineteenth-century transatlantic world.[29] By policing the boundaries of their movements and distancing themselves from Harris, members of outsider religions joined journalists, reformers, and Protestant ministers in creating the category of cults.

It is possible to dismiss Chevaillier's accusations as scandal mongering in a bid for public attention and financial gain—and some observers in the 1890s did exactly that. Indeed, the question of how to interpret Chevaillier's claims is an instance of a dilemma that has plagued the study of new religious movements more broadly: How should we treat the accounts of critics and former members of new religions who claim abuse when those accounts seem to reinforce anti-cult stereotypes? Some scholars have taken a critical look at how "atrocity tales" told by apostates feed into mainstream fears and misapprehensions about cults, while others have accepted such accounts as troubling evidence of authoritarian, sexist, and coercive practices within some new religions.[30] As challenging as this issue is when considering groups active today, it becomes even more difficult when studying the sexual practices of groups, like Harris's, that are long defunct. "Silences mark the history of sexuality," notes historian Elizabeth Elbourne, "reflecting both lacunae in historical records and the hush surrounding certain sexual practices in many times and places."[31] This silence is even greater in the specific case of Fountaingrove because the affidavits and letters Chevaillier based her accusations on no longer exist other than what she fed to the media.[32]

The San Franciscans who attended Chevaillier's lecture in February 1892 probably did not care if her accusations were strictly true or not, nor did most of the reading public who followed the scandal, and it is tempting to follow their lead in declaring that the day-to-day sexual arrangements at Fountaingrove were irrelevant in terms of the scandal's queasy appeal and cultural impact. When I began to research this story more than a decade ago, my initial impulse was to declare the truth unrecoverable and to simply study how the scandal played out. However, the global #MeToo movement, which drew attention to the prevalence of sexual abuse and harassment experienced by women, as well as ongoing revelations of systemic sexual abuse within the Roman Catholic Church, helped me see the importance of grappling with, rather than avoiding, the question at the heart of the scandal: Was Chevaillier right about Harris?[33]

Ultimately, I believe that is both possible and necessary to take seriously allegations of abuse made against *all* religions. In this case it required exhaustive research, scrutiny of thousands of extant primary sources located in more than a thirty archives, and a sometimes-creative reading of those sources to uncover what likely went on behind closed doors at Fountaingrove, while at the same time documenting how Chevaillier's allegations ricocheted all too easily through the broader culture to become fodder for anti-cult narratives. To accomplish this balancing act, it was necessary to consider the evidence as well as the silences of the archive and to delve deeply into the backgrounds, biases, and perspectives of all participants in the scandal.

This story has many beginnings, which comprise Part One of this book. We learn the backgrounds of the central players in the scandal, moving from upstate New York during the revivals of the Second Great Awakening, where Harris received his first visits from spirits; to Boston during the "mind cure" craze, where Chevaillier began her career as a reformer; and on to England, where Harris met his most famous protégé and greatest failure, Laurence

Oliphant, and his eventual heir and "adopted son" Kanaye Nagasawa and the other Japanese men who joined Harris's movement.

Part Two chronicles the scandal itself: Chevaillier's campaign, Harris's counterattacks, and the wide variety of religious and social groups that became involved, including suffragists and spiritualists, Swedenborgians and Theosophists, journalists and politicians, Protestant ministers, and self-styled messiahs. Their interest in the scandal demonstrates the broad and conflicting cultural anxieties about faith, sex, death, marriage, gender, and race that the scandal tapped into. Along the way we will meet both a Mr. X and a Miss X, attend a surprising wedding, and witness a murder investigation at Fountaingrove.

Part Three gives the various endings of this story, including the long shadow Harris cast over the twentieth-century figure of the cult leader, Chevaillier's later-life career as a prison reformer, how Kanaye Nagasawa's heirs were cheated out of a fortune by racist state laws, and—finally—how people in Santa Rosa deliberately misremembered Fountaingrove's once-sordid history.

"The scandal is a public act of abjection, a procedure of expulsion through which we safely distance ourselves from scandal's targets," writes religion scholar Katherine Pratt Ewing.[34] The story of California's first cult scare reveals the long history and persistence of certain cultural preoccupations and procedures of expulsion, concerning which religions are real, rational, and uplifting and which are false, irrational, and degrading; which sex acts and family arrangements are normal and wholesome and which are deviant and indecent; and the urge to protect the purity of white women. Because of the powerful and enduring nature of these concerns, the concept of the cult would have a long life indeed.

PART ONE
BEGINNINGS

1

September 1890

The Pivotal Man

When the greatest breakthrough of Thomas Lake Harris's long and remarkable spiritual life arrived in the autumn of 1890, it arrived gently. It arrived "as suddenly, as pleasantly, as when a deep-laden, storm-tossed ship glides over the harbor-bar from the raging outside sea, and swings at ease in a land-locked haven," he wrote later. For the past three years, Harris had lived in near-complete isolation at Linn Lilla, his hermitage eight miles from the rest of his Fountaingrove colony in northern California, accompanied only by his amanuensis and most trusted follower Jane Lee Waring. He was in his mid-sixties and felt older: "frail, emaciated, and perishing." Physically enfeebled, Harris spent those three years at Linn Lilla practicing "divine respiration," a method of deep breathing, prayer, and meditation that he had discovered nearly thirty years earlier. He studied his old writings—more than twenty books and hundreds of poems written since he was a young man—finding them outdated and incomplete. Sometimes his spirit soared out of his body, and he explored the heavens and communed with celestial beings, especially his counterpart and spiritual bride, Lily Queen. At other times, he battled demons and returned to his body trembling and exhausted.

At Linn Lilla, Harris went deeper and further into himself and into the cosmos than he had ever gone. He vowed to "never publish another word . . . unless I pass safely through this final ordeal." His life literally was on the line; the only outcomes were "success or dissolution." For he sought what he called the "final chord of the rhythmic law." He sought to "overcome the universal racial tendency to physical deterioration and decease." He sought mastery over death itself.

And then, on September 20, 1890, the breakthrough came. His spirit touched the "last rhythmic chord that leads the harmonic vibrations into bodily renewal." Within a week, his decrepit body had returned to full health. His "bent form stood upright; flesh grew upon the bones; the dim eyes found their sparkle; every bodily sense awoke invigorated." Blood flowed into his

Unholy Sensations. Joshua Paddison, Oxford University Press. © Oxford University Press 2025.
DOI: 10.1093/oso/9780197775325.003.0001

organs, creating "one grand consciousness of bodily grandeur, freedom, and, in a sense, of corporate immortality." For three decades, Harris had circulated his major writings only among his followers, unwilling to let outsiders see "crude or partial statements." Now, however, Harris felt ready to re-engage with the American public in a way he had not done since his time as a young spiritualist in New York City. Then, as now, Harris had burned with divine revelations so powerful he could hardly contain them.[1]

The spiritual journey that culminated at Linn Lilla in 1890 began forty years earlier when at age twenty-six Harris first began to understand his cosmic importance. At about ten o'clock one evening in March 1850, while in his bed chamber in his quarters in New York City, Harris had been visited by a spirit who appeared as a tall, beautiful man wearing a Greek toga and a garland of olive leaves and lilies. "His brow was high and massive, his eyes were of a dark-blue color, his hands delicate and with taper fingers, his lips wearing an expression of childlike sweetness," Harris reported. The spirit showed Harris a white book filled with pictures that moved and hieroglyphs that shimmered as if prisms. "Do you perceive that all the knowledge which hitherto you have attained to, is far exceeded by the wisdom contained in the first and most minute of those hieroglyphs?" the spirit asked. Harris agreed, and the spirit vowed to return to him in a few years' time to explain that hieroglyph's meaning.[2]

In November 1853 the spirit had returned as promised. In front of witnesses, Harris fell into a trance and dictated the meaning of the hieroglyph. According to one onlooker, Harris spoke with a "deep-toned and musical" voice, at times chanting, his eyes closed. His dictation ended up lasting twenty-six hours, spanning twenty-two sessions over fourteen days. The result was a four-thousand-line poem, published as *An Epic of the Starry Heaven,* in which a company of spirits takes a human narrator on a tour of the solar system and other celestial realms. In a preface, the spirit-author declared Harris a uniquely powerful medium, possessing a "sacerdotal interior" and "poetic genius," who would serve as a key intermediary between the spirit and human worlds. Though "still in an exceedingly feeble condition," Harris's capacities were destined to grow "more highly vitalized and more luminously expanded" in the years ahead.[3]

Despite his claims of primacy, Harris was far from the only person in antebellum New York being visited by spirits or engaging in trance writing. His assertions of uniqueness, in fact, may have revealed how crowded a field he operated in. Beginning in the 1820s, the so-called Burned-Over District of

Thomas Lake Harris in 1864; courtesy Edwin Markham Archive, Horrmann Library, Wagner College, New York City.

upstate New York produced a host of prophets, seers, and mediums, and New York City soon became second only to London in metaphysical activity. More than two decades before Harris, a young man named Joseph Smith had been visited by an angelic being who informed him of his special destiny and gave him access to holy writings, which Smith published as

The Book of Mormon. In 1847, Andrew Jackson Davis published *The Principles of Nature,* reportedly the "revelations of a spirit freed" channeled by Davis while in a trance. Less than a year later, reports of "spirit rappings" by Kate and Margaret Fox of Hydesville, New York, captured headlines across the nation and helped make spiritualism a popular phenomenon. By the 1850s, tens of thousands of Americans had participated in a séance or witnessed the outpourings of a touring trance speaker. Trance-written books like Harris's *An Epic of the Starry Heaven* were a booming subgenre, produced "by and through" mediums such as John Murray Spear, Nathan Francis White, and E. C. Henck.[4]

Within this crowded and fractious milieu, Harris stood out as an especially divisive figure, a reputation that would follow him for his entire life. Unlike many nineteenth-century spiritualists, Harris rarely used the language of science to explain the supernatural. He considered himself a poet and mystic, not a scientific investigator. Rather than framing his metaphysics in terms of empiricism, natural science, or the Enlightenment, Harris embraced the arcane, the emotional, and the erotic. This put him often out of step with other religious liberals and spiritual seekers. At times Harris took values they admired too far—critics called him too inward focused, too spontaneous, too fervent, too unorthodox, too fanatical. At other times he seemed to represent values that religious liberals felt they were leaving behind; they labeled Harris unscientific, autocratic, patriarchal, indoctrinatory, secretive, and—eventually—predatory.

He was also an inveterate amalgamator of elements taken from a wide range of philosophies and religions. Over the course of his life, he borrowed from Calvinism, evangelical Protestantism, Universalism, mesmerism, spiritualism, utopian communitarianism, Adventism, Swedenborgianism, European mysticism, Theosophy, and Buddhism. More often than not, this pattern of borrowing offended the groups Harris borrowed from, especially when he claimed to have brought their ideas to perfection. He was also a geographical wanderer, spending time in Europe and in the American Northeast, South, and West, in urban as well as rural settings, and he attracted followers from western Europe, Japan, and across the United States. These migrations and controversies, together with the esoteric nature of his writings and his increasing tendency toward seclusion, made Harris a mysterious and infamous figure to religious seekers throughout the world well before his dramatic breakthrough at Linn Lilla in 1890. In particular, his singular ideas about sex would create frictions and suspicions among metaphysicians that would smolder for decades, ready to explode.

Harris's first migration occurred when he was a child. He was born in Fenny Stratford, England, in 1823 and moved to Utica, New York, with his parents, Thomas and Annie Lake Harris, at age five. The Harris family was solidly middle class; his father, an auctioneer, grocer, and crockery merchant, owned his own store called Thomas Harris & Co. However, young Thomas Lake Harris had a difficult childhood. His mother died when he was nine and he also lost a sister. His father was a deacon in a local Baptist church and a proponent of a "hard, narrow Calvinism" against which the young Harris chafed. He later recalled that, as a teenager, he had "learned to abhor myself as indeed born of sin and constitutionally full of latent evil. . . . Notwithstanding a goodness of surface conduct, I was in a great despair." At age fifteen he attended a revival meeting in Utica where "the presence of the Lord was manifested with a sense of quickening as of a new birth." He became filled by an "overflowing love of Christ," vowing to "devote my life to him."[5]

Harris was one of many living in western New York who experienced a "new birth" into evangelical Christianity in the 1830s. Bustling, manufacturing-based Utica was in fact a central hub of the series of revivals known as the Second Great Awakening. Fiery Presbyterian minister Charles Grandison Finney had used the town as a base in the mid-1820s, taking advantage of the nearby, newly constructed Erie Canal to launch his mission work. Abolitionist Theodore Weld was a student at Hamilton College near Utica when he experienced the new birth during one of Finney's sermons, going on to become a leading defender of the revivals. The revivals in Utica overwhelmingly attracted young men and women, like Harris, from the town's growing middle class—he was surrounded by clerks, artisans, and merchants prospering from industrialization yet facing increasing economic insecurity and moral uncertainty.[6]

Harris's teenage new birth experience inspired him to pursue an ecclesiastical career, and he spent the next several years studying to become a Baptist minister. However, his reading of the Bible—along with works by "Emerson, Swedenborg, Carlyle, Shelley, Wordsworth, Coleridge, Goethe, and Schiller"—prompted him to break with the Baptists and join the Universalists. In a move that illustrates his confidence, as young as twenty, in his own spiritual vision, he wrote a letter to Utica's Bethel Baptist Church informing them that their doctrines were "not in accordance with the truth as revealed in the word of God." Bethel promptly excommunicated him for heresy, for which Harris was "sorely persecuted" by his family.[7] Undeterred, Harris started preaching and writing poetry for Universalist magazines. He was a "quiet, bashful, unassuming young man, of very delicate physique" who nonetheless "showed a good deal of vivacity, even brilliancy, of conversational gifts," according to one Universalist.[8]

Harris's unhappy childhood exposure to Calvinism no doubt made the Universalists appealing, for they had arisen in the late eighteenth century in opposition to Calvinist "tyranny" and continued that fight well into the antebellum period. Rather than a fearsome God of damnation and hellfire, Universalists believed in a benevolent God of love who offered salvation to all. Harris was also attracted to the Universalists' reputation as radical foes of orthodoxy, alluring and dangerous because their denial of hellfire supposedly bred immorality.[9]

After apprenticeships at churches in Minden, New York, and Charleston, South Carolina, Harris relocated to New York City in 1845, where he was ordained as pastor of a Universalist church on Elizabeth Street. By far the nation's largest metropolis, New York in the 1840s was, in the words of resident Walt Whitman, a "noisy, roaring, rumbling, tumbling, bustling, stormy, turbulent" city where thousands of immigrants worked in proximity to America's wealthiest plutocrats.[10] Harris was, according to the Universalist press, a "young man of promise" who was "greatly esteemed, both as a man and a preacher, by his people."[11]

However, straightforward Universalism proved constraining, and in 1846 Harris started weaving elements of mesmerism into his sermons. From Franz Anton Mesmer, the eighteenth-century German physician and philosopher, Harris borrowed the notion of "animal magnetism," the invisible spiritual fluid that flowed between and within all living things. In a rare use of quasi-scientific rhetoric, Harris insisted that Christ's miracles had been performed via mesmerism—clairvoyance gave him foreknowledge of Judas's betrayal while magnetism allowed him to heal the sick, as Mesmer had done in Vienna and Paris. These powers, furthermore, were available to any Christian who was properly "developed" in the magnetic arts.[12]

Mesmer's ideas had been brought to the United States in 1836 by French devotee Charles Poyen, whose popular speaking tour of New England featured him mesmerizing and healing volunteers from the audience. As spiritualism would a decade later, mesmerism had spread quickly, embraced by physicians, clergymen, and reformers as well as traveling showmen who made use of the revivalists' circuit. Many of Harris's fellow Universalists, with their rationalist approach to Christian theology, were attracted to mesmerism, which seemed to offer proof of a spiritual-material connection in its salubrious effects on subjects. Universalist minister John Bovee Dods, who substituted the term "mental electricity" for Mesmer's "animal magnetism," lectured widely in the 1840s extolling its capacity to "charm all pain." Other Universalists, however, rejected Mesmer's insights, sparking a fight within the denomination. Boston's *Trumpet and Universalist Magazine* mocked Harris's ideas as "insane" and a "humbug," wondering, if anyone could reproduce Christ's feats, why were resurrections and other miracles not widespread today? Ultimately, mesmerism proved too heretical for most Universalists to accept, in that it threatened to strip Christ of "his divine commission, his Messiahship, and the truth of his doctrine," as one skeptical Universalist put it. Dods would be forced out of the denomination in 1848, by which time Harris had already left.[13]

Following a progression that would become common among New York's booming class of religious experimenters, Harris by that point had already moved from mesmerism to spiritualism. According to his later account, Harris had first experienced a brush with the spirit world as a teenager when his mother Annie, several years deceased, visited him one evening in Utica. "My poor child, always believe that God is your Father and that man is your brother," she told him with "inexpressible soothing tenderness." Such reassuring communications from dead family members were a central appeal of spiritualism. As urbanization and industrialization were making mourning practices less communal, spiritualism offered what historian Ann Braude has called "a unique kind of consolation to the bereaved." In 1854 Harris would also hear from the sister who had died during his childhood.[14]

Unlike the majority of empirical-minded mesmerists and Universalists who gravitated toward spiritualism in the late 1840s, Harris rejected the scientific, political, and popular manifestations of the movement in favor of a more private, mystical vision. By 1846 he had become affiliated with the small New York circle—mostly Universalists or former Universalists—that surrounded the charismatic young spiritualist Andrew Jackson Davis. This was just as Davis was becoming famous as the "Poughkeepsie Seer" whose trance-written *The Principles of Nature* would sell nine hundred copies in its first week. According to Davis, the young Harris was "brilliant" but intense.

Approaching Davis after a reading from what would become *The Principles of Nature*, Harris informed him, "When that Book is published I shall lock up the Bible in the drawer under the desk, put the key in my pocket, and preach the angel-utterances of the New Philosophy!" Davis reported that Harris "emphasized almost every word, as he spoke it, with a firmly clenched fist; his whole frame shook; his eye was oracularly luminous." Harris's zeal caused Davis's "spirit to shrink back as one would shut his eyes against the intrusion of too much light."[15]

Andrew Jackson Davis was early spiritualism's philosopher, and Thomas Lake Harris its poet. Davis's writings, especially *The Great Harmonia,* published in six volumes from 1850 to 1861, were meticulously organized, "encyclopaedical" explanations of his "investigations" of the spirit world, replete with quasi-scientific terminology. Hoping to shape public understanding of the explosion of popular spiritualism after 1848, Davis explained that "electrical vibrations" flowed from the spirit world through the medium via a process that was "simple and physical, philosophical and rational," no more "complicated or wonderful than the principles upon which the magnetic telegraph is daily operating along our great commercial avenues." Davis's books included charts and maps modeled on mathematical, ethnological, and cartographic scholarship of the era. Davis's approach made his works popular among a wide range of spiritualists eager for an intellectual scaffolding to erect around their séances.[16]

Harris, on the other hand, emphasized the ineffable, romantic, and emotional aspects of spiritualism, and his writings would grow more and more lyrical and impenetrable over the years. His earliest poems, published in the *New York Tribune* and Universalist journals in the mid-1840s, were sonnets or had rhyming couplets, conventional structures that mirrored their well-worn subject matter. Some metaphysical themes were present as early as 1844, however. In "A Memorial Hymn," published in Utica's Universalist magazine, Harris described the visit he had received from his dead mother but here called it a dream, culminating with the line, "I waken and weep— thou art gone, thou art gone." Similarly, in "Evening Thoughts" from 1845, his narrator is allowed a glimpse of the spirit world while on a moonlit walk:

> Seraphic strains entrance the raptured ear,
> Melodious warblings of the angel band;
> They sing, to cheer us while we linger here,
> The fadeless glories of the Spirit Land![17]

By the time he had joined Davis's circle, Harris's poetry had become more radical in topic if not form. In the pages of the metaphysical journal *Univercoelum and Spiritual Philosopher,* Harris emphasized the interpenetration of the material and spiritual realms, as in "A Hymn to the Inner Life":

> The friends we mourn as lost have not departed,
> They have but laid aside Earth's frail disguise;
> On your dark way, they pour, you lonely hearted!
> The light of loving eyes.

In another poem, "The Home of the Soul," he described what happens to people after death, a process he claimed to have experienced "in spirit." Having crossed "the dark portal," leaving his body behind, he ascended heavenward to the Land of the Morning, where he was surrounded by departed loved ones. "This, *this* is the Real," he realized.[18]

Such themes—the impermanence of death, the everydayness of the supernatural, the comforts and love offered by the sprits—were common throughout early spiritualist discourse. However, Harris soon began to adopt a more uniquely prophetic voice. In "An Hymn of the Transition Age" from 1850, he assumed the mantle of a Greek oracle, claiming that God "makes his Poets Prophets now at last." He foretold a coming Armageddon in which war and pestilence would "stain with her children's blood the shuddering Earth" and from which "Humanity shall rise and live forever, / Throned in the might of its sublime endeavor, / Divine, harmonious, free, in glorious spirit-birth!" In fact, much spiritualist writing had an undercurrent of millennialism that gave urgency to the movement's many reform efforts, from temperance to antislavery. But most spiritualists preferred a more evolutionary vision of steady moral progress and a God of love, not vengeance. Harris's expanding theology, however, included both evil and Armageddon, and he was becoming more and more convinced of his own primacy in the events he foresaw.[19]

In November 1847, a few months after the publication of Davis's *The Principles of Nature,* the New York Universalist Association passed a resolution requiring its ministers to agree to the following declaration: "I sincerely declare that I receive the Bible as containing a special revelation from God, which is the rule of Christian faith and practice; and I will strive faithfully to preach its doctrines and inculcate its precepts." Intended to drive out the spiritualists in their ranks, similar resolutions were also adopted by

Universalist associations in Boston, Buffalo, Michigan, and Vermont. Even more than mesmerism, spiritualism divided the Universalists; more ministers from that denomination embraced it than from any other, but many others objected on theological or intellectual grounds. Harris responded to the resolution by quitting his pulpit, as did several other spiritualists. He promptly went on the road to explain and defend Davis's *The Principles of Nature.* In Cincinnati, Harris presented himself as a willing martyr to the cause, telling audiences that he had "suffered and lost much for his strict adherence to the new revelation."[20]

Harris could have been both a spiritualist and Universalist (some clergymen managed to be both), but, as he later explained, "I could not with propriety hold any position that subjected me to the inevitable limitations of the sect." In the *Univercoelum,* he described his journey from Calvinist Baptist to Universalist to spiritualist as a right and natural progression that the "best men from among the Universalists, Unitarians, and Friends" were now following as they sought "inward illumination." Such attitudes rankled the Universalists, and Harris received their special scorn. While in Cincinnati, he verbally sparred with local Universalist pastor John A. Gurley. Soon after, the editor of the Universalist magazine in Utica to which Harris had contributed many youthful poems attacked his turn toward spiritualism with venom: "Harris, as we expected when he began his *comet* career, has gone clear overboard, and made complete shipwreck of his former faith. . . . We hope he will never again pretend to be a Universalist."[21]

Harris's progress toward "inward illumination" soon had him questioning the divinity of Davis's pronouncements as well. While in southern Ohio he spent time with a group called the Universal Brotherhood, whose members included radical Quaker abolitionist John O. Wattles and a youthful clairvoyant named James Mahan rumored to be as powerful as Davis. In the mid-1840s, Wattles and Mahan had been part of a failed utopian colony in Ohio called the Clermont Phalanx, one of the dozens of communitarian projects launched in the 1840s based on the ideas of French philosopher Charles Fourier. In his 1820 manifesto *Theory of Social Organization,* Fourier had called for the creation of cooperative "Phalanxes" in which, "free from all pecuniary cares and anxieties," all members would equally share in the labor and planning of the community.[22]

The Clermont Phalanx had broken apart after two years, but a remnant had regrouped outside Cincinnati as a semi-secret Universal Brotherhood now devoted to spiritualism. Harris's visit marked his first exposure to cooperative, agrarian communitarianism, to which he would later devote much of his life. He came away deeply impressed by the "men, ideas, and purposes" of the Universal Brotherhood, especially how they had "gradually harmonized in sentiment" without "dogmatic creed and formula." His time with the Brotherhood also shook his faith in Davis; thereafter Harris vowed to stop defending *The Principles of Nature* because he now, like those in the Brotherhood, saw that it contained "some truth and a great deal of error."[23]

Back in New York City but without a church, Harris formed his own Independent Christian Society and attracted such luminaries as *New York Tribune* editor Horace Greeley, who had donated money to the Clermont Phalanx in Ohio. Harris's new Society declared itself devoted to the pursuit of "Religious Truth, not merely as they are supposed to exist in Miracle and Tradition, but as they are found in Nature, in Providence, in Spiritual Revelation, in all forms of Science, and in the powers and tendencies of the human soul." The main attraction for visitors was probably not this broadminded theology but Harris's captivating performances behind the pulpit. Attendees at Independent Christian Society services praised Harris's "lively, and vigorous, though undisciplined imagination." One onlooker described Harris's preaching as a "truly extraordinary performance, displaying a mighty sweep of intelligence, an amazing fervency of hero-worship, and an unequaled splendor of illustration." Harris delivered sermons with a "vehemence of affection" that made his "frail frame tremble, as though the spirit it encased were struggling to escape its tenement."[24]

Harris's break with Davis quickly turned into something of a feud. Writing in the *Univercoelum* in September 1848, Harris offered "A Few Words of Caution" about Davis. "Mr. Davis's book contains errors and contradictions, in the midst that is truthful," Harris wrote. He went on to warn, "A diseased mental state often exposes those of peculiar mental powers to dangerous hallucinations, and begets fancies which have no foundation in truth or nature." This last comment was probably a reference to Davis's relationship with Catherine DeWolf Dodge, a wealthy patron twenty years Davis's senior. The previous year, Davis had employed his "clairvoyant power of exact investigation" and discovered that she was destined to leave her husband and marry him instead, which she did. Davis's spiritualist circle was appalled, none more so than Harris, who sneered at Davis, "A man blinded by passions—a man who yields to his lusts—who loses himself in sensuality—cannot be in unity with God!"[25]

Harris's disgust toward Davis reveals him to be no sex radical at this point in his life. By the summer of 1848, Harris had been married for three years, to Mary Van Arnum from Albany, and fathered a son. The couple would soon add a second son. Harris was in this sense in line with the early spiritualist movement, which generally celebrated companionate marriage, monogamy, and procreation. However, some antebellum spiritualists advocated the notion that men and women should be guided by "spiritual affinity"—that is, true, uplifting, romantic love with a soul mate—rather than the restrictions of church- and state-sanctioned marriage. Divorce, in other words, was far less of a sin than staying in a loveless and therefore godless marriage.

Harris did not share these attitudes, hewing to a more traditional view of marriage vows as inviolate. In a sermon a few years later, he would mourn the fact that "under the influence of spirits, husbands have deserted their wives and joined themselves adulterously to others." He was especially incensed that Davis had misused his spiritual influence over Catherine DeWolf Dodge and suspected that his former friend acted out of lust rather than love. While others in Davis's circle thought him the "victim of a designing woman," Harris viewed Davis as the lascivious initiator, corrupting his spiritual gifts. Harris also feared that Davis's conduct would hinder spiritualism's spread. "Our movement is embarrassed," he told Davis. "Your friends are troubled in every direction.... It is in every man's mouth everywhere!"[26] With his fear of bad publicity and his distrust of unbridled "sensuality," young Harris comes across as conservative, even prudish. He saw sex as a corrupting and powerful force that needed to be controlled. This notion would grow to become a lifelong obsession for Harris.

After Harris broke with Davis, he began to come into his own as a medium. On January 1, 1850, he published his prophetic apocalyptic poem "An Hymn of the Transition Age," and two months later he was visited by the spirit-angel in the Greek toga with the magical hieroglyph-filled book that would later become the basis for his trance poem *An Epic of the Starry Heaven*. Soon after he received a fateful telepathic summons that directed him to Auburn, New York. Eliza Ann Benedict, a medium whose powers had been unlocked after a visit from one of the Fox sisters in 1849, had gathered around her a peculiar group of clairvoyants called the Apostolic Circle. In the context of early spiritualism, Benedict's Apostolic Circle was unusual in that its members communicated not with ordinary spirits but directly with biblical prophets and apostles, including Daniel, John, and Paul. Benedict and other mediums in the Apostolic Circle then transcribed and published these "Expositions of Scripture."

The Apostolic Circle was also atypical for its inclusion of several Adventists, which gave its "Expositions of Scripture" a strong millenarian cast. The Adventists were former adherents of the New York farmer-turned-prophet William Miller, who had accumulated tens of thousands of followers convinced by his prediction that Christ would return on October 22, 1844. Following the "Great Disappointment"—when Jesus failed to return on that day—Miller's movement had dissipated and fractured. Some Adventists turned to spiritualism, which offered religious truths more direct and seemingly verifiable than those offered by Miller. Mainstream spiritualists in Auburn disapproved of the Apostolic Circle, however. Elias Capron, for example, complained that the "peculiar phraseology of the second advent advocates" in the Apostolic Circle twisted and made ridiculous its spiritual "Expositions of Scripture," which he called "puerile."[27]

Harboring his own millenarian beliefs, Harris arrived in Auburn and found kindred souls. Throughout 1850 and 1851 he visited Auburn frequently, assuming leadership of the Apostolic Circle alongside Eliza Ann Benedict and James Leander Scott, a Seventh Day Baptist minister who, like Harris, had been spiritually summoned from New York City. Scott was known among Seventh Day Baptists as a zealous missionary—in Rhode Island, he had preached forty-nine straight evenings in what was remembered as "Scott's Revival" of 1842–1843—and he brought that passion to the Apostolic Circle. Scott attracted large crowds in Auburn with sermons, according to a follower "*inspired* at the time of their delivery" and originating from the Apostle Paul. Harris and Scott soon began publishing a journal in Auburn titled *Disclosures from the Interior,* "edited, superintended, and controlled" by the spirits of biblical prophets and apostles. In addition to writings dictated by Daniel, John, and Paul, *Disclosures from the Interior* included poems from such dead literary celebrities as Percy Shelley, William Wordsworth, Samuel Taylor Coleridge, and Robert Southey, with Harris acting as their instrument.[28]

In July 1851, Scott—possibly influenced by Harris's enthusiasm for what he had seen of the Universal Brotherhood in Ohio—experienced a vision telling him to relocate the Apostolic Circle to western Virginia. By the time Scott set off in October, he was now communicating not only with prophets and apostles but also God himself. "Flee to the mountains whither I direct," commanded God via Scott. "In that mountain my people shall rest secure.

Above it the cloud of glory descendeth." Following his divinations, Scott and about one hundred spiritualists established a 10,000-acre agrarian community in Mountain Cove, Virginia, which he identified as the original Garden of Eden, the "spot where our first parents sinned" that would "form the center" of the coming redemption of the world. Mountain Cove would be Harris's first experiment in communal living, and his first scandal, one that would haunt him the rest of his career.[29]

Mountain Cove was not the only spiritualist colony founded in the antebellum period, but it gained a reputation as the strangest. Scott's direct revelations from God made him highly unusual among spiritualists, who typically communicated with individual spirits rather than God directly. Harris, who fundraised for Mountain Cove before moving there with his wife and two young sons in early 1852, teamed with Scott to produce a new periodical, the *Mountain Cove Journal and Spiritual Harbinger,* which they filled with particularly dense and high-flown revelatory prose. For example, Scott and Harris produced this mindboggling account of God's creation of the universe:

> And God made two great lights to rule the Zodiac, and to be for creative disclosure, disclosive manifestation, manifest glory, glorious radiation, interpenetrative aggregation; and thence vortices, vortical suns, suns of vortices, solariums, vortical, planetariums, planets, floral universes, universal paradises, paradisiacal heavens, heavens of spiritual universes, celestial heavens, seraphic habitations, seraphimal universes, cities of heavenly seraphima, and final consociative universal intelligence in unity of innumerable individuality, in triunity of unfolding universes, adoring and ascending in beatification unto eternal life.

Such rhetoric won derision from newspaper editors eager for a chance to mock spiritualism; they called the *Mountain Cove Journal* "unmeaning rhodomontade," "rinctum-puppy-diddle-boodle," and "gabble."[30]

It is difficult to reconstruct what daily life consisted of at Mountain Cove because few eyewitness accounts exist. A Universalist minister from New Orleans named Theodore Clapp visited the colony in July 1852 and praised the members' "skillful management" of their "fine fields of wheat, pastures, meadows, orchards, and gardens." Though himself not a spiritualist, Clapp insisted the colonists were "neither vulgar, nor unlettered, nor inexperienced, nor fanatical." He emphasized that they verified all messages received from the spirit world via use of the Bible, immediately discarding anything inconsistent with "this divine standard." Furthermore, they rejected "Socialism" and sex radicalism in favor of private land ownership and Christian marriage. Harris and Scott, Clapp concluded, were "pure-hearted and noble-minded men."[31]

A very different picture emerged from accounts given by I. S. Hyatt, a journalist who had been so won over by the Apostolic Circle that he had quit his job as editor of the *Cortland Democrat* in 1851 to move to Auburn and then Virginia. However, Hyatt left Mountain Cove after a year, disillusioned by the constant "discord, slander, and vindictiveness" that pervaded due to the control Scott and Harris tried to exert over their followers. Soon after arriving in Virginia, Hyatt reported, Scott denied the mediumship of Eliza Ann Benedict, insisting that only he (and Harris after his arrival) had access to the spirit prophets and apostles. According to Hyatt, members bristled at Scott's authoritarianism and his insistence that they turn their finances over to him. Rumors also circulated that Scott was "guilty of licentiousness and adultery."

When Harris arrived, according to Hyatt he found dissension and dissatisfaction tearing the colony apart. The spirit prophets and apostles, however, reassured Harris that Scott had been faithful "in all the work given unto him to do" and that "all discord" was "caused by the presence of the unsanctified, and subsides with their removal." Harris joined Scott in expelling the "unsanctified" troublemakers. By the fall of 1852, when Hyatt left, Harris and Scott were claiming to be the "two witnesses spoken of in the eleventh chapter of Revelation." Hyatt compared the two men to Robert Matthews (also known as Matthias the Prophet), the religious "impostor" who had become notorious in the mid-1830s from charges that he abused his charismatic leadership, financially and sexually exploiting his followers. Matthews, like Harris and Scott, had claimed direct revelation from God.[32]

Other sources support the idea that Harris and Scott increasingly viewed themselves as peerless and infallible mediums. The *Mountain Cove Journal* was filled with defenses of their ornate theology, attacks on Andrew Jackson Davis, Shaker leader Ann Lee, and other perceived rivals living and dead, and ominous visions of the coming apocalypse. They prophesized that the "fearful Era when the Crime of ages shall be finally made manifest and judged and swept away" was at hand. In March 1853, the duo journeyed to St. Louis to deliver public lectures on spiritualism. Harris explained that true, godly mediums—meaning himself and Scott—inevitably faced "scorn, hate, and denunciation, and [were] charged with madness by their bosom friends," likely a reference to troubles at Mountain Cove. Standing side by side with Scott in front of an audience of 2,300 Midwestern Protestants, Catholics, and Jews, Harris asserted their supernatural powers and inerrancy as mediums. "If we are wrong, let us be put down," he said.[33]

The Mountain Cove colony dissolved in the fall of 1853, having lasted two years. Even before its end, mainstream spiritualists distanced their movement from it and its leaders Scott and Harris. Samuel Byron Brittan and Charles Partridge, who had known Harris in New York spiritualist circles for years, published Hyatt's accounts in their journal, the *Spiritual Telegraph*, noting that they had "never regarded the claims of Messrs. Scott and Harris with favor." They praised Hyatt for rejecting the "absurd pretensions" of Mountain Cove and returning to "rational Spiritualism." Similarly, Auburn spiritualist Elias Capron denounced the "arbitrary assumption of power and holiness on the part of the [Mountain Cove] dictators." He regarded it as an exemplar of "religious fanaticism"—the very opposite of true spiritualism. Thirty-five years later, Capron would still view Mountain Cove as "one of the greatest frauds on its victims that has ever been known in the history of Spiritualism."[34] British spiritualist Emma Hardinge, in her participant-history of the movement, dubbed Mountain Cove's leaders "Pope Harris and Cardinal Scott," conjuring up not only Catholic hierarchy but associations of lecherous, decadent priests who sexually exploited nuns and parishioners, popularized in such tales as *The Awful Disclosures of Maria Monk*.[35]

In fact, religion scholar Ann Taves has shown how a wide range of nineteenth-century religious movements—from Methodism to Adventism to spiritualism—used the concept of "fanaticism" as a means of boundary marking. As a way of "designating false religion," charges of fanaticism provided a language with which religious gatekeepers policed their ranks and purified their theologies. By portraying Mountain Cove as excessive, irrational, undemocratic, and corrupt—and therefore outside the parameters of proper spiritualism—these critics sharpened their identity as all the more moderate, reasonable, and equitable. As such, Harris's reputation as a "fanatic" presaged his later reputation as a "cult leader."[36]

The Mountain Cove debacle was a major disappointment for Harris, one that he would learn from. In his future communitarian experiments, he would never again share leadership with another person the way he had shared leadership with Scott. The rumors of "licentiousness and adultery" that swirled around Scott demonstrated to Harris, once again, the explosive power of sex and the need to harness and control it. Mountain Cove was dead, but decades later it would be reborn as Fountaingrove.

Harris's quick reintegration into New York spiritualist circles following the breakup of Mountain Cove shows that his reputation had not yet been irrevocably stained. It is possible that Scott—who moved to Ohio and soon disappeared from the movement—received the lion's share of blame for Mountain Cove's unorthodoxies. Though lacking his own pulpit for a time, Harris preached and lectured frequently in the mid-1850s in New York and was invited to join Brittan and Partridge's New York Conference of Spiritualists, the nation's most prominent circle of mediums and investigators. Beginning in November 1853, Brittan served as Harris's primary amanuensis during the twenty-two trance sessions that resulted in *An Epic of the Starry Heaven,* which was published by Brittan and Partridge in 1854. They then published Harris's two follow-up trance poems, *A Lyric of the Morning Land* and *A Lyric of the Golden Age,* also book-length accounts of Harris's celestial journeys.[37]

As packaged by Brittan and Partridge, the three trance poems bear evidence of Harris's uneasy place in the spiritualist movement. Brittan and Partridge, both ex-Universalist ministers, were tireless champions of "rational Spiritualism," which they promoted in the many books and periodicals they edited and published. Brittan also helped found the conservative Society for the Diffusion of Spiritual Knowledge, comprised of wealthy New York businessmen, clergy, politicians, and other self-styled "men of respectability and standing." Brittan and Partridge surrounded Harris's mind-blowing poetry with introductions and appendices aimed at framing the poems in the trappings of scientific inquiry. In his introduction to *An Epic of the Starry Heaven,* Brittan went to great lengths to "prove" its divine origins, elaborately explaining how Harris's busy activities before and during the trance sessions had permitted no time for him to be secretly writing, how Harris's life was interrupted by trance sessions at inconvenient times, how he had never written a poem of longer than two hundred lines before the sessions, and so on.[38]

Taking a different tack in his introduction to *A Lyric of the Golden Age,* Brittan described the measurable effect the spirits had on the room while they were speaking through Harris, which included audible "vibrations, concussions, vocal and instrumental music," visible shapes "illuminated by a supra-mortal light," and on one occasion the "delicate aroma" of jasmine. In appendices, Brittan provided meticulous logs of the date, location, and names of witnesses present at each trance session. One appendix contained an interview Brittan conducted with a spirit speaking through Harris, during which Brittan attempted to clarify the precise nature and mechanism of Harris's mediumship. However, the spirit provided comically abstruse answers:

> Q. Did Mr. Harris, in spirit, actually visit the planets, and were the localities and scenes described in the Poem disclosed to his interior vision as objective realities?

> A. Spirits who stand in the Sun-sphere perceive by means of an odic emanation from the sun. They become negative at times to other suns, and leaving odylic forms, traverse with inconceivable rapidity the region to which they may be attracted, entering into any given solar system.[39]

Like the spirit in the interview, the poems themselves resisted Brittan and Partridge's efforts to understand the spiritual world in rationalist terms. With their great length, lack of conventional narrative, and highly abstracted baroque verbiage, the poems immerse the reader in Harris's cosmology and overwhelm the rational mind. They are doubly religious poems—they express religious ideas but also enact a religious experience in their reading. In this sense, Harris's poems shared much with such nineteenth-century American scriptures as Joseph Smith's *The Book of Mormon* and Mary Baker Eddy's *Science and Health,* wherein impenetrability, abstraction, and repetition simultaneously confirmed their divine origins and rendered them perfect for prolonged study. Indeed, at least one spiritualist "cherished" his copy of *An Epic of the Starry Heaven* and passed it down to his descendants like a family Bible.[40]

These difficulties of interpretation noted, the three epic poems do contain recurrent themes that would loom large in Harris's maturing theology. First, they established Harris not merely as a powerful medium but as a visionary prophet who could enter unseen spiritual realms at will and whose destiny it was to "shed / Celestial light on Earth." Throughout the remainder of his life, Harris would continue to enter trance states to converse with spirits, explore the heavens, and do battle with demons. Second, the poems established Harris's interest in "fays," or fairies, the "architects of heaven" visible only to children and spiritually advanced mediums such as Harris. "Born from heavenly love," golden, silver, azure, diamond, emerald, and opal fays lived on earth, frolicking mostly unseen and waiting for the coming day when humans would rise sufficiently in spiritual understanding to be able to commune with them.[41]

Most important, these early trance poems began to establish a doctrine that would become notorious: Harris's idea of "counterparts." According to Harris, "every human soul" had a perfect and opposite match-soul—a counterpart—with which it was destined to be "conjoined / In sacramental marriage of the heart." Belief in the existence of soul mates, "match spirits," or "affinities" was widespread among spiritualists, but Harris differed from his contemporaries by declaring that people's counterparts were generally not other living people but spirits, those who had died and gone over to the celestial plane. Harris's counterpart was Lily Queen, a powerful heavenly being with whom he entered a spiritual marriage in 1854. Harris's passages about Lily Queen are rife with intense erotic undertones:

> The Lily Queen lay sleeping, and her head
> Was fanned by swaying turquoise flowers, that fed
> The air with incense. O'er her form was spread
> A mantle sparkling like the ocean foam.
> Her parted lips like dewy sun-stars shone.

"I began to glow in her sweet presence," Harris continued. "My head on her translucent breast was pillowed.... I trembled as a dew-drop."[42]

Harris described his marriage to Lily Queen as akin to the new birth he had experienced as a teenager at the Utica revival: "I felt a new-born life in me begin." His mystical bond with Lily Queen would be a lifelong source of inspiration and authority for Harris. What his earthly wife Mary Van Arnum thought of this development is unknown, but it may not be coincidence that during the composition of *A Lyric of the Morning Land* she was gravely ill from tuberculosis and died before its publication. In 1856, Harris got remarried to a New Orleans spiritualist named Emily Isabella Waters, whom he had met during one of his frequent lecture tours to the city. But, according to Harris, he and Waters would never consummate the marriage.[43]

In fact, after his marriage to Lily Queen, Harris became an outspoken advocate of celibacy; all sexual impulses were to be directed toward heavenly counterparts, he insisted. "When a man is no longer entangled with women, he begins to long for a Social Kingdom of God," Harris would later explain. Human reproduction "must cease, 'til the sons and daughters of God are prepared for the higher generation, by evolution into structural, bisexual completeness, above the plane of sin, of disease, or of natural mortality." Celibacy helped "demagnetize" and "redeem" the body, Harris taught, by restoring it to a prelapsarian state that Adam and Eve had possessed before the fall. "There is no redemption for humanity till humanity shall deny itself the pleasure of the natural marriage bed," he wrote. Harris's concerns about sex, as well as its power to ruin spiritual advancement, had been brewing since Andrew Jackson Davis's marriage to Catherine DeWolf Dodge, and those concerns had intensified after the collapse of Mountain Cove. Celibacy now became his answer.[44]

Harris's public embrace of celibacy was a bigger departure from mainstream spiritualism than his belief in fairies or his apocalyptic prophesies. With their celebration of companionate marriage and procreation, spiritualists tended to be more "sex positive" than the broader culture. But Harris was hardly alone in championing sexual self-control as a means of spiritual advancement. Sexual desire's potential to disrupt piety was in fact a widespread concern in nineteenth-century America. Catholic priests and nuns and Shakers practiced celibacy; many others, from Protestant minister Lyman Beecher to diet reformer Sylvester Graham, urged sexual restraint. Yet many Americans considered celibacy dangerous; in the words of historian Kara French, proponents of celibacy "denaturalized the assumed naturalness of sex within marriage," and they sooner or later found themselves facing accusations that "unmentionable sexual deviance" went on behind closed doors.[45]

What made Harris unique compared to these other groups was his combining of celibacy with his doctrine of counterparts. On one hand, he urged total sexual self-control; on the other, he effused about the delights of counterpartal sex. "Soul-life and sex-life are at one, in the Divine their pulses run," he wrote. In another poem, he declared, "Unsexed existence weaves but desolation."[46] But as he had shown in his response to Davis's marriage to Catherine DeWolf Dodge, he was no fan of divorce, and he criticized "disorderly spiritualism" for its sanctioning of "extramarital spiritual attractions." He taught that earthly marriage vows, once taken, should be honored, and sexual impulses should be directed to celestial counterparts rather than potential soul mates among the living.[47]

On matters of sex, all spiritualists were deeply influenced by the writings of eighteenth-century Swedish theologian Emanuel Swedenborg. Trained as a natural scientist, Swedenborg had turned to spiritual investigation in the 1740s, recording and publishing his visions of the geography and inhabitants of various celestial realms. American spiritualists and other religious liberals admired Swedenborg's opposition to formal church structures, his dedication to personal spiritual exploration, and his conception of interpenetrating seen and unseen worlds.

More than any other thinker, Swedenborg influenced spiritualists' conceptions of sex. Based on his visits to heaven, he informed readers that spirits retain their gender and capacity for sexual desire after death. Not only is there marriage in heaven, there is sex—and lots of it. Holy, blessed, mind-blowing (heterosexual, monogamous) sex—what Swedenborg called "conjugal love"—between male and female spirits for all of eternity. Spiritualists, who strove to create heaven on earth as much as possible, embraced the potential for this kind of spiritual-sexual connection during their lifetimes and sought their soul mates accordingly.[48]

Like other spiritualists, Harris's trance poems borrowed elements of Swedenborg's celestial geography and his penchant for detailed, almost ethnographic description. However, Harris viewed Swedenborg's breakthroughs as partial, a starting rather than an ending point. "I do not think that he saw all truth or that he fully apprehended all that passed before his sight," wrote Harris in an 1853 letter, "but I do believe that in the Essentials of Truth he was correct."[49] When it came to sex, Harris's doctrine of counterparts borrowed from Swedenborg's "conjugal love" but Harris taught that it was usually possible only if at least one partner was in heaven. Sex between people on earth was mere "bodily pleasure"—a fool's gold that distracted and corrupted the spirit. Sexual urges in themselves were not immoral, but they became so unless directed heavenward, to counterparts like his Lily Queen. Perhaps as a result of this sublimation, Harris's writings were more unabashedly erotic than most spiritualists even as he condemned carnal desires between the living. More than anything else in Harris's theology, this unusual combination of sexuality and mysticism—celibacy and counterpartal sex—would disturb outsiders.

Harris's less than fully reverent appropriations of Swedenborg put him at odds with the Church of the New Jerusalem, also known as the New Church or most commonly the Swedenborgians, a small but vocal Protestant sect organized around the Swedish mystic's writings. In fact, a "trialogue" occurred in the late 1840s and 1850s between Transcendentalists, spiritualists, and Swedenborgians over the implications of Swedenborg's insights. Ralph Waldo Emerson and other Transcendentalists rejected the accuracy of Swedenborg's "dogmas" but were inspired by his example of joyful, self-directed spirituality. Some Swedenborgians, such as abolitionist George Bush, at first displayed an openness toward spiritualism before ultimately renouncing it as misguided, unruly, and even dangerous. They accepted only Swedenborg's writings and the Bible as divinely inspired, not the confusing and contradictory outpourings of America's growing ranks of mediums. Spiritualists, for their part, condemned the New Church as overly formal, authoritarian, and "bigoted," and they typically ignored Swedenborg's belief in hell, evil spirits, sin, and historical declension.[50]

More than any other figure, Harris walked the line between spiritualism and Swedenborgianism, borrowing from both movements but embraced by neither. He had first come to the unhappy attention of the Swedenborgians in 1847 while lecturing on Davis's *The Principles of Nature* in Cincinnati. Benjamin Fiske Barrett, a Swedenborgian minister from New York who happened to be in Cincinnati at the time, published a scathing attack on Davis and Harris, calling their theology "a perfect chaos of contradictions— a strange compound of Swedenborgianism, Universalism, Naturalism, Materialism, Infidelity, and Fourierism." By 1857, Harris had moved closer to the Swedenborgian orbit, establishing a new congregation in New York City called the Church of the Good Shepherd attended by both spiritualists and Swedenborgians. That same year he also founded the New Church Publishing Association, a brazen adoption of New Church nomenclature. Harris found support among a subset of liberal "New Era" Swedenborgians who were intrigued by his brand of esoteric spiritualism.[51]

All of Harris's metaphysical interests combined in 1858 in *Arcana of Christianity,* a manifesto laying out his religious cosmology in all its una-bashed weirdness. Harris promoted it as "the most comprehensive book of Philosophy, Morals, Religion, and Spiritual and Historical disclosures ever given to the world." *Arcana of Christianity* volume one—it would eventu-ally swell to thousands of pages over four volumes—had something to en-chant or offend any reader. Harris continued to position himself as God's singular prophet, insisting that his revelations came not from spirits or angels but were "revealed specially by the Lord Jesus Christ."[52] He rewrote sections of the Bible, correcting and interpreting them according to his di-vine visions. He took a tour of the solar system and reported that Mars had strange birds, platypuses, chimpanzees, kangaroos, elephants, llamas, and "camel-leopards."

He conferred with the spirits of Virgil, Confucius, the Apostle Paul, St. Augustine, Martin Luther, Oliver Cromwell, and his own Puritan ancestors.

In that portion of heaven reserved for the French, he asked after Napoleon Bonaparte but was told that his "Snow-phantom has vanished." He traveled with angels, spoke with fairies, and fought with demons. He badmouthed science, Mormonism, Roman Catholicism, atheism, and "pantheism." He gushed about counterpartal sex, the "nuptial blending of an angelic spouse with his companion" culminating in "an inter-blending of spirit with spirit, until the wife is absorbed into the being of the husband." Harris affirmed that "when they have attained to this condition they typify and represent the Lord," who was bisexual, the Two in One, both "the Eternal Masculine and the Eternal Feminine."

If all this was not wild enough, Harris reported that he spoke with the spirit of Emmanuel Swedenborg, who drolly told him, "I hear that you have been writing concerning me." Swedenborg went on to confess that his eighteenth-century writings were "concluded incorrectly," which Harris had long maintained. Swedenborg's spirit then gave Harris his blessing, rejoicing in "the opening of the celestial sense of the Word upon your orb." Harris proceeded to look into the future, when "pivotal men will arise, of a vast and complex genius" to usher in the unfolding of God's plans for earth. Existing nations and religions will fall away, and "the New Church will at last govern the social earth." The first of these pivotal men was, to no reader's surprise, Harris himself.[53]

No group was more offended by *Arcana of Christianity* than the Swedenborgians, who moved to distance themselves from Harris and what they called his "visits to Mars and the 'heaven girls.'"[54] They resented his use of New Church terminology and how he blended Swedenborg's ideas with the "vain imaginations of his own mind."[55] Harris's old foe Benjamin Fiske Barrett, now editor of *The Swedenborgian* magazine, mocked him for daring to "compare himself with Swedenborg, and to assume to write *from a higher plane* than he did."[56] Excommunicated by the Baptists, nearly expelled by the Universalists, and denounced by mainstream spiritualists, Harris had now made lifelong enemies of the Swedenborgians, an enmity that would eventually bring disastrous consequences for Harris.

In April 1859, Harris stepped down as pastor of the Church of the Good Shepherd and announced he was leaving New York for the world's other center of occult activity, London. "I am about to go on a long and painful journey," he informed his congregation.[57] But God had commanded him, "My son, go thou to England, and there I will show you further what you shall do."[58] It would be in Great Britain that Harris would found the Brotherhood of the New Life, the spiritual community that would be the focus of his energies for the remainder of his life. In Britain, he would gain his most famous acolyte, diplomat, and Parliament member—Laurence Oliphant. Although Harris would return to the United States in 1861, he would never again be as engaged and open with the American public as he had been in New York in the 1850s—until his breakthrough at Linn Lilla forty years later.

Now, in the autumn of 1890, Harris prepared to re-enter conversation with a wider world he had ignored for decades. Blessed with supernaturally renewed youth, he was brimming with new poems, new manifestos, and new proclamations. He began planning a Fountaingrove Library pamphlet series to be published quarterly and circulated in California and beyond. The first volume, to be titled *The New Republic: Prospects, Dangers, Duties, and Safeties of the Times,* was to be a full-throated attack on unrestrained industrial capitalism and the spiritual woes it birthed. "No more an old man of nigh seventy, but now renewed in more than the physical and mental prowess of the early prime," he informed the world, "my retirement is at an end."[59]

2

April 1891

The Spiritual Reformer

Alzire Chevaillier decided to write the prophet a letter. She had spent weeks poring over Thomas Lake Harris's works, both his brand-new socialist manifesto *The New Republic: Prospects, Dangers, Duties, and Safeties of the Times*, and some older, rarer books she had managed to find. Deeply impressed by *The New Republic*'s religious attack on industrial capitalism, Chevaillier saw in it "conclusive corroboration" of one of her core beliefs: "The Kingdom of Heaven is not born within, unless it externalizes the Kingdom of Heaven, *i.e.,* of peace, harmony, and goodwill without." This was in fact something to which Chevaillier had dedicated her adult life: the application of spiritual truths to America's social and economic problems.[1]

However, Chevaillier was most taken by one of Harris's earlier, stranger books, the similarly titled *The Great Republic: A Poem of the Sun*, a 250-page lyrical poem describing a utopian civilization on the sun Harris had visited in a dream. Although most of the poem described this solar paradise, Chevaillier was especially struck by some passages discussing the challenges of moral reform here on earth: "Reformers fail because they change the letter, / And not the spirit of the world's design." Harris urged reformers to focus not on the wider world but themselves: "Grow perfect! bide thy time! in thine own being, / Solve, by an actual test, the problems vast, / That vex mankind."[2]

In the spring of 1891, Chevaillier's mounting frustration with her political reform work—and with the doctrines of traditional Christianity—made Harris's advice to turn inward especially appealing. She was forty years old, living in Manhattan, an experienced activist, orator, writer, teacher, magazine editor, and mental healer. Yet she could look back on few concrete victories after more than a decade of political activism. Her mostly thwarted desires to do good in the world had led her to move further and further from the traditional Christianity of her youth and toward metaphysical answers of the sort Harris offered.

Unholy Sensations. Joshua Paddison, Oxford University Press. © Oxford University Press 2025.
DOI: 10.1093/oso/9780197775325.003.0002

Beginning in her late twenties, she had thrown herself into a variety of social movements first in Boston and later in New York City, striving to protect the most vulnerable members of urban society. Boston and New York in the 1880s were central hubs of the Social Gospel, a loosely organized movement of Christian reformers dedicated to solving the many problems engulfing American cities during the Gilded Age. Poverty, crime, alcoholism, disease, the exploitation of workers—the Social Gospel strove to solve these problems and more through the implementation of Christian principles on industrialized society. A graduate of the Boston Girls High and Normal School, Chevaillier was typical of white female Social Gospel reformers, who tended to be middle class and educated.[3] Despite suffering from frequent "nervous" troubles, she longed to help create in the United States what she called the "Brotherhood of Man—which means equal opportunity, equal privilege, equal culture, equal service—no caste, no distinction."[4] However, controversy and disappointment seemed to follow her every move.

The first issue she had felt called to address was America's deplorable treatment of the mentally ill. In 1880, Chevaillier had helped found the National Association for the Protection of the Insane, which strove to modernize urban asylums. Despite the earlier efforts of reformers like Dorothea Dix, American asylums typically operated without governmental oversight. Many were little more than overcrowded holding tanks for people suffering from a wide range of mental and physical issues. "Shall we not put hearts and minds and hands together," asked Chevaillier, to make asylums less like prisons and more "homelike"?[5] She conducted her own one-woman letter-writing campaign to politicians and literary figures, including Massachusetts governor John Davis Long and poet Henry Wadsworth Longfellow, pleading with them to remember "that class of people we are all too apt to forget," namely "the innocent and powerless insane."[6]

However, she and other members of the Association had triggered a tremendous public backlash when they declared Charles Guiteau, the assassin who killed President James Garfield, insane and unfit to be executed. Guiteau claimed that had God commanded him to shoot the president; during his trial, Guiteau's defense attorneys attempted to portray him as criminally insane, but the jury—along with most of the nation—judged him sane enough to be held responsible for the murder. After Guiteau was sentenced to die, Chevaillier visited the White House to plead with President Chester Arthur to delay the execution long enough for a commission of psychiatrists to study Guiteau's mind. However, the idea that he might escape execution due to insanity infuriated many Americans, and the press castigated the National Association for the Protection of the Insane for meddling in the case. Chevaillier felt she was "in the teeth of the fury of this whole *nation.*" The assassin Guiteau was hanged in 1882, and the Association soon disbanded.[7]

Immediately after, Chevaillier was swept into another controversy when she defended Massachusetts Governor Benjamin "Beast" Butler's attacks on Tewksbury Almshouse, which included a hospital for the insane. A loud-mouthed champion of the common man with a nose for making headlines, "Beast" Butler accused Tewksbury employees of a host of macabre crimes, including secretly selling the dead bodies of inmates to Harvard Medical School and tanning "human skin" from corpses to make shoes. According to Butler, Tewksbury employees then sold these shoes to "men of jaded passions, worn out prematurely by their vices. . . . If they can put their feet in slippers made from a woman's breast, perhaps they can feed their imaginations."[8]

During the fallout from these accusations, Butler sent Chevaillier as his representative to the annual Conference on Charities and Corrections in Louisville, Kentucky. After her accusatory report on Tewksbury, she found herself under attack by Butler's political enemies, who called her a liar and struck her report from the official proceedings. Chevaillier fired back in the press, insisting, "my one hobby [is] my hatred of deception, and I happen to have the moral fearlessness to have no temptation to deceive."[9] Butler managed to force out the superintendent of Tewksbury, but the Massachusetts legislature decided there was no basis to most of his inflammatory charges. Butler lost his re-election bid the following year, and Chevaillier looked foolish for having parroted his talk of missing corpses and human-skin slippers.

From there, she became involved in a variety of social issues—helping secure "free soup" for Boston's poor, touring European welfare institutions as part of a federal commission—never staying with any issue for long. Her family's wealth and connections allowed her to dabble. Her father, Jean Charles Chevaillier, had immigrated from his native France to Nacogdoches, Texas, in 1835 on the eve of the Texas Revolution.[10] He prospered in Anglo-controlled Texas, becoming a merchant, rancher, and slaveowner.[11] In 1848, after the United States annexed Texas, he married Sarah Conant Clark, a teenager half his age who hailed from an old Boston family that traced its lineage back to the *Mayflower.*[12]

Named for the romantic heroine of Voltaire's play *Alzire*, Alzire Adrienne Chevaillier was born in Nacogdoches, Texas, in 1850, but her father Jean

Charles died suddenly while she was a toddler. Her mother, pregnant with a second child, took Alzire back home to Boston, but the bulk of her husband's estate ended up staying in Texas to pay off his debts. A widow at age twenty-two, Alzire's mother, Sarah, worked as a teacher and took in boarders to pay for the education of her two children.[13] Young Alzire took private lessons from famed abolitionist Wendell Phillips, a friend of the Clark family. One boarder who stayed with the Chevailliers in Boston described Sarah Chevaillier as "a nervous, brisk, vivacious, and intelligent little woman"; as for Alzire, she "suffered from nervous troubles."[14] Alzire's younger brother Charles moved back to Texas in 1871, where he grew cotton on some of his father's former lands, while she took up reform work in Boston.[15]

Chevaillier's activism sprang directly from her strong religious beliefs, which had earned her the childhood nickname "Faith." She grew up in the Episcopalian church, as had her mother and grandfather before her. In her twenties, she was a devoted congregant of Trinity Church, the wealthy Episcopal church that towered like a Gothic castle over Copley Square in Boston. She had a close friendship with Phillips Brooks, nationally famous rector of Trinity, filling a notebook with abstracts of his sermons and meeting with him frequently about her spiritual development.[16] A central question young Chevaillier struggled with concerned the unfairness of social inequality and God's apparent refusal to change things. She pondered, "Was not God our Father and did he not own everything, all the wealth of the world, and yet he lets some of his children starve and gives others so much."[17] A big man with prematurely silver hair and "large, dark, glowing eyes," the charismatic Brooks espoused a brand of liberal Protestantism that embraced the Social Gospel—to a point. He supported woman suffrage and social programs for the poor but rarely spoke on political matters from the pulpit.[18] Chevaillier later recalled "this white-haired holy man with his large beautiful eyes looking into my earnest distracted ones and taking both my hands in his." He told her not to blame God for poverty, for God "has given a world of plenty for every man, woman and child in it to have." Instead, he placed the blame on humanity's own selfishness, greed, and ignorance.[19]

By the mid-1880s, Chevaillier was increasingly unsatisfied with the answers offered by Phillips Brooks—and traditional Christianity. The "dead-ness of forms and rituals" in the Episcopal Church disgusted her, as did the liturgy with its "numberless repetitions."[20] She also continued to suffer from what she called "ill health and partial invalidism," which made her "human-itarian efforts spasmodic."[21] Later, during the Fountaingrove scandal, she would be accused of spending time in an asylum as a patient rather than a reformer during this period. Like many other white middle-class women of her era, she may have been diagnosed with "neurasthenia," a catch-all term for a range of symptoms including headaches, fatigue, and anxiety. Chevaillier had worked with George M. Beard, the world's leading authority on neurasthenia, on the Guiteau insanity case. There was no known cure for neurasthenia, but by the early 1880s, Beard and other physicians were exploring treatments, such as hypnosis and talk therapy, that emphasized underlying emotional causes.[22] These solutions lacked an explicitly spiritual dimension, however. For a solution to her health problems, Chevaillier turned instead to what newspapers were calling the "Boston craze"—Christian Science.

In the spring of 1885, she began taking classes from Mary Baker Eddy at her Massachusetts Metaphysical College. Eddy's Christian Science movement was based on the idea that "mind alone can save a man's life and heal his diseases."[23] Centered in Boston, the movement was beginning to attract spiritual seekers like Chevaillier who were moving beyond the boundaries of liberal Protestantism. Eddy, then in her early sixties, had founded the Christian Science Association in 1879. Beset by a lifetime of ill health, Eddy had studied spiritualism, mesmerism, homeopathy, vegetarianism, and the water cure before developing her own spiritual system of healing. She taught that "all sensation is Mind, and Mind is God"; she denounced "the use of drugs, hygiene, manipulation, alcohol, tobacco, or anything but Mind to make and keep man well and happy."[24]

Chevaillier took Eddy's course in "Mind Healing," which promised to teach students how to heal physical maladies by convincing the afflicted that their problems did not truly exist. Eddy's assigned readings were from the Bible and her scripture *Science and Health*. Chevaillier embraced Christian Science with her typical fervor. In a letter to Eddy, she vowed to "find out what it is that is wrong in me, and to root it out at whatever cost, until I am absolutely empty, and ready to be filled with the Holy Spirit, and thus declare the God who is power and love to mankind."[25]

By this point, only about 140 people had taken classes with Eddy since she opened the College in 1881; most were middle-class reform-minded women like Chevaillier who longed to heal themselves and the wider world. Compared to Protestant churches like Trinity, with their patriarchal structure and traditional orthodoxies, Christian Science offered theologies and practices that were radical, woman centered, and practical.[26] Christian Science theology was distinctly feminist; Eddy envisioned God as a bisexual

"Father-Mother" and the Holy Spirit as a "Holy Comforter." She celebrated Eve from Genesis as the world's first Christian Scientist. At Eddy's college, women who completed sufficient coursework became certified as Christian Science Association healers, giving them access to the male-dominated fields of medicine and religious leadership. Some established their own Christian Science institutes in other cities, essentially running franchises of the Massachusetts Metaphysical College.[27]

While Chevaillier was taking the Mind Healing course, Eddy invited her to her home on several evenings for conversation. "You are so spiritual and have done so much good in Boston that I feel sure you will make my instantaneous healer," Eddy told her.[28] When Chevaillier came down with pneumonia, she proudly informed Eddy that she refused all medicine, even when Phillips Brooks told her, "God made the medicines and it was my *duty* to take them."[29] However, the women's relationship soon began to sour. Eddy urged her to board at the college while taking a second class, but Chevaillier hesitated. Eddy had said that the first class was free but now was pressuring her for money. Worse, Chevaillier longed to be a mental healer, of herself and others, but she seemed to lack the gift. She declared herself the college's "worst pupil" and hoped that Eddy would "not blame my dullness, for my whole being *longs* to *be good* and to *do* good."[30] And her own health grew markedly *worse* after taking the class.

In November 1885, Chevaillier formally broke with the Christian Science Association. In a long letter to Eddy, Chevaillier gave ten reasons why she was leaving. She objected to Eddy's insistence on secrecy and how Eddy publicly vilified ex-practitioners who left the movement. In a foreshadowing of her later attacks against Thomas Lake Harris, she compared Christian Science to "Romanish doctrine," with its "papal infallibility and the surrender of individual judgment and conscience." Chevaillier was not alone in feeling this way; although Eddy's theology was feminist and her movement offered opportunities for women to become healers, Eddy's authoritarian leadership style tended to alienate her best students.[31] Furthermore, Chevaillier complained, "I have never been able to heal the simplest case of belief in sickness in others." Perhaps worst of all, she mourned that "my life has been practically thrown away the past year.... I have literally *done nothing* except in the smallest private normal ways for Humanity."[32] She had devoted almost a year to Eddy and left with mostly regrets about time squandered.

Chevaillier was finished with Eddy, but not with mental healing. The year following her split with the Christian Science Association, Chevaillier finally found herself able to mentally heal a family friend in Texas named Clara Starr of a rare disease, making her miraculous recovery "the only case in medical history."[33] Chevaillier began associating with other disgruntled former students of Eddy who were hanging up their shingles advertising metaphysical healing, "mind cure," and even Christian Science, much to Eddy's chagrin. Chevaillier took classes from Anna B. Newman, a Boston mind cure healer who counted the author Louisa May Alcott among her patients.[34] In fact, by 1886 Boston had six different mind cure clinics, all borrowing to one degree or another from Eddy or from Eddy's own teacher, Phineas Quimby. A physician and former Christian Scientist named Luther Marston opened a Church of the Divine Unity in Boston in 1888 that became a haven for disaffected Eddyites. Boston's apostates were in contact with those in other cities, especially Emma Curtis Hopkins in Chicago and Mary Plunkett, the "high priestess" of mental healing in New York. They created institutes and schools, published newspapers and journals, and ended up attracting more people to the principles of Christian Science than Eddy ever had. These offshoot movements would later become known as New Thought.[35]

By 1888, Chevaillier advertised herself as a metaphysical healer. She charged one dollar per treatment but waived the fee for those who could not afford it. Like other Christian Scientists, she healed by showing clients that their physical maladies lay only in their minds, a feat accomplished through conversation, prayer, and "thought transference" from Chevaillier to the patient.[36] "My method of treatment is purely MENTAL, through the POSITIVE THOUGHT OF SPIRITUAL TRUTH AND LAW," she explained.[37] In a letter to Mary Plunkett's *International Magazine of Christian Science*, which had a wider circulation than Eddy's *Christian Science Journal*, Chevaillier boasted of curing "a lady suffering from melancholia, with suicidal tendencies"; a woman with "an acute case of dysentery, cured in one treatment"; and patients with typhoid fever, poor eyesight, diarrhea, and cancer. "I now intend to devote all my time to teaching and healing, as I believe it to be of infinitely greater value than literary or philanthropic work," she wrote. Political reform, she now believed, was "simply 'beating the air;' fighting effect instead of cause; resisting evil instead of building up the good; negative rather than positive; iconoclastic rather than constructive; human rather than Divine."[38] By healing one patient at a time, she could do more good than she ever accomplished politically.

Chevaillier had moved beyond traditional Protestant theology but, like many nineteenth-century metaphysicians, she remained committed to a personal identity that was broadly Christian. In another article for the *International Magazine of Christian Science*, she emphasized that she followed the "simple primitive Christianity as taught by the Christ in the four gospels." Yet in that same article she made the unorthodox argument that physical death was not inevitable; rather, it was possible to "change from the natural to the spiritual" so gradually that "we cannot tell when the supreme moment of the complete spiritualization of the body occurs." Death was unnecessary for those with sufficient faith. To support her claim, she quoted the Bible, Phillips Brooks, Mary Baker Eddy, and the Buddhologist Edwin Arnold.[39] From these and other sources, Alzire was concocting her own brand of spirituality that emphasized the power of the mind, the illusory nature of the physical world, and a God of universal love. "God is All—God is Good—All is Good": this is "the one truth of the universe," she insisted.[40] For Chevaillier, this interconnectedness necessitated concern for others, especially the less fortunate. "No one can be happy while his brother has not equal opportunity and privilege as the child of God," she wrote in a letter to Eddy.[41]

Although Chevaillier and other former students of Eddy usually praised their former teacher, Eddy did not return the favor. Instead, she viewed them as perverting her teachings and diluting her brand. She claimed sole authorship of Christian Science and successfully sued one ex-student, Edward J. Arens, for copyright infringement.[42] In print, she labeled non-authorized practitioners "charlatan teachers, healers, and authors [who] are flooding the community" and indicted them for practicing not Christian Science but "mesmerism, *alias* mental mal-practice."[43] Eddy used the terms mesmerism, mental mal-practice, and malicious animal magnetism to describe a misapplication of her principles to cause harm rather than healing.[44] In private letters, she accused certain former students of "exercising all their magic of evil in occultism to kill me."[45] She urged Christian Scientists loyal to her to identify "transgressors" in the movement who were straying from Eddy's approved methods. These transgressors were instructed, "Waken from this spell of Animal Magnetism! You know you are not doing or feeling right to deceive or to turn away from or to hate us or Mrs. Eddy. It is *mesmerism*, and shall not control you."[46] Even students loyal to Eddy could earn her ire. When Christian Scientist Abby H. Corner was indicted for manslaughter in 1888 after her daughter died in childbirth while under her care, Eddy denounced Corner as a "recreant practitioner" and "impostor" in local newspapers.[47] For Eddy, this was not merely a struggle over control of a movement, this was a holy war between spiritual forces of good and evil.

In response to Eddy's slanders, Chevaillier issued a call for unity and peace among mental healers. Addressing "the Eddyites, the Marstonites, the Dresserites, the Plunkettites, the Hopkinites, the Wilmanites, and so on *ad infinitum*," she reminded them that "it is the one Truth we proclaim."[48] Deeply moved by Edward Bellamy's new novel *Looking Backward*, published in Boston in 1888, Chevaillier was becoming interested in politics once again. The novel described a future America in which socialism had eradicated poverty, inequality, class conflict, and pollution. Chevaillier joined mental healer Abby Morton Diaz to help found the nation's first "Bellamy club" in Boston, which sparked a widespread network of so-called Nationalist clubs dedicated to promoting socialism in the United States.[49] "Mr. Bellamy's method of Nationalization of Industries," Chevaillier informed her fellow mental healers, "to me seems the only practical solution" to the human misery created by industrial capitalism.[50] She viewed disharmony among metaphysicians as a distraction from pressing political and moral issues of the day.

In 1889, however, the mental healer wars reached their apex when a scandal erupted in New York that threatened to discredit the entire mental healing industry. Unsurprisingly, it involved sex and marriage, especially dangerous topics for a woman-centered movement like Christian Science. First, in the pages of the *International Magazine of Christian Science*, Eddy's disaffected former student Mary Plunkett alongside her husband John publicly declared their marriage "null and void." They said that they had been celibate for years, living "together as friends."[51] But the two did not legally divorce and in fact would have found it difficult to do so. Divorce laws in New York were among the strictest in the United States, typically granting a divorce only upon proof of adultery or abandonment. Spouses could not both seek a divorce, this was labeled "collusion" and was "morally reprehensible."[52]

Nevertheless, Mary Plunkett soon wed one of her students, Arthur Bently Worthington, in a private ceremony and began calling herself Mary Bently Worthington. She filled the July 1889 issue of the *International Magazine of Christian Science* with a lengthy defense of her actions. She acknowledged the "ignorant malice, envious rivalry, and unreasonable hatred" she now faced from friends and the public, and in fact some newspapers were calling for her immediate arrest for bigamy or unlawful cohabitation.[53] However, Mary insisted she acted not out of "weakness or immorality" nor from "vice and lust." Rather, she had discovered, in Worthington, her soul's true mate. She cited Emmanuel Swedenborg's notion of "conjugal love," a powerful love between a man and a woman that is "spiritual" rather than "sensual." Uniting with Arthur Bently Worthington was nothing less than "the ultimate of all religious inquest," the culmination of her spiritual journey. She insisted that she practiced "Divine marriage," not "free love," which she repudiated and called "free lust . . . conceived of the devil (ignorance)."[54] Similarly, Arthur told a reporter, "We are not believers in free love, but rather perfect marriage."[55]

The Worthingtons were treading carefully—for understandable reasons. Their anxieties about practicing "free love" sprang from a widespread public backlash to sex radicalism that was reaching its peak in the 1880s. Inspired by Swedenborg as well as French philosopher Charles Fourier, feminists in the United States had offered religious, political, and economic critiques of marriage beginning in the antebellum period. These activists insisted that sex must be an expression of love rather than marital duty, and they portrayed loveless marriage as "legalized adultery" and "slavery" for women in particular, who had no legal right to refuse sex with their husbands. Although the vast majority of these sex radicals advocated serial heterosexual monogamy, not what would today be called polyamory, their "free love" movement encountered fierce opposition from newspaper editors, clergymen, and politicians, who portrayed free lovers as sanctioning unrestrained promiscuity and the destruction of families.[56]

The U.S. government criminalized the circulation of "obscene" and "immoral" materials in 1873, especially targeting sex radicals for prosecution. U.S. postal inspector Anthony Comstock hounded Victoria Woodhull, a spiritualist, woman's rights activist, and "varietist," who sanctioned serial monogamy in the pursuit of true love. Dubbed "Mrs. Satan" by cartoonist Thomas Nast, Woodhull and free love were caricatured in the press as demonic.[57] By the 1880s, spiritualists, freethinkers, and woman's rights groups were distancing themselves from the taint of so-called free love.[58] Mary Bently Worthington's denunciation of free love was a form of this distancing, made all the more urgent because she had left an unfulfilling marriage for an emotionally and physically satisfying one, the precise move sex radicals had been championing for decades.

Mary Baker Eddy, however, saw an opportunity to pounce. As an unconventional woman who herself had faced charges of promoting free love when starting her movement, Eddy knew these waters well. She consistently emphasized the "purity" of Christian Science and condemned all forms of desire. Although she married three times, she taught that celibacy was "nearer right" than marriage.[59] In *Science and Health*, Eddy described sex and marriage in distasteful terms, viewing them as—for now—necessary for the reproduction of the species due to humanity's current lack of spiritual development. But she condemned infidelity as a "pestilence" and free love as "depravity."[60] When Victoria Woodhull had lectured in Massachusetts in 1876, Eddy wrote a letter to a local newspaper excoriating her as "one who outrages decency, insults human nature, and disgraces the name of woman."[61]

So when Mary Plunkett became Mary Bently Worthington, Eddy was ready. Her *Christian Science Journal* carried articles in its June and July 1889 issues about her former student. Eddy bragged of having "crossed swords with free-love" back in the 1870s and free love "fell *hors de combat.*" Now, in Mary Bently Worthington, she saw a "phoenix" that was "springing up from the ashes of free-love." Her ex-student's talk of "Divine marriage" was, Eddy said, nothing more than "conjugal insanities" masking "gross sensualism." She emphasized that Mary was no longer a member of the Christian Science Association and "unworthy to use the name of Science."[62] Privately, Eddy warned her students that "Plunkett has exploded in her matrimonial morals." Eddy knew that Christian Science itself was at risk. "Great care must be taken to keep the garments of this Body *clean,*" she wrote to her students. "One defective apple causes the ones at its sides to rot and moulder."[63]

Alzire Chevaillier had long been friendly with Mary Plunkett. When the news broke of her marriage to Arthur Bently Worthington, Chevaillier had a decision to make. Most mental healers were distancing themselves from Mary, but Chevaillier stood by her—cautiously. In the same issue of the *International Magazine of Christian Science* in which Mary announced her new marriage, Chevaillier wrote an article titled "Judge Not." Without mentioning the scandalous marriage, she asked those in mental healing circles to avoid "righteous judgment." She said the Bible as well as Christian Science taught people not to engage in gossip and criticism of other people's sins.[64] This was hardly a full-throated defense of Mary's marriage and in fact implied that it was sinful. Chevaillier's article amounted to a mild show of support for Mary without endorsing her new marriage or anything resembling free love. However, under fire from Eddy and the press, Mary was grateful, praising Chevaillier for her "breadth of thinking" and her "freedom from that most common plague, 'judging.'"[65]

Chevaillier may have regretted this small act of compassion when newspapers reported in late July 1889 that Arthur Bently Worthington was in fact Samuel Oakley Crawford, a "forger, thief, and ex-convict" with a string of abandoned wives in multiple states. This "king of villains," who operated under many pseudonyms, had last been seen a few months earlier posing as a lawyer in Grand Forks, North Dakota, before he skipped town, leaving behind a wife and child.[66] Newspapers initially portrayed Mary as a naïve dupe of Crawford's schemes until she insisted that, in fact, he had told her of his past "troubles" after they married and she had decided to stick by him. Even if Arthur Bently Worthington was not his real name, she defiantly informed the press, "Mary Bently Worthington is the name I have taken, and I shall carry it as long as I live."[67] However, the "Free Love Pair," as the New York Sun labeled them, quickly discovered they could no longer live and work "unmolested" in New York.[68] In September 1889 they left the country, going first to London and then Christchurch, New Zealand, where they went on to found a controversial religious movement called the Students of Truth.[69]

As the Mary Bently Worthington scandal played out, newspaper editors and Protestant ministers seized the opportunity to attack what they dubbed "unchristian science" and the "divine healing business," exactly as Mary Baker Eddy had feared.[70] The Plunkett-Worthington "free love partnership," opined the New York Sun, was a natural outgrowth of "Christian Science humbug."[71] Rev. James Buckley, editor of New York's Methodist newspaper, declared that the Plunkett-Worthington affair illustrated the evils of Christian Science, which "has already destroyed the peace of many families by intimacies which has arisen between female 'scientists' and male patients." Buckley cited the sexually charged privacy required during the treatment process as well as the "peculiar personal influence of the physician over the patient" as evidence of how mental healing led to "unholy alliances."[72] Buckley's comments showed how female-dominated mental healing practices threatened prevailing American norms of religion, gender, and sexuality. Unlike male physicians, female mental healers were suspected of misusing their powers to tempt and seduce men, employing their unorthodox religious doctrines as cover. Mary Worthington's own sister, Viola Buckley, told a reporter, "Christian Science is a cloak for free love."[73]

Christian Scientists in New York who were still loyal to Eddy had to field questions about Mary Bently Worthington and free love. Rev. F. E. Mason, a Christian Science pastor in Brooklyn, insisted that "Christian Science respects the laws of the land in relation to the marriage vow." Mary and her ilk were "so-called Christian Scientists"—unsanctioned practitioners.[74] Bizarrely, Laura Lathrop, another of Eddy's followers in New York, blamed the scandal on Mary's first husband John Plunkett, who she said was "weak" and had allowed Mary to "dominate in everything."[75] Mary, it seems, had overstepped her role as properly submissive wife, and John had not been manly enough to keep her in place and so had been cuckolded.

As for Eddy herself, after the Plunkett-Worthington affair, she began to consolidate control over Christian Science as a brand and a religion. In October 1889 she closed the Massachusetts Metaphysical Association, which had produced as many competitors as loyal acolytes. She began planning the building of a Mother Church in Boston and, in 1894, would change the format of all church services so that pastors read only prearranged passages from the Bible and Eddy's *Science and Health* rather than give their own sermons. And she used copyright law to establish control over her writings and the term "Christian Science."[76]

Alzire Chevaillier had managed to thread the needle of the Plunkett-Worthington scandal, supporting her friend without being tainted by associations with free love. The entire affair must have been eye-opening for her. It showed her how society—including other metaphysicians—treated a woman who insisted on her ability to control her own sexual life. It also showed her the power of the media to exaggerate, distort, and destroy, and how accusations of free love in particular sparked cultural fears of moral ruin. Chevaillier would take these lessons with her to the next phase of her activism: editing her own magazine.

Just before Mary Bently Worthington left the country, she turned control of the *International Magazine of Christian Science* over to Chevaillier. Mary called Chevaillier "the one woman, who during all the storm and fury caused by my announcement of the great truth of conjugial marriage, which she did not endorse at all, has stood calmly heroic" in nonjudgment.[77] Chevaillier took over Mary's office in midtown Manhattan and her subscription list, but she moved quickly to distance herself from the *Journal's* now notorious former editor—and from Eddy's Christian Science. In October 1889, Chevaillier released her first issue, now renamed the *International Magazine of Truth*. She assured readers that "the question of Marriage and Divorce, which has occupied, of late, much space in the Magazine will not hereafter be discussed." Furthermore, she emphasized that her magazine "will not sanction any violation of defiance of the civil law." Instead, the magazine "shall stand for Purity, Peace, Charity, and Righteousness."[78]

An illustration on the cover of her first issue, which Chevaillier drew herself, displayed her spiritual interests at this time, a blend of feminist mental healing and liberal Christianity with a dash of Asian mysticism. A robed white woman embodying Truth advances toward the reader, holding a mirror toward heaven in one hand and a book in the other. "We must keep our mirrors (thoughts) turned towards the Lord," Chevaillier explained. A crescent moon in the sky represents "the Orient ... the Eastern origin of the search for spiritual enlightenment." The entire scene originates from a lamp in the bottom corner of the page representing "Divine Science, as revealed spiritually by the Christ." The pursuit of truth, above all else, would be her new spiritual and political goal.[79]

The following year, which Chevaillier spent in New York, was the busiest of her life. She produced twelve issues of her magazine, each of which contained multiple essays, book reviews, and editorials by Chevaillier in addition to articles she solicited. One of Mary Baker Eddy's biographers would later call Chevaillier's *International Magazine of Truth* an "embryonic *Atlantic Monthly*," and in fact it was more concerned with political issues of the day than most mental-healing periodicals.[80] Chevaillier used the journal to condemn prisons, capital punishment, plutocracy, and industrial capitalism.[81] She steered clear of anything related to sex, winning paise for being "much too smart to sacrifice her prestige by openly flying in the face of decency."[82] She remained involved in the Bellamy-inspired Nationalist movement, served as secretary for New York's first Christian Socialist club, and was president of the newly formed New-York Society for Parks and Playgrounds for Children.[83] She wrote articles attacking child labor and religious intolerance for Boston's progressive journal *The Arena*.[84] She also continued her mental-healing practice in New York and offered courses in the "Divine Science of Spiritual Truth and Brotherly Love," charging fifteen dollars for twelve lessons.[85]

It was a flurry of activity, going in many directions at once in a way that was excessive even for her, and by the fall of 1890 Chevaillier began to feel that she had spread herself too thin. Her magazine was becoming a financial burden, with many subscribers and advertisers negligent in their payments.[86] She decided to merge her *International Magazine of Truth* with another metaphysical publication, *The Problem of Life*, edited by Wilberforce J. Colville. He was a well-known healer and lecturer who had had a colorful career as a spiritualist before turning to mental healing. This background in spiritualism was unusual for most people in mental-healing circles, who, following Eddy's lead, often looked down on popular spirit communication as "mainly

International Magazine of Truth, October 15, 1889; courtesy Mary Baker Eddy Library, Boston.

erroneous, having no scientific basis nor origin, no proof nor power outside of human testimony."[87]

Feminine and small in stature, Colville had been a popular spiritualist trance speaker since age sixteen. Only female spirits spoke through him, and he was an outspoken advocate of women's rights.[88] By 1886, he had joined the Boston mind cure community and was also becoming interested in Theosophy and Buddhism.[89] He then moved to California, where he lectured on metaphysics to audiences in Oakland, San Francisco, Sacramento, and Los Angeles.[90] *The Problem of Life* was more broad-minded than most mental-healing periodicals; "uniformity we despise," Colville wrote in his first issue. "We KNOW there is truth in all systems, but the WHOLE TRUTH in none." And he criticized mental healers who "are often so unfriendly to each other's views—what is the matter with them?"[91] Chevaillier's decision to join forces with him was another step away from Eddy and Christian Science and a step toward a broader metaphysics that included spiritualism. Colville edited the combined magazine, with Chevaillier a regular contributor and editor of a section in each issue.

Giving up the magazine freed Chevaillier to become involved in an issue that had long interested her: woman suffrage. Home to national leader Elizabeth Cady Stanton, New York City had long been an unofficial headquarters for the suffrage movement and a frequent site of parades, rallies, and conferences.[92] In February 1891, Lillie Devereux Blake, president of the New York City Woman Suffrage League, invited Chevaillier to give an address to her members. Presumably this was due to Chevaillier's record of political activism rather than her work as a mental healer, a movement that had an uneasy relationship with woman suffrage. Mental healing had proved attractive to many suffragists in the 1880s, not surprising considering mental healing's woman-centered practices and demographics, creating tensions with evangelical Protestants and freethinkers in the suffrage movement. Raised a Quaker, Susan B. Anthony took classes from Eddy's acolyte Laura Lathrop in 1887 but publicly kept Christian Science at arm's distance.[93] Stanton was openly critical; when a friend moved to Chicago to take classes from Emma Curtis Hopkins, Stanton dismissed mental healing as "mental bewilderment" and called it an "epidemic, which is certainly very contagious and spreading in many latitudes."[94] Stanton and Blake viewed all organized religions as a crucial component of women's subjugation and were working together on *The Woman's Bible*, a chapter-by-chapter denunciation of patriarchy in the Bible. At the same time, more conservative suffragists objected to mental healing because of its unorthodox doctrines and associations with free love and radicalism.[95]

In her speech before the Woman Suffrage League, Chevaillier made no attempt to hide her intertwined metaphysical and political convictions, warning her listeners that her convictions were "radical." Certainly women deserved suffrage, she said, but it was not enough for women to gain political rights—those rights must be accompanied by spiritual growth or women would make the same errors of "conservatism, superstition, and custom" that men had made. "Yes, my friends, woman suffrage, until we rise to the consciousness of our highest birthright, would mean little," she said. Only by strengthening their "faith in the Divinity of Man, male and female, as the manifestation of our Father-Mother God," could women realize their "higher mission to bruise the heel of the serpent of ignorance, discord, and sin." Political questions were in reality spiritual ones, she said. She concluded by challenging women to look beyond suffrage to the many social problems that needed their attention. Her list of pressing political issues included enacting dress reform ("let every earnest woman forswear corsets"); ending child labor; creating public-supported nurseries, kindergartens, and playgrounds; alleviating poverty; passing temperance laws; abolishing capital punishment; and nationalizing all factories and industry.[96]

Unabashedly socialist and infused with feminist metaphysics, Chevaillier's speech won praise from Edward Bellamy, who declared it "excellent."[97] What the women in the Suffrage League made of it is unclear, although Chevaillier did note soon after that her "radical unpopular thought" was ruffling some feathers in New York.[98] She insisted that she had no regrets. For Chevaillier, humanity's spiritual immaturity was the underlying root cause of misery and inequality. How could a reformer address the health of the world and nation without first addressing the health of herself? It was a question she had struggled with throughout her adult life as she had oscillated between focusing on personal spiritual growth and focusing on activism in the world. The social issues she mentioned in her speech were a to-do list of her own unrealized goals and an expression of her frustration with her own career as an activist.

Now, in the spring of 1891, she felt in need of personal renewal once again. After a very busy year and a half in New York, she wanted to leave the city behind along with her many half-realized projects there. In March

1891, she wrote to French metaphysician Marie Sinclair Caithness to inquire about the prospect of teaching classes in mental healing to American expatriates in Paris. Caithness admired Chevaillier and would soon publish a translation of her speech before the Woman Suffrage League in a French newspaper, but she urged Chevaillier not to come to Paris. "My experience of the American colony here, is that you would have no chance of obtaining even five students of anything serious," Caithness informed her. Instead, she advised Chevaillier to come to France on a "pleasure trip, to see the home country of your Father," Jean Charles Chevaillier. But Chevaillier's attention had shifted to the American West.[99]

It may have been Wilberforce J. Colville, who knew California spiritualist circles, who suggested that Chevaillier read the works of Thomas Lake Harris. She had likely also encountered his poems in Mary Plunkett's *International Magazine of Christian Science*, which ran several in the late 1880s.[100] There were also connections between Harris and Bellamy; the solar paradise in Harris's *The Great Republic* may have reminded her of the utopian society in *Looking Backward*, and Bellamy himself had recently praised Harris's newly issued *The New Republic* as "an eloquent and philosophical description of the present social ferment."[101] Harris's reputation as an iconoclastic spiritualist, who had never fit into any religious movement but borrowed from them all, intrigued her; his writings about what he called "divine respiration" appealed to her due to her mental-healing work and own health issues.[102]

So in April 1891 she wrote to Harris, asking if she and her mother Sarah might come to Fountaingrove. She asked not to formally join his movement, the Brotherhood of the New Life, but to "obtain board near him and receive the benefit of his instructions for a few months, that I might both become holier and be able to do more wisely a consecrated work for Humanity." To her delight, she received a prompt telegram from Harris, offering her and her mother the use of a mountain cabin on his lands near Santa Rosa.[103]

Chevaillier began plans to leave for California, making arrangements to offer classes in the science of spiritual healing in San Francisco in June. She informed readers of *The Problem of Life and International Magazine of Truth* that she was going West to "seek the mysteries of God and of our own being on the mountain tops of the Sierra Nevadas, in retirement for several months." Like Jesus on the mountain, she hoped to "receive special messages of Truth and Love that may bless humanity—where we hope to have our spiritual vision opened and our power to heal and speak increased."[104]

But there was yet another religious controversy brewing in Boston that would follow her from the East Coast to the mountain tops of California. It involved her former mentor, Episcopal pastor Phillips Brooks, one of the most famous preachers in the nation. Chevaillier had betrayed him.

3

May 1891

The Wandering Apostate

Laurence Oliphant had been dead for more than two years, but he was back in the world's headlines. Thomas Lake Harris's most gifted acolyte—and ultimately his greatest disappointment—Oliphant had a famous distant cousin, Scottish author Margaret Oliphant, who wrote a book about him. Published May 20, 1891, by Blackwood & Sons in London and soon after by Harper & Brothers in New York, *Memoir of the Life of Laurence Oliphant* was an immediate sensation throughout the English-speaking world. Called "the most notable biography of recent years" and "the most interesting biography written since Boswell's *Johnson*," Margaret Oliphant's book offered an insider account of the life of a man who had been in and out of the public eye for decades.[1] Laurence Oliphant had led a life out of a storybook—he was a diplomat, lawyer, adventurer, novelist, politician, and spy. But it was his connections to Harris, which Margaret chronicled in horrified detail, that propelled the book into international conversations.

She had whetted the public's appetite in February 1889 with an obituary for her cousin published in *Blackwood's Magazine* that briefly laid out the basics: at the height of his fame and political influence, Laurence Oliphant had given up his life of public service and "disappeared into the unknown" to follow Harris to the United States. At his colonies in New York, Harris had stripped Oliphant of "all congenial work, all adventure, novelty, society, everything he hitherto lived for," forcing him to perform manual labor and live communally. In the obituary, Margaret hesitated to call Harris an "illiterate charlatan" out of respect for her cousin's judgment; rather, she acknowledged that Harris "must, to judge by his disciples, have been no common man." She had little further to say about Harris: "I am not able to give any more information about him, for I have none."[2]

Now, however, after two years of research, she was not so reticent. Though better known as a novelist, Margaret actually preferred writing nonfiction and she did it well. *Memoir of the Life of Laurence Oliphant* was her fourth

Unholy Sensations. Joshua Paddison, Oxford University Press. © Oxford University Press 2025.
DOI: 10.1093/oso/9780197775325.003.0003

full-length biography—she had also written several shorter profiles—and for it she used the same methods she had used to write her biographies of clergyman Edward Irving, politician Charles Forbes René de Montalembert, and theologian John Tulloch. In each, she blended personal recollections of the man (except in the case of Irving, whom she never met) with information from letters, interviews, and other primary sources.[3] For her *Memoir of Laurence Oliphant*, she quoted extensively from letters she secured from Laurence's second wife, Rosamond Dale Owen Oliphant, as well as from interviews with his family members and her own conversations with him. This gave her book a degree of detail that made its revelations especially compelling. Her tale, of a powerful man who gave up everything—including his wife—to join a strange commune, only to rebel against its leader in order to follow his own mystical visions to Palestine, was both a riches-to-rags narrative and a tragic love story. Margaret's research provided the bizarre details, and the reading public was riveted.[4]

Published in two volumes, *Memoir of the Life of Laurence Oliphant's* first half chronicled the early exploits of Laurence up to his "disappearance" in 1867, thereby portraying meeting Harris as a life-altering hinge. Volume 1 therefore reads as prelude, telling the story of Oliphant's birth in 1829 to wealthy Scottish parents stationed in Cape Town, South Africa, his privileged education in Ceylon and England, and the wanderlust that took him, in one diplomatic capacity or another, across Europe to India, Russia, the United States, Canada, China, and Japan before age thirty. In 1865 he settled down in Scotland and was elected to the House of Commons. He was a popular lecturer and writer, well known in elite British social circles as a raconteur and flirt. But he had a secret mystical side to his personality that, in Margaret's telling, sadly lured him off course from the life of influence and politics that seemed to lie ahead.

From a young age Oliphant wrestled with reconciling his own spiritual impulses with the evangelical Protestantism of his upbringing. "My conscience is never satisfied with my conduct, nor my understanding with my belief, so that altogether I live in a state of internal conflict," he informed his mother Maria while in his mid-twenties. Soon after, he "completely burst the straight bonds of his mother's evangelical views," becoming interested in spiritualism and rejecting the divinity of the Bible. He said he longed for "a supernatural revelation of a faith" and had a "yearning for the fountainhead"—that is to say, direct, personal experience of the divine. These desires, Margaret wrote in the final line of volume 1, were the "latent spark of the

Laurence Oliphant, frontispiece; Margaret Oliphant, *Memoir of the Life of Laurence Oliphant and of Alice Oliphant, His Wife.* Vol. 2. London: William Blackwood and Sons, 1891.

revolution [that] had been lying for years in his heart, awaiting the hand that should stir it to life." That hand, of course, would belong to Harris.[5]

A Free Presbyterian turned Anglican, Margaret Oliphant portrayed her cousin's metaphysical yearnings as a regrettable flaw of character and intellect. But in fact Margaret well knew that Laurence was not the only spiritual seeker in Britain during the early Victorian era who "burst the straight bonds" of Christianity. Many of her friends had dabbled in spiritualism, and, though she was skeptical of what she called the "freaks of table turning and rapping," she hosted at least one séance in her own drawing room.[6] Nor was Laurence the only person in Britain to be intrigued by Harris's prophetic utterings. In fact, when Harris had left New York for London in May 1859, he found a receptive audience for the weekly sermons he began delivering, first at Store Street Music Hall and then at the Marylebone Institution, a library and lecture hall on Portman Square.[7]

In fact, spiritualism was surging in late 1850s London after a series of American mediums had visited and given demonstrations of "spirit rappings." Private séance groups such as the Charing Cross Spirit-Power Circle, established in 1857, sprang up to cultivate the mediumship of local spiritualists, giving thousands of Londoners a chance to observe spirit communication for themselves.[8] Upon arriving in London, Harris was impressed by British spiritualism, calling it "a fairer form than in America, and grows more healthily by far."[9] In London and Manchester, he filled lecture halls with spiritualists, open-minded Swedenborgians, and others simply curious to see this singular visitor from New York. British spiritualist William Howitt—an acquaintance of Margaret Oliphant's—attended his free-form sermons and was taken by Harris's "eloquence; at once full, unforced, outgushing, unstinted, and absorbing."[10] Another attendee recalled Harris's whole-body preaching style: "He stood apparently on tiptoes; he sank down to his desk; he pointed with his finger and shrugged up his shoulders in a manner not at that time familiar to the British public."[11]

Predictably, Harris soon stirred up controversy as his initially positive impressions of England's spiritual state soured. "Men walk in a half dream, oppressed by the nightmare of dead and dying institutions," he informed his American friends in December 1859. "England is now at the ebb of the tide in spiritual things."[12] A month later at the Marylebone Institution, he delivered what amounted to a shot across the bow of British popular spiritualism, warning that many of the messages imparted by mediums were in fact the handiwork of demons rather than kindly spirits. "Murder, adultery, suicide, and the most revolting blasphemies, may be traced directly to the communications and puttings forth of impure spirits," he thundered. Demons manipulated naïve mediums, he insisted, spreading wickedness, sin, and disease. "Shun the séance," he commanded. "If you do not wish to become yourselves demoniacs, shun the place, and shun the occasion." Only the "experienced self-crucified disciple of Christ"—extraordinarily powerful and holy mediums such as himself, in other words—"are safe in venturing in the perilous border land between the world of nature and the world of spirit."[13] A few of his listeners may have known that Harris was in fact an experienced demon fighter, as shown in his recent book *The Song of Satan,* published as an appendix to his magnum opus *Arcana of Christianity,* which was filled with feverish trance poems he had received during "temptation-combats" with "Infernal Spirits."[14]

The crowd of more than three hundred spiritualists at the Marylebone Institution was "enchained, transfixed, and utterly confounded," according to James Grant, a journalist in attendance. Harris's words "fell like so many bombshells, bursting for nearly an hour, in rapid succession, among his audience." Grant, himself a disillusioned ex-spiritualist, ignored Harris's defense of own mediumship, portraying him—bizarrely for anyone the least bit familiar with Harris's writings—as an "evangelical" opposed to all forms of spiritualism.[15] Harris denounced Grant's report as "one-sided and extremely incorrect," but newspapers in Britain and the United States, always eager to run criticisms of spiritualism, picked up the story, using variations of the headline "Spiritualism Abandoned by the Rev. Harris."[16]

All of this did little to endear Harris to spiritualists on either side of the Atlantic. London's spiritualists scrambled to discredit Grant's report as a "scandalous misrepresentation" of Harris's words while simultaneously distancing themselves from Harris's attacks on other mediums.[17] The matter quickly became a referendum on Harris's theology and career. William Howitt defended Harris's sermons as grandiloquent "prose poems," not intended to be taken literally, while other British spiritualists saw the sermon as an example of his megalomaniacal tendencies. "In all his changes" over the years, complained the editors of London's *Spiritual Magazine,* "he only has been always right, and he must always be the founder of a new and true church, outside which there is no salvation."[18] In Boston, the *Banner of Light* noted the irony of mainstream newspaper editors who "for years have only recognized in Mr. Harris 'the visionary,' 'the fanatic'" were suddenly praising his warnings about spiritualism.[19] Harris's former New York publisher

Charles Partridge took this as an opportunity to attack the "peculiarities of Mr. H." and to remind readers of the Mountain Cove debacle. According to Partridge, all of Harris's strange talk of counterpartal sex with Lily Queen had made him unmanly, "like a tender, sensitive plant, which expands or shrivels up at the approach of the slightest influences." This overload of feminine "sensation" explained why Harris was always "speaking in favor of spiritualism in one lecture, and *against* it in the next."[20]

British Swedenborgians were divided on the subject of Harris as well. He had supporters: the well-respected physician J. J. Garth Wilkinson, who had translated Swedenborg's works into English in the 1840s, hosted Harris and his wife Emily in his home for several weeks when the couple first arrived in London in 1859; and William White, who ran the bookshop of the Swedenborg Society, published several volumes of Harris's newest sermons.[21] However, after greater exposure to Harris's "blasphemous pretensions," London's *Intellectual Repository for the New Church* ran a series of articles in 1860 denouncing Harris as a false prophet and a "habitual and systematic deceiver."[22] In July, the Swedenborg Society banned the sale of his books in the bookshop and commanded William White to stop publishing Harris's writings. White refused, and the conflict escalated to the point that White, accompanied by "about a dozen pugilists and roughs" including bareknuckle boxing champion Jem Mace, physically "plunged over head and ears" rival Swedenborgians out of the bookshop. Legal suits and countersuits followed.[23]

In fact, Harris's ideas were sowing dissension among Swedenborgians around the world. Swedenborgians in Boston suspended a minister named Woodbury Fernald due to his open admiration for Harris, whom Fernald viewed as the first person since Swedenborg "chosen to break the first seal of the celestial mysteries." Rather than accept the suspension, Fernald resigned from the church.[24] In Australia, Harris's "mad folly" was making "great trouble" among Swedenborgians there.[25] All told, the Swedenborgians by this point had earned the reputation of being "Harris's chief opponents, his most bitter calumniators, his most vindictive enemies."[26] Harris would long hold a grudge against the Swedenborgians: two decades later, he would tell a follower that "all the greatest troubles and worst lies that have ever been sent by the evil powers against him, were sent through that sect."[27]

Undeterred, Harris continued to preach at the Marylebone Institution and at Mechanics' Hall in London throughout the spring and summer of 1860. It was during this period that Harris's life began to fatefully intersect with that of Laurence Oliphant. Surprisingly, it was Oliphant's mother, Maria, a life-long member of the evangelical Protestant Reformed Church, who showed the initial interest in Harris. Her husband, Laurence's father Sir Anthony Oliphant, had died recently, which perhaps encouraged her interest in spiritualism. She, having either attended one of Harris's lectures or read about him in the press, desired to meet him. Laurence reached out to J. J. Garth Wilkinson, a family friend, but Wilkinson—who like other Swedenborgians was coming to regard Harris as a "colossal delusion"—refused to introduce the Oliphants to Harris "with the expressed opinion that the acquaintance was not for Oliphant's good." Nonetheless, Laurence showed up uninvited where Harris was staying and "walked outside of Harris's lodgings for some time in doubt, and finally introduced himself to 'the Prophet.'" Laurence was impressed by Harris and would inch, closer and closer, toward him over the next few years.[28]

By October 1860, Harris had moved on to Edinburgh, Scotland, where he began delivering weekly sermons in the Calton Convening Rooms. During the following eight months that Harris spent in Scotland, he met his important disciple and future biographer Arthur A. Cuthbert. Harris would soon preside over Cuthbert's wedding to Emily Fawcett, a spiritualist Harris had crossed paths with while in England. But Harris continued to keep the Oliphants at "arm's-length" over the next few years, testing their seriousness, which seemed to pique Laurence's interest all the more.[29] This was a strategy Harris used with other affluent would-be followers as well: denying them access. Irish politician and writer Justin McCarthy years later wrote a novel, *Comet of a Season,* based on Harris's visit to England. In the novel, the celebrity-prophet "repelled with cold contempt the invitation of a duchess." The result was that "even duchesses were now more anxious than ever to have him under their roof, and fanatics and sectaries of all kinds were disposed to put full faith in him."[30]

At the outset of volume 2 of *Memoir of the Life of Laurence Oliphant,* which chronicled the rise and fall of Laurence's devotion to Harris, Margaret grappled with the conundrum of why her cousin grew so attracted to the man. She knew her readers would expect an explanation, but she struggled to give one that did not portray Laurence as a naïve dupe, a picture she found too unflattering. In the words of a friend, Margaret succeeded in "telling the whole truth without showing how his 'divagations' made him absurd."[31] Instead, Margaret portrayed Laurence's attraction as a virtue carried too far. She explained that Harris offered "the greatest novelty of all—that men should put what they believed into practice." Harris embodied "absolute— nay, remorseless—obedience, at the cost of any and every sacrifice, to the principles of a perfect life." Laurence had spent his life looking for something "genuine and true," she wrote, in Harris, "at last he had found it."[32]

Neither Margaret nor future biographers could locate any letters from this period documenting the process in which Laurence came to join Harris's movement, so it is difficult to judge the veracity of Margaret's explanation. It is clear, though, that living in England and Scotland during 1859 to 1861 changed Harris. No longer the pastor of a church, actively involved in the world, he was becoming the leader of a brotherhood, removed and protected from society. As such, he offered Laurence things more specific than "principles of a perfect life"; he offered a safe haven, an adopted family, and set of spiritual practices that promised to make Laurence healthy, powerful, and pure.

While in Scotland, Harris founded the Brotherhood of the New Life, a name he would use for the rest of his life to refer to his international group of followers. "Brotherhood" suggested the broad equality of all people; "new life" carried echoes of both the "new birth" Harris had experienced as a teenager in Utica as well as the Swedenborgian New Church he was leaving behind. Long interested in the Advent, Harris viewed the emergence of the Brotherhood of the New Life as a fulfilment of biblical prophecy and a harbinger of the coming apocalypse. His final London sermons had been filled with descriptions of "what signs should precede His second coming," signs that were "rapidly being fulfilled." What he had seen of British industrialization—"the factory operatives in England, grim, and soiled and stained" living "one step above chattel slavery," exploited by "the do-nothing classes"— had convinced him that God's final judgment of humanity was imminent.[33] Rather than engage with this wicked world, the Brotherhood of the New Life would set itself apart: communal rather than competitive, rural rather than urban, sacred rather than profane.

Central to the Brotherhood of the New Life was a spiritual practice Harris had been experimenting with for several years, which he called divine respiration, open respiration, or simply "the Breath." This was a combination of deep breathing, prayer, and meditation that brought the practitioner's mind and body into "unified intellectual and physical harmony." Emanuel Swedenborg had engaged in different types of "internal respiration" that he had learned from spirits: holding his breath while respiring "inwardly for a considerable time," breathing "from the umbilicus towards the heart, and so upwards through the lips," and other techniques.[34]

Building on this, Harris's divine respiration was a way to feel the Holy Spirit within the body, revitalizing and protecting it. While in London, Harris had demonstrated divine respiration to several Swedenborgians, who were impressed. "I am satisfied that he possesses a mode of breathing of a nature widely differing from any other person I have ever known," reported one Swedenborgian. "The breaths are sometimes of an incredible length and volume. But at other times, in states of trance, the breath seems suspended for incredibly long periods, as though life had ceased." J. J. Garth Wilkinson noted with a doctor's eye that Harris's chest looked "weak and contracted" until he engaged in divine respiration, during which his "ribs came forth and opened out, and the breast swelled to huge proportions. I never saw such capacity for respiration in any other person."[35]

Harris's discovery of divine respiration was another sign of his role as a pivotal man set to usher in earth's final age. "A pivotal-respirative man stands in the perfection of health and life, through the respirative and regenerative unity of the body," he noted in the final volume of *Arcana of Christianity*, which he began writing while in England. The pivotal man, "physically located in Great Britain," would teach divine respiration to the Brotherhood of the New Life, who would spread out "from America to the extreme east of Asia." Breathing in unison, members of the Brotherhood would "uplift, solace, and reinforce the pivotal man"; in turn, he would "inter-unite himself with them and interflow through all their faculties." He would take upon himself their "bodily maladies and mental distresses."[36] Divine respiration, in other words, spiritually connected practitioners to Harris and to God while freeing them of disease, illness, and neuroses.

In May 1861, the Harrises returned to the United States, bringing Arthur Cuthbert, Emily Fawcett, and a few other founding British members of the Brotherhood of New Life with them.[37] Harris informed his friends in New York that his time of "public uses" had ceased; going forward, he would be committed to agrarian communitarianism. He invited those who wished to achieve "equilibrium"—mind, body, and spirit in harmonious balance—to join him.[38] The Civil War had just broken out, and though Harris had previously signed antislavery petitions and contributed poems to William Lloyd Garrison's *Liberator* and Frederick Douglass's *North Star*, he now turned his back on politics altogether.[39]

Over the next six years, Harris established three colonies in succession in New York state, each larger than the previous: first at Wassaic, then in nearby Amenia, and finally in Brocton on the banks of Lake Erie. Members of the Brotherhood of the New Life pooled their finances to buy the land. Several, but by no means all, of Harris's followers were wealthy, including Cuthbert, his fellow Scot James A. Fowler, and Jane Lee Waring, who hailed from a "well-known highly-respected New England family."[40] Waring had been a parishioner at Harris's Church of the Good Shepherd in New York City and would become his primary amanuensis and the manager of day-to-day life in his colonies. Other than Harris, who generally devoted his time to study, writing, and spiritual journeys, everyone in the Brotherhood engaged equally in physical labor. "Upon this base of industry, the temple of our spiritual work is now to stand," Harris explained.[41]

These new communal efforts differed from Harris's failed Mountain Cove colony from a decade earlier in several important ways. There was no co-leader like James Leander Scott to destabilize Harris's authority; now, Harris was the sole and unchallenged leader. Rather than publish and widely distribute a newspaper, as had been the case with the *Mountain Cove Journal,* Harris's new publications were now only sent to select interested parties rather than the "indiscriminate public," creating an aura of mystery around his teachings and protecting him from public ridicule.[42] Financially, Harris's new colonies had better support from his new, wealthier supporters, and he seemed more interested in making money than when at Mountain Cove, opening a bank at Amenia and experimenting with commercial wine-making. The historical moment was also different: the onset of the Civil War made Harris's colonies seem like appealing escapes from a society tearing itself apart, and several white Southern families, "fleeing from the land of slavery," moved to New York to join.[43] Finally, Harris's religious thinking had evolved from his early days as a spiritualist; in his words, he had been "too immature in mind and experience" to succeed at Mountain Cove.[44] Now, he offered a unique and fully formed metaphysical theology with divine respiration at its core.

And divine respiration worked. He taught it first to his wife Emily and then to his twelve or so initial followers at the Wassaic colony, and their accounts attested to its miraculous effects. Emily Fawcett, now Emily Cuthbert, wrote, "The Breath sustains us, not only in the discharge of laborious daily duties, but enables us to watch for hours at night when watching is needed. It removes disease and tendency to disease in the system, and makes the heart

glad and peaceful when it would naturally be sad and depressed." Divine respiration was effective in "demagnetizing against disease, and energizing for
increase of physical health and strength." It was "full of comfort to mind and
body." As one progressed, it unlocked a person's ability to see fairies, normally
hidden to human eyes, and thus to live "surrounded a hymning, joyous mul-
titude." The fairies, whose names included Bussie Darling, Sister Bell, King
Good, Comfort Good, and Great Mr. Rabbit, communicated with colonists
via Harris's mediumship. Perfecting divine respiration was an emotional experience, causing people to weep and to become more loving toward God
and others. "I never felt anything like it before, and it is a love which makes
every other sink into insignificance, and I could cheerfully give up all for it,"
said one female practitioner.[45]

Meanwhile, the Oliphants were moving further into Harris's orbit. By
1865, Laurence's mother, Maria, had left Britain and joined the colony at
Amenia, which now had more than thirty-five members. Her generous do-
nation allowed the colony to buy enough farmland in Brocton to relocate
the expanding colony there in late 1867.[46] Laurence was in the House of
Commons but growing disillusioned with politics. Elected as a member of
the Liberal Party, he had no patience for partisan gamesmanship and broke
with Liberal leader William Ewart Gladstone to back a reform bill supported
by the Conservative Party. Visiting the House of Commons in spring 1867,
future biographer Margaret Oliphant met Laurence for the first time, and he
told her that politics "was a life unendurable, which he at least could support
no longer." The two distant cousins began a correspondence, with Laurence
sending Margaret a copy of Harris's London sermons and offering to try to
get her a meeting with the prophet, who was back in London for a brief visit.
She declined.[47]

Laurence had already visited the Wassaic colony twice, but Harris had
refused to admit him.[48] Now, with Harris back in London in 1867, Laurence
had another chance to make his case for membership in the Brotherhood
of the New Life. Unlike Harris's earlier high-profile trip to Britain in 1859
to 1861, this visit was conducted quietly, done only to oversee the private
printing of two new books. "Mr. Harris, though he has been in London for
some week, has not been seen by anyone," huffed the editors of London's
Spiritual Magazine, still antagonistic. "He is probably going through one of
his periodical spiritual 'states,' when he is supposed to be receiving instruction for his future guidance, and during which he keeps [to] his bed for
days and weeks."[49] This new low profile was part of Harris's turn away from

"public uses" and public controversies. He met with Laurence, however, and the younger man's "urgent persistence" finally won Harris over.[50] Before the year was over, Laurence was writing to Margaret Oliphant on his way to New York, about to leave behind "his position, his prospects, politics, literature, society, every personal possession and hope."[51] He formally renounced his seat in the House of Commons but offered no public explanation for his absence. "What has become of Laurence Oliphant?" British newspapers asked. Where is the "handsome, clever, fascinating young diplomatist" who had "taken all hearts as it were by storm"?[52]

Rumors of his whereabouts reached the press in early 1869. Oliver Dyer, a reporter for the *New York Sun* known for his exposés of urban "wickedness," visited Brocton in April and confirmed Oliphant's presence in a "most unusual community" there. A bemused Dyer reported that Oliphant "works side by side, and on terms of perfect equality, with fellow laborers who are without culture, or wealth, or anything except a love for God." Oliphant, though, looked well: "He is robust. There is no dyspepsia or morbidness in him. He is cheerful and fond of jokes." Despite getting up "to work at 4 o'clock in the morning," he "is as blithe and jocund as a boy." Dyer asked Oliphant if he missed his old life in diplomacy and politics, to which Laurence replied, "Not in the least." Oliphant insisted that divine respiration, together with manual labor and communal living, was helping him "eradicate the evils of my nature. When I shall have accomplished that work, and become so spiritually pure that I can touch pitch and not be defiled, I may return to public life."

Dyer left skeptical about Harris's doctrines but impressed by the colony's industry and apostolic living. Brocton seemed less strange than Oneida and many of the dozens of other utopian colonies that had sprung up across the United States during the mid-nineteenth century. Indeed, another journalist from the *New York Tribune* soon visited and declared Brocton nothing more than "a banding together of a body of men and women, desirous of leading as pure a Christian life as possible." If Oliphant was happy there, "what are you going to do about it?"[53]

Margaret Oliphant's book filled in more details, and she took a much less sanguine view of Laurence's time in Amenia and then Brocton. In her account, Laurence was "plunged into the severest and rudest elements of life." The labor demanded of him was demeaning: cleaning out stables, driving a team of horses, harvesting strawberries. Worked to the bone, exhausted from lack of sleep, fingers frostbitten in the New York winters, Laurence struggled to keep a positive attitude, and his mother, Maria, fared even worse, Margaret reported. "She, a woman always delicate and much regarded and studied by her husband and son, was made to lay her ladyhood aside and all the habits of her life, and to engage in manual or menial labor," including "washing, cooking, and cleaning of the house." This was an overturning of class hierarchies that Margaret could not stomach. Furthermore, Margaret reported with horror that Harris required Laurence and Maria to live separately and not communicate in the "close and confidential" way they had always done. In a passage that would be much quoted by newspapers, Margaret wrote, "all ties of relationship were broken ruthlessly, and separations made between parents and children, husbands and wives."[54]

The dozens of letters Laurence Oliphant wrote to his friends William and Georgina Cowper, which Margaret did not have access to, paint a more complex picture. The Cowpers were well-to-do British spiritualists and admirers of Harris; Oliphant had introduced them to Harris in London in 1867 and, from America, kept them apprised of his spiritual journey.[55] Oliphant confirmed that he was at times separated from his mother "but the change in her is quite wonderful, and the separation is not very serious, for I can look at her going about her daily avocations out of any window, with a light step and a merry laugh, such as I never saw or heard before."[56] He found the physical labor and long hours difficult but isolation from Harris, which the prophet enforced during Oliphant's first few months as he "demagnetized," was worse. Oliphant embraced his new "freedom from worldly care—the facilities it offers for concentration on Divine things, the possibilities of silence." The colony's lack of class distinctions was humiliating, as when he had to work alongside "three or four common Irish Navvies" as equals. However, he said that the "mortification which I had to endure was most valuable discipline."[57] Fannie Brownell, a woman from Georgia who joined the Brocton colony in 1869, confirmed that Oliphant "took his place joyfully" there. "He never showed that he felt any superiority to the humblest brother in the school," Brownell recalled.[58] What Margaret Oliphant saw as debasement, Laurence saw as purification.

This included an opportunity for sexual purification. Oliphant admitted that he had once lived a life of "open infidelity and most reckless dissipation."[59] As a young man, his father had taken him to see an exhibition in Paris of the "horrible diseases incurred through sex license . . . represented in lifelike, colored papier-maché figures." Oliphant later reflected, "I deeply regret that the lesson did not bear the fruit it ought to have done in my youth."[60]

Rumors circulated in London that he had contracted syphilis in the years prior to joining the Brotherhood of the New Life.[61] Whether this was true or not, he embraced celibacy while in the Brotherhood. "Here I am removed from the whole class of sins and temptations to which I am liable in London," Oliphant wrote to William Cowper, "and I hope that while propensities to these sins are lying dormant, they may be removed."[62]

Not all colonists shared Oliphant's commitment to sexual abstinence. Newlyweds Arthur and Emily Cuthbert had a son, Arthur Jr., at Wassaic, and Harris wrote to an inquirer in 1877 that "one young pair in our borders have had three children, I am sorry to say." But Harris continued to preach that celibacy was central to spiritual advancement and most colonists seem to have abided by it. "They have become, in the natural sense, celibate as I am: some entering from a state of monogamic marriage, but others virginal from the first," Harris claimed.[63] In addition to its other salutary effects, divine respiration helped practitioners overcome sexual desire and free their impulses from becoming "exaggerated and perverted to cupidities and lusts."[64] Most couples lived together as a unit in the three New York colonies, but Harris at times commanded family members to live separately, telling them that their devotion to each other was a spiritual hindrance. "'Familism' was an evil to be broken down," Arthur Cuthbert Jr. later explained.[65] Arthur Jr. and a few of the younger children present were raised communally: "they feel they have many Fathers and Mothers who all love them or are trying to do so, with an equal devotion," Laurence told Georgina Cowper.[66]

In Harris's official doctrine of counterparts, sexual desires were carefully controlled and expressed only with spirits, not partners here on earth. Like divine respiration and belief in fairies, the doctrine of counterparts became part of daily life in Harris's colonies. It was not, according to the Brotherhood, "free-love," which Laurence Oliphant decried as "an abomination in the sight of God."[67] Rather, meeting your counterpart was a holy, private moment full of sexual-spiritual significance. One female colonist described in detail it in her diary: "When I awoke I heard the strangest little noises in my breast, and everything there all day long has seemed to be in a flutter, as if little wings were moving." Thereafter, she felt "a wonderful fluttering, stirring, rushing, and rapid movement within me." Her counterpart delighted her but also made her feel "utterly exhausted and worn out. . . . The breathing, the circulation, rushing, flutterings, turnings, and I scare know what, make me never free from a consciousness of my body all the time." She struggled to put the experience into words: "I wish I could describe what this is like, somebody inside of you all over, lately it seems to be so much about my mouth and tongue, almost like a kiss." Meeting one's counterpart was an intensely erotic, bodily experience that carried no danger of pregnancy, disease, or sin. It was thrilling, but safe.[68]

Some people discovered that their counterpart was a deceased spouse, making the encounter a joyful reunion. Maria Oliphant, for example, discovered that her counterpart was her dead husband Anthony, with whom she began having "constant communications."[69] However, sometimes counterparts were not what they seemed; Arthur Cuthbert Jr. recalled one overeager colonist "joyously declaring that he had felt his counterpart in the night, and then afterwards sadly discovering that he had only overeaten of newly baked brown bread!"[70]

By May 1870, Laurence had not yet met his counterpart, but Harris judged him spiritually advanced enough to be allowed to return to Britain where he might be able to do good for the Brotherhood of the New Life. Laurence visited Margaret Oliphant in London, and she found that his three years of hard labor had not changed his belief in Harris, which was "as profound and unshaken as ever." Furthermore, she found Laurence to be "as serious, as humorous, as entertaining, as delightful a companion, and as much disposed to social enjoyment as when he had been one of the most popular men in London."[71] Indeed, the mystery surrounding his disappearance had made him more sought after than ever. His satirical novel *Piccadilly,* originally published in *Blackwood's Magazine* in 1865, was newly released as a book and sat "on every table at the West-end."[72] The novel's obvious semi-autobiographical elements—it tells the story of a wealthy young man's romantic adventures in decadent London and ends with its hero leaving for the United States under the care of a mysterious spiritual healer—fueled its popularity and revived a new round of gossip about Oliphant.[73]

During the next year, he returned to a semblance of his old life, working for the *London Times* as a foreign correspondent in France during the Franco-Prussian War and rise of the Paris Commune. When his mother, Maria, joined him in Paris for a time in 1871, British newspapers assumed that they had given up their religious "craze," but he corrected them: "I have not separated myself from Brocton," he wrote. "I never felt myself in more close and intimate union with it than now."[74] In fact, Oliphant told a Swedenborgian friend that "my internal union with Mr. Harris is such, that he would instantly become conscious of any serious departure from the strict line of my use."[75]

That union would soon be tested, however, for in Paris, Oliphant met Alice Le Strange, a wealthy Englishwoman from Norfolk. She was twenty-six, sophisticated, and "very pretty," possessing "the sweetest and frankest nature that I ever met," according to Oliphant, still a bachelor at age forty-two.[76] Within a few months they were engaged to be married.[77] Maria Oliphant approved; Alice's family did not, perhaps due to Laurence's devotion to Harris. Knowing full well Harris's attitudes about romantic and sexual entanglements, Oliphant was filled with anxiety about navigating marriage while advancing the state of his soul. He worried about what Harris would think of Alice, and vice versa. Oliphant tried to teach divine respiration to her and how it would connect them to God via Harris, telling her, "His functions are pivotal, and we in a sense meet in him; for our breath is in some mysterious way enfolded in his." Oliphant tried to convince her (and himself) that marriage would help their spiritual advancement: "if I have you to help me, I should rise higher, and get from your strength and support what no one else could give."[78]

Although Alice Le Strange does not enter the book until almost halfway through volume 2, Margaret Oliphant gave her equal billing with Laurence in its full title: *Memoir of the Life of Laurence Oliphant and of Alice Oliphant, His Wife*. Alice's entrance changes Margaret's story from that of an earnest man's misguided mystical quest to a tragic tale of star-crossed lovers made miserable by an evil "tyrant." Margaret's version of Alice Le Strange is an idealized embodiment of upper-class British womanhood; she is "beautiful and delightful," "one of the most perfect flowers of mankind," "sympathetic, clear-headed, yet an enthusiast," "a fine musician as well as a brilliant conversationalist," with "beautiful diction and melodious speech." Margaret chalked up Le Strange's willingness to join the Brotherhood of the New Life as a sad byproduct of her love for Laurence as well as her youthful desire for "something more exacting and authoritative, than the calm and indulgent Christianity which she generally met with."[79]

In fact, Le Strange was another Victorian spiritual seeker who, like Alzire Chevaillier, had come to question traditional Christianity out of anger and sorrow about the world's injustices. In a letter Le Strange wrote to Harris from Paris in early 1872, she chronicled her history of "doubts of God's existence, or at least of His benevolence" that arose from her "extreme horror of and pity for the suffering in the world." Her personal conscience and inner sense of right and wrong had led her out of traditional Christianity and, she told Harris, also made her balk at giving up authority to him as spiritual

Alice Le Strange Oliphant, frontispiece; Margaret Oliphant, *Memoir of the Life of Laurence Oliphant and of Alice Oliphant, His Wife*. Vol. 2. London: William Blackwood and Sons, 1891.

mentor. But she vowed to try, promising to "put myself and ourselves under your direction in all matters." She let Harris decide their wedding date and promised to turn over to him her wealth "for any purpose to which you might see fit to apply it."[80]

Laurence and Alice wed in St. George's Hanover Square Church in London in June 1872; his mother and the Cowpers were present but none of Alice's family attended.[81] In keeping with Harris's teachings, the couple would never sexually consummate the marriage. Laurence later told his second wife, Rosamond, "I learned self-control by sleeping with my beloved and beautiful Alice in my arms for twelve years without claiming the rights of a husband. We lived as a sister and brother. I am a passionate lover, and so it was difficult, very difficult."[82] They stayed in Paris and, it seems, lived happily there, practicing divine respiration and aiding the Brotherhood of the New Life from afar. Now friendly with the Cowpers, Alice told Georgina in December 1872 that she counted herself lucky to be one of Harris's "special children who have never seen him nor the spot where his labors have to be concentrated."[83] However, in April 1873, British newspapers reported that Laurence, "like Lot in Sodom," was fleeing Paris for Brocton once again. His mother and new wife went to New York with him.[84]

No records seem to exist documenting Alice's first weeks at Brocton, so Margaret Oliphant was forced to speculate how mortified "a flower of perfect civilization and ladyhood" such as Alice must have felt when expected to take up hard physical labor. At one point, Alice and her mother-in-law Maria lived together for eight months, cut off from the rest of the Brotherhood, in order "to learn to do things for ourselves." Maria said that Alice "has been going through the ordeal, a very hard one, of putting off all the old and much-admired refinement, polish, intellectual charm, etc." The two women cooked, washed, ironed, and raised chickens, but "the internal work was by far the hardest," Maria reported.[85] Alice seems to have accepted her new life, writing to Georgina Cowper in July 1876, "It is two years since I wrote last and they have been more than two wonderful years to me and to us all." She urged Cowper to join her at Brocton: "*That* is here which you have looked for so long," adding, "things more wonderful than any imaginings become the simple realities of everyday experience."[86]

Meanwhile, Laurence went on the road to New York City and Canada, raising money for the Brotherhood. This was necessary because Harris felt called by the spirits to move the colony once again, this time 2,600 miles west to Sonoma County in northern California. While composing his solar trance poem *The Great Republic,* he had experienced a vision of himself "in future time, as dwelling in the vicinage of the great forests of sequoia, near the Pacific, where, mingled with the sighing winds among the evergreens, might be heard the murmur of the not far distant ocean."[87] In February 1875, Harris and a few trusted acolytes took the overland railroad to California, purchasing a tract of land just north of Santa Rosa for $21,000 in order to build "a fine residence" in the "style of an English park," as he told a local newspaper.[88] The new colony supported itself at first as a dairy and poultry farm and then as a vineyard.[89]

In looking to California, Harris followed in the footsteps of many other nineteenth-century seekers who, ever since the Gold Rush, imagined the Golden State as a land of personal freedom and spiritual renewal.[90] Spiritualist James J. Owen, who moved to California from upstate New York in 1850, believed that there was "something in the atmosphere of the Pacific Coast particularly conducive to psychical phenomena," either due to the physical environment or the "heterogenous and peculiar character of our people."[91] This reputation must have influenced Harris's decision to look to California, along with the cheap land and mild climate of Sonoma County, perfect for wine cultivation. Harris may have also encountered the writings of Sonoma winegrower-turned-booster Agoston Haraszthy, who throughout the 1860s had championed the "extraordinary productiveness" of the region's soil to Easterners and Europeans.[92]

Harris named the new colony Fountaingrove, a clear echo of Mountain Cove. Fountaingrove was his chance to take what he had learned in his earlier colonies and put in place, finally, a true utopia on earth. Here, unlike in Brocton, men and women would be segregated into separate living quarters, with men in the Commandery, women in the Familistery.[93] Fountaingrove also saw another innovation: communal bathing. Harris had long believed that "water streams and springs themselves are surcharged with qualities from the three Heavens, promotive of health, longevity, and new vital conditions."[94] In addition to its restorative effects, communal bathing encouraged a breaking down of people's feelings of modesty, embarrassment, and lust. "Our father says that before we can be in any true condition we must all be so innocent that we can stand naked before each other without a thought of shame, and wash and dress each other," wrote one woman at Fountaingrove.[95] Only the most spiritually advanced people at Brocton were invited to Fountaingrove. Alice arrived in October 1876; Laurence was still in New York and did not receive an invitation.[96]

To Margaret Oliphant, this "complete severance of a married pair" was the ultimate sign of Harris's cruel "despotism." Unaware of the couple's celibacy, Margaret saw their separation as an unnatural violation of romantic and procreative marriage. In her *Memoir,* she described Laurence's "great depression and misery" when he turned up at California only to be sent back to Brocton by Harris.[97] Once again, Laurence's letters to the Cowpers told a different story. "Alice went to California about two months ago and I am very glad she is there," he wrote in January 1877. Six months later, he told them that he had not heard from Alice, "but I know she is going through deep spiritual experiences and am happy in thinking what the results may be. . . . I hear she is well and happy and progressing."[98] As in all his letters to the Cowpers, it is hard to know how much of this cheerfulness was due to the fact that his friends were, from the beginning, potential converts to the Brotherhood that Harris had tried to raise money from.[99] Whatever his true views on the matter were, Oliphant was planning a trip to England, France, and Turkey, "most probably without my wife."[100]

Another explanation for Oliphant's benign attitude about the separation from his wife was that his understanding of his marriage had changed. In the fall of 1880, Oliphant was in England awaiting the publication of his new book *The Land of Gilead,* about his travels in the Middle East.[101] He met with Margaret Oliphant and confided to her "an extraordinary discovery": he had finally made contact with his counterpart, and it was not Alice. Rather, as Harris taught, Laurence's counterpart was a spirit " 'on the other side'—that is, already passed into the unseen state—of whose communications he had been increasingly conscious." Laurence then read an "astonished" Margaret some poems his counterpart had revealed to him. This incident was "the only sign of mental aberration which I ever saw in him," she wrote. Margaret saw his "boyish" excitement about his counterpart as a desperate cover "for the clouds and weariness in which life was being lost."[102] But for Oliphant, the encounter with his counterpart and his newfound ability to communicate with the celestial realm after thirteen years of patience and self-sacrifice must have felt like the breakthrough of a lifetime. He was finally unlocking his mystical powers.

Oliphant's counterpart did more than deliver poetry—she was his spiritual guide and newfound source of authority. About this time, Oliphant paid a visit to Anna Kingsford, a British spiritualist attending medical school in Paris because, unlike in England, France's medical schools admitted women. Kingsford was an outspoken vegetarian and animal rights activist as well as a medium who received spiritual "illuminations" in her sleep. Oliphant's first visit was friendly but a few days later, he returned with a warning: his counterpart had informed him that Kingsford "had been deceived by evil influences." He urged Kingsford to stop her own mystical investigations and to follow Harris, "the appointed medium between the earth and the world of counterpartal angels, reunion with whom can only be accomplished through him." Kingsford felt "utter repulsion" toward this idea and toward the insipid counterpartal poetry—"doggerel," she said—that Oliphant read to her. She distained his "fanciful sex-relations and doctrine of 'counterparts,'" distrusting Oliphant's talk of the "sensuous delights of the most exquisite kind" that union with her counterpart offered. Like many metaphysicians, Kingsford recoiled from the frank eroticism of counterpartal doctrine, distrusting its combustible mixture of spirituality and sex.[103]

He gave no indication to Margaret Oliphant nor to Anna Kingsford, but in fact Laurence was beginning to have his own doubts about the infallibility of Harris's mediumship. In October 1880, he wrote to a London spiritualist newspaper to reiterate that he was "as much a member of Mr. Harris's community as I ever was," but in truth his commitment to Harris was waning.[104] At this point, Oliphant had not seen Harris in person since 1874; as a result, much of his spiritual progress had been made under his own supervision.[105] Following the other Brocton colonists, Oliphant called Harris "Father" but had always felt uneasy around him. "Father's presence is an awful pressure, though a blessed one," Laurence told Margaret at one point. "Because he feels our states so terribly, the watchfulness over ourselves has to be unceasing."[106]

Now, Oliphant was coming into his own as a medium and beginning to question some of Harris's decisions, especially involving finances. When Harris asked Oliphant to "dishonorably" use inside business information Laurence possessed "in order to make a large sum of money," he refused. Finally, while in Egypt in early 1881, Oliphant "received from Harris a peremptory and unreasonable command. . . . I was preparing, as usual, to obey him, when suddenly the words came to me, 'It is finished.'" Oliphant knew he had to leave the Brotherhood of the New Life. Immediately, "new powers awoke in me, fresh inspirations, an exhilarating energy," a spiritual confirmation that his decision to leave was a blessed one.[107]

Shortly before his transformative Egypt trip, Alice had moved back to London. Desiring to "share the experiences of other women who work for their living," she had left Fountaingrove in January 1878 and supported herself giving lessons in "music, French, and German" for four dollars a month in nearby Calistoga and Benicia, California.[108] Margaret Oliphant, predictably, was horrified that Alice had had to educate "the children of miners and other uneducated persons," but Alice had enjoyed the work, and by the time she left Benicia she had "many friends" wishing her a "happy visit and safe return" in the local paper.[109] Alice also did not seem especially upset about the spousal separation that so troubled Margaret. "I have always exacted of Laurence that he should leave me free to make my own personal experiments that I may think needful for my usefulness in the world," Alice informed her mother upon her return to London.[110] But Alice accompanied Laurence to Egypt, where he had his epiphany about breaking with Harris. By this point, she had not seen Harris for three years; she, too, was ready to leave the Brotherhood.

In May 1881, Oliphant went to Brocton to collect his mother, and he found the New York colony in crisis. Maria was seriously ill and "certain rumors" about Fountaingrove—possibly the adoption of communal bathing—had disillusioned some of those still left behind at Brocton.[111] Laurence confirmed that "abuses had crept in of which I wholly disapproved." He convinced a few of the colonists to follow his lead in leaving, a group that included one of its founding members, Emily Cuthbert.[112] The Oliphants then took the train to California, and Laurence gained admittance into Fountaingrove for the first and only time. What transpired there between Oliphant and Harris is unknown; Margaret Oliphant could report only that mother and son were "far from graciously received." They stayed a few days, and Laurence spoke with Harris only for one hour before they left for nearby Cloverdale, where Laurence took his mother to a local folk healer who administered "decoctions of herbs and faith." To no avail, for Maria died on October 25, 1881. Laurence buried her in the local Cloverdale Cemetery under a headstone that announced her elite Old World credentials, identifying her as the "widow of Sir Anthony Oliphant, K^T CB [Knight Commander, Order of the Bath] of London, England."[113]

What followed, in Laurence's words, was "a struggle." A legal and financial struggle, as Oliphant sought title to lands he had provided funds for in Brocton and as Harris attempted to get Oliphant committed to an insane asylum. Even before Laurence had left Fountaingrove, Harris had sent a telegram to Alice in London asking her permission to "put her husband in a madhouse" due to his "mediumistic mania."[114] She refused and eventually Laurence received a portion of the more than $100,000 he and his mother had turned over to Harris. The Brocton colony collapsed and the lands were liquidated, with a large chunk purchased in 1882 by future Massachusetts governor Benjamin "Beast" Butler.[115] A few of the remaining Brocton colonists went to Fountaingrove but most left the Brotherhood, some siding with Oliphant, others going their own way.

Publicly, Harris claimed the rift with Oliphant was over money—greedy Oliphant had "swindled" Harris and the other colonists. Privately, however, members of the Brotherhood explained Oliphant's defection within their religious worldview. Oliphant had left because he "opened himself to the evil proprium"—that is to say, the evil spirits that Harris had warned about back at the Marylebone Institute in 1860. These spirits "whispered doubts and treason against Father, into his ears." Specifically, these spirits convinced Oliphant that his counterpart was in fact Harris's own Lily Queen, who supposedly told Oliphant that he, not Harris, was "her true and loyal knight." Furthermore, Alice, while at Fountaingrove, had used "occult magic" to assume Lily Queen's form and she then tried to kill Harris with a "current of deadly magnetic force, sharp as a spear." This usurpation of Lily Queen, who provided much of Harris's spiritual authority, was a clear sign of the Oliphants' having succumbed to the "magical powers of the underworld." To the faithful within the Brotherhood, the story was "deeply instructive," a cautionary tale they told each other about remaining on guard against carnality and evil spirits, and also a sign that "things must be in the times of the End." The fact that Maria Oliphant died a few days after the schism at Fountaingrove was, in their eyes, "judgment."[116]

The final two chapters of *Memoir of the Life of Laurence Oliphant* are anticlimatic. The reunited couple, "with the happiness of a boy and girl going forth upon a new world," went to Palestine. Laurence had been advocating the creation of a Jewish state in Palestine since 1878, working with Jews and Christian Zionists interested in "fulfilling prophesy and bringing on the end of the world," he said.[117] When these efforts stalled, he and Alice bought land in Haifa on the Mediterranean Sea alongside a colony of German American Templers, a millenarian Lutheran sect.[118] Some ex-colonists from Brocton, including Emily Cuthbert, joined the Oliphants at Haifa, and they were soon living communally once again, with Alice and Laurence serving in the Harris role as spiritual co-leaders. They also advocated to the Ottoman government on behalf of Jewish and Druze neighbors.[119]

In 1884, Alice and Laurence together wrote their first mystical text, *Sympneumata,* a strongly Harris-inspired vision of humanity's budding spiritual evolution. Rather than "counterparts," they spoke of "complements," every person's "real love." Once a person was united with his or her (always heterosexually matched) complement, they would "learn to perceive a mighty order of nature in which they may co-operate with higher beings of hitherto undreamed-of type." God was bisexual, and complementary (i.e., spiritual, i.e., counterpartal) sex would soon replace "earth-peopling after the fashion of the past."[120] Anyone familiar with Harris's writings would find it derivative, but by this point few of his newer works circulated outside of his private circle of admirers. Margaret Oliphant found it thrillingly romantic that Laurence and Alice wrote it together, she speaking and he holding the pen, finishing each other's sentences, but Margaret also admitted that she could not understand a word of *Sympneumata*'s "confused and torturous phraseology." British reviewers at the time called it "mere mystical jargon" and "vague, vast, and impalpable." It soon became a book "many have seen but few have read."[121]

According to Margaret, the couple's time together in Haifa was one of "absolute and peaceful happiness."[122] But it would not last long. In January 1886, Alice Oliphant died at age forty from a "slow fever," probably malaria; Laurence believed the true cause of death was "spiritual pressure." Her death did not end their relationship; in fact, Laurence reported they were "more firmly wedded now than we could ever be" when she was alive.[123] He wrote his next esoteric manifesto, *Scientific Religion,* in the same manner as *Sympneumata*: Alice dictating, now from beyond the grave, with Laurence holding the pen.[124] And it turned out that Alice had been his counterpart/complement after all. Laurence said that Alice could now "invade my frame, thrilling my nerves" in ways she could not when alive. They were finally having sex.[125]

However, Laurence outlived Alice by less than three years, himself dying from lung cancer in London on December 23, 1888. Just a few months before his death, Laurence had surprised his friends by impulsively marrying Rosamond Dale Owen, a woman suffrage activist and dress reformer who was the daughter of spiritualist Robert Dale Owen and the granddaughter of famed utopianist Robert Owen. Laurence had been so impressed by one of Rosamond's letters that he had traveled to New Harmony in Indiana to ask her to come to Haifa with him.[126] Laurence's friends, including Margaret Oliphant, were dismayed, but he said Alice's spirit blessed the new union.[127] When he and Rosamond married in August 1888, Laurence was already looking "wretchedly ill" from cancer. As his condition worsened throughout the fall, Rosamond used her "magnetic powers" to ease his pain but could not save his life.[128] The obituaries for Laurence focused on his diplomatic work, his world travels, his short political career, and his popular books. Mention of his time in the Brotherhood of the New Life was scarce; most newspapers omitted it altogether.[129] His much-publicized disappearance back in 1867 had been mostly forgotten.

That is why the arrival of Margaret Oliphant's *Memoir of the Life of Laurence Oliphant* in May 1891 delivered such a wallop. She steered clear of any mention of sex—or its absence—not mentioning Harris's nor Laurence's theories about celibacy, and she did not know enough about the inner workings of Fountaingrove to discuss communal bathing. But her descriptions of Laurence's, Maria's, and Alice's engagement in manual labor, their years of "enforced" separation, the great sums of money they turned over to Harris, and their eventual break with him made for gripping reading. Her saintly portrait of Alice, who suffered for love, and her villainous portrait of Harris drew on archetypes from popular sentimental fiction of the era. *Memoir* was a sensation from London to San Francisco, selling out its first British printing of 1,500 copies in a week.[130] It shone a light of international publicity on Harris like never before in his long and winding career. But by the summer of 1891 Harris was no longer in retirement. His youth and vigor had been recently restored, and he was ready to respond. The media attention would arrive just as he was re-entering the broader world around him, and just as he was welcoming an inquisitive guest from the East named Alzire Chevaillier.

4

June 1891

A Samurai in Fairyland

On June 7, 1891, Kanaye Nagasawa met Alzire Chevaillier and her mother, Sarah, at the Santa Rosa railroad station and brought them to Fountaingrove in the colony's carriage. Japanese men's presence in the Brotherhood of the New Life was not widely known and meeting Nagasawa must have been a surprise to the Chevailliers. It is possible that the two women had seen a few immigrants from Japan during their time in New York City—there were about six hundred *Issei* living in the city in 1891—but this was likely their first conversation with someone born in Japan.[1] Alzire was impressed by Nagasawa's clear devotion to Harris, but Sarah took an immediate dislike to the man, later calling him "educated" but "lordly."[2] The fine carriage was drawn by a team of expensive Hambletonian horses, the women's first glimpse of Fountaingrove's dazzling financial resources.

The visitors would have been further surprised to learn that Nagasawa had been part of the initial group of Brocton colonists who accompanied Harris to Santa Rosa in 1875 to purchase the lands for Fountaingrove, and he had been living there ever since.[3] As such, he was situated to be an excellent tour guide for the women as they made the three-mile journey north from the railroad station to the colony. He may well have told them how much Santa Rosa had changed from those days. In 1875, the town had still bore some of the marks of the Mexican trading post it had been founded as in 1833. Now in 1891, however, Santa Rosa was a town of about 5,300 and growing quickly. A mid-1880s construction boom had added numerous brick buildings to the downtown, including a new courthouse and an enormous opera house called the Athenaeum that could seat almost half the town. Santa Rosa was now surrounded by miles of orchards and vineyards stretching north to the Mayacamas Mountains and west to the coastal redwoods. The broader Sonoma County was on its way to becoming a recognized wine region, specializing in transplanted European grapes, but its chief export was still redwood timber.[4]

Unholy Sensations. Joshua Paddison, Oxford University Press. © Oxford University Press 2025.
DOI: 10.1093/oso/9780197775325.003.0004

As the carriage arrived at its destination, it turned off the main road and up a graveled driveway lined by gorgeous trees, shrubs, and flowers. In the years since 1875, Harris had made a series of land purchases from neighbors to add adjoining properties to Fountaingrove, paying in total $50,820 for almost two thousand acres.[5] Those acres now stretched ahead, with sculptured gardens, graveled walkways, and fountains giving way to orchards, vineyards, and forested hills beyond. These lands along with the rest of the Santa Rosa region had once been part of a land grant given by Mexico to Maria Ygnacia Lopez de Carrillo in 1841. She had employed local Pomo men and women as laborers to herd cattle and grow wheat, corn, and beans. Like other Californio families, the Carrillo family slowly but surely lost title to their lands after the U.S. military takeover and invasion of 1846–1848.[6] In a local history of Sonoma County published in 1889, Harris had won praise for "converting the apparently barren hills into lands teeming with wealth and abounding in beautiful homes."[7] Whatever else he was, Harris was part of the Anglo-Americanization of California as his efforts to create heaven on earth overwrote the Pomo and Mexican landscape.

Nagasawa guided the carriage up a hill toward three large white buildings: Aestivossa, the central manor house; the Familistery, where the colony's women lived, and the Commandery for the men. Back in New York, Chevaillier had written Harris asking if "he could find me some secluded place in the mountains where I could be alone with myself and my books and nature."[8] So she was surprised when Nagasawa took them to the palatial, two-story Aestivossa. When the structure was built in 1875, it had attracted local attention for its gas-powered lights, hot and cold running water, and bathrooms with marble washstands.[9] It boasted arched doorways, four parlors, multiple fireplaces, a large dining room, a ballroom, and "the most extensive library in northern California." Harris had named the mansion Aestivossa because the word meant "high country of divine joy," he said.[10]

Jane Lee Waring, who oversaw management of Fountaingrove as she had previously done at Brocton, greeted them at Aestivossa. Waring was in her early sixties but "one of those women who never look old," according to Sarah, due to her "sweet face." Waring showed the Chevailliers to a bedroom lavishly furnished with artworks and antiques, as was the rest of Aestivossa. "In our room was the finest bed that I ever saw," noted Alzire. "It was of highly polished mahogany, exquisitely carved. It was draped with a canopy of old gold satin and rich lace work." Alzire and Sarah were "astonished" at the wealth on display but also "delighted with the atmosphere of art and literature that pervaded the place." Expecting something more rustic in the "wilds" of California, Alzire found herself "in a fairyland of art and learning." Waring informed her that Harris was not at Aestivossa but that she and Nagasawa would convey the Chevailliers to him tomorrow at his hermitage Linn Lilla, eight miles from the colony's main buildings. There was a cottage near Linn Lilla where the Chevailliers would spend the summer.[11]

After dropping the visitors off, Nagasawa likely reported to the winery building, which he managed alongside fellow colonist Ray P. Clarke. Since 1885, Nagasawa, Clarke, and a follower of Harris in New York City named Jonathan W. Lay had been distributing Fountaingrove's wines under the name Lay, Clarke & Co. They omitted Nagasawa's name even though he knew more about winemaking than his partners; he had worked in the vineyards at Brocton and was at this point an experienced viticulturist. Lay, Clarke & Co. wines had quickly gained a "distinguished reputation for purity and excellence," distributed by friends of Harris in New York, London, Liverpool, Manchester, and Glasgow.[12] According to a May 1888 edition of the *Fountaingrove Wine News,* likely the first winery house newsletter in U.S. history, they produced 225,000 gallons that year of "high class Mountain Wines. The Burgundies, Clarets, and Champagnes promise an unusual excellence." Lay, Clarke & Co. had an arrangement with the Union Pacific Railroad to transport their wines from California to New York in special refrigerated train cars. Fountaingrove boasted one of California's largest wine production buildings, a three-story, steam-powered, state-of-the-art brick factory with the capacity to make and store 600,000 gallons of wine. The winery building was known for its "extreme cleanliness." According to one visitor, "A lady's silk and satin garments would not be soiled in taking a tour of the place."[13]

As with everything in Harris's colonies, winemaking carried special spiritual significance. Arthur Cuthbert claimed that the wines they had sold at Brocton gave people "an incipient ability to organic openness to the pure Breath of God." With each bottle of wine sold, they were, "in a small way," helping humanity to spiritually advance.[14] The Fountaingrove wines were even more powerfully holy. In a letter to his Lay, Clarke & Co. office in New York, Harris insisted that Fountaingrove wine "reduces the potentiality in the organisms of the frame that are operating by an inversive action against the divine life." This was because a spirit had "passed three times within the last few days through the finer electro-vinous spirit of the collective body of the Winery."[15] Furthermore, Harris maintained that Fountaingrove wine was so instilled with "the Divine aura" that "it would be impossible to cause drunkenness by its use."[16]

Other than the occasional visiting spirit, Nagasawa was the person most responsible for the Fountaingrove winery's successes. In fact, he was among the best-educated and most well-traveled people in Sonoma County. Born Hikosuke Isonaga in 1852, he grew up in a wealthy samurai family in Kagoshima, Japan, and had been educated in the Chinese Confucianist classics as well as translated European works from an early age. In 1864, he was selected to be a student at the Kaiseijo, a new school of Western studies in Kagoshima that aimed to develop a European-style military in Japan. Commodore Matthew Perry and his armada of U.S. gunboats had forcibly opened Japan to outside trade in 1853, and Japan's government was beginning to embrace Westernization as a means of protecting its sovereignty. At the Kaiseijo, young Hikosuke Isonaga focused on British Studies, learning English as well as science, engineering, and medicine.

When he was thirteen, the shogunate government selected him to be a part of a secret overseas mission. He and eighteen other young men from Satsuma samurai families were to travel to Great Britain to learn about Western military strategy, agricultural practices, politics, and technology. Because Japan officially banned outmigration, they had to travel under aliases to protect their families. The youngest member of the group, he adopted the name Kanaye Nagasawa, one he would use for the rest of his life.[17]

He and the other student-spies arrived in London in June 1865, where they enrolled at University College. Their presence immediately attracted media attention, with British newspapers commenting on their "bronze countenances, high cheek-bones, thick lips, and the oblique expression of their eyes" as well as their "remarkable *physique*" of the "Mongolian type."[18] Too young for university, Nagasawa left the others later that summer and moved to Aberdeen, Scotland, to go to a secondary school there with the younger brother of Thomas Blake Glover, a merchant who had opened a firm in Japan. Nagasawa excelled at the Chanonry House school, popularly known as the Gym, earning certificates of merit in English, French, Latin, history, geography, art, and—significantly—biblical scripture.[19]

Christianity was banned in Japan and would be until 1873, so this was probably Nagasawa's first exposure to the religion. Alexander Anderson, the longtime headmaster at the Gym, was a staunch Baptist who required students to attend two church services every Sunday plus a prayer meeting every Thursday. "No boy, unless we were hopelessly unsusceptible, could

Kanaye Nagasawa at age thirteen, 1865; courtesy Museum of Sonoma County, Santa Rosa, California.

have stayed a few years at the Gym without getting a good working knowledge of the Bible," recalled one student.[20] Nagasawa's first experience of Christianity was one of Protestant strictness and holistic involvement, which perhaps prepared him for his later entry into the Brotherhood of the New Life.

At some point during the 1865–1866 school year, the Japanese students living in London met Laurence Oliphant. He had first visited Japan in 1858 as private secretary to Lord Elgin, British diplomat to the Far East, and he had returned to Japan in 1861 as first secretary. A week into this post, a Japanese man—seemingly motivated by patriotic fervor—had attacked Oliphant with a two-handed sword, slashing his arm and almost killing him.[21] Nevertheless, Oliphant remained interested in Japan, particularly its religious and moral development, and when he encountered the Japanese students in London he told them about Harris, calling him a "living Confucius of the present day." In September 1866, two of the students—Naonobu Sameshima and Kiyonari Yoshida—traveled with Oliphant to Boston and New York on an educational "tour through America."[22] This occurred while Harris was still testing Oliphant's dedication, prior to his famous "disappearance" to America in 1867. In New York City, Oliphant introduced Sameshima and Yoshida to Harris. According to their later retelling, the students were "strangely moved; one of them shed tears from the effect produced upon him." Harris sat between them, "grasping the hand of each of them," causing one student to feel his "right arm tremble, and for many weeks it was affected by a nervous trembling which he could not explain." They left unable to think of anything other than Harris and his teachings.[23]

Sameshima and Yoshida returned to London and told the other students about their experience with Harris. They kept in touch with him via Oliphant for a few months, with Harris offering to pay their passage to New York if they wanted to join the Brotherhood. In May 1867, Harris visited London and while there met with some of the students. At that moment, the Japanese shogunate government was facing trouble and would be overthrown by forces loyal to the emperor later that year. Funds for the Japanese students in London were drying up and they found themselves in debt. In June 1867, six of the students took Harris up on his offer, motived by a mix of religious enthusiasm, financial need, and a desire to learn about the United States. Sameshima and Yoshida sailed to New York accompanied by Kanaye Nagasawa (then age fifteen), Arinori Mori, Yoshinari Hatekeyama, and Kanjuro Ichiki. They were some of the very first Japanese immigrants to move to the United States. They went to the colony at Amenia and then, joined by Oliphant, to Brocton. They corresponded with other Japanese students traveling abroad, urging them to come; ultimately, about twenty different Japanese young men would spend time in the Brotherhood.[24]

At Brocton, Jane Lee Waring initially put Nagasawa to work caring for dairy cattle; other Japanese men did the laundry, cooked, chopped wood, and other chores. Like Oliphant, they were unused to the rigors of farm labor, but their backgrounds in Confucianism and their elite educations had made them no strangers to concepts of self-discipline and hard work. Oliphant informed Georgina Cowper, "I see them, dear souls, every day hard at work with their countenances beaming with delight. They feel the effects of the sphere and of the influx that comes with labor, and they say that they never knew what happiness was before."[25] In another letter, Oliphant wrote that two newly arrived Japanese men now believed that "their past lives in Japan had been very wicked, and that any punishment which Faithful [Harris] saw fit to inflict, they would willingly bear. They are now learning to wash clothes, make beds, wash dishes, and other humble uses."[26] The journalist Oliver Dyer, during his visit to Brocton in April 1869, reported seeing a "tawny pagan"—one of the Japanese men—studying his Bible. "How happy he was!" wrote Dyer. "His face shone as though it were reflecting rays from the Sun of Righteousness."[27]

Like other colonists, the Japanese members of the Brotherhood practiced divine respiration; in fact, Sameshima and Yoshida had begun trying it out even while still in London, feeling "at times a certain fluttering or trembling of the heart, as if their whole system was touched by the influence of His presence in them."[28] The Japanese men were, according to Oliphant, especially "demonstrative" in their divine breathing: "you hear from their own lips their experiences."[29] God's breath "came sensibly pushing through their frames and they at once accepted from their own sensations what was taught."[30] Sameshima and Yoshida had first described divine respiration to the other students as *zazen,* the practice of seated meditation that is central to Japanese Zen Buddhism, and it may be that their familiarity with *zazen* readied them for divine respiration.

They also practiced the celibacy asked of the colonists. Samurai men did not traditionally refrain from sex, but one of the Japanese men at Brocton, Arinori Mori, had previously written that a good samurai should "root out the sexual passion."[31] Perhaps due to his youth, Nagasawa became Harris's messenger to Brocton's various households, especially when Harris sensed an outbreak of carnal desires among his followers. "I was called out many times in the midnight hour from warm bed, to go out into the freezing air, as a messenger from him," Nagasawa later recalled, "to many houses to rouse the brothers and sisters to fight and break up the environment then existing [in] these houses, caused by the coalescing of the spheres, especially amongst the opposite sexes."[32]

For his part, Harris praised Asian people as being more "subtle," "virtuous," "gentle," "cleanly," "abstemious," and "capable of the loftier religious impulses" than other groups.[33] He regarded Buddhism as a "magnificent system, fearfully powerful and fascinating to the intellect," but one that was "*crumbling at its centre.*"[34] In its place, he envisioned a blossoming of the Brotherhood of the New Life in Asia; once planted in Japan, he prophesied, "it will go like lightning."[35]

A diary that Nagasawa kept while at Brocton in 1871 showed him to be a diligent student of Harris's teachings. His days were filled with physical labor and constant self-scrutiny of his spiritual state. Along with other colonists, he struggled to "annihilate utterly and absolutely our natural selfhood and aims which we held dear to us." On January 1, he pledged himself to greater "self-abnegation commencing with the new year." He had studied briefly at Cornell University the previous year but dropped out because Jane Lee Waring told him that "study hurts me and instead of using [i.e., spiritually advancing] I am sinking down very fast. Books keep my mind downward instead of lifting it higher and higher to the Lord."[36] Every sin or act of disobedience by a member of the colony caused Harris tremendous physical and mental suffering, he said, and Nagasawa paid careful attention to Harris's daily ups and down of health.

A breakthrough came for Nagasawa on January 23, 1871, when "after breakfast Fairies gave me [a] name: Phoenix." Expertise in divine respiration allowed colonists to see fairies and to receive their fairy name: Jane Lee Waring was Dovie, Laurence Oliphant was Woodbine, and Maria Oliphant was Viola. According to Harris, fairies helped the faithful "demagnetize" and "slay the lust that smites." The fairies at Brocton gave colonists a rhyme to repeat when feeling sexual desire: "Cats yun away! Cats yun away! His little wife, the Will, will say: Cats yun away! Love, hear what I say! Turn out the billygoats; cats yun away!"[37]

After receiving his fairy name, Nagasawa "began to feel nearer to them all." Rejuvenated, the following day he wrote, "I began to feel such strange things as I recalled my past misery and sorrow." However, he was soon in torment again, recording, "in the night I could not hold my state and cried great parts of the night with full of misery." Celia Requa, known by her fairy name Golden Rose, often reprimanded Nagasawa for his "carelessness in taking care of myself etc etc.," he wrote. Celia and her late husband James had been followers of Harris since his days as pastor of the Church of the Good Shepherd in New York in the late 1850s. "I felt miserable and in despair for my weakness," Nagasawa wrote in April 1871. "I got a hard scolding from Aunt G.R. nearly all day." A few days later, he wrote: "Aunt Dovie and Golden Rose scolded me very much for my impudence and working more than my body can bear. I felt very sad and wept and Aunt Dovie explained me minutely why they are so anxious about me."[38] Throughout these trials, Nagasawa remained committed to the Brotherhood, with its exhilarating ups and excruciating downs.

As Nagasawa moved into the inner circle, the other Japanese men were drifting away. Some, such as Arinori Mori, felt called to return to Japan to "discharge our duty to our country." He went on to become a prominent diplomat and proponent of Western-style education and religious freedom in Meiji Japan. Other Japanese students left because they "felt somehow badly toward the teachings" of Harris, coming to the conclusion that they were "many strange superstitions."[39]

By the time Harris was thinking of moving the colony to California, only Nagasawa and one other Japanese man remained at Brocton: Ōsui Arai, who had arrived in 1871. Arai was a samurai from Sendai, Japan, who had been exposed to Christianity during the early Meiji era via a Russian Orthodox priest. He met Arinori Mori in Tokyo and Mori brought him to Brocton while on a diplomatic mission to the United States.[40] Both Nagasawa and Arai were part of the small group that rode the railroad west with Harris to Santa Rosa in 1875 to found Fountaingrove. While Aestivossa was under construction, Nagasawa and Arai slept on site in "rough board tents."[41] Harris initially put Nagasawa in charge of landscaping and then, in 1879, the planting and operation of the vineyard. Arai ran the colony's print shop, which produced Harris's privately distributed works of poetry and theology.

In the 1880s, the Japanese government had begun to allow—even encourage—outmigration as a safety valve for population growth and to elevate Japan's reputation around the world. In 1891, there was a total of seventy-four Japanese immigrants in Sonoma County.[42] Nagasawa and Arai had encountered moments of racial hostility in Santa Rosa, as when a white competitor to Fountaingrove had advertised that "milk sold by me has no Japanese or Chinese flavoring."[43] However, in general Nagasawa and Arai stood apart from other Japanese immigrants in the area, and not only because of their inclusion in the Brotherhood. As was typical of migrants from Japan who entered the United States via New York City, the two men were wealthier and better educated than most Japanese immigrants on the West Coast, who had entered via San Francisco.[44] The majority of those immigrants worked as low-paid agricultural laborers, filling a void created by the passage of the Chinese Exclusion Act of 1882. As Fountaingrove wines grew in reputation, Nagasawa in particular moved in circles highly unusual for a Japanese immigrant in California. In June 1891, at the time of the Chevailliers' arrival, he was a member of the Sonoma County World's Fair executive committee charged with creating exhibition materials for the upcoming fair in Chicago.[45]

The next morning, on Monday, June 8, Nagasawa helped the Chevailliers back into the carriage and, joined by Jane Lee Waring, drove them ten miles to the cottage where they would spend the summer. Entering a mountainous area of Sonoma County known as the Los Guillicos Valley, the carriage climbed up a steep dirt road that ran alongside a deep ravine. They finally reached a plateau where they saw a little white house nestled against a towering wall of black rock. The cottage was surrounded by wildflowers and dense shrubbery, and they could hear the gurgling of a nearby stream. Alzire regarded the house as "a very plain building and rather small, but it was quite a homelike little snuggery." She felt "much pleased with the idea of living in it."[46]

After dropping off their luggage, Nagasawa and Waring led the Chevailliers on a short hike to Harris's mountain home Linn Lilla, where the autumn before he had discovered the secret of eternal life. Linn Lilla proved to be a handsomely furnished, six-room house with bright white siding and a shingled roof. Sarah found it "beautifully embowered" and surrounded by "lovely flower borders."[47] Inside, in the booklined study, Alzire laid eyes on Thomas Lake Harris for the first time. She discovered him to be a "rather thin old man, with a long gray beard, highly intellectual face, piercing dark eyes, very deep set, and who stood erect as a statue." He came forward and, much to the Chevailliers' surprise, greeted each woman with a kiss. "It was such a kiss as a spiritual father might give to his child," Alzire noted, "and I received it in that way."[48]

According to Chevaillier's later retelling, Harris sat down and, "with an air of great dignity," said to her, "Now read me. What do you find?"

Taken aback, Chevaillier replied, "I see in you great spiritual illumination and power. I see towering intellect and a strong will. I have come all the way here from the East to learn from you how I may receive some of this illumination and to imbibe all the spiritual truth that I am capable of receiving. I have come for light that I may increase my power for good in the world."

"Child," said Harris, "you must be as wise as a serpent in these days. Let me see."

Coming forward again, Harris "with a dramatic gesture" put his hand on Chevaillier's solar plexus and "gave a most unearthly grunt."

"U-g-h-hh," he exclaimed. "Oh, these vampires. These vampires of preachers. These great preachers and others have fastened on you and drawn from you until they have nearly deprived you of your spirituality." Removing his hand, he informed her that he had stayed up all of the previous night fighting off the demons that infested her. "It was a fearful struggle," he said, one that had almost killed him.

The idea that malevolent spiritual forces might attack and weaken someone was not a foreign one to Chevaillier. Her former teacher Mary Baker Eddy taught that "malicious animal magnetism" could do harm. Chevaillier's own mental healing practices included "thought transference" from herself to a patient as a way of cleansing them of illness. It was not preposterous that Harris, with his powers, could protect her from evil spirits. She felt "very grateful for one who would do so much for me and was very anxious to show my gratitude."

Harris told her, "Come onto my grounds any time you desire. It is not a privilege that is often accorded, but it will be accorded to you. You, little one, will be received into the inmost circle."[49]

Everything about this first conversation demonstrated that Harris was not like other men. The kisses and touching of Chevaillier's solar plexus were intimate gestures that violated norms of proper comportment. His talk of sleepless nights spent battling demons in order to protect her established his spiritual powers as a pivotal man. His invitation to grant her access to the "inmost circle" promised special treatment and esoteric knowledge. By calling her "child," he put himself in the role of a wise father—exactly what Chevaillier sought. Her years of her spiritual seeking, which had led her out of the Episcopalian Church into Christian Science and then to her own practice of mental healing, had brought her to this place and this moment.

At this exact moment, in fact, she was entangled in a religious controversy involving her first spiritual mentor, Phillips Brooks, rector of Trinity

Church in Boston, a controversy that was about to intrude on her solitude in California. A few months earlier, in March 1891, Episcopal bishop of Massachusetts Benjamin Henry Paddock had died, and Brooks was elected to be his successor. But as his election awaited confirmation from the national Episcopal body, rumors began circulating that Brooks's theology was more liberal than he publicly acknowledged. It was said that Brooks privately denied the validity of the historical episcopate, the Nicene Creed, and even the divinity of Jesus.

Benjamin F. De Costa, powerful rector of Church of St. John the Evangelist in New York City, emerged as the leader of the opposition to Brooks's confirmation. De Costa told the press that he had proof of Brooks's heretical beliefs—a letter written by an unnamed "friend and correspondent" from Boston who had had private conversations with Brooks. This friend reported that Brooks viewed the divinity of Jesus as a matter that should be left to individuals to decide for themselves. "Surely," this friend informed De Costa, "he is most unfit to be a bishop, if, as all say here, he would let everybody stand on his head if he wants to do so, and avow that no doctrine is essential, not even the evangelical one of the Trinity and the Divine Incarnation." De Costa did not name this "friend" from Boston but mailed a copy of the letter to Episcopal bishops throughout the United States and shared it with the press in order to forestall Brooks's confirmation.[50]

Alzire Chevaillier was the "friend" who had written the letter. She wrote it right before leaving for California. She knew De Costa from her reform work in New York, having served with him on the Society for Procuring Playgrounds for Children.[51] She wrote the letter out of frustration that her former mentor Brooks would not publicly embrace what she believed to be the true liberality of his views, which he had expressed to her in private. Rather than hide his true beliefs, Chevaillier longed for him to leave the Episcopal Church behind, as she had done. Without naming her, De Costa confirmed that this was his correspondent's motivation, saying that she was "practically done with the Episcopal Church" and angry that Brooks lacked "the honesty to come out and follow the example of their pupil."[52] Given the former closeness of Chevaillier's relationship to Brooks, he must have viewed her letter to De Costa as a shocking betrayal of trust. But Chevaillier, in her striving to do good in the world, believed exposing Brooks's supposed heresy would encourage others to question the confinements of traditional Christianity and move on, as she had done, to a more "advanced" spiritual state. "Until we have a spiritual church allowing every latitude of interpretation, the brightest lights, intellectually and spiritually, will find no room for them in the inn of ecclesiasticism," she believed.[53]

On June 7, the day Chevaillier arrived at Fountaingrove, the *New York Times* broke the news that De Costa's anonymous correspondent was none other than "Miss A. A. Chevaillier, who will be recalled as having come to this city from Boston and revived the *International Magazine of Christian Science,* founded and run for a time by Mrs. Plunkett." The fact that De Costa's informant was a woman—something he had tried to hide, even calling Chevaillier "him"—immediately discredited her as a source for many. In connecting Chevaillier to the notorious Mary Plunkett-Arthur Bently Worthington scandal of two years prior, the *Times* further cast her as an "absurd" person for Episcopal bishops to trust.[54] Other newspapers followed suit, running such headlines as "It Was a Woman" and quoting Episcopalian ministers who said Chevaillier's name "would not carry any weight with the church" because she was an "ardent Christian Scientist."[55]

The *Springfield Republican* went further, printing a letter from someone who claimed to know Chevaillier from Boston. This writer said that Chevaillier had a history of "backbiting": "I suppose there is not a conspicuous person who has done Miss Chevaillier an act of kindness in the past dozen years who has not been repaid by her secret or open enmity. . . . She has that peculiar nature to which slander and spite are essential."[56] Brooks himself refused to comment, but his friends in Boston attacked her for the "baseness of her ingratitude" to her former pastor.[57] The matter had quickly become a referendum on Chevaillier's past, personal conduct, religious beliefs, and trustworthiness as a woman and witness.

California newspapers picked up on the story and reported that Chevaillier was currently residing in the state. On June 10, an intrepid *San Francisco Chronicle* reporter went so far as to track her down at Fountaingrove and even hiked in to pay her a visit at the secluded cottage where she and her mother were staying. "Yes, I am Miss Chevaillier," she confirmed when he knocked on the door. The reporter found her to be a "slight little woman . . . apparently past the age of thirty. Her most striking feature were her two bright blue eyes that sparkled with intelligence and constantly twinkled in company with a ready smile which was as gracious as her manner." When asked about her letter to De Costa, she replied, "I am too insignificant to be drawn into this fight, but if it has been accidentally done I cannot help it." She went on to confirm that Brooks was too unorthodox in his beliefs to be a proper bishop. "He is broader than the canons and dogmas he is bound there to uphold," she said. But she emphasized that she regarded him as a "noble, great-hearted man."[58]

Chevaillier preferred, however, to discuss her current spiritual beliefs and mental healing practices, topics the reporter found "unconventional." She took him down to the bubbling mountain stream where she and her mother had been spending the last couple of days reading. She informed him that she had come to Fountaingrove to "gain by study and meditation a deeper insight into the truth; to try to lose all bitterness against the classes in which I find so much of the cause of human misery; to gain a more perfect love and a deeper spiritual power." The reporter left with the impression that Chevaillier was an "intense" and "earnest" woman who "wished to help humanity" above all else. "Such, in past, was the woman found struggling with mysticism, occultism, and social errors up in the hermitage of Thomas Lake Harris, the mystic," he concluded.

Chevaillier, probably suspecting that the reporter might portray her as a kook, decided to take matters into her own hand the next day by writing a letter to the *Boston Herald* to explain her side of the story. Writing from what she called the "Primeval Mountain Wilds" of California, she claimed that she had originally written to De Costa not intending to fuel his campaign against Brooks but simply as De Costa's confidant. However, she said, God chose to use her as an instrument to lead others beyond the narrow creeds and dogmas of traditional Christianity, which she called "churchianity." She could only hope that Brooks was "too full of divine consciousness" to hold it against her, "whatever the result to himself." As to whether her name would "carry weight" in the Episcopal Church, she declared that she cared not and loved only "absolute truth." She felt compelled to also clarify that she had left Eddy's Christian Science after finding it "as selfishly individualistic and non-ethical, practically, as churchianity." Finally, perhaps sensing that his confirmation was assured at this point, she reversed course and urged the Episcopal Church to confirm Brooks as bishop precisely because of his liberal views: "Surely the church ought to be large enough and Christly enough to welcome a man of such convictions and tolerance."[59]

Chevaillier's letter to the *Boston Herald* was her attempt to turn the Brooks controversy into an opportunity to promote her broadminded spiritual values. She emphasized the purity of her motives, refuting the idea that she had acted out of spite or ingratitude. However, her unorthodox religious views, which she heartily defended, together with her attacks on "churchianity," hardly would have endeared her to Episcopal bishops. She had already been discredited and De Costa humiliated when her identity emerged. The day after she wrote to the *Boston Herald*, Episcopal ministers around the country learned that the national body had confirmed Phillips Brooks as bishop of Massachusetts. He had never publicly addressed the charges of heterodoxy and remaining masterfully above the fray proved to be a sound strategy. He never spoke to Chevaillier again.[60]

Meanwhile, Harris was engulfed in his own media controversy as Margaret Oliphant's *Memoir of the Life of Laurence Oliphant* began to be reviewed in newspapers across the United States.[61] Though less of a sensation in the United States than in Great Britain, the book directed negative attention toward Harris and Fountaingrove. Its portrayal of Harris as a megalomaniacal despot who had manipulated Oliphant, robbing him of a fortune and forcing him to live apart from his wife and mother, disrupted the quiet, respectable reputation Harris had tried to maintain since founding Fountaingrove in 1875. Disaffected members of the Brotherhood of the New Life fed the fire. On June 21, the *San Francisco Chronicle* ran an article that claimed to give insider information, provided by a former member of Harris's communities, about the "big, fat spiritist spider, Thomas Lake Harris." This apostate offered little that was new to the reading public other than a few bizarre details—such as Harris forcing Alice Oliphant to take dirt baths—but it fed the growing story.[62] Another ex-member told the *New York Tribune*, "there is no question that 'Prophet' Harris is a hypnotist of greater power than anyone who has ever made a study of mesmerism, for he controls the intelligent and ignorant with the same skill."[63] If wealthy and accomplished Laurence Oliphant had fallen into his "web," no one was safe. Given the extent of his occult powers, Harris "should have been executed years ago before he wrecked the lives of so many bright people," thundered a writer in San Bernardino.[64]

Harris's devoted supporters in Britain had recently organized themselves into a Department of Great Britain of the Brotherhood of the New Life, led by Arthur Cuthbert in Birmingham and Charles Pearce in Glasgow, and they attacked Margaret Oliphant's book as a pack of oversights, exaggerations, and outright lies. They insisted that Laurence and Alice Oliphant had joined the Brotherhood willingly and fully aware of the sacrifices—the self-denial and manual labor—communal living required.[65] But Cuthbert could not help but imply that the Oliphant family's string of deaths—Maria in 1881, Alice in 1886, Laurence in 1888—were a byproduct of them having left the Brotherhood, to which Margaret Oliphant responded, "Does Mr. Cuthbert believe his chief [Harris] to hold the keys of life and death?"[66] Cuthbert believed exactly that, in fact, though he refrained from saying so in print.

In years past, Harris would have tried to ignore the media maelstrom, but now, with his youthful vigor renewed, he decided to issue a public rebuttal. Published as volume 2 of his new Fountaingrove Library pamphlet series and also as a letter to the local *Sonoma Democrat,* Harris titled his response *Brotherhood of the New Life: Its Fact, Law, Method, and Purpose: Letter from Thomas Lake Harris with Passing Reference to Recent Criticisms.* Before addressing Margaret Oliphant's book and its fall out, he revealed for the first time the news of his breakthrough at Linn Lilla the previous September—his discovery of eternal youth. Not only was he restored to his "early prime," but, he told the public, "this gift that I hold is the coming inheritance of all." Just as the truth of Jesus's ministry had been demonstrated by the "resurrection of His corporate fleshy image from the grave," Harris's miraculous youthfulness was an "attestation to the truth of the New Life." Those who would follow him would likewise be transformed, "their bodies in gradual transportation to that glorious image of the divine-human Lord." Calling forth once more his old apocalypticism, Harris warned that "civilization is verging to a crisis"—now was the time to heed his warnings and accept his invitation to join in the "relations of communion in the New Life."

Finally he addressed the rumors and accusations swirling around him. "The first thought of the vulgar is, that secrecy and mystery, isolation and home-keeping, imply depravity," he noted. In fact, he and his followers were "industrious, peaceful, harmless, and non-aggressive." In reference to Margaret Oliphant's book, he directed Americans to the rebuttals made in the British press by Cuthbert and Pearce. Beyond that, Harris refused to comment, noting, "men do not bandy words with carrion." As for the newspapers, he praised "respectable" journalists but lambasted "the nasal purveyors of the Sensational Press, who prowl about the kitchen middens, and who from the smell of the waste-pipes presume to sit in judgment on the aromas of the *salon.*" He ended the letter by promising "this American People, whom I love, and to whose best interests my life is pledged and consecrated," that the current controversy would soon pass. "I have no fear that I shall ever cease to be regarded as a loyal and honorable son and servant of a great and glorious People," he said. He promised more publications soon, for he was writing at a fevered pace, producing new revelations, uncovering new "verified facts," and unlocking new spiritual powers to be shared with the public.[67]

Harris also gave a rare interview to a reporter from the *New York Sun*, who visited Fountaingrove at the end of June. Harris informed the reporter that he had not read Margaret Oliphant's book and had no intention of reading it, but he was "tolerably familiar" with its contents. "I cannot reveal the truth about Laurence Oliphant's coming into my family without giving pain to persons now living," he said. "If Mrs. Oliphant has made mistakes it is because she did not take sufficient care to ascertain the facts." Harris then steered the conversation to the "underlying motive of his life": "bringing about social reform and regeneration."[68] Soon after giving this interview, Harris fired off a letter to the *Religio-Philosophical Journal*, a major spiritualist newspaper in Chicago. Reviewing the history of spiritualism, Harris refrained from criticizing mainstream spiritualism as he typically did. Instead, he said that all the unruly séances, trance writings, and spirit photography of the past forty years had led humanity to this moment—1891—the beginning of a "human renaissance" that he would lead. "Spring is in the air," he concluded. "The grim, scarred veterans of thought grow young again; we taste the free, delicious breath of the advancing and influent God-time."[69]

Harris also sent *Religio-Philosophical Journal* a strange, erotic poem called "The New Day," which editor John Bundy declined to publish, noting "I do not understand it" and "My readers would not understand it."[70] Privately, Bundy complained that the poem was "utter *rot* to my 'undeveloped' understanding. It has too the same libidinous touch as does nearly all he writes. Suppressed menstruation and moral male masturbation beget strange mental and psychical states."[71] Once again, Harris's singular mixing of erotic and spiritual themes, along with his much-publicized celibacy, put him outside the metaphysical mainstream.

Far from shrinking from the media attention, Harris was using it as an opportunity to spread his spiritual message and potentially broaden his movement. His remarkable claims of newfound youth and his promise to help others achieve it was the boldest public statement he had made since his denunciation of popular spiritualism in London in 1860. Whether due to his magically renewed youthful vigor, his long-brewing apocalyptic beliefs, or the Oliphant book, he was putting himself squarely in the public eye, confident he could rise above the speculations and accusations of the "Sensational Press." Behind the scenes, Jane Lee Waring wrote to Harris's friends and followers confirming he had "recently attained to the full and final solution of the human problem." All of his previous writings were to be regarded as "*obiter dicta* (notes by the way)," superseded by his newest writings. A new era was dawning, in which Harris would have "direct relations with the world."[72]

Aware that Alzire and Sarah Chevaillier may have already learned of the storm surrounding *Memoir of the Life of Laurence Oliphant*, Jane Lee Waring paid a visit to their mountain cottage toward the end of June. She brought both volumes of Margaret Oliphant's book as well as a packet of newspaper clippings containing "all the most pronounced criticisms upon the community." Waring told Chevaillier that "outrageous attacks" on Harris were an inevitable part of his "earthly martyrdom." She assured Chevaillier that they were "fabrications of the basest sort," but she wanted Chevaillier to read them for herself.[73] Impressed that Harris would encourage her to read criticisms made of him, Chevaillier glanced at the materials but soon set them aside. She was more interested in reading *Lyra Triumphalis,* Harris's forthcoming volume of songs and poems dedicated to the "disinherited and outraged Common People," which Harris allowed her to see before publication. *Lyra Triumphalis* was filled with attacks on immoral industrial capitalism, appeals to socialism, and declarations of woman's special role in spiritually perfecting the world, such as this verse from a poem titled "Religion in Socialism":

> O ye of the first resurrection;
>   Ye daughters of sorrows and sweets;
> Ye toilers in whom the affection
>   Of God its society meets;
> Lift up, yea, lift up! be it spoken,—
>   The word and the will of Twain-One,—
> The bonds of the breathless are broken;
>   The soul breathes to sun.[74]

The book seemed to be written especially for her.

5

Autumn 1891

Enter Mr. X

Alzire and Sarah Chevaillier ended up spending more than three months as Harris's guests, departing on September 11. They mostly filled their days reading by the stream, taking walks in the mountains near their cottage, and enjoying "healthful rest and meditation." With Alzire's history of poor health, the summer at Fountaingrove was precisely what she needed following the stressful, busy year and a half she had spent in New York City.

Periodically, Kanaye Nagasawa took them by carriage back to Fountaingrove proper so they could dine at Aestivossa. There, they became acquainted with some the colony's twenty-five members. Alzire took an immediate liking to Ōsui Arai, whom she found to be sweet natured and well spoken. She was especially impressed with the Parting family: Emma Parting, her sister Eusardia Nicholas, and Emma's two daughters Margaret and Alice, both in their twenties. Emma Parting was a wealthy British widow whose husband, the late John Parting, had worked with Emma's brothers to found the first photographic studios in British India. The Parting women had moved to Fountaingrove in 1886. Chevaillier found them to be "persons of high education" who were "accustomed to the best society." Margaret played the pianoforte prettily, and Alice was "an artist of considerable experience, who handles pencil and brush with true art feeling." Alice's painting of Aestivossa had run on the front page of a San Francisco newspaper in 1889 as an exemplar of "the more costly class of California rural homes."[1] At Aestivossa, Chevaillier also met Celia Requa, still one of Harris's most committed acolytes. Golden Rose had been part of the core group that accompanied Harris to California in 1875.[2]

Chevaillier was surprised to see these cultured women, young and old, engaged in physical labor at Fountaingrove. Harris did employ some hired hands in the vineyard, but the day-to-day operations of the colony were carried out by its members, just as had been the case at the New York colonies. Margaret Parting helped Ōsui Arai set type in the print shop while

Unholy Sensations. Joshua Paddison, Oxford University Press. © Oxford University Press 2025.
DOI: 10.1093/oso/9780197775325.003.0005

Alice Parting, illustration of Aestivossa at Fountaingrove, *Pacific Rural Press*, May 18, 1889.

Alice did the laundry. Chevaillier also noted that the women were "plainly dressed," despite their backgrounds of wealth and refinement. For all her radical political and religious views, Chevaillier remained a middle-class white woman from a respectable Boston family, and she was taken aback by these aspects of communal living at Fountaingrove.[3]

As the summer passed, she also visited Harris at Linn Lilla from time to time. He gave her advance access to the string of new writings he was producing for public consumption: first *Brotherhood of the New Life: Its Fact, Law, Method, and Purpose,* with its declaration of Harris's renewed youth; then *Lyra Triumphalis,* with its thrilling populist hymns; and finally *God's Breath in Man and in Humane Society,* a 300-page treatise on how divine respiration could bring "psycho-physical transformation, renaissance, and transposition to the organic lines of the eternal life."[4] As a working mental healer, Chevaillier read this last work with professional interest. Harris claimed that divine respiration "wars against disease, expels the virus of hereditary malady, renews health its foundations, [and] stands in the body as a sentinel against every plague." He had been making such claims privately for decades—in fact, much of *God's Breath in Man* had been written in the 1860s—but he was now making them boldly and publicly. For proof, he offered himself: "old age and its wintry senses" had fallen away, he said, for he was "reborn as the Divine-Human Twain-Oneness."[5]

In a dispatch to her magazine *Problem of Life and the International Magazine of Truth,* Chevaillier declared *God's Breath in Man* the "book of the century for those who really wish to destroy *proprium,* i.e., to lose sense life that they may find their life in God."[6] However, the broader press reaction was not so kind. Already in the news due to Margaret Oliphant's *Memoir of the Life of Laurence Oliphant,* Harris's disclosure of his discovery of eternal youth brought another round of mocking press coverage. Newspapers likened him to Ponce de León and Methuselah and wondered why he still looked every one of his sixty-eight earthly years.[7] London's *Pall Mall Gazette,* which under its muckraking editor William T. Stead had a long-standing fascination with Harris, ran a nasty piece by a "North California Neighbor" of Harris calling him "deeply pathetic." His recent claims notwith-standing, Harris remained "very stooping and aged in appearance: his hair and long beard are almost white and his frame fragile."[8] Not to be outdone, the *St. James's Gazette* asked to "put to the test his account of the marvelous transformation he has undergone. What a flutter there will be among septuagenarians when the news arrives that the aged Prophet has reappeared in all the bloom, let us hope, of early prime!"[9]

In response to these kinds of sarcastic challenges, Harris issued a statement of clarification. It was true that his external appearance had not radically changed—he still looked sixty-eight years old, not showing his transformation "as some might suppose." However, he did look "more natural," he said. And though "for a time, he would wear the appearance of old age upon the surfaces," he insisted that "these surfaces would appear vivified and penetrated by a divine-natural youthfulness and radiance." This implied that, soon enough, his "surfaces" would change more radically to reflect his new youthfulness.[10]

In the meantime, Harris faced a different kind of attack from spiritualists and other metaphysicians who used the controversy over his claims of youth and Margaret Oliphant's book to mock and denounce Harris's "squalid fanaticism."[11] Just as they had done during Harris's earlier years, spiritualists in the United States and Great Britain portrayed Harris as unscientific, greedy, and dangerous—exactly what skeptics said about spiritualists themselves. Chicago's *Progressive Thinker* called Harris's claims of renewed youth "preposterous, verging on idiocy."[12] In London, the editor of *Light* declared Harris an "evil genius" possessing a "remarkable magnetic influence over those who submit themselves to his power." Harris was nothing more than a "modern Messianic pretender."[13] In the *Religio-Philosophical Journal,* spiritualists mocked Harris's "strange" poetry and decried his "love of power, to lead and allow none to question, to command and be obeyed."[14] Once again, Harris was giving spiritualism a bad name.

A newer transatlantic metaphysical movement—Theosophy—likewise worked to distance itself from Harris's resurging infamy. Founded in New York City in 1875 by Helena Petrovna Blavatsky and others, the Theosophical Society emerged from spiritualism but was a semi-secret organization more like the Freemasons than the popular séances of the 1850s and 1860s. Blavatsky said her trance writings were the work not of spirits but Tibetan masters—advanced spiritual beings here on earth—and her writings borrowed from European esoteric traditions such as Hermeticism as well as Buddhism and Hinduism. Though founded in the United States, Theosophy thrived in England. The British Theosophical Society, founded in London in 1878, attracted spiritualists, mystics, and Orientalists interested in Eastern sources of wisdom. Their secretive structure and study of arcane texts from Europe and Asia in turn inspired the creation of other occult groups, most notably the Hermetic Order of the Golden Dawn in 1887.[15]

The Brotherhood of the New Life and the Theosophists had things in common: they both had their roots in spiritualism but had shifted toward esotericism, they both believed in an "occult" spiritual world accessible via ritual practice, and they both advocated the practice of celibacy as a path toward spiritual advancement. Yet for all they shared, the two movements remained highly critical of each other. They were frequently linked in the press, much to the chagrin of both groups.[16] In 1884, Harris had written a book called *Wisdom of the Adepts,* privately circulated among the chosen, that simultaneously attacked Theosophy as an "esoteric Buddhist cult" and appropriated some of its ideas, albeit filtered through Harris's own theology. Like Blavatsky's books *Isis Unveiled* and *The Secret Doctrine,* purportedly lost histories of the "archaic truths which are the basis of all religions," Harris's *Wisdom of the Adepts* was a stupefying world history of esoteric thought that included stops in ancient Greece, Rome, Egypt, India, Japan, Lemuria, Atlantis, and the Land of Ob.[17] More openly hostile than Harris, Laurence Oliphant had regarded Theosophy as a "delusion and a snare" and mocked it in a short story called "The Sisters of Thibet."[18]

The Theosophists were not amused. Toward the end of her life, Helena Petrovna Blavatsky attacked Harris's theology in the pages of her journal

Lucifer (named for the Greek name for the planet Venus, not for the devil of the Bible).[19] After her death in May 1891, her successor as editor, the women's rights and labor activist Annie Besant, continued the tradition. In September, Besant printed a piece describing the "abhorrence" with which Theosophists regarded the idea of putting Blavatsky and Harris "side by side as guides and prophets." A month later, with Margaret Oliphant's *Memoir* making headlines, Besant wrote a lengthy takedown in *Lucifer* of Harris's "false mysticism." She described reading his works "with an overpowering sense of nausea" due to his "mania for dwelling on the sex-idea; no thought that does not center in sex, revolve around sex." Besant explained that Theosophists strove to rise "above sex to the plane where sex is not," whereas Harris reveled in "impure sensual images that there abound, drugged and poisoned by the emanations of passion and of sexual desires."[20] Once again, Harris's unabashed and seemingly hypocritical mingling of the sexual and the spiritual provided fodder for critics eager to display their own purity.

These various strands of opposition to Harris converged in London's St. James Hall in late November 1891. J. Cuming Walters, a young admirer of Harris's writings but not a member of the Brotherhood, delivered a scathing lecture attacking Margaret Oliphant's *Memoir* as "ignorant" and full of "wholesale misrepresentations" about Harris. Walters called Margaret "vindicative and unjust" for taking her "demented" cousin Laurence's side in a dispute she did not understand.[21] Walter's lecture filled St. James Hall with a rowdy mixture of Harris's followers, spiritualists, socialists, Theosophists, and Swedenborgians; a journalist in attendance declared that "on more than one face in the room religious fanaticism was written clearly."[22]

The discussion following Walters's lecture "grew rather hot," according to one attendee; "many rose desirous to speak and all had not the opportunity." The colorful crowd included stalwart Department of Great Britain of the Brotherhood of the New Life member Charles Pearce, visiting from Glasgow; occultist C. M. Berridge, who published expositions of Harris's theology under the pseudonym Respiro; ex-Theosophist Edward Maitland, who had recently founded the Esoteric Christian Union and who sat looking "intensely amused" by the evening's proceedings; and a group of no doubt baffled balloonists from the Balloon Society of Great Britain who had for unknown reasons sponsored the talk. The heated discussion included a moment when an "old white-haired Swedenborgian got up"; "his eyes shot fire" as he denounced Harris for corrupting Swedenborg's ideas. Another man in the audience accused Walters of "suppressing the horrible impurity of the sexual doctrine that was the main thing" lurking in Harris's theology. Walters managed to end the evening by proposing two resolutions, approved by the majority of the crowd, that Harris's works deserved "unprejudiced consideration" and that Margaret Oliphant had judged Harris based on "insufficient evidence."[23]

By this point in the autumn of 1891, Chevaillier was living in Oakland, where she offered mental healing services—she charged one dollar per treatment—and taught classes in the Science of Gospel Healing by Spiritual Law.[24] After leaving Fountaingrove in September, the Chevailliers had stayed for a few days in the Grand Hotel in downtown Santa Rosa; there, Alzire gave another interview to a reporter about her religious views. Billed as "the leader of the new movement known as 'Spiritual Science,'" Chevaillier gushed about the "delightful summer" she had enjoyed in Harris's mountain cottage. "It would be impossible to find a more beautiful spot for healthful rest and meditation," she said. Asked if she believed in Theosophy, spiritualism, or Christian Science, she replied that all three held partial truths but none was complete. As for Harris, she regarded him as a "grand man, and a powerful and profound thinker. Some of his doctrines I concur in, while others I regard as being in advance of the times." She added, "His theory is very beautiful, and I never saw a happier and more harmonious set of people than those whom I met in his colony at Fountaingrove."[25]

Chevaillier had similarly glowing things to say about Harris and his followers in a dispatch she sent in September to the *Problem of Life and International Magazine of Truth*. "It has been our priceless privilege, a privilege never before extended, to be the guest of this man of God for nearly four months," she wrote. She felt certain that "divine guidance" had brought her to Harris's doorstep so that her "soul could be most deeply fed for divine *use.*" She further enthused that Harris "is not merely a mystic, but has demonstrated divine socialism and the death of egotism in his unified families of diversified personalities." She promised that she would soon have much more to say about the new spiritual truths, including the efficacy of divine respiration, that she had learned from Harris.[26]

But in fact some tensions had arisen between Chevaillier and Harris by the end of the summer, tensions that prompted her to leave his mountain cottage a bit sooner than planned. Considering Chevaillier's broken relationships with her two former mentors, Mary Baker Eddy and Phillips Brooks, and her own strongly held spiritual worldview, these tensions were probably inevitable, all the more so given Harris's insistence on his own primacy. First,

Chevaillier's middle-class sensibilities were offended by Harris's sometimes strange and immoderate behavior. During one visit to Linn Lilla in August, Chevaillier witnessed Harris spiritually doing battle with a demon. "He was sitting on a sofa," she recalled. "Of a sudden he straightened out, threw back his arms, kicked up his legs and began some queer convulsive motions." Harris then adopted the voice of the spirit in hell whose soul he was trying to redeem, using "the coarsest kind of language, in which profanity and vulgarisms abounded." Shocked, Chevaillier rose to leave, but Jane Lee Waring asked her to stay and "see what he suffers." Chevaillier reluctantly agreed. "I never listened to anything half so horrible before," Chevaillier later said. After defeating the demon, Harris—still inhabited by the damned soul—called for communion wine, which he gulped, "spilling it over his face and letting it drool down his whiskers." A thought popped into Chevaillier's head at this moment: "Anti-Christ." On another occasion, she saw Harris sitting with his feet in Jane Lee Waring's lap, a surprisingly intimate scene that gave Chevaillier pause.[27]

Second, Chevaillier resented the plans Harris began to make for her, which violated her much-cherished independence as a reformer, healer, and activist. He told her that she reminded him of Alice Le Strange Oliphant: "You have her brilliancy and grace and are well fitted to take her place." He imagined her returning to Boston or New York and using "her great talent and ability" there to "teach others the doctrines of the new life." During one conversation, Harris informed her, "Oh, you are to share in all our spiritual joys, and our worldly ones too. You are to be our little queen of the East." Chevaillier responded that she did not desire to be a queen nor his agent in the East. When Harris persisted and she demurred, he told her, "Child! Child, it will mean death to you!" Brotherhood member Jonathan W. Lay, visiting from New York, similarly warned her at Linn Lilla not to question Harris's plans. "If you do," he said, "Father will give you up, and that would mean death to you. I have known some to die in ten days after Father ceased to work for them!" Chevaillier laughed at Lay's "ebullition of fanaticism, superstition, [and] servile fear," but she was inwardly chilled by these threats.[28]

Finally, Chevaillier began to question some of Harris's religious teachings. When he told her that she possessed a spiritual counterpart—her soul's true love in heaven—named Sir Knight Peace, she asked, "Father, how will I know when my counterpart is about to make himself known to me?" Harris blurted, "Oh, you will feel him in your toes." The fluttery, embodied sensation

Alice Parting, oil painting of Thomas Lake Harris at Fountaingrove, 1893; courtesy Museum of Sonoma County, Santa Rosa, California.

of first meeting one's counterpart had been joyfully experienced by many in the Brotherhood, but Chevaillier recoiled. "I felt a revulsion and was for a moment sickened of the whole concern," she recorded. "What I had deemed a sublime thought was rendered ridiculous by his vulgar words." Toward the end of August, Chevaillier argued with Harris about some of the ideas in his books, especially the idea of his "kingship or primacy." "We had a spirited argument," according to Chevaillier, "and I fancied that I had got the better of him in the controversy."

Soon after, Alzire and Sarah paid a final, fateful visit to Aestivossa, where they had always been treated as honored guests. This time, however, the Chevailliers were taken in via a side door and informed they could not dine at the main table but were instead given dinner in a small room near the kitchen. Waring said that Harris was busy writing and "in his deep state could not see anyone." Insulted, Chevaillier wrote Harris a "highly indignant" letter informing him of her desire to leave immediately. "Mamma and I have been in the habit of visiting where people lead busy literary lives, and we have sufficient tact and *savoir faire* not to interfere with their round of duties or to permit ourselves to be entertained by them," she told him. "But we do expect as guests to meet at the table with our host and are unwilling to be guests under any other circumstances. I detest kings." Sarah, also offended, complained that Harris was "trying to show his kingly authority."

Harris and Waring apologized and told Alzire that "Fountaingrove was her home, to which she could always come." Alzire was mollified but Sarah less so. The Chevailliers returned to their cottage, but Sarah wanted to leave and after a few more days, they informed Harris of their decision. Kanaye Nagasawa came with the carriage to take them to the Grand Hotel in Santa Rosa. Soon after, a "huge bouquet of choice flowers" arrived from Waring along with a gracious note. When Alzire sent Harris a check $100 for their summer room and board, he refused to hear of it and returned her check "with the most exquisite refinement and delicacy of manner."[29]

Overall, Chevaillier appreciated her summer in Fountaingrove and felt she had grown spiritually and intellectually from her exposure to Harris. She left with reluctance.[30] In her comments to the reporter while staying in the Grand Hotel and in her September dispatch to *Problem of Life and International Magazine of Truth,* Chevaillier was universally positive about Harris, his teachings, and Fountaingrove. She felt profoundly fortunate to have been gifted "more than a few hours" with "this mystic, who, like his Master, has come down or rather ascended to the extremest external needs of fellow man."[31]

Then she met Mr. X. That is what she called him later, to protect his identity, for he said he wished to stay out of the public eye. In early November, he invited her and her mother to pay him a visit at his house in San Francisco. Mr. X had read of her summer at Fountaingrove and of her esteem for Harris, and he knew what he had to say would most certainly upset her. Mr. X had spent the past decade speaking to ex-members of the Brotherhood of the New Life and gathering their accounts. He had in his possession more than a dozen letters and affidavits from these apostates—including one from Laurence Oliphant, written from Palestine a few years before his death. When Alzire and Sarah paid him a visit, Mr. X urged them to read these documents, which he promised would shock them. He said they showed the depraved truth about Harris and what truly went on in his colonies.

Mr. X's true identity was in fact Alfred W. Manning, a name well-known to longtime San Francisco residents. Born in London, Manning had come to California in 1859 and gained local fame in the 1870s as the proprietor of Manning's Oyster Grotto, where he served pan-roasted oysters with "real French bread, the appetizing, sourdough sort beloved of all that know good bread when they taste it." By 1891, he had left the restaurant industry and owned a carpet-cleaning company and an apartment building downtown. He was also, crucially, vice-president and librarian of the Swedenborg Library and Tract Society in San Francisco.[32] Like many Swedenborgians, Manning had dabbled in spiritualism, helping to publish and circulate an account by British visionary James Johnston among Swedenborgians in the United States. And like many Swedenborgians, Manning had studied and ultimately rejected the visions of Thomas Lake Harris as contrary to the writings of Emmanuel Swedenborg, which Manning devoutly regarded as divine revelation. Manning disliked how Harris positioned his own revelations as superior not only to Swedenborg's but also to the Bible itself, and he was confounded by the fact that some Swedenborgians remained sympathetic to him.[33]

So Manning began gathering information that could expose Harris as a fraud. He wrote letters to former members of the Brotherhood asking them about their experiences in Harris's colonies. He hired several ex-members to work for his businesses, then interviewed them about Harris and had them make out affidavits. He asked about finances—how much money and property they gave over to Harris. He asked about labor arrangements—how much they toiled compared to Harris. And he asked about sex—were the colonists truly celibate, as Harris maintained? Or did secret debauchery go on behind closed doors?

Probably to protect his business interests, Manning did not want to be publicly linked to what he was learning about Harris, so he sought ways to spread the word indirectly. He wrote private letters to Swedenborgians in the United States and Great Britain detailing his findings.[34] He knew Michael de

Young, publisher of the *San Francisco Chronicle*, from his days as an oyster restauranteur. In February 1885, Manning had drawn on that connection to feed information to a *Chronicle* reporter for a hit piece on Harris titled "A Spiritist Spider." After comparing Harris to Helena Petrovna Blavatsky and discredited spiritualist brothers William and Horatio Eddy, the *Chronicle* writer gave a mostly inaccurate history of the Brotherhood of the New Life, emphasizing the weirdness of Harris's teachings, the separation of family members including husbands and wives, and the profits Harris reaped over the years from his followers. At least two former members, according to the reporter, had committed suicide after leaving the Brotherhood penniless. Using information provided by Manning, the reporter mentioned—for the first time in print—the co-ed "Japanese system of bathing" employed at Fountaingrove. Going further, the reporter said that "licentiousness" reigned behind the scenes, justified by Harris's doctrine of heavenly counterparts. "By a special arrangement with the unseen powers, the female spiritual counterpart, which had hitherto been reserved for the other world, were allowed to descend and take material shape in first one woman and then another," the *Chronicle* reported in 1885, "all restraint between the earthly and spiritual counterparts being then put aside."[35]

Virtually every utopian colony in nineteenth-century America faced insinuations of licentiousness at one point or another. Sensationalized books such as John B. Ellis's *Free Love and Its Votaries; or, American Socialism Unmasked,* published in 1870, had made the Oneida colony in upstate New York—and utopianism more broadly—synonymous with sexual immorality and the destruction of Christian marriage.[36] During the 1880s, long-standing attacks on Mormon polygamy had reached a fever pitch as hundreds of Mormon men were imprisoned after passage of the Edmunds Anti-Polygamy Act of 1882.[37] Harris's colonies had encountered much less hostility from outsiders compared to Oneidans and Mormons but some rumors about sexual improprieties did circulate among neighbors. At Brocton in 1869, Laurence Oliphant mentioned in a letter that "attacks upon the purity of the life continue to reach us from various directions. The 'movement' is said to be 'more odious in its character than that of Brigham Young.'"[38]

Oliphant dismissed these rumors as "preposterous slanders," and Harris ignored them, just as he publicly ignored the *Chronicle* article Manning planted in 1885. Harris did respond privately, however; nine days after the article appeared, he transferred almost all of the Fountaingrove lands out of his own name and into the names of Jonathan W. Lay, Ray P. Clarke, and Kanaye Nagasawa.[39] This was a clear attempt to shield himself from accusations made in the article that he was enriching himself by amassing valuable lands while his followers toiled in poverty. Lay, Clarke, and Nagasawa were the heads of the Lay, Clarke & Co. wine business, so turning lands over to them made the colony seem more like a business than a religious community.

This strategy seemed to work, for the 1885 "Spiritist Spider" piece barely made a ripple in the public consciousness.[40] In Santa Rosa, the local chapter of the fraternal organization Knights Templar, of which Harris was a member, still threw him a party in 1886 "as a public expression of the esteem and affection" they held for him.[41] Anyone familiar with Harris's biography would have noticed the article's many historical inaccuracies, making it easy to ignore its talk of suicides and co-ed "Japanese baths." Much to Manning's frustration, a few Swedenborgians even rose to Harris's defense after its publication. "They have made him a free-lover and the keeper of a free-love establishment," complained William Holcombe in the *New Church Independent*, a Chicago Swedenborgian journal known for its broadmindedness. "To those who are acquainted with the singular beauty, purity, and goodness, we may say, of his published writings, the charge is revolting and improbable."[42] Harris also had his defenders in spiritualist circles, such as West Virginia oilman Marius C. C. Church, who had taken over Harris's pulpit in the Church of the Good Shepherd after Harris left for England in 1859. Church assured fellow spiritualists that Harris believed in "absolute continence—the annihilation of the animal instinct." Church rejected the accusations made by Manning's line-up of Brotherhood apostates as "absolutely false."[43]

Now, in 1891, Manning had another opportunity to expose Harris, and it came in the form of Alzire Chevaillier. He must have known about her role in the recent Phillips Brooks confirmation controversy, when she had turned on him and positioned herself as a pious champion of "absolute truth." Manning gave his stack of letters and affidavits to Chevaillier, which she reluctantly agreed to read. She read, and she believed. The fact that Manning was "a gentleman of high social repute, and a prominent Swedenborgian" reassured her that the statements were legitimate. Her recent outpourings of praise for Harris and for the "happy and harmonious" people at Fountaingrove now made her burn with "humiliation." She had made a terrible "blunder," she now saw, "in so widely commending this remarkable two-sided man, an angel of light and an angel of darkness, bringing moral wreck and ruin."[44]

Feeling embarrassed, betrayed, and confused, Chevaillier wrote Harris a long, anguished letter in mid-November laying out what she had learned from Manning. "How did you dare to allow mamma and me to go to such a place when you knew that I would not have been in sympathy with anything impure or immoral," she asked, "and that all I wanted was spiritual growth that I might be able to do more good in the world?"[45] She included again the check for $100—though it was her "last penny"—so that she would be under "no obligation" to Harris.[46] But she concluded the letter with a reiteration of her love and respect for Harris, an indication that she was still in the process of sorting out her feelings. She then wrote a rather tepid piece for the November issue of *Problem of Life and International Magazine of Truth* on "The Dangers of Occult Science," in which she warned her readers to avoid those who "are claiming 'Kingship,' 'Messiahship,' to be 'the Pivotal Man of the age,' etc." She did not mention Harris by name, however.[47]

At Fountaingrove, Chevaillier's November letter set off alarm bells. Between Margaret Oliphant's book, Harris's stream of new writings, and his much-mocked claims of renewed youth, Harris's name had already been in the newspapers extensively this year; these earlier stories would be mere kindling for an even bigger fire if Chevaillier went public with Manning's accounts. Jane Lee Waring sent Chevaillier's letter to Arthur Cuthbert in England, and he responded with concern. "Very little reliance, I fear, is to be placed on such expressions of love for Father as Miss C. concludes her letter with," Cuthbert wrote. "Oliphant and Alice kept making the same professions almost to the last. So did Judas Iscariot." Cuthbert acknowledged that Chevaillier could do great harm to the Brotherhood, for "she has been drawn near, and taken to the very bosom, and so has that vantage ground, giving her the ability to wound cruelly if she please to take advantage of it." But he felt confident they could withstand an assault by her, for "Miss C. is really of too coarse a quality to be able to do much serious injury. There is not good enough in her character to give the evil any subtlety of power."[48]

Those at Fountaingrove were not so sure, however, and a week later, on November 29, Nagasawa sent a note to Harris's friend, the poet Edwin Markham, who lived in Oakland. Markham was a frequent dinner guest at Aestivossa and an admirer of Harris's poetry, though not a member of the Brotherhood.[49] "If you can arrange your business, please come *tomorrow afternoon* without fail as there is an urgent business that we wish to consult with you," Nagasawa told him. "That Oakland woman is attempting to cause trouble. We (Lady Dorie and I) are on our way to the mountain to see Father."[50] If Chevaillier was about to go to war, they would be ready.

PART TWO
SCANDAL

6

December 1891

Worse than Mormons

Alzire Chevaillier's campaign to destroy Thomas Lake Harris began in the pages of the *San Francisco Chronicle* on Sunday, December 13. An interview with her, titled "Hypnotic Harris: Miss Chevaillier's Strange Story," took up four full columns and included two pen-and-ink illustrations. The first drawing showed Chevaillier in profile, looking to the right, her hair pinned atop her head, her expression determined. Her long neck was exposed, and she wore a white blouse, suggesting feminine purity. Just below it and one column to the right, the second illustration showed Harris, also in profile, looking left, wearing a dark suit, his expression neutral and his lower face hidden by his long white beard. The two profiles faced each other as if locked in combat.

The article began by giving Chevaillier's background, identifying her as a "woman suffragist, sociologist, spiritual scientist, philanthropist, nationalist, magazine writer, and reformer." She was also, according to the article's writer, a "charming young lady and a deep student of psychology, sociology, and other -ologies." Furthermore, she was "young and vigorous," a "brilliant talker," and a "woman of experience in the world of reform." She had come to Fountaingrove the previous summer hoping to "imbibe spiritual knowledge" from Harris, assuming that he was the "pure and holy spiritual guide that she had read him in his writings."

Her youth (she had actually just turned forty-one years old), intellectual credentials, and pious intentions now established by the *Chronicle* reporter, the writer then turned the article over to Chevaillier and her account. She explained her initial reasons for going to Fountaingrove and described the troubling things she saw there, specifically the manual labor carried out by the Parting women and other members of the colony, as contrasted to the wealth and leisure that Harris enjoyed. As he dined on "oysters and champagne" like a decadent European lord, they ate the "plainest kind of food." Chevaillier could not "reconcile the prophet's pretensions to a higher

Unholy Sensations. Joshua Paddison, Oxford University Press. © Oxford University Press 2025.
DOI: 10.1093/oso/9780197775325.003.0006

Miss Alzire A. Chevaillier.

Alzire Chevaillier, *San Francisco Chronicle*, December 13, 1891.

Thomas Lake Harris, *San Francisco Chronicle*, December 13, 1891.

spiritual and social state for his people with the hard facts which now appeared before her." Emma Parting and other "dupes" at Fountaingrove had turned over great sums of money to Harris and willingly lived "under his severe ordinances."

This was nothing new and repeated what Margaret Oliphant's *Memoir of the Life of Laurence Oliphant* had reported. But then Chevaillier turned to a subject Oliphant had refrained from addressing in her book: sex. "After a man has been taken into the inner circle he is given a heavenly counterpart, which after a time is permitted by the prophet to descend and take material form in whatever woman he may see fit to designate as the affinity of the disciple," Chevaillier said. "The condition of the morals of these people is vile. It is what I may describe as refined sensualism." Here, the *Chronicle* writer broke back in: "As she said these words Miss Chevaillier, who is one of the most modest young ladies that Boston has produced, looked pained." She visibly steeled herself so as to not "flinch in the performance of her duty of exposing the false prophet."

Her tale culminated in her final, insulting visit to Aestivossa and her "flight" from Fountaingrove. Not mentioning Alfred W. Manning or his role in this story, she said she left because "I could not bear to think that Harris was trying to introduce me to the nameless practices of which I heard so mysteriously." She was now planning to take the matter to the governor, U.S. Congress, and the president himself in order to break up Fountaingrove. "This accursed doctrine of the counterparts is worse than anything ever revealed as to the Utah and Oneida practices," she said. "It is a new sexology, holding the virus of a refined and subtle sensualism in whose web many a pure soul has become hopelessly entangled." She said she had testimony from ex-members, including Laurence Oliphant, to prove her allegations that Harris's "teachings were worse than those of Mormonism." She concluded by emphasizing her own purity once again: "Now that I have come out from his influence without a stain, I feel that it is given to me as my bounden duty to fight this demon with whatever weapons I may be able to lay hold upon," she said. "I thank God that my dear mother was with me in that awful time when I was under the spell of the hierarch of Fountaingrove."[1]

Chevaillier was an experienced writer, lecturer, and reformer, but she had never before entered the public sphere to talk about something so incendiary—sex, and "vile" sex at that. During the Mary Plunkett-Arthur Bently Worthington scandal of 1889, she had managed to mildly defend her friend while steering clear of the associations with "free love" that were so often applied to mental healers, suffragists, and socialists—women like her. Now, in making her attack on Harris, she ran the risk of being tainted by the very sexual depravity she decried. The *Chronicle* piece was constructed to mitigate that danger. A presumably male reporter framed and introduced her account and vouched for her by giving assurances of her youth and modesty. By expressing her reluctance to speak on such topics, and her shock and moral indignation, Chevaillier assured the public that she acted only out of the purest and bravest of motives. Lacking a husband, she made frequent mention of her mother as way of demonstrating that she had had maternal protection from Harris's evil intentions.

By emphasizing that she brought this unsavory matter to the public only out of sacred, feminine duty, Chevaillier was following a line of argument that had been made by other woman suffragists and social purity reformers during the Gilded Age. They insisted that to be good women— morally upright, virtuous, and feminine—they *needed* to enter the public sphere as speakers, activists, and, yes, voters. "Women's voice and influence in the affairs of State," declared the delegates of the California State Suffrage Convention of 1870, would bring "charity, mercy, and forgiveness" to politics, thereby "purifying, elevating, and humanizing" government.[2] California's woman suffrage movement had nonetheless faced accusations of promoting immorality and free love. Laura de Force Gordon, a spiritualist who as a teenager had toured the East Coast as an itinerant trance speaker, had her lectures on woman suffrage interrupted by hecklers and was attacked as a "masculine woman" who was trying to "invade the natural precincts of man."[3] By 1891, Gordon and other spiritualists in California had joined forces with the more conservative Women's Christian Temperance Union (WCTU) to deliver petitions and briefs supporting woman suffrage to the state legislature. Invoking women's innate domesticity and religiosity, the WCTU argued that "she who keeps the home fires burning and cares for the children" deserves as much political voice as "he who ... goes out to battle in the world."[4]

All women entering the public sphere had to make such calculations, and those who discussed sex in public had to be especially strategic. The public demonization and legal harassment that Victoria Woodhull and other sex radicals had faced in the 1870s made the stakes abundantly clear. Female anti-polygamy activists, however, had shown a possible way for women to discuss sex safely. Fanny Stenhouse, in her 1872 exposé *Tell It All: The Story of a Life's Experience in Mormonism,* had emphasized that she was a reluctant activist, acting only because she was "enthusiastically urged" on by her friends. Putting aside her own "personal delicacy," Stenhouse had said she strove to "tell my story in the plainest, simplest way, and to avoid exaggeration, but never shrink from a straightforward statement of facts."[5] Ann Eliza Young, a former wife of Brigham Young, had begun her anti-polygamy campaign via an interview with a male reporter, who described Ann's youth, beauty, and "remarkably sweet face." In her tell-all book *Wife No. 19*, Young said she acted only out of the "warmest and tenderest feelings" toward Mormon women.[6] Chevaillier's interview in the *Chronicle* appropriated these women's strategies. In calling Harris's doctrines "worse than that of Mormonism," she not only cast Fountaingrove in terms of a well-known and reviled religion, but she also portrayed herself as the inheritor of female anti-polygamy reformers' efforts.

It was no coincidence that Chevaillier's crusade began in the pages of the *San Francisco Chronicle*. Manning's longstanding relationship with its publisher, Michael de Young, had led to the 1885 "Spiritist Spider" attack piece on Harris based on Manning's materials. With his brother Charles, Michael de Young had made the *Chronicle* the largest newspaper in the West through its innovative and often sensationalistic tactics, attacking public figures in proto-muckraking fashion. In 1891, the *Chronicle* was locked in a circulation battle with William Randolph Hearst's *Examiner*, which Hearst had taken over from his father four years earlier. Both newspapers borrowed from the methods of Joseph Pulitzer's scandal-obsessed *New York World*.[7] In California, the murder trials of Laura Fair, who had killed her lover and "spiritual husband" Alexander Crittendon in 1870, as well as the lawsuits made in the 1880s by Sarah Althea Hill against politician William Sharon, whom Hill claimed was her husband, had provided years of fodder for newspaper editors eager to share the salacious details with their readers.[8]

San Francisco had a reputation for being a "wide open town" in terms of personal freedoms, especially sexual freedoms, dating to the Gold Rush era.[9] However, historian Amy Sueyoshi has shown that mainstream newspapers in the city were overwhelmingly conservative in terms of enforcing "white supremacy and heteropatriarchy."[10] Scandal stories sold newspapers and tended to reinforce the status quo by policing society's sexual, religious, and racial borders, and Chevaillier's attack on Harris was no exception. Harris was not as well-known nationally as someone like Henry Ward Beecher, the Congregationalist minister who had faced a sex scandal in the 1870s after Victoria Woodhull accused him of adultery.[11] But Harris's fame had risen over the course of 1891 due to his new writings and Margaret Oliphant's book to the point that his name—if not his doctrines—had become recognizable to the reading public.

The article's "Hypnotic Harris" headline—almost certainly not written by Chevaillier—played on public fears of mesmerism and hypnotism that had simmered for decades. Chevaillier's old ally in insane asylum reform, George M. Beard, had conducted public experiments in the 1880s demonstrating that hypnotism was a "subjective condition," not a product of "animal magnetism" or anything metaphysical, but newspapers still roused fears of villainous hypnotists who misused their occult powers to take financial or sexual advantage of, usually, women.[12] In the weeks after Chevaillier's article, the *Chronicle* would run a story about a "female spiritualistic medium" who drove another woman insane through hypnotism as well as an exposé of a hypnotist at San Francisco City and County Hospital who was forcing other patients to sleepwalk.[13] The *San Francisco Call*, chasing the *Chronicle* and *Examiner* in circulation, had recently published an article with titillating illustrations describing how hypnotists could take complete control of women's bodies.[14] In California, stage hypnotists were coming under suspicion for causing madness and imbecility; legal experts debated how to handle crimes committed by hypnotized people as if this was a common occurrence; and Protestant ministers speculated about whether it was "divine power" or "purely magnetic or psychological forces" at work. These cultural concerns would soon take fictional form in the character of Svengali, the hypnotist villain of George du Maurier's wildly popular novel *Trilby*, serialized in *Harper's Monthly* in 1894.[15]

It did not matter that Harris had rejected mesmerism after dabbling in it in the late 1840s. Because he seemed to have powerful influence over others, the *Chronicle* labeled him a hypnotist. The figure of the evil hypnotist was powerful in part because it offered an explanation for why people like Laurence Oliphant and Emma Parting—wealthy white people—devoted years of their life to communal living and a strange religion. Decades later, a similar explanation would be offered by anti-cult activists and the media in the 1970s: namely, that people who joined new religious movements were "brainwashed" by cult leaders. The assumption behind both the hypnotism and brainwashing tropes was that no one—especially well-to-do white people—would willingly join or give money to a "cult."[16] As historian Rebecca Davis has observed, concerns about hypnotism and brainwashing revealed wider anxieties about "possible weaknesses within the American psyche that exposed the mind to subjugation."[17] If anyone could be brainwashed, no one was safe.

Chevaillier's crusade continued in the *Chronicle* a week later, on December 20, when she drew on the publicity that had been created by Margaret Oliphant's *Memoir of the Life of Laurence Oliphant* to bolster her arguments. When given the book by Jane Lee Waring the previous summer, she had barely glanced at it, but since meeting Manning she had read it with a new appreciation. Now, she wrote in the *Chronicle* that, "to one like myself, who has been inside the charmed circle" of Fountaingrove, it was obvious that Margaret Oliphant's book contained "many omissions and crudities." But she reported that the book contained enough "to astound one that a man of the world like Laurence Oliphant should have been the dupe of such a craze."

Chevaillier said that she knew the true reason Oliphant had broken with Harris: "It was the same thing that that tore the veil from my trusting eyes. It was the 'celestial amours' of the 'counterparts.'" She then printed a letter, given to her by Manning, written by Oliphant from Haifa in 1885. The letter in fact directly contradicted Chevaillier's suggestion that Laurence had left due to matters related to sex; instead, Oliphant said he left because of Harris's dishonesty and financial improprieties. Harris manifested a "reckless disregard for truth," according to Oliphant, and was "selling for gold and his own private ends the gifts with which God had entrusted him for the service of humanity." Nonetheless, Chevaillier insisted Oliphant had broken with Harris due to his supposed "disgust" over immoral sexual practices.

She then hastened to remind readers that she herself "saw no impurities at Fountaingrove," unless you counted seeing Jane Lee Waring smoking Harris's used pipes and sitting with his feet in her lap. However, she was satisfied that "ninety-nine out of every hundred girls who might be drawn under the spell of this wonderful and unscrupulous hypnotizer and mesmerist could by no means on earth escape from his power, and they would be dragged down to ruin." Only the presence of her mother, together with a "will that is stronger than that of most girls," had saved Chevaillier from that ruin. "I trusted myself in the lion's den, and with these great safeguards I could defy the beast," she said. "This lion's den is still open, and into it may be thrust many other women."[18] She wept "tears of pity" when she thought of "those poor young Parting girls, who have been so sadly led astray by that awful man."[19]

Chevaillier's focus on protecting young white women from ruin was consistent with the anti-polygamy narratives she was drawing on as well as her own history of moral reform work. In Boston and New York, she had striven to protect society's most vulnerable members—the mentally ill, prisoners, workers, the poor, children, and women, all condemned to live outside what historian Barbara Young Welke has termed the "borders of belonging" due to their dependent status and curtailed rights.[20] While her heart went out to Fountaingrove's young women, Chevaillier mentioned the white men of the colony (other than Harris) only in passing; the only saving they seemed to need was in terms of their finances. The sexual double standard of the Gilded Age, which chastised sexuality in women while valorizing it in men, made the "purity" of white men much less in need of protection.[21] Chevaillier likely suspected that it would be difficult to raise much public sympathy for Fountaingrove's adult white men, and furthermore it might have appeared overweening for her to try.

The idea of saving young white women from sexual and moral peril also resonated with cultural anxieties about prostitution that were rising in the 1890s. Anti-prostitution reformers were beginning to use the term "white slavery" to dramatize the plight of urban female prostitutes "enslaved" by corrupt male pimps and traffickers. This new focus on saving young white women from a life in sex slavery was a shift in rhetoric from earlier campaigns that had demonized sex workers, often portrayed as racialized immigrants, as threats to public health and morality.[22] In San Francisco, the Pacific Society for the Suppression of Vice would soon form in 1893 to curb prostitution and pornography due to mounting concerns that "white slavery" was "dragging, driving, drawing, duping" the city's "daughters" to "infamy."[23] Chevaillier's focus on saving young white women from the "lion's den" of sex and sin at Fountaingrove drew power from these broader fears of unchecked male power and fragile white womanhood, fears that journalists were amplifying during this period through high-profile exposés of prostitution similar to Chevaillier's campaign.[24] "Already I think I have saved a number of girls from going there to be introduced to his licentious system of counterparts," she boasted.[25]

On Christmas Eve, however, Chevaillier's campaign took a surprising turn when she paid a visit to Sutemi Chinda, Japanese consul in San Francisco. Accompanied by a *Chronicle* reporter, Chevaillier asked the consul to investigate the wrongs being done to "his countrymen" Kanaye Nagasawa and Ōsui Arai at Fountaingrove. "Both Ari [*sic*] and Nagasawa feel convinced that should they leave 'the Use,' Harris has the power to strike them dead at any time," she informed the consul. Arai in particular needed help, she said, because Harris worked him ragged in the print shop for, of course, no pay. "There is no jinriki-hiki in all Yokohama who has one half the burden put upon him that is thrust on Ari's shoulders," she said. Though he was a "well-educated young man," he sadly was the "most abject slave of the whole colony." He was "simple as a child and Harris can do anything with him that he pleases," she said, due to Arai's "blind, simple faith." Chevaillier trusted that Chinda would take the matter seriously lest it create an international scandal.[26]

Three days later, Chevaillier's mother Sarah wrote a front-page article for the *Chronicle* that continued this new focus on the Japanese men at Fountaingrove. Sarah's account, like her daughter's initial report, was introduced by a male writer who emphasized her beauty and youthfulness; though age sixty-one, she moved with an "ease and grace that many girls of eighteen might envy." Sarah backed up Alzire's narrative—"we saw nothing impure or immoral at Fountaingrove," she insisted—and added new details about Nagasawa and Arai, whom she called "Prince Kanaye Nagavassa" and "Ari." According to Sarah, the Japanese men had helped introduce the "Edenic bath system which still flourishes" at Fountaingrove. Nagasawa "drives the carriage for Harris and lords it over the one servant who is given over to his tender care," Sarah said, while Arai "has a hard time of it working night and day for the prophet." Included within Sarah's report were pen-and-ink illustrations of Jane Lee Waring, Nagasawa, and Arai, the only Fountaingrove colonists apart from Harris that the newspaper visually depicted in this chain of articles.[27]

Clearly, the editors of the *Chronicle* believed the presence of the Japanese men at Fountaingrove made the story especially newsworthy. In fact, there was tremendous public fascination with Japan and all things Japanese during the 1890s, a fascination the Fountaingrove scandal played into. In 1853, when Commodore Perry and his armada of gunboats officially opened Japan's doors to the West, most Americans knew little about Japan. However, the next fifty years saw an explosion of accounts penned by diplomats, scholars, artists, and missionaries interpreting Japan. Early visitors had tended to portray the Japanese as exotic and inferior, "diminutive" and heathen, backward and stunted in terms of both religion and race. However, Japan's rapid industrialization, modernization, commercial expansion, and rise to become an imperial power following the Meiji Restoration of 1868 had given many thinkers in the United States pause. How could a "Mongolian" and "heathen" nation be, by most available benchmarks, so "civilized"?[28]

Ōsui Arai, *San Francisco Chronicle*, December 27, 1891.

Prince Kanaye Nagavassa

Kanaye Nagasawa, *San Francisco Chronicle*, December 27, 1891.

By the early 1890s, the industrialization and militarization of Meiji Japan, accomplished through heavy taxation and conscription, was beginning to trigger what would become a massive wave of outmigration. The 1890 U.S. Census was the first to include "Japanese" as a separate racial category, recording 2,039 Japanese men and women living in the United States. Over the next two decades, however, at least 200,000 Japanese migrants would move to Hawai'i and another 180,000 would come to the U.S. mainland, mostly to California.[29] Even in 1891, at the beginning of this process, the arrival of Japanese immigrants was triggering a range of reactions among Americans, from anti-Asiatic nativism to Orientalist attraction and everything in between.

The long-standing presence of Chinese immigrants on the West Coast meant that, upon arrival, the *Issei* were viewed at times as part of a generalized "yellow peril" and at times as specifically Japanese. The passage of the Chinese Exclusion Act of 1882 had created a new demand for agricultural labor, which the Japanese began to satisfy. According to the *San Francisco Call,* San Fernando Valley orchardists initially preferred the Japanese to white or Chinese laborers because "they work harder and take less pay."[30] Generally more literate than Chinese immigrants due to compulsory education in Meiji Japan, the *Issei* in California agriculture soon established a reputation for militant labor activism, winning higher wages and significantly less appreciation from white growers.[31]

Japanese immigrants' success in agriculture prompted outcry from white laborers, especially Irish Catholics, who expanded and recycled the arguments they had used a generation earlier against Chinese "coolies" to solidify their own whiteness, patriotism, and Christianity. Denis Kearney, whose Workingmen's Party of California had helped rewrite the state Constitution in 1879 to ban employment of the Chinese, pivoted in the early 1890s to this new "menace," now crying "the Japs must go!" Following the example of the still ongoing anti-Chinese movement, California's anti-Japanese movement interwove economic, ethnological, and religious arguments, portraying the Japanese as racially debased and sexually depraved. Said Kearney in reference to Japan's mixed-gender bathing practices: "There is no such thing as virtue in Japan. The men and women of that country are as free to mingle together as are the beasts of the field."[32]

However, others welcomed the arrival of the Japanese not as workers but representatives of an "orderly," "artistic," and "mysterious" society, leading to something of a Japan craze in California during the 1880s and 1890s. Women's clubs hosted lectures on Japanese crafts; galleries displayed exhibitions of Japanese art; and Japanese restaurants and tea gardens appeared in San Francisco, Sacramento, and Los Angeles.[33] The leading purveyors of the Japan craze were San Francisco's Deakin brothers—Walter, Frederic, Edwin, and Harry—whose company imported not only goods, arts, and crafts from Japan but also the artists themselves, most prominently Toshio Aoki. The Deakin brothers had also offered a "trip through Japan" in the form of an exhibition in San Francisco's St. Ignatius Hall in 1885. Three times a day, for two-and-a-half months, San Franciscans had witnessed a "living panorama of the industrial and art life of the Japanese," filled with "Skilled Japanese Artisans Constantly at Work Manufacturing all Classes of Japanese Goods," including painters, potters, coppersmiths, weavers, tailors, and even barbers. Like nearby Chinatown, only more idealized and controlled, the Deakin brothers' "Japanese village" cashed in on white Californians' growing Orientalist interest in Japanese culture.[34] In fact, across the Atlantic world in the 1890s, Japanese food, commodities, architecture, and design were becoming popular, with Japanese art prominently on display at international expositions in London, Paris, Philadelphia, and Chicago.[35]

In California, however, the Japan craze existed side by side with the nation's most virulent anti-Japanese movement. Due to San Francisco's size, location on the Pacific Rim, and history of both anti-Asian hostility and Orientalist tourism, the Japanese were discussed more often, and in more polarized extremes, there than in any city in North America during the 1890s. Were they superior to the Chinese or ultimately part of the same Asian "menace"? Were the *Issei*'s high rates of literacy and labor success, together with Japan's aggressive modernization, comforting or disconcerting trends? Were they intractable Buddhists, potential Christians, or something else?

These questions made the presence of Ōsui Arai and Kanaye Nagasawa at Fountaingrove all the more sensational. The Chevailliers drew on different aspects of prevailing racial attitudes about the Japanese in their portraits of the two men. Alzire portrayed Arai as hard-working, tractable, and simple—a more sympathetic version of the depictions of Japanese agricultural workers offered by Denis Kearney and other unionists. Whereas she ignored Fountaingrove's white men, she viewed Arai as an appropriate subject of her help and pity. His Japanese ethnicity and supposed passivity made her feel comfortable in positioning herself as his would-be savior.[36] Nagasawa's business acumen and greater power at Fountaingrove made him harder to conform to the stereotypes of Japanese agricultural workers that Alzire invoked with Arai. Instead, Sarah portrayed "lordly" Nagasawa as a different kind of tragic figure—ludicrous and twisted, bossing around his "one servant" as a miniature version of Harris. As white abolitionists had done to certain "distinguished" enslaved Africans, Sarah wrongly dubbed Nagasawa a "prince" to make his subjection to Harris all the more tragic.[37]

In fact, Alzire and Sarah Chevaillier had spent little time with Fountaingrove's two Japanese men and knew almost nothing about them. They misspelled the men's names, and the biographical information they provided was mostly wrong. Alzire did not know how for sure how many Japanese men were in the colony, at times saying two and at other times saying three. Though she called them "young," both Nagasawa and Arai were in their mid-to-late thirties, only a few years younger than her.[38] By casting herself as their protector and emphasizing their naïveté and youth, especially Arai, she drew on racialized notions of the Japanese as feminine, childlike, and delicate. Perhaps for these reasons, she failed to rouse the interests of Consul Sutemi Chinda, who "took the testimony of Miss Chevaillier with little show of interest."[39] Chevaillier may have been surprised to learn that a predecessor of his, Saburō Takagi, had helped the Brotherhood of the New Life purchase the initial lands for Fountaingrove in the 1870s.[40]

By emphasizing the presence of Japanese men at Fountaingrove, the Chevailliers added an element of potential miscegenation to the scandal, invoking fears of racial impurity and Asian contamination. This was perhaps an inadvertent move on Alzire's part, as she seemed to view the Japanese men as piteous victims; but if unbridled "free love" was happening at Fountaingrove, then must not interracial sex between white women and Japanese men be happening as well? California's Gilded Age popular literature often depicted Chinese men as taking advantage of their supposedly feminized or asexual nature to gain the trust of white women so as to seduce them.[41] By the 1890s, Japanese "houseboys" were on their way to becoming distrusted for the same reason.[42] To the California white public, Chevaillier's portrayal of the Japanese men as feminized may have made them *more* rather than less of a threat to white female purity, contrary to what she seemed to intend.

The *Chronicle*'s portraits of Arai and Nagasawa showed them to be not youths but adult men who looked back at the viewer with bold gazes. This was consistent with another component of Gilded Age America's ornate Orientalist popular culture: cartoons. By the early 1890s, San Francisco readers had been exposed to dozens of anti-Chinese cartoons in the *Wasp*, *Jolly Giant*, and other publications, some of which stirred racial animosity by depicting a Chinese man proudly embracing his white wife (sometimes with "unnatural" mixed-race children in tow).[43] The *Chronicle*'s pictorial representations of the two Japanese men, to the exclusion of virtually all other Fountaingrove members, conjured up such earlier images. The California legislature had banned marriage between whites and "Mongolians" in 1880; though initially directed at Chinese men, the "Mongolian" designation proved useful to block marriages between Japanese men and white women as well. In a case that would draw widespread media attention in 1909, Gunjiro Aoki and Helen Emery would have to travel from San Francisco to Washington state to wed.[44] During this period, controversies were erupting at Protestant mission schools when Asian male students became romantically involved with white female missionaries.[45] For all these reasons, Fountaingrove's combination of Japanese men and white women was explosive.

The presence of Japanese men at Fountaingrove also served to underscore the Asiatic foreignness of the "Japanese bathing" that went on there. Within Japanese Buddhist practice, bathing was an important ritual of purification that was both communal and intensely personal. But mixed bathing in Japan had both shocked and titillated Americans as early as Commodore Perry's visit in 1853. In his diary of the expedition, one naval officer had noted with disgust that a few American officers were paying visits to a "bath house where old and young, male and female are mingled promiscuously in a state of unblushing nudity to the gaze of strangers."[46] Artist Wilhelm Heine's depiction of co-ed bathing at a *sentō*, which appeared in early editions of Perry's narrative, stirred up enough controversy that it was removed from subsequent printings.[47] While some Americans saw Japanese bathing as a sign of presexual innocence (hence the term "Edenic," also used in the Fountaingrove scandal), most onlookers judged it vulgar, indecent, and animalistic.[48] Suspecting immorality, San Francisco health officials frequently investigated Japanese bathhouses in the 1890s, despite the fact that they usually featured a bamboo wall segregating the sexes, a reflection of both American gender roles and a shift away from mixed bathing occurring in Meiji Japan.[49] Talk of Japanese-style bathing at Fountaingrove therefore conjured up powerful racial and religious associations that cast the colony as doubly deviant.

Chevaillier portrayed the colony in other Orientalist terms as well. She declared that "Fountaingrove was no fit place for any one who had not first been a follower of Mohammed or other sensualist of equal power."[50] Jane Lee Waring dressed "in the most Sybaritic fashion imaginable," Chevaillier said, a reference to the ancient Greek city of Sybaris, notorious for its hedonism.[51] Waring's attire reminded Chevaillier of Frederic Leighton's famous 1880

Orientalist painting *The Light of the Harem*.[52] By calling Harris specifically a "prophet," Chevaillier drew on a tradition of Islamophobic discourse that linked Harris to the original so-called false prophet, Muhammad.[53] Similarly, by comparing Fountaingrove to Mormon Utah, she tapped into a long history of anti-Mormon rhetoric that frequently depicted Mormons as Orientalized facilitators of interracial mixing due to their religious and sexual practices.[54] Japanese Buddhists, Muslims, and ancient Sybarites, along with homegrown Mormons and Oneidans, all converged in the specter of Fountaingrove, marking it as foreign, racially debased, iniquitous, and profane.

By the end of December, Chevaillier's allegations about Fountaingrove had begun to garner headlines across the United States and Great Britain. To ensure maximum exposure, Chevaillier gave an interview to a re- porter from Pulitzer's *New York World, which ran it under* the headline "Worse than Mormons." Hundreds of versions of her account appeared in newspapers large and small across the English-speaking world.[55] In Britain, where Laurence Oliphant's fame had been much larger than in the United States, at least twelve newspapers ran summaries of Chevaillier's account in the first week of the scandal alone.[56] These abridged stories emphasized Oliphant's supposed disgust with counterpartal sex, Harris's diet of "oysters and champagne" and his "marvelous hypnotic power," and the presence of Japanese men at Fountaingrove. Some American newspapers acknowledged Chevaillier's involvement in the Phillips Brooks controversy before noting that "the fact that Miss Chevaillier is not the most reliable of persons cannot destroy the effect of the evidence she has gathered."[57]

Several of these news accounts employed the word "cult" to describe Harris's Brotherhood of the New Life and groups like it. This was new; in all the discussion of Harris over the years, the first time his movement had been called a cult was in the fall of 1891 during mocking coverage of his claims of eternal youth, when the *London Pall Mall Gazette* referred to the "Harris cult."[58] Chevaillier's charges accelerated the word's usage and newly deroga- tory connotations. An editor in Harrisburg, Pennsylvania, took the scandal as an opportunity to lambast all the "cults and isms" that had proliferated in nineteenth-century America. "Nine-tenths of such communities, wherever found, are either blasphemous or lewd," the editor thundered. "The leaders of these communities are all swindlers, and some of them a curse to society and a shame to the name of religion."[59] Similarly, the *London Anti-Jacobin* announced with concern that the "Harris cult is amazingly on the increase, and that the cult is likely to take on the proportions of a boom." This piece, reprinted in the *San Francisco Chronicle,* stirred up fears that the "Harris cult" was growing in England, preying on "that motley crowd of zealots who revel in the new and strange."[60] According to the *New York Times,* communities led by "Harris and other prophets of his sort" could reliably be identified by "the absence of clothes in both sexes."[61] Other editors put the blame on not cult leaders but followers for their naïveté, upon which "such impostors as Harris count."[62] Day by day, as the story spread, the Fountaingrove scandal was creating the modern notion of the cult, a word that Chevaillier, ironically, had never actually used.

Up to this point Chevaillier had hesitated to divulge the exact contents of the materials Manning had given her other than Oliphant's letter. She had breathlessly described immorality at Fountaingrove but skimped on specifics. "I would not dare to give to the general reading public," she said in mid-December, the "graphically described" accounts she held. "I fully feel that I have not overstepped the bounds in which such subjects should be retained in their public discussion."[63] But what if the public wouldn't listen? How far could she go, in describing the licentiousness of Fountaingrove, without becoming herself guilty of corrupting the public? How far *should* she go?

Chevaillier must have also known that Harris and his supporters would soon be making a counterattack on her, her trustworthiness, and her reputation. Ever since her involvement in the assassin Charles Guiteau's insanity case in 1882, she had been impugned in print due to her association with one controversial cause after another: asylum reform, Christian Science, socialism, woman suffrage, and opposition to Phillips Brooks's confirmation. The attacks she had suffered only confirmed her confidence in her own moral, spiritual, and political vision, however. In the face of whatever assaults from Fountaingrove might come, she felt "determined to devote the next few years of my life at least to breaking up that horrible place."[64] The battle was just beginning.

7

January 1892

Disorderly Doctrines

The Brotherhood of the New Life's counterattack against Alzire Chevaillier began by Jane Lee Waring writing a letter to her brother. George E. Waring Jr. was a well-known sanitary engineer who had designed the drainage system that created the ponds in New York City's Central Park. Now living in Rhode Island, George was a popular writer on such topics as anti-contaigonism, sewer systems, and public sanitation.[1] Due to his modest fame, newspapers reporting on the Fountaingrove scandal sometimes mentioned the connection between Jane Lee and George Waring. In her dispatch to the *San Francisco Chronicle*, Sarah Chevaillier had gone so far to claim that George had "tried in every way possible to induce Miss Waring" to leave Fountaingrove, "but she would not go."[2] So Jane wrote to her brother about the "storm that continues to howl around our heads here" and to give him "the facts about Miss Chevaillier's visit" so he would know the "*truth*."

She proceeded to lay out a version of events that emphasized Harris's purity and Chevaillier's deviousness. According to Waring, Harris had extended the initial invitation to Chevaillier and her mother out of "chivalry" and because he had wanted to learn more about Christian Science and mind cure. Soon after the Chevailliers arrived, however, Waring saw that a "trap was being laid" for Harris, a trap of seduction, making Waring wonder who was after Harris, "the mother or the daughter?" After Alzire insisted on speaking to Harris at Linn Lilla without Waring present, he retreated to Aestivossa. Chevaillier responded by sending "the most tender, urgent appeals for him to come back" because she and Sarah were "so lonely," and Harris invited them to dine at Aestivossa for what would be the final time. In Waring's recounting of events, Chevaillier became insulted when she found that she "could not sit all over her host, so to speak, and ransack every corner of the place, and possess herself of the man, his work, and his friends." Thoroughly enraged, Chevaillier left Fountaingrove and "ransacked the English-speaking world for evidence against Mr. Harris's purity."

Unholy Sensations. Joshua Paddison, Oxford University Press. © Oxford University Press 2025.
DOI: 10.1093/oso/9780197775325.003.0007

Waring told her brother that she did sometimes sit with Harris's feet in her lap and smoke his used pipes—"a funny picture, looked back upon"—but there was nothing impure about it. "The life here is so utterly away from the world's un-innocence and ourselves so long out of its habit, that we may often, unawares, give offense to prurient prudes," she wrote. The impure one was Chevaillier herself, she insisted. "This woman saw an unmarried man of powerful intellect, delightful social qualities, the center of the most beautiful house in Northern Cal. and she considered herself the gem of all in the world peculiarly fitted to deck that bosom and house, and to *ruin* all for her own glory." Furthermore, Waring reminded her brother that Chevaillier was "the one who tried to prevent Phillips Brooks from being made bishop, and for the love of whom, we are told, she went mad, years ago, and was in an asylum in Philadelphia."

As for Chevaillier's accusations about "free love" going on at Fountaingrove, Waring assured George they were "wholesale *lies.*" But she admitted that strict celibacy had been a struggle for some in the Brotherhood in years past. "Chevaillier bases her vile insinuations on events that occurred many years ago, when, as has been the experience in every effort at social association—the sex question threatened to destroy the society," she wrote. "With us, men and boys were kept demagnetized by healing baths, among many methods tried, and the mothers of the society did the scrubbing." Nevertheless, "cases of nymphomania, with other phases of sexual insanity arose, and for a time it looked as if every effort to cast out devils, and restore the obsessed would fail." Laurence Oliphant, she said, had been the "chief breeding place for the germs of sex-disease" because he had bedded "over a thousand women." Soon, though, Harris won spiritual victory against these demons of "infernal scortation," a term Swedenborg had used for dangerous physical lust. Nowadays, at Fountaingrove, she could "unhesitatingly affirm, with certain knowledge, that every man and woman lives in absolute continence."[3]

In Waring's account to her brother, Chevaillier was nothing more than a scheming "adventuress" who was seeking revenge against Harris for spurning her advances. Chevaillier was "Sarah Althea Hill No. 2," Waring said. Hill's lawsuits against former U.S. Senator William Sharon, whom she claimed was her husband, had made for sensationalistic headlines in California throughout the 1880s. Sharon's defense lawyers had maintained that Hill was a prostitute he had paid for sex, not his wife, and that she had used Haitian "hoodoo" spells to inflame his passions. Media accounts of the trials portrayed Hill as mentally unstable and, in February 1892, Hill would be declared "hopelessly insane" by the *San Francisco Chronicle* due to her involvement in spiritualism. She would spend the rest of her life in the California state insane asylum.[4] By calling Chevaillier "Sarah Althea Hill No. 2," Waring conjured up the image of a deranged, sexually immoral woman on the make.

Harris so approved of Waring's letter to George that he sent out mimeographed copies of it to friends of the Brotherhood. To these he appended a note stating that Chevaillier's attack was actually a spiritual one against him, the pivotal man of creation. Demonic forces, he said, were behind Chevaillier's actions; their goal was to "arrest the new divine respirations, destroy the organisms of the tender people who are growing on towards the renaissance, and break up the quiet and secluded homes in which such are gathered for protection." As he did with everything from a good batch of wine to Laurence Oliphant's apostasy, Harris interpreted this event in terms of a larger spiritual battle that he was waging for the salvation of all humankind. Chevaillier's campaign was one more confirmation that he bore "the stamp of the Crucified One," as Waring told her brother.

Harris asked his followers to redouble their efforts at divine respiration in order to aid in this newest spiritual struggle, and they faithfully complied. "I trust that we, all who love Father for his Race work, will hold around him as an impenetrable phalanx, so that he may not be hurt in this last assault," urged one member of the Brotherhood. "It makes my heart melt to think of the consequences that might ensue, if by failure in my part of the ranks the enemy broke through."[5] The crisis was strengthening, not undermining, their devotion to Harris. Another admirer of Harris decided that "at least one good will result" from Chevaillier's revelations in the *Chronicle*: "The worst that can be said has been uttered. The treasury of filth is exhausted."[6] This prediction would prove to be far from true, for Chevaillier was just getting started.

Across the Atlantic in Glasgow, Charles Pearce did his part by conducting his own letter-writing campaign as British newspapers picked up on the story. Chevaillier's reports were "a tissue of falsehoods from beginning to end," he said. She had barely spent time in Fountaingrove proper and greatly exaggerated the manual labor the colonists performed as well as the wealth enjoyed by Harris. The Parting women, he said, did no more labor at Fountaingrove than they had done in their private homes before joining the colony. As for sex, "the idea of free love has no place in the honest purity of their lives," Pearce insisted. The idea that Harris would take Jane Lee Waring as his mistress was preposterous, as she was "a lady of sixty-two years of age" and a "member of one of the old Boston families." The only "avarice and immorality" on display lay in the "the foul imagination of the accuser."[7] Similarly, in London, the brother of Fountaingrove colonist Emma Parting released a statement to the British press vouching for the moral upright-ness of his sister and assuring the public that the "impurities" Chevaillier discusses "exist only in her own morbid imagination."[8] Harris's supporters defended him by shifting the focus to Chevaillier's supposed depravity and away from Harris's conduct.

Harris also distributed mimeographed letters of support written by people inside and outside the Brotherhood. Someone identified as a "Distinguished English Authoress, Who Has No Personal Acquaintance with Mr. Harris," pointed out that Chevaillier had written several glowing reports about Harris earlier in 1891. "The question for those who believe in her to decide is—which of her statements is to be believed—those written in praise or those in blame," the "Authoress" wrote. "She is a cleft stick."[9] To those wondering why Harris had invited the Chevailliers to Fountaingrove in the first place, longtime Brotherhood member Samuel Clark reported that it was because of Harris's newfound determination to "come successively into rapport with every society and class both religious and secular, in the world, for purposes of instruction." Harris's holy mission thus made the "Chevailliers' persecu-tion appear the more terribly cruel," he said. Clark was confident that ulti-mately this was part of God's plan, for "good is made to come out of evil."[10]

In mid-January, Harris wrote his own lengthy letter addressed to an in-quirer but distributed to friends as another mimeograph. The inquirer was an Episcopalian who wrote to Harris to ask about his doctrines of counterparts: "*According to the papers,* your system includes sexual rela-tions among the unmarried, and I have seen the system compared to that of Oneida."[11] In his reply, Harris vacillated between trying to stay above the fray and engaging in further character assassination of Chevaillier. "It is utterly useless to contradict any falsehood originating in the diseased imaginations of perverted minds and adopted in the consensus of the mercenary and sen-sational press," he said. Nonetheless, he reported that Chevaillier suffered from "mediumistic hallucinations, from having tampered with spiritism" and "dark sciences." She was therefore utterly unreliable.

Harris explained that Chevaillier had begged him to "take her under my protection, to make a home for her, and to employ her as my accredited agent before the public," which he refused to do. She then tried to seduce him, he said, asking to stay with him at Aestivossa "as a guest without her mother." He again refused and expelled her. "I believe in *absolute purity of body, soul, and spirit*," he said. "I believe in a chastity that reaches from the outposts of the body to the deepest thoughts and intents of the heart." At the same time, he acknowledged that there existed "a sexual holiness that is the consummate flower and celestial crown of all holiness"—sex, that is, between the spiritually advanced and their heavenly counterpart, not between people here on earth. This was something Chevaillier could never understand, as she was "rotted down in her sexual beastliness, and has no more conception of the holiness of nuptial life than have the swine."[12]

Altogether, these counterattacks by Harris and his supporters drew on prevailing gender stereotypes of bad women. They accused Chevaillier of being lustful, jealous, scheming, power-hungry, and insane. As women like Chevaillier increasingly challenged the doctrine of separate spheres for women and men during the late nineteenth century, opposition to women's rights had hardened. Anti-woman-suffrage activists, both male and female, attacked outspoken feminists by portraying them as unladylike, un-Christian, and dangerously aggressive.[13] Harris and his followers employed these broader gender anxieties in their attacks on Chevaillier, casting her as not just unreliable but also mentally ill, sexually aggressive, and dissolute.

At the same time, Harris endeavored to make the young women of Fountaingrove more visible in the nearby community of Santa Rosa. Chevaillier had portrayed them as locked away, trapped in "servile positions." To counter this, Harris put Eleanor Clarke, Ray P. Clarke's twenty-year-old daughter, in charge of buying beef and other supplies from Santa Rosa vendors. She drove a spring wagon into town with the instructions to "be polite and cheerful, and never mention the 'mess,'" she recalled many years later. "Miss Chevaillier unintentionally did us good," Eleanor insisted. "Turned me into a woman able to meet the business world, from a girl so sensitive and retiring as to usually blush when spoken to."[14] Ironically, Chevaillier would have no doubt approved of Eleanor's personal transformation, an inadvertent side effect of her campaign, had she known of it.

In mid-January, Chevaillier tried to wrest back control of the headlines by paying a visit to Republican California governor Henry Markham at his home in Pasadena. She turned over "a load of books and documents" related to Fountaingrove and asked him to order an investigation. According to the *San Francisco Chronicle*'s write-up, Chevaillier furnished "pages and pages of foolscap written about the Edenic baths, counterparts, and other features of Harris's patent improved sexology." In all, Markham now possessed enough "passion literature" to "run afoul of the officers of the Society for the Suppression of Vice." Markham promised to look into the matter.[15]

As news of her charges spread from newspaper to newspaper, an artist added two illustrations that became appended to many accounts. In the first, Harris warns Alzire of the "vampire ministers" that prey on her. In the second, Harris is shown dining on raw oysters and champagne. He wears a Moroccan-style fez hat with tassel, reminiscent of Ottomans as well as semi-secret masonic groups in the United States such as the Shriners, founded in 1872, who wore the fez. With his luxurious meal and fez, Harris was portrayed as an Orientalized sultan with a harem. At the same time, the two illustrations mock Harris as old and foolish—a laughable false prophet "not like Christ," as a common headline trumpeted.[16]

One periodical that surprisingly did not cover the growing Fountaingrove scandal was Chevaillier's own magazine: *The Problem of Life and International Magazine of Truth*. Its editor, Wilberforce J. Colville, refused to publish Chevaillier's accusations about Harris and ended their working relationship by dropping the *International Magazine of Truth* from the magazine's title beginning with its January 1892 issue.[17] Colville had known of Harris from his time in California spiritualist circles and was an open admirer of his writings. In dropping the *International Magazine of Truth* from the masthead and Chevaillier as co-editor, Colville had the support of his New York City publisher, Frank F. Lovell, who was also an admirer of Harris. Colville then penned a gushing review of Harris's *God's Breath in Man and in Humane Society*, calling it a "wonderful book written by an extraordinary man," an indirect rebuke of Chevaillier's accusations. Despite his lifelong advocacy of women's rights, Colville chose to side with Harris over his own editorial partner Chevaillier. Her magazine, which Chevaillier had inherited from Mary Plunkett, had been killed off.[18]

Undeterred, Chevaillier issued her book review of Margaret Oliphant's *Memoir of the Life of Laurence Oliphant*, rejected from *The Problem of Life*, as a privately printed pamphlet. An expansion of her *Chronicle* piece from December 20, the review quickly turned into a reflection on Chevaillier's own experiences at Fountaingrove. She emphasized that she was acting out of "love, not hate, in tenderness, not bitterness" toward Harris. The lesson to learn, she said, was to "look to *Principle* and not to *Personality*" and to trust "our own purity of heart to sift all the error, the chaff," from any spiritual

THE VAMPIRE MINISTERS!

Thomas Lake Harris and Alize Chevaillier cartoon, *Topeka Daily Capital,*
January 19, 1892.

leader's teachings. Chevaillier acknowledged that her name was being
tracked through the mud as a result of her campaign but insisted that it "shall
not deter us a single instant, from what we feel to be a solemn duty laid upon
us by the most High." Returning to the book at hand, she felt certain that
Harris's "black magic" was the only explanation for how he had wrung years
of service out of Laurence, Alice, and Mary Oliphant. Harris was nothing
less than a "bright-winged Lucifer"—the most dangerous man alive.[19]

Meanwhile, Jane Lee Waring's letter to her brother George was proving
effective. Reassured that nothing resembling free love was going on at

HE LIVES ON OYSTERS AND CHAMPAGNE

Thomas Lake Harris cartoon, *Topeka Daily Capital*, January 19, 1892.

Fountaingrove, George penned a statement, released by Harris as another mimeograph and picked up by the press, addressing the allegation that he had tried to induce his sister to leave the Brotherhood. George acknowledged that he had never "been in sympathy" with Harris's weird religious ideas. However, "knowing the constant purity of her life," he had made no attempt to get his sister to leave and did not ask her to do so now. The entire matter was a lie concocted by the "Chevaillier women, who are selling sensational articles to the newspapers—gathering in the crop that the *Memoir of Laurence Oliphant* manured," George said.[20]

George did not stop there, however. He also reached out to his longtime friend William Dean Howells, the well-known writer and editor of *Harper's Monthly*. The previous fall, Howells had reviewed Margaret Oliphant's *Memoir* and, like most readers, lamented the Oliphants' delusional "bondage" to Harris.[21] Now, after hearing from George Waring, Howells published a retraction. He had been too hasty in dismissing Harris as an evil hypnotist, he now declared. According to information he had received from George, Howells now believed Harris had been unfairly maligned in Margaret Oliphant's book. Referring to Harris's recent claims of restored youth, Howells refused to mock them and went so far to say, "we must respect the dreamer; it may be, in fact, that we stand at the verge of a great realm, hitherto strange, which our steps are about the penetrate."[22] Harris was so delighted by Howells's retraction that he sent the editor two cases of Fountaingrove wine, which Howells promptly sent on to his friend George Waring.[23]

Howells's piece did not mention Chevaillier at all, but his newfound generosity to Harris infuriated her. She was especially galled because she held Howells in "profound reverence." After six anarchists had been found guilty of the bombing of police officers in Haymarket Square, Chicago, in 1887, Howells had been one of the few mainstream voices that had questioned the verdict and called for clemency.[24] Chevaillier was heartbroken that he was now publicly defending Harris. Suspecting that Howells would refuse to publish a rebuttal in *Harper's Monthly*, Chevaillier decided to place an open letter to Howells in a San Francisco magazine called the *California Illustrated World*. Unlike the *Chronicle*, which tended to edit her writings or cast them as interviews, the *California Illustrated World* was willing to give her six-and-a-half full columns and print her words under her own byline. Describing her own change of heart regarding Harris, she begged Howells to rethink his position "in the name of public morality against indecency, in the name of democracy against theocracy, [and] in the name of liberty against accursed and criminal mental slavery."

Up to this point, the only letter or affidavit in her possession that Chevaillier had put in print was Laurence Oliphant's 1885 letter from Haifa, which had not mentioned sexual matters. She had made many references to the materials she had gained from Alfred W. Manning but had refrained from quoting them directly or naming their authors. Now, however, to convince Howells and the greater reading public, she felt compelled to back up her claims, which, she admitted, "if not provable, should justly put me in State Prison, else no man's reputation is safe."

The first letter she printed in the *California Illustrated World* piece was by none other than Arthur Cuthbert Jr., son of Arthur Cuthbert and Emily Fawcett, two of the very earliest members of the Brotherhood. Arthur Jr. had grown up in Harris's colonies and had left the Brotherhood as a young adult. In his letter, written in 1885, Arthur Jr. described first seeing co-ed bathing at

Fountaingrove "by looking through a crack in the wall" of the Commandery. "The women were washed by the men at other times," he continued. "I remember one instance where Harris was washed in the naked state by two women (one was Miss J. L. Waring)." Eventually, Arthur Jr. took part in communal bathing himself. He concluded his letter by asking for help to "overthrow this great and cruel deceiver and keeping men from falling into this Hell hole."

Chevaillier next printed a "testimony from a gentleman"—presumably Manning—"who took written notes from another ex-member." This ex-member reported seeing Harris in bed with the man's own mother. Harris also forced this man to marry "a girl he scarcely knew" when he was seventeen but commanded him to never to have sex with her. "Yet three children were born of her," this ex-member said, in spite of his celibacy and in spite of "the queen regnant (Miss Waring, or Miss Requa) kneading and pounding the women to produce abortion."

As shocking as this was, Chevaillier was just warming up. "Another ex-member's written testimony tells of a boy of seventeen being ordered by Mr. Harris to co-habit six times a day with a married woman, in order to save his mother's life," she wrote. "The boy became feeble-minded in consequence." Yet another unnamed ex-member swore that "married couples were almost invariably separated and each given spiritual counterparts through human organisms—old men with young women and young men with old women." According to this testimony, the young men resented this, "setting their teeth and muttering 'the old hag,' as they went to the task called 'medicine.'"

"Mr. Howells, is it not most horrible immorality to teach such disorderly doctrines?" Chevaillier asked. She begged him to stand up for "purity, morality, justice, and righteousness," rather than for "deception, fraud, cruelty, and lust."[25]

In her open letter to Howells, Chevaillier's words were more graphic and more forthcoming with bizarre sexual details than ever before. Forced marriages, intergenerational sexual couplings, secret abortions, voyeurism, mass co-ed bathing, people driven to insanity—these were all new, highly salacious details sure to capture the imaginations of the reading public. Rather than back down due to the counteraccusations being made against her, Chevaillier doubled down. The way that Howells had simply ignored her surely was a factor in this shift. Perhaps her encounter with Governor Markham—who said he would look into Fountaingrove but never did so—fueled her as well. Or perhaps she felt that she had little left to lose in terms of her public reputation; holding back the sexual details out of modesty was not protecting her. The only way to preserve her womanly honor, it seemed, was to convince respectable people like Howells that Harris could not be ignored or underestimated. "There is not a Social Purity, Woman's Club, or Church in this land that should not aid this uncovering of iniquity and help uproot this impostor's power for harm," she informed Howells.

How true were Chevaillier's accusations? How reliable were the sources she got from Manning? Anyone following the story in January 1892 must have wondered about these questions, and they remain pressing questions for anyone looking back on the scandal today. Yet those questions were and are excruciatingly difficult to answer, even for historians with access to primary sources that newspaper readers in the 1890s lacked. Herbert W. Schneider, a Columbia University professor of religion who co-wrote with George Lawton a 600-page dual-biography of Harris and Oliphant in 1942, sidestepped these questions entirely by simply reprinting newspaper articles from the scandal in an appendix and stating, "it must be left to the reader to find the truth if he can."[26] Yet those questions seem crucial to try to answer, for they color the central meanings of the scandal. If Chevaillier was entirely wrong, it means that she was a misguided reformer who tried to destroy a group of earnest, celibate communalists; if she was entirely right, then she was an intrepid activist who brought to light the abusive conduct of a hypocritical religious leader.

The affidavits and letters that Manning turned over to Chevaillier unfortunately no longer exist; according to a letter Manning wrote in 1913, the originals all burned in the fire that followed the San Francisco earthquake of 1906.[27] All that remains are the quotations that Chevaillier included in her *San Francisco Chronicle* and *California Illustrated World* articles; in these, only Laurence Oliphant and Arthur Cuthbert Jr. are named as authors. The most damning allegations—Harris seen in bed with women of the colony, Harris ordering colonists to have sex, colonists conducting abortions— are made by ex-members whom Chevaillier never named. Her quotations lack dates, making it impossible to know if the events described occurred in Fountaingrove or in the New York colonies decades earlier. All the affidavits and letters were written by ex-members of the Brotherhood who may have held grudges against Harris and their former community, giving them reasons to exaggerate or even fabricate their stories. Furthermore, the affidavits and letters were solicited and compiled by Manning, who worked for years to undermine Harris's reputation among Swedenborgians and the general public.

We do know the identity of one additional informant. In a letter from 1920, Manning named a Scottish immigrant named Henry G. Craigie Gordon, who had been expelled from Fountaingrove. According to Manning, Gordon told him that "he used to commit adultery with one of the married women," and "her husband and Harris sanctioned it" because "it was not with her, the man's wife, but with his own counterpart who came into her and occupied her frame."[28] Gordon was hardly an ideal witness, however. In addition to possibly harboring a grudge due to his expulsion from Fountaingrove, Gordon suffered from lifelong "religio-erotic" hallucinations to the point that he would be written up as a case study of "paraphrenia"—what would later be called schizophrenia—in the *British Journal of Psychiatry* in 1922. At the time of Chevaillier's campaign, Gordon had become a devotee of a phrenologist, occultist, and self-described messiah named Alesha Sivartha. Gordon was known for displaying "morbid eroticism, speaking about marrying young girls. . . . Love in the abstract and sexual relation were his constant theme, and it was difficult to determine the actual experiences from his imaginations."[29] This could be why Chevaillier omitted Gordon's name from her accusations—he was simply too unreliable.

These evidential challenges noted, the notion that a man like Harris—who had absolute power over his followers, who lived with them in an isolated location, who controlled virtually all aspects of their lives, and who was believed by them to be a pivotal man of creation—might have abused that power is not hard to imagine. It accords with the many examples of abusive Catholic priests, pastors, yoga instructors, and other spiritual leaders that have come to light in recent decades, not to mention numerous historical examples of powerful men who have used their religious authority to take advantage of subordinates and parishioners. All of these examples provide compelling reasons not to dismiss Chevaillier's accusations too quickly.

Certain things can be known. There is no doubt, for example, that some of Harris's wealthy followers, including Maria Oliphant, Laurence Oliphant, and Jane Lee Waring, turned large sums of money over to him. There is no doubt that his followers spent their days toiling in physical labor while he studied, wrote, and conducted spiritual explorations. There is no doubt that Harris separated wives from husbands and children from parents in the name of their spiritual advancement. There is no doubt that colonists at Fountaingrove lived in gender-segregated housing but sometimes bathed together. Cuthbert Jr.'s description of co-ed bathing, including male and female colonists washing Harris, is confirmed by other sources, including Jane Lee Waring's letter to her brother.

However, none of these things—if done voluntarily—necessarily constitute an abuse of power by Harris. Most members of the Brotherhood—including Oliphant until he broke with Harris—did not seem to have regarded these arrangements as inequitable; they spoke of giving their money and labor willingly in exchange for an immersive utopian spiritual experience outside the mainstream. In the case of his Japanese followers, Harris paid for their passage to the United States, provided free room and board, helped them master English, and included them fully in communal life.

On questions of sex, the issues become thornier. Unlike "complex marriage" at Oneida or polygamy among Mormons, for which copious documentation exists, there is little surviving evidence from within the colony suggesting that anything other than sometimes-frustrating celibacy was going on in Harris's colonies. Jane Lee Waring's tantalizing comment to her brother that "the sex question threatened to destroy the society" in the Brocton period due to "cases of nymphomania" suggests that at least some colonists struggled to practice celibacy. In 1878, Harris acknowledged the birth of five children at his colonies in seventeen years.[30] Of course, a few births to married couples is a far cry from the kinds of things Chevaillier alleged.

Sources from outsiders provide other pieces of evidence that Chevaillier and Manning did not have access to. Hannah Whitall Smith, an evangelical Protestant reformer who helped found the Women's Christian Temperance Union, compiled records related to what she regarded "religious fanaticism" in the United States. Appalled and fascinated by Harris's writings, Smith twice visited Fountaingrove to speak with the poet. "One thing I did not like about him; he wanted to sit too close to me," Smith wrote later. "I could not feel that this was any great spiritual experience on his part, but was decidedly of the flesh."

More damningly, Smith also recorded an account given by an "especial friend" of hers whom she called Miss X—a fitting parallel to Chevaillier's informant Mr. X. After meeting Harris on a transatlantic ocean voyage, Miss X considered joining Harris's Brocton community. She corresponded with Jane Lee Waring for several years and met once with Laurence Oliphant before paying the colony a visit. While at Brocton, Waring told Miss X about the doctrine of counterparts and about Harris's Lily Queen. According to Smith's account, Waring told Miss X that colonists communed with Lily Queen through a "peculiar" method: they "go to Mr. Harris's room and get into bed with Lily Queen."

"'But what became of Mr. Harris?' asked Miss X.

"'Oh, Lily Queen is inside of Father, and consequently he, of course, stays in the bed, and by getting into his arms we get into her arms,'" Waring supposedly responded.[31]

When considering the veracity of this story, there are several troubling aspects. Like most of Chevaillier's sources, Miss X's experiences at Brocton were undated and uncorroborated. The story comes to us from Hannah Whitall Smith, an evangelical Protestant leader unabashedly hostile to Harris and other religious "fanatics." And even if it were true that Harris used the idea of counterparts to get into bed with his followers, it might seem unlikely that Waring would reveal something like that to a potential recruit before she had joined the colony.

However, it turns out that Miss X was a highly unconventional woman. Sleuthing in Smith's archive reveals the identity of Miss X: Sarah Frances Smiley, a "preaching Quakeress" from Philadelphia who enjoyed a successful career as a traveling minister throughout the post–Civil War era, both on her own and as part of evangelist superstar Dwight Moody's revival team.[32] Despite her public reputation as an "eminent and most evangelical minister," Smiley had a secret interest in mysticism and would eventually convert to Roman Catholicism.[33] In the 1870s, Smiley spent time at a sanitarium in Clifton Springs, New York, run by Henry Foster, a Methodist doctor with unusual methods. In addition to using water cure, mind cure, and homeopathic techniques, Foster taught that "the Baptism of the Holy Spirit was a physical thing, felt by delightful thrills going through you from head to foot." According to her friend Smith, Smiley was so impressed by Foster that she "felt it her duty to ask him to stand naked before her, and also to do the same thing herself before him." Apparently Foster taught Smiley how to feel the Holy Spirit physically, because soon after Smith witnessed her friend "experience right there thrills of rapture from head to foot, which completely carried her away." Smiley was soon teaching this technique to a circle of friends, kissing them to "produce in them those physical thrills which she believed were the actual contact of the Holy Ghost."[34]

Knowing that Miss X was Sarah Frances Smiley makes the notion that Waring would share intimacies about counterparts to an outsider much easier to believe. If, during their years of correspondence, Smiley had told

MISS SARAH F. SMILEY, THE QUAKERESS PREACHER.
[From a Photograph by W. H. Williamson, Brooklyn.]

Sarah Frances Smiley, *Harper's Weekly*, March 2, 1871.

Waring about her own rapturous experiences with the Holy Spirit and about her openness to nudity and spiritual-sexual physical contact, Waring might well have been willing to discuss secret counterpartal practices employed by the Brotherhood. In fact, Waring might have thought such secrets would entice Smiley all the more. However, Smiley "left the community troubled and distressed," though she would continue corresponding with the Brotherhood for several more years before breaking it off.[35]

The experiences of Mary Emerson are more incriminating. Emerson was a young woman in the 1860s when she joined the Brocton community along with her parents and brother. Anointed with the fairy name Rosa, she was "a beautiful young woman, of a statuesque, regal type," according to one male colonist's recollection, and "remarkable in so many ways it was only natural that all the men of the community should have fallen in love with her." She and her parents left the colony after a few years because, according to her parents, "Harris tried to make Rosa Emerson marry him."[36] This allegation was repeated in the *Fredonia Censor* in 1912 when a former Brocton colonist, probably Mary's father J. M. Emerson, told the paper that he had left the community "because Harris made improper advances to my daughter."[37]

In 1884, Mary Emerson published a thinly fictionalized novel called *Among the Chosen* recounting her experiences at Brocton. In one scene in the novel, Father John (a stand-in for Harris) approaches the female protagonist Rosalie. "He took her hand caressingly in his and led her to the parlor; he sat down upon the sofa and drew her to a seat beside him," Emerson wrote. Father John tells her, "'I love you, Rosalie, with a love your natural parents never knew for you, and I would make you good and noble. But you must trust me child.' The last words were spoken pleadingly, caressingly, as he touched her chin and raised it." In the novel, Father John planned to force Rosalie to marry not him but his son Jack, a future that Rosalie rejects when she hurls a dagger at Father John and flees in the middle of the night. Father John dies that same night when an accidental fire burns down the colony's main building with him inside, so deep in a trance he cannot wake up. Throughout the novel, Emerson depicts Father John as manipulative and controlling, suggesting that she harbored anger toward Harris in real life.[38]

All of this raises more questions. During the period when the Emersons were at Brocton, Harris was still married to his second wife Emily Waters Harris, who would live until 1885. So did the Emersons believe that Harris wanted to enter a polygamous marriage with Mary? If so, would that marriage necessarily be a sexual relationship, given his claims of practicing celibacy with his wife Emily? The Emersons clearly thought it was "improper." Or did Harris try to pair Mary Emerson with one of his two sons, John or Thomas Jr., as in her novel?

Mary Emerson, ca. 1870; courtesy Bancroft Library, University of California, Berkeley.

Sexual intercourse did not need to be happening between Harris and his followers, or between colonists under Harris's direction, to make the goings-on coercive or abusive. If we widen our definition of sex to include anything erotic, it is clear that Harris's colonies were highly sexualized spaces. His poetry and theological writings were so rife with erotic passages that other spiritualists and metaphysicians routinely condemned him. His doctrine of counterparts promised nothing less than sexual ecstasy to his followers once they were visited by their counterpart. One female colonist at Fountaingrove called the experience better than sex: "The first time that it came into my body, that is the trunk, it seemed to enter through the generative organs, and with it came the thought, this is like sexual intercourse, only infinitely more so." She later recorded, "I feel currents of life flowing into me continually and Father says that they are from him." Colonists bathed together at Fountaingrove where, she said, they "literally wash each other's feet and the rest of their bodies as well."[39] In a private letter to his sister, a male Fountaingrove colonist described bathing Harris, granting him "a great relief recently, and in the baths [Harris] finds a help and an unburdening such as he never had hoped for; I have given him more than twenty vapour and warm sitzes, rubbings, etc."[40] With her own eyes, Chevaillier saw Harris sitting with his feet in Jane Lee Waring's lap. He liked to surround himself with adoring women, as shown in a photograph taken at Fountaingrove in 1876 or 1877 that shows him sitting with thirteen female colonists, including Alice Le Strange Oliphant, Jane Lee Waring, Emma Parting, and her young daughters Alice and Margaret Parting.

We also know for certain that Lily Queen sometimes spoke through Harris, giving credence to Smiley's account of colonists getting into bed with Lily Queen. During one of Chevaillier's visits to Linn Lilla, when she rose to leave, Harris "suddenly assumed the state of the 'Lily Mother,' and in a high piping voice, which was, of course, assumed, he said, 'We want the child to stay—let her stay.'"[41] Similarly, a female colonist at Fountaingrove described in her diary how, in 1881, she "slept in the Mother's house [Aestivossa], Lily talked with me through father, and the singular thing about it was that though I fully understood everything that was said, yet as soon as it was said, it was completely blotted from my memory."[42] Her forgetfulness could have been a coping response to what she experienced with "Lily Queen" that night.

Whether or not Harris was having sex—in the conventional, physical sense—with his followers, and whether or not he was commanding them to have sex with each other, it is clear that everyday life in his colonies was

Thomas Lake Harris with female Fountaingrove colonists, ca. 1876–1877; courtesy Museum of Sonoma County, Santa Rosa, California.

sexually charged. At the center was Harris. He taught that spiritual and sexual matters could not be separated, and he created communities that catered to his obsessions, needs, and desires. His followers believed that their divine respiration literally kept him alive and allowed him to "inter-unite himself with them and interflow through all their faculties."[43] He routinely threatened that those who betrayed him died as a result. Although he was clearly not hypnotizing them, as Chevaillier maintained, he exercised tremendous power over his followers. He could—and did—exile followers, separate them from loved ones, isolate them, bless them or curse them, rename them, and dictate how they spent their time and labor. His banished his own wife Emily to separate quarters at Brocton and then Fountaingrove, forbidding all from speaking to her due to her supposed mental illness. Arthur Cuthbert Jr. recalled how he and other "naughty boys" would mock her as a crazy "Old Hag," never considering how "her mental state would hardly be at its best when she knew in her banishment that other ladies were in high favor and living in [Harris's] house."[44] Anyone could suffer this treatment if Harris—or Lily Queen—saw fit.

Chevaillier insisted that she "saw no impurities at Fountaingrove," but she picked up on an undeniable sexualized atmosphere and an imbalance of power. She saw a patriarch whose erotic imaginings ordered the lives and spiritual practices of his followers and who had untrammeled access to their minds, emotions, and bodies. This was especially true when she arrived in the summer of 1891. No longer ill or self-isolating, his recent spiritual breakthrough at Linn Lilla had restored his manly vitality—in his words, "fountains of blood seemed to flow as by a vortical motion, rounding in each recuperative organ to one grand consciousness of bodily grandeur."[45] Upon first meeting her, Harris had greeted Chevaillier with a kiss and put his hand on her solar plexus. In fact, Harris was known for his "excessively demonstrative" manner of greeting girls and women.[46] Hannah Whitall Smith, Mary Emerson, Alzire Chevaillier, and other women all remarked on how Harris sat too close or touched them in ways that made them uncomfortable. They felt he acted out of something more carnal than fatherly concern for the state of their souls. They saw him as a predator.

It may be relevant to note here that Laurence Oliphant, who based so much of his theology on Harris's, had faced his own accusations of sexual impropriety in the final months of his life. A British widow named Jennie Tuttle, who had spent time with Oliphant in his Haifa colony after Alice's death and before his second marriage, began spreading "sickening details" about him. Tuttle told Hannah Whitall Smith, for example, that Oliphant "began to take personal liberties with her" in Haifa, "and at last induced her to share his bed, with the idea that the personal touch would bring about the sympneumata," Oliphant's term for counterpartal ecstasy. Oliphant then "began to urge her to spread the blessing by herself enticing young men into the same relations with her as his own." Tuttle went so far to complain to the National Vigilance Association, a British anti-vice society founded in 1885 to stamp out prostitution, homosexuality, and other sex crimes. Oliphant's death had stopped the investigation from going far, however.[47] Given that Oliphant borrowed so much from Harris's spiritual ideas, Tuttle's accusations may reveal something about Harris's secret counterpartal methods.

Ultimately, there are too many silences in the historical record to fully reconstruct the sexual lives of the members of the Brotherhood of the New Life. As is typical for historians studying sexuality, much-needed primary sources are missing or destroyed, or they never existed in the first place, and the sources that do exist are fraught with interpretive problems.[48] Yet the existing evidence suggests that Harris used his religious authority over his followers to satisfy his own erotic impulses in ways that were not fully consensual, at least for some. As we will see in how the scandal played out, he also lied to cover up what actually went on at Fountaingrove, denying that co-ed bathing occurred, for example. These lies make his statements about practicing strict celibacy all the more suspect. Like so many other religious leaders before and after him, Harris misused his power for his own gratification and lied and issued threats when that power became endangered.

This does not change the fact that Chevaillier made her case to the public in ways designed to inflame preexisting anxieties, and media outlets magnified those anxieties as the story spread. In this as in many other ways, the Fountaingrove scandal established a pattern that would be repeated in subsequent cult scares. The challenge of separating truths from lies by weighing insiders' accounts, apostates' stories, reformers' accusations, and media exaggerations remains today a vexing issue for those studying groups labeled cults. From the Brotherhood of the New Life to the Branch Davidians to NXIVM and beyond, the contested murkiness of the truth would make cults all the more compelling to the public.

8

February 1892

Spirit Versus Flesh

On February 10, the scandal approached its crescendo when Chevaillier announced that she would take her message directly to the people of San Francisco via a lecture, titled "Mysticism and Harrisism: Secrets of the Sonoma Eden Unveiled," to be held on February 16 in Irving Hall. This was a bold move. When speaking in public, women rarely addressed topics of a sexual nature, let alone the kinds of acts Chevaillier had described in her *California Illustrated World* article. In deciding to stand before a mixed crowd of men and women in a large lecture hall and discuss sexual matters, Chevaillier knew that she would make herself even more vulnerable to charges of pollution of public morals. Accordingly, her announcement emphasized that her remarks would be "given in such a manner as propriety will permit" and claimed that she had the "warm endorsement of many clergymen and others interested in public morality and social purity." But she also promised "startling revelations" of "revolting promiscuous sensuality."[1]

In the meantime, the press salivated over the new details Chevaillier had doled out in the *California Illustrated World*. Newspapers as far away as New York, Washington D.C., and Sydney, Australia, printed detailed summaries of her open letter to William Dean Howells on their front pages.[2] Thanking Chevaillier for "fighting the devil with hellfire," editors competed to denounce what was increasingly being called the "Harris cult" in loudest fashion.[3] The *San Francisco Wave* probably won that competition when it called for the Grand Jury of Sonoma County and Governor Markham to investigate the "iniquitous debaucheries" of Fountaingrove, where it said "both sexes of one family bed together like dogs in a kennel."[4] The *Chronicle* reported that Alzire's revelations were causing former admirers of Harris, including European members of the Brotherhood of the New Life, to cut ties with the man.[5]

In recognition of this bad publicity, Harris decided to suspend the Fountaingrove Library series, begun with such optimism the previous year.

Unholy Sensations. Joshua Paddison, Oxford University Press. © Oxford University Press 2025.
DOI: 10.1093/oso/9780197775325.003.0008

"I think Father is beginning to realize that his present thought is beyond the grasp of those who are, as yet, children in the religion," explained Jane Lee Waring to an inquirer.[6] Discretion, rather than bold public pronouncements, was now necessary. "We are coming to a point where extreme reticence and caution must be observed and appearances kept in accord with the world's ways," Waring warned Arthur Cuthbert.[7]

Harris conducted further damage control by writing a letter, distributed once again as a mimeograph, to the New Church Independent, a liberal Swedenborgian journal in Chicago that had kept an open mind about Harris over the years. With his typically ornate prose, Harris dismissed Chevaillier's accusations as "absurd, preposterous ... simply the effusions of baffled greed and insane lubricity, or the artifices of an iniquitous conspiracy." Harris said this was only the latest example of the "stream of diabolical insinuations" he had faced throughout his long career as a mystic. "Laboring, as I do, for the cleansing of mankind, I must encounter the stench, as Hercules did when he was seeking to turn the cleansing river though the Augean Stables," he wrote. He predicted that the current "slander" would "recoil on the heads of those who originate and diffuse it," reminding readers what had happened to Laurence Oliphant after his betrayal: "He died."[8]

Editor John S. Weller responded in print with an editorial in which he reluctantly addressed the "new, or newly revived, newspaper scandal." Weller admitted that he had "maintained a generally friendly attitude" toward Harris over the years, despite hearing rumors circulated among Swedenborgians (a reference to Manning's efforts). "We sincerely hope that all we have heard is greatly exaggerated or untrue," Weller wrote. As for Chevaillier, Weller wondered how much she acted out of "malice, jealousy, or a craze to get her name before the world." Weller also printed an extract from a letter from someone from Boston who claimed to have known Chevaillier there. This Bostonian asserted that she was "not reliable; she has been treated for insanity more than once, and some of her friends think she is not perfectly sane at any time."[9] This was the first time whispers of her alleged history of mental illness made it out of Harris's mimeographs into print. Harris then took the letter and distributed it as a new mimeograph.

One question that loomed for supporters of Harris was, given his tremendous spiritual powers, how could he have so misjudged Chevaillier in the first place? Jane Lee Waring addressed this conundrum in another mimeographed letter sent to extended members of the Brotherhood. Just as Jesus "had an Iscariot among his chosen disciples," so too did Harris allow

Chevaillier to come close to him. And just as Judas's betrayal of Jesus helped bring about the crucifixion and resurrection, Chevaillier's betrayal "had to be gone through" to bring the final stages of Harris's apotheosis. True believers should rejoice, not mourn or question, insisted Waring: "It is a good thing to have a conspiracy reveal itself and play its last card, as this is doing, and so have the reservoir emptied of its infernal filth; and this is but the 'afterbirth of the Oliphant abortion.'" In this time of crisis, Waring cited the scandal as further proof of Harris's Christlike powers and a necessary step toward the "final judgement" of the world.[10] If some admirers of Harris were stepping away, as the *Chronicle* reported, this was an attempt to leverage the scandal by portraying it as the final test before the glorious apocalypse Harris had long predicted. Waring attempted to alleviate whatever doubts or feelings of cognitive dissonance the scandal was sparking among Harris's admirers by doubling down on the broader spiritual meanings of Harris's persecution. For Waring and the faithful, the scandal confirmed rather than cast in doubt Harris's holiness.[11]

On the evening of February 16, Chevaillier delivered her lecture on Fountaingrove before an audience of about two hundred people in Irving Hall. She was introduced by Jerome Anderson, a prominent local Theosophist. Chevaillier began, surprisingly, by praising Harris's poetry and writings for their "inspiration, poetic fire and genius, vivid imagery, oratorical display, and uplifted exaltation up to and over the brink of spiritual intoxication." But his rhetorical gifts only made his evil all the more pernicious, she said. Chevaillier proceeded to give an overview of his checkered career as a spiritualist, including a description of the failed Mountain Cove commune. Long held up as an example of "unscientific" spiritualism run amok, Mountain Cove now became mere prelude to the excesses of Fountaingrove. Chevaillier then chronicled Harris's treatment of the Oliphant family, recycling the by-now well-known stories in Margaret Oliphant's *Memoir of the Life of Laurence Oliphant.*

Finally, Chevaillier turned to what listeners in the audience must have known was coming: sex. It was the promise of hearing "the most delicate matters publicly handled by a woman" that had attracted many to come in the first place, according to a hostile report in the *San Francisco Examiner.*[12] She approached the topic as lightly as she could. "It is with great hesitancy, delicacy, and reluctance that I just touch upon the leading features of evil," she declared. She then listed the topics she simply could not discuss in a public setting: "I cannot go into the shocking details of Edenic baths given by opposite sexes to each other." And: "I cannot particularize authenticated written statements of how force and deception were used by Harris." Of course, by saying she could not discuss these things, she was indirectly doing just that. Perhaps knowing her urban audience craved something salacious, she added, "Husbands and wives are separated, old men are given to comely young women, and young men to old women, according as Harris directs." She repeated the charge that one young man saw his mother taken as Harris's mistress, now adding a new detail: when the son confronted his mother about this, she told him, "It is for the Lord." Sympathizing with this woman, Chevaillier editorialized, "No doubt she was as pure in heart and motive as you and I."

She concluded with an explicit call to action directed to California's women. She called on the Women's Christian Temperance Union, White Cross Guild, and the social purity movement to take up the cause of saving the "hypnotized victims" of Fountaingrove and "wiping this foul den from the face of the earth." If Governor Markham failed to act, she vowed to "go before the authorities at Washington and urge that action be taken against Harris's fold such as has been had against the Mormons," who had been pressured into publicly renouncing polygamy just two years earlier. She ended her speech by demanding "investigation in the name of purity, justice, and liberty."[13]

As in her earlier writings for the *Chronicle*, her focus was firmly on saving the white women of California from Harris's clutches. By casting her crusade as a women's issue, she more safely couched her topic within acceptable bounds of feminine propriety. And by invoking the social purity movement, she drew on a rising discourse that challenged the sexual double standard and demanded that men exercise as much sexual restraint as women. Central to the claims of the social purity movement was the idea that women's economic and political dependance on men made them vulnerable to sexual exploitation.[14] Her depiction of Fountaingrove was an exaggerated microcosm of this broader situation; Harris represented absolute male power and the women of Fountaingrove complete female victimhood. Though she had initially portrayed Jane Lee Waring as Harris's willing accomplice, she made no mention of her in this speech, likely because Waring's role as facilitator and co-conspirator complicated her narrative of rampant patriarchy.

She also made no mention of the colony's Japanese men, who had loomed so large in her earlier campaign efforts. It is unclear why she dropped them from her narrative. As she spent more and more time in California, she may have decided that her largely white audience would not accept Japanese men as sympathetic victims. Or, now that she had shifted from writing articles to delivering public lectures, she may have judged it too dangerous to position herself as a savior of men (though Japanese). Perhaps she decided that trying to save Nagasawa and Arai muddied her argument against the male dominance represented by Harris. A final possibility is that accentuating the presence of Japanese men at Fountaingrove had already served its purpose in terms of casting the colony as exotic and un-American.

It is noteworthy that her introduction at Irving Hall came from Jerome Anderson, a Theosophist, rather than a local Protestant minister. In fact, California's Protestant press ignored the scandal altogether.[15] This is surprising given the prominent role Protestant ministers would soon have in creating—and demonizing—the category of cults. Though it is safe to assume that Protestant leaders disapproved of Harris and his unorthodox teachings, he was so outside the bounds of traditional Christianity that they surely felt no danger of being tainted by association. To wade into public discussion could only lower their respectability. Chevaillier's identity as a socialist and mental healer might have been another reason Protestant ministers kept their distance from her campaign.

Instead, it was metaphysicians outside the Protestant mainstream who leapt into the fray to attack Harris. Chevaillier, of course, was a practicing mental healer and former student of Mary Baker Eddy. Her behind-the-scenes ally was Alfred W. Manning, a prominent Swedenborgian, and San Francisco's Swedenborgian journal, the *New Church Pacific*, went on record to back up Chevaillier's accusations. According to its editor, Harris's "rottenness" was "long known" to Swedenborgians. Only Chevaillier's "innate purity" and "sublime effort of will which few are able to use" had saved her from his hypnotic powers.[16] Among Swedenborgian publications in the United States and Great Britain, only the broad-minded *New Church Independent* in Chicago expressed skepticism about Chevaillier's campaign.

Never fond of Harris, Theosophists quickly joined the chorus against him. Local Theosophist Jerome Anderson introduced her at Irving Hall and in his journal, *New Californian*, he urged Harris's admirers to "correspond with Miss A. A. Chevaillier, care of this Magazine," to learn the awful truth that lurked behind Harris's religio-erotic writings. "Judge the tree by its fruit," admonished Anderson.[17] In New York, Theosophist leader William Q. Judge lambasted Harris's "disgusting doctrines" and emphasized, "with it the Theosophical Society has nothing in common. . . . Our Society must be kept as free as possible from being mixed up with these enterprises."[18] In London, Theosophist leader Annie Besant continued her hostility to Harris, begun the previous year. Though she hesitated to "accuse him of vice on the strength of newspaper paragraphs," she reiterated her hatred for his writings and noted that "publicity is the best cure to insidious mischief of this kind."[19] Chevaillier had in fact met Besant during the Theosophist's lecture tour in New York City the previous spring, just before Chevaillier had left for California. The two women had conversed on "health consciousness" and their shared distrust of "hypnotic or mesmerist" mental healing techniques, giving Besant another reason to side with Chevaillier over Harris beyond wanting, like Judge, to distance her movement from his.[20]

Many spiritualists likewise publicly separated themselves from Harris, the culmination of his troubled relationship with mainstream spiritualism dating to the 1850s. Chicago's *Progressive Thinker* printed Chevaillier's accusations, adding, "Verily, what next?"[21] Henry Lafayette Williams, leader of the Summerland colony near Santa Barbara, felt compelled to affirm his community's commitment to keeping it "free from all sensualists." Touting California's salubrious "climate, soil, and scenery," Williams and other spiritualists had founded Summerland in 1888 as a haven for those seeking spiritual and physical restoration.[22] With Harris's spiritualist colony now dominating the headlines, Williams wanted to address the "numerous inquiries I have received, as to whether this is a free-love colony." Summerland, he insisted, housed only "those whose aspirations are higher than the gratification of the animal nature." He tolerated no "free-lovers" nor "confirmed sots," a reference to Fountaingrove's vineyards.[23]

All of these movements—Christian Science and mental healing, Swedenborgianism, Theosophy, and spiritualism—had been targeted at one time or another with charges of practicing "free love" and undermining Christian values. With the exception of the Swedenborgians, they were all notably woman-centric. Unlike Protestant ministers, leaders of these movements felt a need to separate themselves from the taint of Harris and his Brotherhood. The scandal provided a new opportunity for these marginalized groups to affirm their dedication to mainstream values of chastity, marriage, and family. These groups joined with newspaper journalists in enlarging and maintaining the scandal.

California's newspapers carried stories about Chevaillier's lecture with lurid headlines like "Spirit Versus Flesh," "Iniquity Exposed," and "The Sonoma Blot."[24] The *San Francisco Call* demanded "immediate steps to break up" Fountaingrove and all "spiritualistic communities" like it.[25] Her lecture also had a profound effect on at least one member of the public, a San Franciscan man named Lawrence Sasso who wrote the Chevailliers a personal note. "It was the noblest, the holiest, the most womanly defense of truth, purity, and morality," he wrote, "that I had ever heard issue from the lips of a human being." He added that he had previously given up all religious beliefs, but Chevaillier's "lofty womanhood" was rekindling his hunger for the divine.[26] Chevaillier kept this note among her papers for the rest of her life, suggesting that Sasso's response was exactly the effect she was hoping for.

Her lecture in Irving Hall was such a success, in fact, that she immediately announced a second lecture a few nights later in a surprising location: the enormous Athenaeum opera house in downtown Santa Rosa. An advertisement in the *Santa Rosa Daily Republican* promised a "fearless exposé of the secret immoralities at Fountaingrove."[27] This would be the first time she had returned to Santa Rosa since leaving the previous fall. She had decided to take her campaign directly to Harris's backyard.

She also dispatched an angry letter to Santa Rosa's *Sonoma Democrat*, which had printed a defense of Harris written from Glasgow by Charles Pearce. The editor of the *Democrat*, Thomas Larkin Thompson, had added a comment that the Fountaingrove colonists "have maintained a quiet and orderly existence in this community for many years," having "converted a vast acreage of unproductive hill lands into profitable vineyards."[28] Fountaingrove's winery was good for the economic prosperity of Santa Rosa, so Thompson saw no reason to ask questions about the colonists' private sexual lives. Chevaillier was appalled. She urged Santa Rosa residents to attend her upcoming talk to hear and "judge calmly" her evidence. However, Thompson bowdlerized her letter, omitting from print any sex talk on the ground that such matters were "intensely personal."[29] If people in Santa Rosa wanted to hear such things, they would have to attend her lecture on Saturday night.

At Fountaingrove, the colonists prepared for this latest assault. Harris wrote a "*strictly confidential*" letter to Thompson of the *Sonoma Democrat* thanking him for his "chivalrous southern spirit"—Thompson was from Virginia—and promising "such business advantage as may result from the exposure of this infamy." Harris was on good terms with Thompson; the previous summer, the *Democrat* had run Harris's *The Brotherhood of the New Life: Its Fact, Law, Method, and Purpose* in its entirety on the front page, along with a flattering introduction calling Fountaingrove "a materialized dream of agricultural thrift, comfort, and abundance."[30] Harris now promised Thompson an interview that "will ring through three continents." Harris repeated his charge that Chevaillier sought "simply the revenge of a scorned, detested, and infuriated female." He also explained the "conspiracy" he and his followers were now nurturing: the wild idea that Chevaillier acted as an agent of Margaret Oliphant and her London publisher Blackwood & Sons. This theory combined the two major media assaults of the previous year into a single diabolical enemy. "I will strike, and strike hard, and strike fatally, just as soon as their last blow at me through Miss C. makes it a public duty," he said ominously.[31]

As a Democrat, Thompson may have also been predisposed against Chevaillier's campaign. Ever since its birth in the 1850s, the Republican Party had been aligned with northern middle-class Protestants and moral reform movements such as temperance, anti-polygamy, and abolition. The Democrats, conversely, made room for white Protestant Southerners, Irish Catholic immigrants, and western Mormons, which made the party less inclined to support Protestant moral reform efforts. This predisposition helps explain why William Randolph Hearst's Democratic *Examiner* gave little space to the scandal compared to other papers in San Francisco such as the Republican *Chronicle* and *Call*.[32] There were many exceptions to this trend, however, most notably Joseph Pulitzer's Democratic *New York World*, which loved a good scandal story more than it cared about moral reform politics.

What was on Chevaillier's mind as she and her mother took the train back to Santa Rosa? She knew that Harris was generally regarded by locals as a successful—if eccentric—landowner and entrepreneur whose Fountaingrove wines were "sold all over Europe, and in the East," according to a glowing piece published by the *Santa Rosa Daily Democrat* in the midst of the scandal.[33] Earlier in the month, Chevaillier had registered charges against Harris with the Grand Masonic Lodge of California on behalf of "Masons' wives and daughters," but he remained a member of the local Knights Templar, an indication of his good social standing.[34] The audience for her talk in Irving Hall had been San Francisco urbanites eager for salacious tales; people in Santa Rosa were more likely to be suspicious of any woman speaking openly about sex in public, especially one involving a local prosperous landowner. Chevaillier also had to wonder if Waring, Nagasawa, or even Harris himself might show up at her lecture to confront her.

Sure enough, in Santa Rosa, the Chevailliers found a chilly response from locals. Sarah Chevaillier later complained that Harris had "privately circulated hundreds of printed, malignantly libelous circulars, against my daughter." Due to the circulation of these mimeographs, "on every hand, in Santa Rosa, we heard his underhanded, slanderous reports." The crowd that turned out to the Athenaeum that night was "small but appreciative," according to a short write-up in the *Santa Rosa Daily Republican*. The two local Democratic papers carried no report whatsoever. Given the paucity of the media coverage, it is impossible to know if and how Chevaillier altered her speech from the version she gave in San Francisco, other than the addition of two new flourishes: she claimed Harris had intercepted her mail while at Fountaingrove, and she now corroborated her charges against him by reading from "the bible she said was in use at Fountaingrove, which she had procured in Scotland and which she said could not be secured at any price." It is unclear which of Harris's privately circulated, erotic-spiritual writings Chevaillier had procured; he had plenty that would raise the eyebrows of those outside the Brotherhood.[35]

But public sentiment in Santa Rosa seemed stacked against her, at least among the town's powerful men. Rather than cover her speech, Thomas Larkin Thompson devoted a column of the next issue of the *Sonoma Democrat* to defenses of Harris submitted by local elites. Charles H. Thompson, a doctor who had served Fountaingrove for fourteen years, attested that Harris was "always the same, a gentleman of exalted mind." Having "been into every apartment on the premises," the doctor assured the public that no "immoral atmosphere" existed at Fountaingrove. Jonathan Avery Shepherd, a local Episcopalian minister and a friend of Fountaingrove's, contributed a statement in support of Harris undersigned by thirty Santa Rosa capitalists, merchants, and bankers, many of whom were in the Knights Templar with Harris. They insisted that the Fountaingrove colonists were "respectable, honorable, and in every way worthy people" and that Chevaillier's attacks were "unkind, unwarranted, and not prompted by any good motive." Finally, the *Sonoma Democrat* included a short letter from Harris thanking the good people of Santa Rosa for their support during Chevaillier's visit.[36] He never did grant Thompson the interview he had promised, however.

Harris called the statements of support by Jonathan Avery Shepherd and other elites "unsolicited," but in fact he had been working behind the scenes to secure this support for weeks. He had been friends with Shepherd for many years, and the minister had spoken at Emily Harris's funeral in 1885.[37] Just before Chevaillier's lecture, Harris summoned Shepherd to Fountaingrove and read to him Chevaillier's long, anguished letter from the previous November. Shepherd left convinced that Chevaillier was a "Jezebel" who acted out of "thirst for money," as did her "equally scheming mother." As a minister, Shepherd was disgusted by "the polecat revellings of her impure nature," especially Chevaillier's allegations that co-ed bathing went on at Fountaingrove. Such thoughts "could never enter the brain of man or woman unless drunk with their own innate impure thought revellings," concluded Shepherd.[38] Harris clearly had failed to inform Shepherd that co-ed bathing actually did occur at Fountaingrove.

Harris similarly had reached out to Dr. Charles H. Thompson in a letter in which he dismissed Chevaillier as a "traveling whore" and compared the two Chevaillier women to characters from Shakespeare's *Henry IV.* Sarah Chevaillier was Mistress Quickly, the bawdy tavern owner who strove to maintain a respectable reputation, and Alzire was Doll Tearsheet, a prostitute in Quickly's employ.[39] Finally, Harris had used his financial clout to influence Thomas Larkin Thompson in publishing these letters of support in the *Sonoma Democrat* and suppressing Chevaillier's side of things.

The experience in Santa Rosa suddenly left Chevaillier on the defensive. Knowing that the *Sonoma Democrat* would not print a rebuttal, she and her mother penned open letters to the newspaper and printed them as a letter sheet. "My daughter was never insane, and her word is thoroughly reliable," wrote Sarah. "I never knew a clearer, more logical mind, which ever for one moment in her whole life, has been clouded." Alzire called Harris's mimeographs "cowardly and despicable." She insisted that her mental health background was not pertinent: "The truth or falsity of what I say is the only question at issue." Despite these personal attacks, she said that "I fear not the *final* result, however strongly the carnal forces of evil, deception, and ignorance are, for the moment, arrayed against the cause of Purity, Justice, Truth, and Liberty."[40]

Chevaillier had to recognize that moving the scandal to Santa Rosa had been a mistake. She now found herself arrayed against an array of wealthy, professional white men—doctors, Protestant ministers, businessmen, and newspaper editors—who personally vouched for Harris. As a woman, she lacked the cultural authority, social standing, and economic power to compete. Rather than indicting Harris, she found herself on trial. Prior to this turn, a few newspapers had questioned her motives by suggesting that she acted "for newspaper notoriety" rather than out of altruism and that she was "not the most reliable of persons."[41] Hearst's *Examiner* had scoffed that she "believed in all the 'isms,' except the one with a Harris before it."[42] Now, however, she found herself defending her sanity, her sexual history, and her womanly virtue. During the Phillips Brooks confirmation controversy the previous summer, newspapers had called her a "backbiting," ungrateful woman. What she faced now was far worse.

It was at this moment that the scandal took a turn that Chevaillier could not have predicted. As she left Santa Rosa in late February, a wildly colorful figure arrived in town to pay Harris a visit: an occult scientist, communist, and self-styled messiah named Cyrus Teed. This was their first meeting, but the two men had much in common, and they would become intertwined as "messiahs" and "cult leaders" in the public imagination.

Like Harris, Teed grew up in Utica, New York, during the Second Great Awakening. Teed was sixteen years younger than Harris, so it is unlikely the two men met, but it is possible that as a boy, Teed passed Harris on the bustling streets of Utica. After serving for the Union in the Civil War, Teed had become interested in homeopathic medicine, chemistry, and alchemy, conducting experiments in his own "electro-alchemical laboratory" in Utica. He sought an "occult or hidden principle" of medicine that would grant him "victory over death," an obsession he shared with Harris. And like Harris, Teed had his breakthrough: one night in 1869, using homeopathic batteries and gold dust, he "succeeded in transforming matter of one kind to its equivalent energy" and then back again. This alchemical breakthrough was accompanied by a spiritual one: his body was overtaken by a "gently oscillating ocean of magnetic and spiritual ecstasy" as his body transformed into "spirituous essence." He was visited by an "exquisite" Divine Mother who informed him, "thou art chosen to redeem the race," and returned to his body. Overcome by the "chasteness" of the goddess's virginity, Teed knew he must thenceforth reject "the old sensual proprium" and practice strict celibacy.[43]

After that breakthrough, Teed began gathering followers in a series of utopian communities in upstate New York and, beginning in 1886, Chicago. He taught that celibacy would allow Teed—the "Messenger, Messiah, anointed Savior"—and eventually the entire human race to "dematerialize" their gendered, corporal bodies and be reborn as immortal "man-woman beings."[44] He called this process of transformation "theocrasis."[45] His ideas drew on the writings of Emanuel Swedenborg, John Humphrey Noyes, Andrew Jackson Davis, and particularly Harris, whom Teed admired but regarded as too cautious, too reclusive, and too afraid of "the wrath of the public. He does not come to ultimates," wrote Teed in 1885. "He fears the consequences. I shall walk undaunted into the fiery flame."[46]

True to his word, Teed attracted plenty of hostile media attention for his messianic proclamations and for supposedly bilking money from wealthy patrons.[47] Now calling himself Koresh, a Hebrew word for Cyrus, he clashed with Christian Scientists in New York and mental healers in Chicago when he criticized their methods and commandeered their schools.[48] Newspapers roundly mocked his 1887 pronouncement that astronomers had it all wrong: the sun was actually at the center of the earth, Teed believed, and "we are on the inside of the sphere, not the outside."[49] Though widely discredited, the notion that the earth was "hollow and habitable within" had been promoted by several geographers during the early nineteenth century, most notably would-be explorer John Cleves Symmes Jr., who had tried to launch an expedition into the inside of the earth via "holes at the poles" he never found.[50]

In 1890, Teed had inadvertently helped create the new category of "cults" by giving it a name. In an interview with the *Chicago Daily Tribune*, Teed called his movement "a complete system of cult, universal in its scope." He used "cult" in its traditional meaning of religious veneration. The *Daily Tribune* ran "In Short, a 'Cult,'" as a mocking subhead in the article, one of the first uses of the word "cult" in its newly emerging, derogatory definition.[51] Other newspapers around the United States reprinted the article, helping to spread the new definition of the word.[52] A month later, the *Chicago Daily Tribune* complained of the "kaleidoscopic cults and crazes in this departing century."[53]

In 1890, Teed had established a branch of his movement in San Francisco, which went by various names: Home of the Koreshan Unity, Bureau of Equitable Commerce, Golden Gate Hippocampus, and Ecclesia. As they had in New York and Chicago, Teed's followers immediately garnered hostile press attention in San Francisco; the *Call* mocked them as "long-haired men and short-haired women."[54] This was a phrase long used to denigrate supporters of women's rights; by the 1890s, it was becoming a conservative, all-purpose label for reformers, academics, bohemians, and homosexuals.[55] As in the Brotherhood of the New Life, the celibacy Teed and his followers openly practiced was a challenge to marriage and procreation, especially for married women for whom a spiritual vow of celibacy disrupted a husband's legally enshrined right to have sex with his wife.

This exact issue had flared up in 1891 when several well-to-do San Francisco women had moved into the Home of the Koreshan Unity, much to the consternation of their husbands. "My conscience is clear though they do say I have 'deserted my family,'" one San Francisco woman told readers of Teed's journal, *The Flaming Sword*. "Cutting loose from old ties has been fraught with grief; but the *joy* I feel in being counted worthy to come up through sin and suffering to become a follower of this new Savior of the people is inexpressible."[56] Disgruntled husbands turned to the media to assert their marital rights. After his wife, Mary Mills, joined Teed's movement, wealthy geologist James Mills complained that Teed was "working the old confidence game of Harris, who so successfully duped the Oliphants out of thousands of dollars."[57] This was in August 1891, when Margaret Oliphant's *Memoir of the Life of Laurence Oliphant* was making headlines; by comparing Teed to Harris, Mills attempted to make use of Harris's newfound publicity to tar Teed with the same brush. Mills was also a former Swedenborgian minister, which may have made him especially suspicious of Harris.[58] Newspapers played up Teed's threat, running headlines such as "Wrecked by 'Koresh': A Family Broken Up." According to the *Examiner*, Mills's youngest daughter was so distraught by the departure of her mother that she "lost her reason" and had to be confined to an asylum.[59]

Things got worse for Teed in October 1891 when Royal O. Spear, director of the Home of Koreshan Unity, broke with Teed. In a lecture at Metropolitan Hall in San Francisco, Spear accused Teed of "duping all of his converts into giving him all their worldly possessions" as well as using his powers of "hypnotism" to "ruin many a woman." According to the *San Francisco Chronicle*, Spear's exposé was "incoherent and disjointed," lacking "names, dates, or any proof," but newspapers gleefully picked up on the story.[60] Writers insisted that Teed expressed "his sympathy for the ladies by hugging and kissing them"; according to the *Call*, he was "the most sensual looking man" in San Francisco.[61]

All of this was so similar to the subsequent Harris scandal that casual readers might be confused, even before Teed's visit to Fountaingrove, about the differences between the two men. As in the case of Harris, Teed's "hypnotic" powers, strange religious beliefs, and "false" claims of celibacy loomed as public threats to families, Christian marriage, and the safety of white women. And just as Harris was Orientalized in the public imagination, newspapers called Teed "fakir," misappropriating the term for an Islamic or Hindu holy man, and made reference to his "Eastern harem."[62] The Teed

PLATONIC INSTRUCTION.

Cyrus Teed embracing female followers; *Chicago Inter Ocean*, September 13, 1891.

scandal received considerably less press attention than the Harris one but played to similar cultural anxieties.

When Chevaillier launched her campaign against Harris, Teed was one of the few metaphysicians outside the religious mainstream who defended rather than attacked Harris. Rather than distancing himself from Harris, Teed empathized—and saw opportunity. In *The Flaming Sword*, Teed dismissed Chevaillier's charges as "the one-sided testimony of an adventuress, full of insinuations" but lacking evidence.[63] When Chevaillier wrote Teed a letter of rebuttal, insisting that "there is no malice in my heart towards Mr. H., tho' I believe him to be a scoundrel, an antichrist, a fallen Lucifer," Teed printed a lengthy reply. He explained that Harris was the leader of the "church of respiration," one of seven churches of "organic life and unity" necessary for the impending purification of humanity and end of corporeal death. Long inspired by Harris's writings, Teed now folded Harris's divine respiration into his own cosmology by naming it essential to Teed's impending theocrasis. Teed also attacked the morality of Chevaillier's informant Mr. X, writing, "If there is an abomination in earth it is this man."[64] It is unclear how Teed knew Mr. X was Manning or what he had heard about Manning's private life; nonetheless, Manning continued to be able to keep his name out of the papers while Chevaillier took the full brunt of public scrutiny.

Teed then published a letter from a woman from Santa Rosa who claimed to have visited Fountaingrove the previous summer during the Chevailliers' stay. This woman clearly had been reading Harris's mimeographs and borrowed many of their talking points: Chevaillier's "lower nature is leading her on to her ruin," she said, going on to repeat the rumor that Chevaillier had gone "insane" and sent to an asylum in Boston due to her unrequited love for Phillips Brooks. "I think her present symptoms look like a return of the old malady."[65] Once again, Harris's counterattacks against Chevaillier were making their way into print through indirect means.

As Chevaillier left Santa Rosa following her ill-advised lecture, Teed arrived. He came up from San Francisco, where he was overseeing the closure of the Home of Koreshan Unity and the transfer of his followers there to Chicago.[66] Teed must have known that paying a visit to Fountaingrove in the middle of the scandal would win him another round of media attention. Though he denounced the "heartless, infidel, politic, and merciless public press," Teed consistently gave interviews to reporters and seemed to revel in his notoriety.[67] In fact, just before his trip to Santa Rosa, Teed wrote an editorial for *The Flaming Sword* thanking the press for the "immense amount of gratuitous advertising" he was receiving, noting that "our growth accelerates proportionably to the exaggeration of the reports and the publicity given them."[68]

Sure enough, his visit to Fountaingrove immediately spawned reports that Harris and Teed had decided to merge their movements in a "spiritual and temporal combination." According to the *Chicago Daily Tribune*, Harris, his counterpart Lily Queen, and Teed "will now be three in one, with Teed as the third member of the firm."[69] Given that Harris openly discussed his erotic-spiritual relationship with Lily Queen, the notion of Teed joining them in a threesome carried connotations of both homosexuality and deviant free love run amok.

Furthermore, if Teed sent "a portion of his flock" to Fountaingrove, as the paper reported, it would mean a strengthening of Harris's movement and the public threat it represented. Rather than shrinking in the light of scandal, Harris's influence seemed to be expanding. Most of Teed's followers in San Francisco were "buxom, young and middle-aged women," according to the *Call*, so this would put more California women into direct moral peril.[70] But the threat was even bigger than California. According to news reports, Teed hoped to link together numerous "celibate" communities around the country, including the Economites of Pennsylvania and the Shakers of New York, into one confederacy co-led by Harris and Teed.[71] This kind of pooling of cash, lands, and resources would greatly magnify the reach of both men. As dangerous as they were thought be separately, together they represented nothing less than a nationwide threat to Christian morality and the institution of marriage.

The union was not to be, however. Back in San Francisco in late February, Teed told the *Chronicle* that though both his Koreshanity and the Brotherhood of the New Life endorsed celibacy, "their creeds were too divergent to permit any closer social union between the two." Teed added that "there have been lots of lies told" about Harris, "as there have been about me," but "there are no purer people in America" than those at Fountaingrove.[72] Ultimately, Harris and Teed were probably too alike, each convinced of their singular spiritual importance and committed to their unique theologies, to cooperate for very long. It is hard to imagine either man ceding authority to the other, and Harris certainly would have chafed at the idea that divine respiration was but a step toward Teed's theocrasis. Nevertheless, false media reports about their team up revealed broader anxieties about the potential coming together of "queer little societies" around the United States into a web of sexual and spiritual danger.[73] The threat was bigger than Harris, bigger than Teed—it lurked inside any community, any family, and any marriage.

9

Spring 1892

No More a Celibate

On March 3, readers who had been following the scandal woke to surprising news: Thomas Lake Harris and Jane Lee Waring had gotten married. A few days earlier, Harris and Waring had quietly married in Fountaingrove; the officiant was Harris's friend J. Avery Shepherd, the Episcopalian minister who had defended Harris's character a few days earlier. Kanaye Nagasawa had secretly driven Shepherd from Santa Rosa to Fountaingrove after asking him to acquire a marriage license. The twenty-five members of the Brotherhood of the New Life living at Fountaingrove gathered in Harris's famous library in Aestivossa for the ceremony. Nellie F. Buckley, a friend of the community though not a member, also attended and filed eyewitness reports for the *San Francisco Examiner* and *London Pall Mall Gazette*.

"Whilt thou have this woman?" asked Shepherd, to which Harris replied, "By the Divine Power I will."

When Shepherd read out "till death do us part," Harris paused before finally repeating the vow; as Buckley noted, "it will be remembered that Harris does not acknowledge the inevitability of death."[1]

Newspapers interpreted the wedding, coming as it did in the midst of Chevaillier's campaign, as a concession of defeat on the part of Harris. "No More a Celibate," trumpeted the *San Francisco Call*. "Old Fakir Harris Takes an Aged Lady for a Bride," laughed the *Los Angeles Times*. "Better Late Than Never," hooted the *Sacramento Record Union*. A Louisville paper dryly reported the event as "the leaders of a notorious communistic sect in California, have married after living in the same house thirty years."[2] In London, spiritualist Emma Hardinge Britten, who had dubbed him "Pope Harris" after the Mountain Cove debacle decades earlier, could not resist taking another opportunity to poke at Harris. In her journal *The Two Worlds,* she wondered, "What has become of his bi-sexual counterpart, his spirit-bride who issued from his side? Has she departed, or was she a myth?"[3]

Unholy Sensations. Joshua Paddison, Oxford University Press. © Oxford University Press 2025.
DOI: 10.1093/oso/9780197775325.003.0009

Newspapers gave Chevaillier credit for this turn of events. The heat of the scandal, commentators said, had made Harris afraid that the Knights Templar would expel him, and so he was taking "every means in his power" to defend himself against charges of sexual immorality.[4] The *San Francisco Chronicle* insisted that Harris wed in order to "put a stop to the tongue of scandal that has been put in motion by his enemies."[5]

The coverage of the Harris-Waring wedding took place within a larger conversation about marriage going on in the 1890s. Over the course of the nineteenth century, Americans had taken an increasingly sentimental view of marriage, now conceiving it above all else as an expression of a couple's feelings of romantic love for each other. By the 1890s, however, divorce rates were spiking, leading to widespread concerns that American marriage was in crisis and so too was American Christian morality.[6] California's divorce law allowed a woman to file for divorce on grounds of adultery, desertion, cruelty, impotence, intemperance, conviction of a felony, and failure of financial support.[7] More liberal than New York and many other states, this law prompted complaints by ministers and politicians who complained in the early 1890s about California's "divorce craze."[8] At the same time, public concern about so-called contract marriages—informal and common-law marriages—was also cresting. This would culminate in a revision of California law in 1895 requiring that weddings be "licensed, solemnized, authenticated, and recorded."[9] Marriage, understood as an expression of romantic heterosexual love, seemed to be losing its foundational place in American society.

In this context, the Harris-Waring wedding seemed a mockery of companionate marriage and one more example of the institution's fragility. The union seemed to spring not from love but from Harris's need to counter accusations of sexual impropriety. It was nothing more than "a matter of form and a concession to the prejudices of California society," according to the *Chronicle*. Newspapers presented the wedding as fraudulent, mere cover for Harris's perverse immorality. The fact that Harris had Shepherd, an Episcopalian minister, officiate and file a California marriage license made the wedding all the more provocative, suggesting that ministers and licenses were not enough to protect marriage from schemers like Harris.

Though Waring was sixty-four years old, newspapers emphasized her youth and beauty to better fit the narrative of Harris's danger to young white women. Waring "looks and dresses as though she were not more than forty," reported the *Chronicle*. The *Call* agreed that she "does not look more than forty," adding that she had turned $60,000 over to Harris upon joining the

Brotherhood in the 1860s. Both newspapers printed illustrations of Waring that showed her with an unlined face, hair stylishly piled atop her head, of indeterminate age. (In contrast, the *Examiner*, which ran Buckley's sympathetic account of the wedding, published an illustration of Waring in profile with a double chin and wrinkles that made her look much older.) In Chevaillier's accounts, she had portrayed Waring as a facilitator to Harris's schemes rather than as one of his victims, but press coverage of the wedding presented her as one more "dupe of this impudent fakir."[10]

Nellie F. Buckley's accounts included what was perhaps an even bigger bombshell, overlooked by other newspapers: the newly married Mr. and Mrs. Harris had left California. The day after the wedding, on the morning of Sunday, February 28, the two had boarded a Southern Pacific train car headed, according to Buckley, "presumably to New Orleans, though it is not definitely known." The wedding was Harris's attempt to protect Waring's reputation, Buckley said, so that the two could travel together as man and wife without arousing further scandal. "Because of the recent cruel accusations to which Miss Waring had been subjected he felt it to be the right thing in taking her with him to give her the protection of his name," wrote Buckley. The wedding was intended to be a protection of Waring's womanly virtue, the exact opposite of how newspapers presented it. As radical as Harris's spiritual-sexual views may have been, in this moment of crisis he turned to the legitimacy offered by a minister- and state-sponsored marriage to shield the two of them as they traveled together.

Why did Harris decide to leave Fountaingrove at this moment? He had just used his financial clout and personal connections to marshal the elite men of Santa Rosa to his defense, much to Chevaillier's frustration. However, Harris knew that Chevaillier was not about to stop her campaign despite his best efforts of self-defense. She had already met with California's governor, the Japanese consul, and the Grand Masonic Lodge of California, and she vowed to go to the U.S. postmaster general, U.S. Congress, and even the president. The ceaseless barrage of negative media reports, begun the previous summer in the wake of Margaret Oliphant's *Memoir of the Life of Laurence Oliphant* and escalating with Chevaillier's campaign, had to be taking a toll on Harris's well-being. According to Buckley, Harris left Fountaingrove in search of "a change of air and scene, as a restorative to the Prophet's overstrained nervous system, which, notwithstanding 'the divine respiration,' seems to have experienced a shock by recent calumnious articles."

Mrs. Jane Lee Waring.

Jane Lee Waring Harris, *San Francisco Chronicle*, March 4, 1892.

MISS JANE WARING.
[*From a sketch by an "Examiner" staff artist.*]

Jane Lee Waring Harris, *San Francisco Examiner*, March 4, 1892.

Harris had also begun to fear for his personal safety. According to another friend of Fountaingrove, "Harris became very fearful of being mobbed while in Santa Rosa" following Chevaillier's "scorching lecture against him."[11] Jane Lee Waring Harris, writing while in exile to Richard McCully, a member of the Brotherhood in Glasgow, explained that "the Oliphant Chevaillier storm" of the previous year, coming as it did after Harris's discovery of eternal youth, had surprised and alarmed Harris. "We left home at a few hours notice making a forced march against or rather to foil another impending attack," she explained. "The strain would have been too great going out into the world as marked characters, bearing our former relations, therefore Mr. Harris gave me his name, it being needful for me to travel with him." She assured McCully that the marriage changed nothing: "Father (Mr. Harris) & his Lily stand *alone* the same as ever in their pivotal service and I am the same as ever their humble little handmaiden."[12]

The *San Francisco Call* reported that members of the "Harris cult" were feeling shocked and betrayed by the wedding; if this was true, the new Mrs. Harris's letter to McCully was a way to reassure him that Harris's primacy and spiritual-sexual union with Lily Queen were unchanged. In a letter to Arthur Cuthbert, Jane acknowledged, "I had feared the marriage might seem a stumbling block to many." However, "Father stands alone, in his pivotal place as much as ever," she assured him. Her "holding the representation wifely position in externals," she said, had "become a necessity recognized by the outside world."[13] Of course, Harris had been married twice before, a fact that most newspapers neglected to mention.

Harris predictably offered a more mystical explanation of the marriage and their flight from California. He told McCully that in late January 1892 he had achieved another spiritual breakthrough and no longer had to "bind" evil spirits via divine respiration as he had done the previous forty years. However, this breakthrough had required him to draw spiritual energy from Waring's "organism breaking the column of resistance that passed into her organism, and leading her into the advanced position." She now took, he said, "a position by my side, to which, by the same ordering, there has been given the external legal sanction."[14]

The morning of the wedding, Harris sold the last two parcels of land he still held in his own name in Sonoma County to two of his followers for $11,500.[15] He now no longer owned any property in California. This pointed to another possible reason he legally married Jane Lee Waring—it gave him the ability to reconcentrate control over Fountaingrove lands by putting them in her name. This is exactly what would happen a year later—the colonists would sell all the Fountaingrove lands to Jane Lee Waring Harris in 1893, giving Thomas Lake Harris de facto control but still shielding him from accusations that he was enriching himself through real estate purchases.[16]

Flush with $11,500 in cash, the new couple headed for New Orleans, but metaphysical forces intervened. In a letter to Nagasawa, Jane reconstructed their harried trip. The couple took the Southern Pacific line toward Los Angeles but, "a feeling of great anxiety as if of warning made us feel that there was a danger there to be avoided so we got off at Bakersfield." They stayed there overnight and left the next morning for Albuquerque, "there to rest, and for Father to see which way we should go." In New Mexico, Harris experienced a new vision: "He saw an utter breaking up in the occult condition of people in the States and was told to leave the country without delay." They then went by train to Philadelphia and on to New York, where they boarded a steamship bound for Southampton, England. However, they found too much occult activity occurring in England, and so "we fled to Wales as was the case in 1867."[17] In this time of trouble, Harris had retraced his steps from decades earlier, ending up in the village of Old Colwyn in northern Wales.

Fearing an onrush of reporters, the Harrises kept their presence in Wales secret from everyone except a few trusted followers, including Nagasawa, Cuthbert, and McCully. "The long strain of the past months of persecution, with all its consequent extra labor, and the whirl of our journey from Fountaingrove to this place, leave me with but little power to do anything but sleep," Jane told Cuthbert.[18] However, soon Harris was working on a new book. "We are living very quietly, rarely leaving our rooms, for the concentration has to be continuous," Jane reported.[19] They remained vigilant against external threats, on the lookout for "traitors and betrayers turning up at any time."[20] Harris had no plans to return to the United States any time soon: "The prospect (and this is a secret)," Jane told Cuthbert, "is that he will remain in this country a long time, this being the intellectual center of the earth."[21]

Back in Oakland, Chevaillier had to feel vindicated by this sudden turn of events. Her campaign had driven Harris from Fountaingrove and, though she did not know it yet, from the United States entirely. But due to Harris's secrecy, she had no idea where he was or how long he would stay there; the *Sonoma Democrat* incorrectly reported on March 5 that Harris had only left for "a brief visit in the southern part of the state."[22] The only U.S. paper that reported that Harris was headed out of the state was the *Examiner,* which had persistently been hostile to Chevaillier when not ignoring her; she had good reason to doubt the veracity of its report. And so the campaign continued.

Beyond simply trying to thwart Harris, Chevaillier was at this point struggling to defend her good name against his counterattacks. The public questioning of her sanity must have especially galled her, given her history of reform work with the mentally ill. Her work in the field of asylum reform had sprung from her concern for those society deemed insane—she had endeavored to improve their treatment and living conditions, but at no point had she questioned the validity of labels like "sane" and "insane." She was now learning how easily someone, especially a woman writing and lecturing about sexual immorality, could be labeled insane, undermining her accusations about Harris as well as her reputation and ability to make a living as a mental healer.

In early March, she distributed a new letter sheet containing a statement from Dr. Henry A. Hartt, the medical director of the Columbian Institute in New York, attesting to her sanity. He said that he had known her twenty-one years and that the "charge of insanity against her" made him think of Abraham Lincoln's remark regarding General Ulysses S. Grant's drunkenness: "I wish that all my generals would partake of his whiskey." Hartt concluded, "It would be well if the mind of every woman in the land were 'touched' with an inspiration like that which actuates her."[23] Though this was not quite the ringing endorsement of her sanity that Chevaillier might have wanted, at least it came from a well-respected New York doctor. In the court of public opinion, the voices of elite white men carried so much more weight than all other voices that Chevaillier felt she had to line up her own doctor to counter the Santa Rosa doctor Harris had on his side.

The letter sheet also contained a letter by Chevaillier to John S. Weller's *New Church Independent,* which was now being filled with pro- and anti-Harris statements by Swedenborgians and others. Harris had printed portions of the journal's February issue and distributed them in Santa Rosa prior to Chevaillier's talk there, infuriating her and her mother. Chevaillier was shocked that Weller, a lifelong Swedenborgian, would question her motives considering that Manning—whom she still did not name—had shown Weller his affidavits years prior. "Surely no woman would select so distasteful a task, as this *exposé,* and which only conviction of Duty to God and man could have induced me to undertake," she informed Weller. "No one who knows me, can question my word. I am too strong morally for the temptation to lie." She had too much belief, she said, in Revelation

21:27: "*Whosoever maketh a lie, shall not be written in the Lamb's Book of Life.*" Though Chevaillier had left behind traditional Christianity many years before for a more metaphysical path, she still saw herself as a Christian broadly defined and could quote the Bible to defend her honor.[24]

Chevaillier's letter made a passing reference to Harris's marriage, the only statement she made on the matter. She referred to Waring as "now most properly Mrs. Harris, the materialized human organism through whom '*Mrs. Lily Crysanthia Harris*' [manifests], whom Mr. Harris has asserted for years is his counterpart and true and only wife."[25] It is telling that Chevaillier made reference to "Crysanthia," a misspelling of "Chrysanthea," the name Harris had given Lily Queen in an obscure 1876 book printed in Brocton; Chevaillier had clearly been deeply reading his oeuvre.[26] By assuming that Lily Queen now "materialized" within the body of Jane Lee Waring, Chevaillier joined the newspapers in seeing the wedding as a further sign of Harris's hypocrisy. Sex necessarily occurred within a marriage, according to this line of thought, so Harris marrying Waring was a sign that he had never truly been celibate.

In the *New Church Independent*, Weller printed Chevaillier's letter and one by her mother defending her daughter's sanity but followed them with a missive written by a Swedenborgian Texas lawyer and judge named Thomas Nugent who heaped further scorn on Chevaillier. He called her an "erratic young woman" whose writings were "superficial, illogical, utterly wanting in the common elements of sound sense and consistency," betraying "a most unfortunate spirit." Nugent found it preposterous to think that Harris could hide gross sexual immorality for forty years "so successfully, that even now not a single *act* of immorality can be proven against him."[27] As had happened in Santa Rosa, a professional white man was publicly vouching for Harris and attacking not just Chevaillier's evidence but also her rationality and personal character.

Between Chevaillier's ongoing campaign, Cyrus Teed's visit to Fountaingrove, and now the unlikely wedding, press coverage of Harris had reached a thunderous climax. "No one on two continents is more talked of by mouth or pen," commented a writer for the *Boston Globe*, "than Thomas Lake Harris."[28] To capitalize on all this press, Margaret Oliphant's London publishers released a new edition of *Memoir of the Life of Laurence Oliphant*, which had begun so much public scrutiny of Harris the previous summer. In a new preface, Margaret Oliphant took credit for having "lighted up lanterns everywhere" on Harris and his activities. In reference to Chevaillier's campaign, she said, "My table is covered with American papers" giving sensational details of "his spiritual despotism." Oliphant had written a supportive private letter to Chevaillier at the beginning of the scandal, informing her that Harris had threatened Laurence shortly before his death with the words, "*I killed Alice for her rebellion and I will also kill you.*"[29] But just as in her *Memoir,* Oliphant steered clear of any hint of sex in the new preface. She instead focused on Harris's "luxurious seclusion" and "fairy tale" claims of restored youth. Her overall tone was one of self-satisfaction for having exposed the "Magician in California" as a public threat to naïve followers like her dead cousin Laurence.[30]

As for Cyrus Teed, he was back in Chicago playing up his meeting with Harris at Fountaingrove. Teed told the Chicago press that Harris had "endorsed my doctrine"—a claim that seems unlikely to be true, considering Harris's personality—but acknowledged that the two communities had not entered into a confederacy.[31] Teed had returned from California accompanied by a "young heiress," reportedly worth $200,000, and her two children, evidence of another broken marriage.[32]

Unlike Harris, Teed had long courted public attention, giving frequent interviews to newspapers and publishing *The Flaming Sword*, which his followers distributed on the streets of Chicago. He was now learning the downside of this media attention, however, as he attempted to buy a mansion in Chicago's Washington Heights neighborhood to make room for the members of his San Francisco commune who were headed east. In response, the largely German and Irish immigrant residents of Washington Heights organized a vigilance committee and held a mass meeting in opposition to Teed. They swore to tar and feather him, declaring that "even lynching would be far too merciful."[33] Teed began to receive death threats, and, a few weeks later, someone planted a bomb outside his residence.[34] Teed also began to face a series of "alienation of affection" lawsuits by husbands accusing him of stealing away their wives.[35]

All of this was eerily reminiscent of what was happening to Harris in California. At the same moment that threats of mob violence swirled around Fountaingrove, Teed faced his own threats; just as the San Francisco papers competed to denounce Harris, Chicago's *Tribune, Times,* and *Inter Ocean* were outdoing each other with sensationalized articles about Teed's "hypnotic" powers over women. Newspapers frequently compared the two figures—mockingly called "self-styled messiahs" and "fakirs"—and debated who had the stronger powers of influence over their hapless followers.[36] The *San Francisco Argonaut* joked that Harris provided the "oldest and richest sisters" at Fountaingrove with male mates "mercifully endowed with virile youth and abounding good looks," while Teed "labored long with us in the same beneficent direction, but recently departed for Chicago with his women and boodle."[37]

Alongside Harris and Teed, newspapers often mentioned two other "modern messiahs" also making headlines: George Jacob Schweinfurth and "Prince" Michael Mills. Schweinfurth was a former Methodist minister who ran what one newspaper termed a "high religious cult" near Rockford, Illinois, called the Church Triumphant. Schweinfurth claimed to be "the perfect man and also God," Jesus Christ reborn in human flesh, able to "raise the dead, cure disease, and do all the miraculous things which I accomplished when I was on earth before."[38] In Detroit, "Prince" Mills led an American branch of the British Christian Israelite movement dedicated to triggering the apocalypse by gathering together 144,000 descendants of the lost Ten Tribes of Israel mentioned in the Old Testament. Mills's mostly female group of followers regarded him as a healer, a prophet, and an "inspired being," incapable of sin. Like Harris and Teed, both men were facing intense public scrutiny in spring 1892 for their "hypnotic powers" and "immoral influence" over women. Like Teed, Schweinfurth faced alienation of affection lawsuits and a steady stream of newspaper exposés that mocked the women in his colony who insisted that their children had been fathered by the Holy Ghost rather than by Schweinfurth.[39] Meanwhile, Mills was arrested for adultery, lewd cohabitation, and carnal knowledge of a fifteen-year-old girl, ultimately resulting in a five-year prison sentence.[40]

Far from isolated singularities, men like Harris, Teed, Schweinfurth, and Mills seemed to represent a growing threat. Complained the *Detroit Journal*, "It is getting so every state of any size has its messiah."[41] Overlooking the four men's many differences of theology and practices, newspapers lumped them together as representatives of a rampant "Messiah-craze" that revealed something troubling about the United States as a whole. Too many Americans—"a certain class of disordered intellects"—were falling for these "frauds."[42] The *Boston Globe* opined, "so many messiahs have appeared with the past few years their numbers almost constitute a new profession."[43] Americans' "infinite gullibility" was to blame, as well as the liberality of the nation's laws permitting a too-free expression of religion. "In this free and enlightened age the individual has a recognized right to believe any absurdity, no matter how great, and even to teach it," lamented the *Chicago Tribune*. These messiahs needed to be stopped, their "vast social evil" curbed one way or another, to protect Americans from their own weaknesses.[44]

Newspaper illustrations of Schweinfurth and Mills portrayed them with wild, thick beards, creating a visual parallel to the bearded faces of Harris and Teed.[45] During the mid-nineteenth century, beards had been popular among American men of all social classes, from clergymen to presidents, as a marker of manly vigor and virtue. By the 1890s, however, beard growing was on the decline as youthful, clean-shaven faces—considered "hygienic" and "modern"—were becoming the new masculine ideal.[46] Beards—especially the long beards favored by Harris and the other "messiahs"—now seemed unruly and a sign of deceitful character. In terms of religion, long beards were particularly associated with Jews, Eastern Orthodox Christians, Muslims, Sikhs, and Hindu gurus, all racialized figures outside the white Protestant mainstream. Newspaper accounts often made mention of Harris's "full black and grey beard"; one British paper said he had "the nose of a Moses and the beard of an Aaron."[47] Chevaillier likewise had described his "long grey beard."[48] Teed had actually shaved off his beard just before visiting San Francisco, perhaps to avoid the increasingly negative connotations of facial hair, but for the other three "messiahs," long beards continued to mark them visually as rebellious, unkempt, and out of step with Protestant masculine norms.[49]

Several newspapers likened the four so-called messiahs to another recent "Messiah-craze"—the Ghost Dance, a religious movement among western Native American groups that had dominated headlines in the fall of 1890. Newspapers had castigated Wovoka, Sitting Bull, and other "red messiahs" for spreading "deviltry" and "strange superstition" and for supposedly planning to "wipe out the whites."[50] These kinds of articles were so common that by 1892, the term "messiah" had become racialized from its association with the Ghost Dance, just as how "prophet" was racialized from its long association with Muhammad.[51]

Many articles discussing Harris, Teed, Schweinfurth, and Mills made this racialization clear by comparing the four men to "Indian messiahs" and calling for the same violent treatment the Lakota Ghost Dancers had received at Wounded Knee Creek in 1890, when the U.S. Army massacred nearly three hundred Lakotas. "When painted savages are deluded by some wandering mountebank, calling himself the messiah, into turbulence and insurrection the superior whites scornfully pronounce them mad, and mow them down with Gatling guns," pointed out a writer for Chicago's *Progressive*

GEORGE JACOB SCHWEINFURTH, THE FALSE CHRIST.

George Jacob Schweinfurth, *Chicago Tribune*, May 8, 1892.

Thinker, a spiritualist newspaper. The writer wondered why "the spectacle of white women yielding up that which is dearer to womankind than life, merely to follow the fortunes of some canting hypocrite and blasphemous rogue" spurred no such response by the U.S. government.[52] The *Oregonian* agreed, recalling that during the Ghost Dance, "we called them miserably ignorant, superstitious, barbarous, and a dozen other adjectives," yet these

PRINCE MICHAEL.

"Prince" Michael Mills, *Louisville Courier*, June 18, 1891.

"white messiahs" were permitted to remain "outside the penitentiary walls" where they belonged.[53]

Hiding out in Wales, Harris likely did not see these articles linking him to Teed, Schweinfurth, and Mills, but the threats of mob violence and legal troubles those men were facing reveal what might have happened to Harris had he not left Fountaingrove. Given the intensity of Chevaillier's campaign, and his own international notoriety, which dwarfed that of the other "white messiahs," it had probably been a matter of time before he faced an investigation or arrest warrant. "Open and notorious cohabitation" was against the law in California, as was adultery, abortion, and the seduction of unmarried women, any of which Harris could have plausibly been charged with.[54] Working in his favor was the fact that Chevaillier could make no eyewitness charges against him that would stand up in a court of law, and no ex-members of the Brotherhood came forward during her campaign to accuse Harris of a specific crime. No husbands said that he alienated the affections of their wives, as they said of Teed and Schweinfurth; no one from within Fountaingrove accused him of a sex crime, as had happened to Mills. But the declining fortunes of these other "messiahs" showed how scathing media attention could lead to real-world ramifications, including arrests and violence.

In fact, this looming threat over Fountaingrove materialized on June 2 when a massive fire destroyed the colony's magnificent three-story wine production building. The fire started in the brick building's wooden belfry, and it quickly turned the building into a "furious cyclone," bursting the casks holding thousands of gallons of wine inside. "Streams of burning brandy are running all over the place," reported the *San Francisco Chronicle*, presenting a "magnificent sight from Santa Rosa."[55] When Nagasawa and the other colonists attempted to use Fountaingrove's water hydrants, connected by pipes to a nearby spring, they discovered that the force of the water supply was mysteriously too low to be useful. "If there was any suspicion of incendiarism, this fact would give it color," noted the *Sonoma Democrat*.[56] By the next day, the wine building had been reduced to "a few shattered and scarred walls and a labyrinth of iron hoops, pipes, twisted machinery, and tangled iron roofing."[57] The financial loss was at least $100,000. "The Primate may now exercise his occult powers in discovering who set fire to the place," joked the *Chronicle*. The paper saw the fire as a natural result of the scandal that had begun in its pages six months earlier: "Incendiarism in such a community as the Brotherhood of the New Life shows dangerous discontent."[58]

Informed of the fire by cablegram, Harris "takes it very calmly," Jane reported in a letter to Cuthbert. The couple was grateful that no one at Fountaingrove had been hurt, especially Nagasawa, who was "so daring and so keenly alive to his responsibilities in Father's absence that he scarce thinks of himself." Publicly, colonists at Fountaingrove said they doubted the fire was the work of an arsonist, but privately they were not so sure. Jane could not help but wonder how it had happened given the precautions they had taken against fire. "How it could have got beyond saving I do not see except through incendiaries in the night, there was so little wood work," she wrote.

Her thoughts immediately went to a possible culprit: "Chevaillier said to Father, during the scene at his house when she got angry at not being invited to his table, 'if you put upon me I can burn your house down.'"[59] Chevaillier's burning indignation had become a literal firestorm.

Harris prayed on the matter and received a comforting message from God instructing him to "dismiss all sense of loss, all feeling of regret, and all anxiety." After all, the wine at Fountaingrove was no ordinary wine, for it had been blessed by Lily Queen and it was where she "stored her fluids." The fire had released those heavenly fluids, and they were now "being drawn vitally through atmospheric diffusions into the bodies of many people."[60]

Nonetheless, Harris began considering a plan to sell off Fountaingrove and move the Brotherhood to a new frontier: Mexico. A group of American socialists had founded a utopian colony at Topolobampo Bay on the west coast of Mexico in 1886, and Harris had been keenly watching their progress. In February 1892, during the height of the scandal, Harris had found time to send a check for $200 to the colonists there along with a note praising the "brave good men and women who are toiling there at Topolobampo." Mexico, he said, was about to become a crucial metaphysical location due to the "advance of energies focalizing, from the world of other causes, upon the region occupied by the colony, evolution there of a state of fraternal and heroic men."[61]

Alongside Harris's occult interests in Mexico, he knew that leaving the United States in this time of trouble offered practical benefits. Harris was enjoying the relative anonymity Wales provided, where—according to Jane—"no one has any idea of who Father is."[62] Mexico would provide even greater anonymity, as well as inexpensive land and the potential help of Mexico's government, which under President Porfirio Díaz was encouraging American immigration and business investment.[63] Harris liked the idea of buying a "great landed property in Mexico in a supremely healthy climate."[64] The Mormons had founded several colonies in Chihuahua and Sonora in the mid-1880s to escape persecution by the U.S. government; similarly, Harris imagined a Topolobampo colony as a potential "asylum where our dear people, those at Fountaingrove as well as elsewhere, may have a safe home free from the calamities and danger that must ensue." The United States was no longer safe for the Brotherhood, but Mexico could be a "gathering place for our scattered people, who are now in the bondage of the world's adverse and ruinous conditions." Harris told Cuthbert, "I see no permanent safety anywhere else."[65]

Jane acknowledged that, like her wedding to Harris, this Mexico plan might look to outsiders like a sign of defeat. "The *Chronicle* and Chevaillier will think they have driven us out," she told Cuthbert. "If they have, they will soon see that they have done us a good turn while their aim was to destroy us."[66] Like the fire, which Harris had decided was "no calamity," the Chevaillier scandal had resulted in a chance for a glorious future in Mexico "if each at home holds faithful through the crises and thus supports me and the onward movement."[67]

Meanwhile, only the inner circle knew that Harris and his new bride were in Wales. They had disappeared "utterly from public gaze," according to the *San Francisco Call.* Some people speculated, wildly, that Harris had gone to Asia to take control of a group of Theosophists who had "left the Blavatsky fold and gone over to him." Others thought he was somewhere in Europe or that he was dead, his recent claims to eternal youth notwithstanding.[68] By June, Chevaillier was also making plans to leave California. She had been waging the campaign against Harris for six months by this point, as well as dealing with the counterattacks made by him and his supporters, which had dripped their way into the media. She had lost her magazine and her mental-healing practice in Oakland had failed to prosper, perhaps due to what one newspaper termed the "cheap notoriety" she had gained from the scandal.[69] With Harris gone indefinitely, she and her mother had decided to go back to Boston.

On her way back east, Chevaillier stopped in Chicago where she met with John S. Weller, editor of the *New Church Independent.* Weller was a second-generation Swedenborgian who, unlike most members of his church, had continued to keep an open mind about Harris over the years. During the past six months, his journal had featured vigorous back-and-forth debate about Harris and Chevaillier. In the July issue, his final word on the subject, Weller devoted a full forty pages to the scandal, including his personal interview of Chevaillier. He began the section with a photograph of her, which had been the basis of her portrait in the original *San Francisco Chronicle* exposé article. As in the *Chronicle*'s illustration, she is in profile, her eyes bright and determined, wearing white. Unlike some female reformers such as Elizabeth Cady Stanton, who rejected conventional beauty standards for women, Chevaillier always took care to present herself as attractive, something oft-noted in sympathetic news articles.[70]

Weller also included a photograph of Harris in the issue so as to provide readers with "portraits of the leading actor and actress" in the scandal.

Miss A. A. Chevaillier.

Alzire Chevaillier, *Chicago New Church Independent*, July 1892.

THOMAS LAKE HARRIS.

Thomas Lake Harris, *Chicago New Church Independent*, July 1892.

In the photo, Harris is seated, wearing a black suit; several rings attached to a gold chain dangling against his chest, suggesting both wealth and arcane power. He appears dignified and utterly calm, the master of his world. Weller seemed to delight in the hubbub, filling the "Harris-Chevaillier number" with reprinted newspaper articles and letters written by most of the major players: Chevaillier, Harris, Laurence Oliphant, Arthur Cuthbert, Dr. Charles H. Thompson, William Dean Howells, John Pulsford, and others. Kickstarted by a Swedenborgian in Alfred W. Manning, it was fitting that the Chevaillier scandal ended in a Swedenborgian journal run by Weller.

The most surprising piece came from Laurence Oliphant, who fittingly weighed in on the scandal from beyond the grave. Weller had been holding on to a letter written to him by Oliphant in 1885 in response to the "Spiritist Spider" hit piece on Harris published in the *Chronicle* that year. The letter was the first and only statement by Oliphant regarding sexual relations within Harris's colonies that surfaced during the scandal. Oliphant said that the "charges contained in the *San Francisco Chronicle* are much exaggerated, and in some respects quite incorrect." He was writing about the 1885 *Chronicle* article but eerily seemed to be addressing Chevaillier's recent pieces in that same newspaper. The members of the Brotherhood, Oliphant said, were "actuated throughout by the purest and highest of motives, and are in no way open to the gross charges in which they are included." As for Harris, Oliphant insisted that evil spirits had "taken possession" of his former mentor, turning Harris into "a fearfully infested and most dangerous medium for a debased and powerful class of spirits." Regarding the sexual "impropriety" that Harris was accused of, Oliphant hinted that "in certain matters this is not exaggerated."[71] What exactly that meant, he failed to say.

Another new letter in the *New Church Independent* section was from a Swedenborgian in Los Angeles who claimed to know someone who had spent nine years at Fountaingrove, where he lived like "a common *ranchman* on a California *farm,* but he had his *counterpart* and indulged in the Edenic baths." The Swedenborgian resuscitated old stories about Harris's Mountain Cove colony and claimed that, ever since that failed venture, Harris had been using "his abilities to secure financial and sensual pleasures for his own especial use."[72]

The penultimate piece was Weller's emotional conversation with Chevaillier in Chicago. She reiterated that she had seen nothing impure with her own eyes at Fountaingrove. "I left there reluctantly (with mamma), for I *did* love and worship him as a father," she admitted. "Papa having died in my early childhood, I have so craved a father's love and a father's hand to lead me in the dark." This revealing statement helps explain the fury of her campaign; she felt personally betrayed by Harris, not only in his role as a spiritual mentor but also as a father figure she said she loved. She had similarly turned against her former father figure Phillips Brooks, trying to block his ascension to bishop of Massachusetts, when he had let her down by publicly denying his unorthodox beliefs. Harris maintained that Chevaillier had wanted to seduce him, but that was surely a deliberate misreading of the intensity of her emotions—she had wanted an intimate relationship with him, a father-daughter relationship. When Manning approached her with his evidence, she experienced it as a personal betrayal by Harris that had launched her crusade.

In regard to her campaign, now reaching its close, she insisted, "I do not regret what I have done, however much Mr. H. may attempt to defame my character. It will result in good, and *he* cannot harm me while I hold my Father's hand—He will protect and care for His child." God the Father would never let her down, she said, even if earthly fathers did. "*Mr. Harris knows I am pure;* and he knows how I shrank back from all allusions of a sensuous nature," she told Weller. "I never was drawn to gentlemen except on an intellectual plane." This last statement was remarkable for its candor, considering the overwhelming heteronormative sexual culture of the United States where women were expected to romantically if not sexually desire men. Chevaillier's unmarried status had always made her social position more vulnerable, allowing critics to dismiss her as an "adventuress" or a "crazy old maid."[73] But here, she put forward her lack of sexual and romantic interest in men as proof of her purity. Throughout the campaign, she had emphasized Harris's "hypnotic" powers over women, which violated their ability to consent to everything from counterpartal sex to manual labor. By saying that she was never "drawn to gentlemen," she insisted on her own self-determination and ability to control her own romantic and sexual life, societal expectations be damned.

After meeting her, Weller was impressed by Chevaillier's "genius, rare intellectual culture," as well as her "physical charms." But he still mockingly called her the "Joan of Arc in this siege" and "our little Nemesis," a reference to the Greek goddess of retribution. He no longer doubted her sincerity, as he had done earlier in the scandal, but he still looked down on her methods, wondering, "Is it anything but Christian or Christ-like, to sit in judgment upon [Harris's] *reported* errors, and sins, and parade them before the public?" Weller recommended that, going forward, Chevaillier should focus on "a higher Christian work in her philanthropic, charitable, and healing spheres of activity, than in this relentless persecution and martyrizing crusade."[74] In fact, Chevaillier was making plans to do just that, in the form of a new magazine tentatively titled *The Comforter.* She hoped to bring to the magazine her "ripened experience" as well as "eighteen months of special occult and mystical study of the deepest hidden treasures of truth." Her year in California had certainly not gone as planned, but she vowed to take what she had learned from the experience to further her life's goal: "The cultivation of the kingdom of heaven upon earth."[75]

Weller gave the last word to Harris, publishing a recent letter Harris had written him before he left California for Europe. Harris once again played it both ways, saying that he would "make no reply" to Chevaillier's charges before proceeding to call them "simply absurd," "preposterous," "the effusions of battled greed and insane lubricity," and "the artifices of an iniquitous conspiracy." Harris ended his letter by likening himself to Emanuel Swedenborg, recalling that, during Swedenborg's celestial travels, the Swedish mystic had learned that devils in hell were "circulating extravagant slanders" against him. "For the last thirty or forty years I have been followed, as Swedenborg was, by a stream of diabolical insinuations," Harris concluded, "and I expect this to go on till the Kingdom of God has introduced divine order into the debauched and perishing natural society." Harris was Swedenborg, Chevaillier was a devil, and the only thing that would stop the accusations against him was Armageddon.[76]

10

January 1896

The Victim of an Ungodly System

On January 2, 1896, a fifteen-year-old girl named Mary died at Fountaingrove. This tragedy probably would have gone unnoticed by the wider public were it not for the fact that Mary was the granddaughter of Thomas Lake Harris. As such, Mary Harris's short life and death became fodder for rumors, speculation, and conspiracy theories, all of which played out in the media. Mary's death seemed proof of everything Alzire Chevaillier had said during the scandal a few years earlier—Fountaingrove was a ruinous place for California's young white women.

Mary's father was Thomas Lake Harris Jr., the younger of the two sons Harris had with Mary Van Arnum in the late 1840s. Thomas Jr. had lived at the Brocton colony in its early years, but by the 1890s he had been estranged from his father for decades. He had moved to Montana, got married, and had two daughters, Mary and her younger sister Pearl. After Thomas Jr.'s wife died, he sent Mary and Pearl to live with admirers of his father in Oakland, where the girls attended Lincoln Elementary School. By 1893, the two sisters had moved to Fountaingrove, becoming by far the youngest colonists there. Mary disliked life in the colony and attempted to kill herself in 1895 by throwing herself out of a second-story window of the Familistery. She recovered but continued to show signs of depression, to the point that in late December 1895, Kanaye Nagasawa and others at Fountaingrove feared she would again attempt to take her own life. According to Nagasawa's statement, on the evening of January 2, they heard screaming coming from Mary's room. "We found her stretched out on a chair with her arms above her head, writhing in agony," Nagasawa told the *San Francisco Chronicle*. "She said she had taken strychnine but only a little in order to scare us." She died less than an hour later. Nagasawa added that Mary drank the strychnine "while in one of her fits of temporary insanity."[1]

Dr. Charles H. Thompson, the Santa Rosa physician who had vouched for Harris in 1892 after Chevaillier's lecture, paid a visit to Fountaingrove

Unholy Sensations. Joshua Paddison, Oxford University Press. © Oxford University Press 2025.
DOI: 10.1093/oso/9780197775325.003.0010

as did the Sonoma County coroner, who declared Mary dead from "strychnine poisoning administered by her own hand while under despondency." The colonists held a small funeral the following day, presided over by Episcopalian minister J. Avery Shepherd, another public supporter of Harris who had officiated his marriage to Jane Lee Waring a few years earlier.[2]

No doubt fearing what could happen if the media got wind of Mary's death, Nagasawa went to the offices of the *Santa Rosa Republican* the day of the funeral to inform them and to request that they print only a brief notice.[3] However, other California papers immediately picked up on the story. In the years since the fire and end of Chevaillier's campaign in June 1892, Harris and Fountaingrove had hardly been in the news at all. Harris and his new wife, Jane Lee Waring, had been spotted in New York City, where they relocated after deciding to leave Wales, but their address was a closely guarded secret known only to the Brotherhood of the New Life.[4] They kept a low profile, as did Fountaingrove, which stayed out of the headlines entirely. Under the direction of Nagasawa, the winery recovered from the fire and was "running in full blast" by mid-1893.[5]

The death of Mary Harris provided California newspapers with an opportunity to resurrect the Oliphant and Chevaillier scandals and to rail against "free love" and the "Harris cult." Journalists portrayed Mary's death as a "mystery" and a "secret" rather than as a straightforward tragedy. Hinting at a possible murder, they wondered how Mary had gotten ahold of strychnine, why the coroner had accepted the Fountaingrove colonists' version of events, and why there had been no autopsy. They asked why the "brief" and "perfunctory" funeral was held so soon after Mary's death—what were the Fountaingrove colonists hiding?

Newspapers also speculated as to why Mary—supposedly a "a very attractive girl" and "one of the brightest members of the community"—might have tried to kill herself. Unbothered by a complete lack of evidence, the *Chronicle* printed rumors that Mary, as a "pure, high-minded girl," had committed suicide rather than be forced into "free love" practices at the colony. "Some repugnant command was forced upon Miss Harris," the paper suggested, "rather than submit to it she went to the medicine chest, secured the strychnine, repaired to her room, and took the fatal dose." Mary Harris "Loathed Free Love," declared a *Los Angeles Times* headline. The *Examiner* printed an illustration of Mary, purportedly based on a photograph, that portrayed her as a sad-looking young woman with dark rings around her eyes. She wore a high-necked cotton dress, suggesting chastity. The accompanying headline dubbed her "The Victim of an Ungodly System."[6]

This portrayal of Mary as a pious victim was a complete media fabrication, based on almost no actual information about her personality or life. Those who knew her painted a different picture. Nagasawa called her a "very high strung girl" who was "very much addicted to outbursts of temper, and while in them was very rude." Dr. Thompson agreed that she was "high strung and high tempered." She could be at times "violently obstinate and perverse," Thompson said, followed by times when she would be "all contrition." He

The Girl Who Met Death in the Fountain Grove Community.
(From a photograph of Miss Mary Harris.)

Mary Harris, *San Francisco Examiner*, January 12, 1896.

had treated Mary for "slight trouble with her bowels" a few days before her death but had not detected any suicidal intentions.[7] Like neurasthenia, "high strung" was a gendered term mostly applied to women, suggesting a feminine weakness of character and self-control. Calling her "high strung" was likely a way of saying that Mary Harris pushed too strongly against the many restrictions of the colony.[8] Considering Mary's situation—dumped at Fountaingrove with no say in the matter, and required to partake in the demanding physical labor all colonists participated in—it is not surprising that a fifteen-year-old chafed against life there. In fact, most young people who grew up in Harris's colonies left as soon as they could, including Arthur Cuthbert Jr., Mary Emerson, and Harris's own sons.

The media outcry was loud enough to convince Santa Rosa authorities to launch a grand jury investigation into Mary's death. The district attorney issued subpoenas to Pearl Harris, Kanaye Nagasawa, Emma Parting, and Margaret Parting, who testified before the grand jury. Nagasawa repeated the story he had told the *Chronicle*: On the evening of January 2, he heard screams, entered Mary's room, and found her in "great agony"; she told him she had taken strychnine and died soon after. The other colonists backed up Nagasawa's account. Asked about her life at Fountaingrove, thirteen-year-old Pearl Harris reported that she had not seen her sister Mary for about a month prior to her death because the two girls slept in separate buildings and were "never allowed to roam."

From this meager soil, newspaper writers cultivated a portrait of Mary and Pearl as "the saddest stories of desolate childhood that ever were listened to." Mary—"motherless and renounced by her father"—had suffered through a "wretched" and "desolate" life within Fountaingrove's Aestivossa, now dubbed the "House of Mystery." She was "practically a prisoner" there, and so she had "sought escape by death." The *Chronicle* added a new wrinkle, suggesting that Mary hated life at Fountaingrove because she was a devout Catholic, a faith supposedly passed to her by her deceased mother. As a good Catholic girl, she detested the spiritualist practices of the colonists at Fountaingrove.[9]

Nagasawa became the central target of the media's hostility, not a surprise given the anti-Japanese racism of the era. Newspapers described him using racialized language, calling him a "a very shrewd Japanese," "short, stout, and phlegmatic," and Fountaingrove's "little, shrewd-faced, black-eyed manager." *Chronicle* artist George E. Lyon created a portrait of Nagasawa that featured extensive cross-hatching around his eyes and lower face, making him seem swarthy and menacing. The *Examiner* complained that Japanese "foreigners" served as pallbearers at Mary's funeral and that the coroner had naively accepted the word of "a Japanese." Furthermore, Nagasawa had hired Japanese workers in the Fountaingrove vineyard, "displacing white labor" with "Japs." Nagasawa ruled over Fountaingrove "as Harris ruled it before," supposedly going so far to personally destroy any photographs taken there by outsiders.[10]

More explosively, media accounts speculated that Mary might have killed herself to avoid having to accept Nagasawa as a sexual partner. The *Chronicle* reported that "he has said that he does not believe in marriage"

KANAGE NAGASAWA, THE JAPANESE WHO IS NOW AT THE HEAD OF THE COMMUNITY OF THE BROTHERHOOD OF THE NEW LIFE.

Kanaye Nagasawa, *San Francisco Chronicle*, February 14, 1896.

and that he "has also made many remarks to show his admiration for young American girls."[11] In this version of events, Mary did not merely loathe free love but miscegenation as well, drinking strychnine to preserve her sexual and racial purity. Ever since Chevaillier's initial exposé of counterpartal sex at Fountaingrove, the specter of miscegenation had loomed due to the presence of Japanese men and white women at the colony. Mary's death became enmeshed in broader racial animosities and fears of Japanese men "scheming" to seduce white women.

Nagasawa tried to quell the "free love" rumors by telling the *Chronicle*, "stories that men and women ever bathed together nude at Fountaingrove is not true." This of course was a lie, one consistent with the lies Harris had told people in Santa Rosa during the Chevaillier scandal. Furthermore, Nagasawa insisted that "the marriage relations among us are the same as among other people." Fountaingrove was simply a "business proposition," not a "community," he said.[12] In fact, Nagasawa and the other colonists remained in constant contact with Harris, who continued to issue religious and logistical instructions from New York. The Fountaingrove lands were owned by his wife Jane Lee Waring Harris, giving Harris firm financial control. But advertising Harris's involvement would have been bad publicity for Fountaingrove during this moment of crisis.

Much to the San Francisco media's dismay, the grand jury declined to issue a murder indictment in the death of Mary Harris. The jurors said they "could not find that anyone was to blame for the young woman's rash act." One juror declared, "I believe there is something rotten at Fountaingrove," but in the matter of Mary's death, the jury concluded that no crime had been committed.[13] Undeterred, the *Chronicle* issued an editorial declaring that "the blood of this child is upon the heads of those at Fountaingrove." The paper also laid the blame at the feet of Thomas Lake Harris, who had agreed to take Mary in at the colony: "The criminal law cannot reach him, but the moral law, which says no one shall escape penalty of evil-doing, will not permit him to escape." The *Call* pointed out ominously, "Pearl Harris is still a prisoner there."[14]

She would not be for long. A few years after the death of Mary, Pearl would also leave Fountaingrove; in 1904, she turned up living with a "kind Swedish lady" in Colorado. Now calling herself Bettina, she corresponded for a few years with Jane Lee Waring Harris, who sent her twenty dollars a month. After Harris's death, Jane would convince Bettina to waive any claim to her grandfather's estate, noting in her diary, "Little Bettina has won our love and confidence in signing a 'Waiver' to any claim."[15]

Sequestered in his townhouse in Manhattan's Upper West Side, living "solitary and apart in a city of millions of people," Harris made no public comment on his granddaughter Mary's death.[16] His plans to establish a new colony in Topolobampo, Mexico, had languished after an ill-fated attempt to bring in Japanese investors to build a railroad.[17] But he continued receiving spiritual revelations, all recorded by his wife-amanuensis Jane, though often she found there was "no earthly language in which to clothe them."[18] The breakthrough he had made in Linn Lilla in September 1890, when he had discovered the secret of eternal youth, continued to grant him episodes of "vigor and divine lightheartedness," though more and more infrequently.[19]

His celestial travels and communications with Lily Queen revealed to him that the end of the world—a preoccupation for Harris since the 1840s—was finally about to be ushered in. A "divine fire" would soon cleanse the earth, destroying "ninety-nine in one hundred" people due to "the natural atmosphere bursting as a bubble from within." The "wicked and unfit" would melt away, leaving behind only the purest, most skilled practitioners of divine respiration. The "saved of all peoples" would then form into a New Jerusalem, heaven on earth. "Even so come, Lord Jesus—come quickly!" Harris wrote a few days after Mary's death. "Amen."[20]

PART THREE
ENDINGS

11

The Original Cult Leader

Thomas Lake Harris died in his posh Manhattan apartment in the early morning hours of March 23, 1906, at the age of eighty-two. "We did not think he would be taken from us," Jane Lee Waring Harris admitted in a letter to the other members of the Brotherhood of the New Life. "He was so alive that there seemed to be no place of entrance for death. Yet the extremely sensitive and vital structure could not—as it proved—endure the strain forever."[1] A few days later, she reluctantly held a private funeral, attended by Nagasawa, Edwin Markham, and a few others, after hoping to detect "signs of remaining life, in vain, till decomposition showed on the body." She instructed the Brotherhood to "not drop the fight against death, but in all things, inward and outward, try to carry out Father's wishes." There would be no death notice sent to the press because "he is not dead but intensely alive, making his presence palpably felt since his translation in all the groups who follow in the way of his teachings."[2]

The lack of a death notice meant that very few newspapers published an official obituary.[3] Loyal to the end, the Knights Templar of Santa Rosa issued a belated tribute in July, declaring that Harris was "beloved by all who passed under the spell of his heavenly genius." They also insisted that he "firmly believed and taught that Jesus is the Christ," a willful erasure of Harris's unique theology.[4] That same month, however, *Harper's Weekly* mistakenly commented that Harris "was still alive at last accounts."[5] It was a surprisingly quiet end for a man who had been in the public spotlight off and on since the late 1840s and whose name had become a household word during the Oliphant and Chevaillier scandals.

In fact, Harris's final years had been mostly spent in seclusion. He produced only two new volumes of poetry, privately printed by Charles Pearce in Glasgow and distributed to friends. He made one final trip to Glasgow to oversee their printing, and he also spent time in New Brunswick, Canada, and in Florida, where he purchased land, but he and Jane spent most of their days sequestered in their Manhattan apartment. As his health declined, Harris continued to insist that he was "redeemed, transformed, rejuvenated,"

Unholy Sensations. Joshua Paddison, Oxford University Press. © Oxford University Press 2025.
DOI: 10.1093/oso/9780197775325.003.0011

that he had won a struggle with death "that mortal man never triumphed through before."[6] His later visions included a visit with the spirit of Abraham Lincoln and its counterpart, who turned out to be Sojourner Truth.[7] Harris also had a final visitation from the spirit of Laurence Oliphant, who appeared to him as a "black man." Harris "wound his arms firmly around the creature and commenced crushing the black form which was only an appearance and at last he broke it and tore it to pieces." This released Oliphant's spirit from the "apostasy" that had consumed him during his lifetime, ending "the cruelest human episode since the betrayal in Gethsemane." Harris and Oliphant were finally reconciled, at least in Harris's mind.[8]

Sarah Frances Smiley, Hannah Whitall Smith's Miss X, gave an unflattering account of Harris in these years. The report is particularly unreliable in that it comes thirdhand: we have only Smith's recording of what Smiley heard from the matron of a New York City hospital where Jane Lee Waring Harris received treatment. But according to this matron (by way of Smiley and Smith), Harris "had become a driveling, sensual old man; that his only thought appeared to be hugging and kissing women; that he had tried to do it to her and that she had to avoid ever being alone with him." Encountering this matron alone in a hospital hall, Harris "threw his arms around her and exclaimed, 'I love you! I love you! I love you! You do not know how I love you!' And she was obliged to make her escape in order to avoid further demonstrations." The matron also reported that Jane Harris worked hard to prevent her husband from ever being alone with women.[9]

In these final years, Harris managed to avoid publicity with one exception: in late 1900, news broke that Jane Lee Waring Harris had turned the Fountaingrove properties back over to his followers once and for all. In what the *San Francisco Call* deemed "queer terms," Jane gave the real estate to several members of the Brotherhood—Kanaye Nagasawa, Margaret Parting, Eusardia Nicholas, Robert M. Hart, and Mary Hart—with the instructions that everything would be held in trust and ultimately go to the person who remained alive the longest.[10] Still nursing a long-standing grudge, one spiritualist newspaper reported that Harris had finally "retired from the business of controlling other people." The paper rejoiced that the "sensational" news media could no longer "fasten upon Spiritualism this conscienceless fakir." Harris and his infamy would finally cease to be a taint on mainstream spiritualism.[11]

The *New York Sun* managed to get a short interview with Harris, the last he would ever give. At age seventy-eight, he remained a "splendid looking old man with eyes that burn with undimmed fire," according to the *Sun* reporter. Harris informed him, "All it amounts to is that I was getting old and my wife was getting old and so we decided to get rid of the property." Harris proceeded to sing the praises of Nagasawa, whom he called "a man of remarkable qualities" and "really my adopted son."[12] Under Nagasawa's management, the Fountaingrove vineyards were enjoying tremendous success, selling their wines throughout the United States and—due to Harris's far-flung network of followers—in Scotland, Ireland, and Japan. The first California wine distributed internationally, Fountaingrove vineyard was helping to solidify Sonoma Valley's reputation for fine wines around the world.[13]

The *Call* marked the news of the land sale by publishing a full-page story on "The Passing of the World-Famous 'Primate' Harris Colony." Artist Willis Thorndike provided a lurid illustration that dominated the page. Harris, sporting long unkept hair and a pointed, graying beard, wore the embroidered robes of a wizard, suggesting wealth, knowledge, and occult powers. His eyes were slightly crossed, making his gaze seem feverish or crazed. Arms outstretched, he appeared to be in a trance or in the middle of an arcane ritual. Beneath each arm was an inset image of violence—a bullet whizzing by the head of Laurence Oliphant, a near-miss Harris had supposedly prophesized, and the crumpled body of granddaughter Mary Harris. The artist crammed in two more portraits, one a profile of Harris wearing a more respectable-looking suit, the other an image of "Prince Tokuma Konoye" (yet another misspelling of Kanaye Nagasawa). The accompanying article gave a brief history of Fountaingrove, which it called "the weirdest communal scheme ever perpetrated." For Harris was "no ordinary man," the writer reminded readers. "He was a human magnet who drew after him thousands of converts who were as clay in his hands, turning over to him all their worldly goods and obeying his dictates as humbly as a slave."[14]

The *Call* illustration and article crystalized the ways Harris had been portrayed in the Oliphant, Chevaillier, and Mary Harris scandals, casting him as the prototype of a newly emerging public villain: the cult leader. Media reports had used the term "cult" with increasing frequency over the course of the 1890s to describe Harris's movement. This new meaning of "cult" emerged to serve a journalistic need: it marked certain religious groups, like the Brotherhood of the New Life, as an imminent danger to the public. Unlike terms such as sect, community, or society, a cult demanded intervention from outsiders. Cults were, by definition, coercive, strange, and

San Francisco Call, May 19, 1901.

violent; they were lorded over by cult leaders who were manipulative, fraudulent, and sexually perverse. Above all else, they were fascinating, especially to an urban reading public coming to terms with rapid changes in gender roles, sexuality, immigration, and race relations. In their competition for readers, Pulitzer, Hearst, de Young, and other editorial pioneers of what was by 1895 being called "yellow journalism" had created the idea of the cult in order to protect the public from the very menace they helped create.

Ironically, Chevaillier herself had never used the word cult, but her campaign had helped establish the category with Harris as the quintessential cult leader. Older terms of religious excess and power such as "enthusiast," "fanatic," "prophet," "mesmerist," and "messiah"—all of which Harris had been called over the years—converged in the 1890s in the figure of the cult leader with Harris as the ultimate example.

As the media labeled the Brotherhood of the New Life a cult, they did the same to other groups; in fact, by the late 1890s, cults seemed to be everywhere. It was not just new religions like Cyrus Teed's Koreshanity that were labeled cults; older movements that had long been outside the U.S. mainstream became labeled cults as well, including spiritualism, Christian Science, Theosophy, and the Church of Jesus Christs of Latter-day Saints.[15] At the same time, British and American missionaries, scholars, and other writers began speaking of "Shinto cults," "Buddhist Tibetan cults," "Hindu cults," and "voodoo cults" in Asia and the Caribbean.[16] The demands of the British and U.S. empires fueled this new concept of cults, working alongside and replacing older religio-racial categories of "heathen" and "pagan." Unlike those older categories, the term "cult" acknowledged differences between religious groups—a Shinto cult was different from a Hindu cult—while still casting them as threatening and illegitimate. This discourse further reinforced the racial dimensions of all cults as existing outside both Protestant Christianity and whiteness.[17]

During the Chevaillier scandal, mainstream Protestants had ignored the matter even as Harris's career was thoroughly debated in secular and metaphysical periodicals. However, by 1898, conservative Protestant ministers in the United States seized on the term "cult" as a useful way to consolidate an American Protestant identity and body politic. That year, an Episcopalian minister named Arthur Barrington published *The Anti-Christian Cults*, the first of what would become an evergreen seller in evangelical circles: the counter-cult reference guide. Barrington made the case that Christian Science, Theosophy, and spiritualism were "false, subversive of the Christian faith, and totally unable to afford true comfort and consolation." The book's introduction, written by Episcopalian bishop Isaac Lea Nicholson, insisted that Christians needed to become vigilant against the "anti-Christian cults" as the newest battle in "the long spiritual combat of truth against error, of the Church against the Devil, of Christ against Belial, of God against the worldly mammon of unrighteousness."[18] Cults did not just appeal to newspaper readers; their existence could spark Christian piety and revival as well. Encyclopedic books on cults soon became a cottage industry, with such works as George Hamilton Combs's *Some Latter-Day Religions* (1899), John Elward Brown's *In the Cult Kingdom* (1918), Gaius Glenn Atkins's *Modern Religious Cults and Movements* (1923), Charles W. Ferguson's *A Confusion of Tongues* (1928), and J. K. Van Baalen's *The Chaos of Cults* (1938) following the model established by Barrington's *The Anti-Christian Cults*.[19]

Although the term "cult" had a wide and flexible range of application, it was from the beginning especially associated with California. By the time of Harris's death in 1906, California newspapers were overflowing with accounts of "cults" and "cult leaders" who used their "hypnotism" to defraud and seduce followers, especially young white women.[20] In a typical cult story from 1909 that could have been recycled from the Chevaillier scandal, the *Oakland Tribune* denounced one supposed cult leader's "immorality, lewd and improper conduct, interference between husbands and wives, coercion of prospective young women converts, and flagrant insincerity."[21]

Speculating in 1908 why California had so many cults, the *San Francisco Chronicle* blamed it on the state's sunny climate, which attracted "innumerable swamis and avatars, prophets and mystics."[22] The prominent presence of Asian religions in California, a byproduct of Chinese, Japanese, Korean, and Indian immigration, helped cultivate this reputation, as many of the groups labeled "cults" in the early twentieth century had Asian elements or leaders. These groups included Raja Yoga Academy at Point Loma and Krotona in Hollywood, both run by Theosophists; Shanti Ashrama in Santa Clara County, a spiritual center based on the teachings of Indian guru Ramakrishna; and the Mazdaznan Society in Los Angeles and Stockton, a neo-Zoroastrian group often called a "sun cult."[23]

"Sun cults," "sex cults," "strange cults," "love cults," "hill cults," even a "silk underwear cult": California had them all by the 1910s.[24] Taking stock of Southern California's "dubious cults and equivocal occultisms" in 1919, Catholic writer Michael Williams deemed them "too numerous, too bewildering in their variety and their fantasy to be briefly catalogued." Looking at the California religious landscape, he saw only a "vertiginous confusion of modern idolatry and sorcery and superstition and mania."[25]

Media coverage of Harris during the early 1890s had created the mold of the California cult leader, and he continued to be a touchstone for journalists writing about cults throughout the early twentieth century. G. W. Wilderman, founder of the World's Christian Cooperative Society in Baja California; Rev. F. F. Young, the so-called terrorist preacher of Oakland; Mnason, the bearded prophet and founder of the Lord's Farm in New Jersey; Willard P. Burke, an osteopath who opened a sanitorium in Santa Rosa only to be accused of the attempted murder of a woman and baby under his care—all of these men garnered comparisons to Harris. He was, according to Pulitzer's *New York World*, the "first of the century's rich crop of messiahs." Harris failed to overcome death as he had hoped and expected, but he lived on in popular culture as the original California cult leader.[26]

12

The Angel of the Jails

A few months after Alzire Chevaillier returned to Boston in 1892 following the Harris scandal, she found herself at the funeral of her other former mentor Phillips Brooks. He had died, shockingly, from heart failure in January 1893 at the age of fifty-eight, only having served as bishop of the Episcopal Diocese of Massachusetts for a year and a half. Protestant ministers around the country eulogized him as the "best-loved man of his time."[1] The Boston press, remembering Chevaillier's letter in opposition to Brooks's promotion, asked her for a comment. "When one tries to put a great man inside a bishop, he has about as much difficulty as when he tries to put a quart into a pint measure," she said. "The great soul of Mr. Brooks burst through its caged environment and tore his body to pieces in the freeing process."[2] Her rather gruesome description of Brooks's death suggested that becoming bishop had killed him. Even as she memorialized Brooks, she defended her prior opposition to him assuming the role.

Chevaillier threw herself back into moral reform work in Boston, becoming involved in the Church of the Carpenter, an Episcopal parish led by William Dwight Porter Bliss devoted to labor justice and Christian socialism. Rather than starting her own magazine, as she had planned, she helped Bliss edit *The Dawn: A Journal of Christian Socialism*.[3] However, California continued to call her. Within a year, she and her mother had sold their home in Boston and relocated to Los Angeles and then San Diego. Writing to a friend, Chevaillier said she now took "no stock in the East, as we look ahead at the tribulation and 'sea of trouble' soon to cover the earth."[4] She referred to the widespread unemployment and labor unrest that was occurring in the wake of the Panic of 1893, when hundreds of banks and businesses closed. When the American Railway Union went on strike in the summer of 1894 to protest wage cuts made by the Pullman Palace Car Company, the union in Los Angeles invited Chevaillier to give an address. She excoriated the two-party system, imploring the railway workers in the audience, "Will all rise who have forever and forever shaken off the fetters of these two parties of the Railroads and the Banks, and who have cast their last

Unholy Sensations. Joshua Paddison, Oxford University Press. © Oxford University Press 2025.
DOI: 10.1093/oso/9780197775325.003.0012

ballot for the Republican or Democratic parties, which have enslaved the American people for so long?"[5]

More typical of Chevaillier's worldview was a speech she gave a few years later, during a coal mine strike in 1900. In this speech, she blamed the "misery, suffering, sorrow, sickness, poverty, sin, and death that is everywhere rampant today" on humanity's lack of spiritual enlightenment. "Christianity must become political," she said, "using the good as its organ, for the government needs religion for its redemption and perfection." Just as she had done in her earlier years of reform work in Boston and New York, she insisted that only spiritual advancement could solve social and political problems. "May the God within each one of us co-operate with the infinite love and wisdom in hastening this blessed day," she said.[6]

The idea that God was "within each one of us" was common in the Christian Science and mental-healing circles Chevaillier traveled in. By the turn of the twentieth century, many practitioners of those methods had embraced a new name for their movement: New Thought. More eclectic and flexible than Christian Science, mind cure, or mental healing had ever been, New Thought appealed to Christian socialists and moral reformers like Chevaillier as well as a wide range of Americans looking for self-help strategies based on the power of positive thinking.[7] Unsurprisingly, Southern California became a "hotbed of New Thought," with a wide variety of churches, clubs, Unity Centers, and Homes of Truth.[8] Chevaillier became involved in New Thought in California and continued to practice mental healing but no longer did so for money, "not daring to sell the gift of the Holy Spirit."[9] However, as New Thought became increasingly popular and male dominated in the early twentieth century, to the point that it became known as a "get-rich-quick religion," Chevaillier drifted away from what had originally been a woman-centered movement, forging her own spiritual path once again.[10]

In a revealing letter Chevaillier wrote in 1900 to Septimus J. Hanna, editor of *Christian Science Sentinel*, she reflected on her former days as a student of Mary Baker Eddy in Boston. She could not help but compare Eddy to Harris—both were former teachers she had loved but became disillusioned with. She wished she had learned more from Eddy about "malicious mesmerism," one of Eddy's terms for the misapplication of mental healing to control others and cause psychic harm. In her battle with Harris, she was armed with "fearlessness and purity," she said, but "I was not armed with *the knowledge* which if I had accepted what Mrs. Eddy taught, would have made me invulnerable. The result is I have been laid on the shelf of uselessness, the longing for service, ever since I was there" at Fountaingrove.

Chevaillier now vowed to "never again attack any wrong but wait until *lifted up* spiritually to a height when I could *draw* others by Love and Truth into Holiness and Health. Probably that is why I am useless; because not yet *lifted* up."[11] Chevaillier seemed chastened by her experiences during the Harris scandal, blaming her lack of spiritual preparation for the "uselessness" she felt in its aftermath. Rather than attacking "wrong" in the world, with all the counterattacks that they had brought upon her, she once again now focused on her own personal spiritual growth.

Her mother Sarah died in 1904, leaving Chevaillier without her lifelong companion.[12] She had lived with Sarah her entire life and now found herself profoundly alone. "I have lived in this house alone, day after day, not seeing a human being," she wrote to a friend soon after. "I am *alone* at any rate—eat, sleep, and stay alone. It is not natural or wise." Her family wealth was nearly gone; "Momma often blundered and made mistake after mistake in our business matters from twisted people and been 'done up,'" Chevaillier lamented.[13]

Despite her financial straits, Chevaillier decided to go to Chicago to study with Alice Bunker Stockham, "simply because I must break up the strain here, even if I have to walk to find a human friend who will bind up my wounds."[14] Stockham was a New Thought healer and well-known if controversial authority on women's health and sexuality. For couples, she advocated a practice she called "karezza"—lengthy sexual intercourse without male orgasm—for its physiological and religious benefits. After karezza, Stockham said, "the physical tension subsides, the spiritual exaltation increases, and not uncommonly visions of a transcendent life are seen and consciousness of new powers experienced."[15] A year after Chevaillier's visit, Stockham's feminist, metaphysical, pro-sex writings would get her arrested for violation of the Comstock Act.[16]

On sexual matters, Chevaillier was more conservative than Stockham and believed, as she said during the Harris scandal, that "spirituality and sensuality must be divorced."[17] Unlike Stockham and other radical reformers of the era such as Ida C. Craddock and Lillian Harmon, who championed sexual desire as an essential component of spiritual liberation, Chevaillier had always held fast to more traditional ideals of propriety and chastity.[18] But just as she had pursued studying with Harris despite the unabashedly erotic nature of his poetry, she was drawn to Stockham in this time of loneliness and grief in search of "new vibrations and a noble human bond to hold me up until I am ready to hold others up."[19]

Sarah Chevaillier was dead but, bizarrely, she became involved in a kerfuffle in 1906 involving Mary Baker Eddy. *McClure's* magazine ran a photograph of Sarah, mislabeled as Eddy, as part of an investigation into Christian Science, which it predictably labeled a "cult."[20] Outraged, the Christian Science church released a press release condemning the photo mistake, which it insisted was emblematic of the "utter unreliability" of *McClure's* journalism.[21] In the photo, Sarah Chevaillier's eyes were ringed with darkness, making her look older and more sinister compared to the "genuine picture of Mrs. Eddy" that the Church supplied. As such, the erroneous photo undermined Eddy's claims that Christian Science allowed practitioners to "grow in beauty and immortality, instead of lapsing into age and ugliness."[22] The Church included an affidavit from Charles Chevaillier, Alzire's brother in Texas, attesting that the photo was indeed of his dead mother. Alzire was more famous than her brother but, given her break with Eddy and the up-and-downs of her reputation, it was not surprising that the Church reached out to Charles rather than Alzire for the affidavit. Charles was also, of course, a man.

By this point, Chevaillier was living in Los Angeles in a small bungalow near Hollenbeck Park. Supporting herself by writing, lecturing, and the financial help she received from wealthy friends, she finally found the issue that would consume her attention for the remainder of her life: prison reform. This was a natural extension of the work she had done years earlier in asylum reform; a new way to help society's most vulnerable members. It was simultaneously political, economic, and spiritual work, her way of doing "my own special little part, in the world's awakening to God's good purpose of universal love, prosperity, and peace for all his children."[23] Now going by the name Faith, an apt childhood nickname, Chevaillier gave lectures about the "torture chambers at San Quentin," worked with the Woman's City Club of Los Angeles to curb gambling and add night classes for prisoners in the city jail, and advocated for the legal rights of the accused.[24] She denounced the death penalty as "judicial murder" and convict leasing, prevalent in Los Angeles since the 1880s, as "degrading and inhuman."[25]

More than anything, she spent her days visiting inmates in Los Angeles's overcrowded city jail. Built in 1881, the city jail had become "filled to five times its capacity, swarming with vermin, reeking with vile diseases and filth," according to an exposé Chevaillier delivered to the Woman's City Club in 1916 that made front-page news.[26] Los Angeles's penal system, which

Sarah Chevaillier (misidentified as Mary Baker Eddy), *McClure's*,
December 1906.

included a stockade and county jail as well as the city jail, housed more people than any other U.S. city of similar size. A war on poor white and Mexican male itinerants—denounced as "tramps" and "hobos" by city leaders—had put Los Angeles on the path to becoming, in the words of historian Kelly Lytle Hernández, "the carceral capital of the United States."[27] Chevaillier's tireless work on behalf of prisoners in Los Angeles earned her the moniker "Angel of the Jails." She administered legal advice to prisoners, petitioned judges and politicians on their behalf, organized entertainments, and raised money for celebrations and gifts, all the while calling for "a radical change in our social, economic, and ethical structure" via Christian socialism.[28]

By the early 1930s, Faith Chevaillier had become a cherished elder figure in philanthropic and literary circles in Los Angeles. She was in her eighties but "still as active as if forty," she told the dancer Ruth St. Denis, "still trying to add my quota of happiness and help to the underdog, the sorrowful, and needy."[29] She was still an inveterate spiritual seeker, a student of "God, Buddha, Allah, Jehovah, Confucius, Zoroaster too."[30] Surprisingly, her circle of friends included Edwin Markham, the California poet whom Kanaye Nagasawa had summoned to Fountaingrove in November 1891 to help prepare a counterattack against Chevaillier's impending campaign. Forty years later, Markham remained convinced that Harris was a misunderstood genius, having spent decades working on an edited collection of the prophet's unpublished writings.[31] Chevaillier and Markham must have discussed their shared history with Harris at some point, but their existing correspondence leaves no trace. In a list of the twenty-two greatest accomplishments of her life that she compiled during this period, Chevaillier omitted any mention of her campaign against Harris, raising questions about how she looked back on the scandal.[32]

Two sources from her final years provide clues. The poet Ruth Le Prade, Chevaillier's closest friend during her final decade of life, interviewed her several times for a biography Le Prade hoped to publish called "The Angel of the Jails." The biography emphasized Chevaillier's connections with celebrities such as Wendell Phillips and Phillips Brooks and her many accomplishments in various arenas of moral reform. Completed after Chevaillier's death and embellished with many fictionalized details, Le Prade's "The Angel of the Jails" portrays Chevaillier's encounter with Harris as a gothic horror story, with her the plucky heroine and him the melodramatic villain. At Fountaingrove, Harris attempts to hypnotize Chevaillier with his "deep, mesmeric eyes" before "he gathers her in his arms and kisses her passionately on the mouth. At the touch of his lips she recoils. 'Let go of me! Let go of me!' she cries, struggling wildly."[33] This was probably an invention of Le Prade; if Harris had actually grabbed and kissed Chevaillier, she almost certainly would have used it as evidence against him during her campaign.

In another likely invented scene, Chevaillier returns to Fountaingrove to confront Harris face-to-face before launching her crusade. When Harris threatens to "discipline" her using his mental powers, Chevaillier defiantly stands up to him: "Her lifted face shining and resolute, she looks up into the deep cavernous eyes of the enraged man who towers above her like some mighty cliff, his furious face black as Lucifer, and says with strong determination—'No, I am not afraid! You serve the powers of darkness. I serve the powers of Light.'"[34] It is impossible to determine how much of this came from Chevaillier's memory of events forty years later and how much Le Prade invented to make a compelling story, but to whatever degree it came from Chevaillier, it suggests she looked back on her campaign with more than a little pride. She stood up to Harris—literally, in "The Angel of the Jails"—and triumphed over his evil. Ultimately, however, Le Prade failed to find a publisher for her biography, leaving Chevaillier's life story untold.

The second source, which did make it into print, was an article by a *Los Angeles Times* writer named Bailey Millard, who interviewed Chevaillier shortly before her death in 1935 at age eighty-four. As a young man in the early 1890s, Millard had been city editor of the *San Francisco Call*, and he harbored a long-standing suspicion of the "free-love Communist" Harris and his "mystical cult."[35] Titled "The Lady and the Satyr," the 1935 article recapped the by-now largely forgotten story of the Chevaillier-Harris scandal. As in Le Prade's "The Angel of the Jails," the tale was simplified, presented as the triumphant tale of a "comely young woman" who "assailed California's religio-free-love community at Fountaingrove, broke it up, and drove its leader, Thomas Lake Harris, from the State." The *Los Angeles Times* was well known for its exposés of numerous Southern California "cults," and, predictably, Millard labeled Fountaingrove a cult several times in the article.[36]

"Harris never had me fully psychologized," Chevaillier is quoted as saying, but "he would have fooled any susceptible person believing in occult affairs, and I admit that at that time I was uncommonly devoted to and influenced by the supernatural." This remark suggests that it was a regrettable interest in metaphysics that led her down a dangerous path toward moral ruin, turning her story retroactively into a cautionary tale about straying from the

"At First She Sat Enthralled at the Feet of the Prophet, Listening to His Speeches,"
Los Angeles Times Sunday Magazine, June 16, 1935.

Christian mainstream. Considering Chevaillier's lifelong interest in metaphysics, this seems a likely fabrication by the author, a final example of how
the media made use of Chevaillier to craft narratives they thought would appeal to readers.

"The Lady and the Satyr" included an illustration of Chevaillier portrayed
as an "attractive young woman," sitting at a table with Harris as he stares into

her eyes, his body shrouded in darkness. Harris's wicked, "supersensual" poetry books sit on a table between them. Lace curtains hang behind them, suggesting decadence and secret sensuality. Both Harris and Chevaillier were dead when the article appeared, but they lived on as stereotypical cult leader and cult victim, still facing off behind the curtains.[37]

13

The Baron of Fountaingrove

Kanaye Nagasawa ended up inheriting the Fountaingrove lands, outliving or outlasting all the other Fountaingrove colonists. His countryman Ōsui Arai, who had traveled overland to California with Harris and Nagasawa in 1875, was banished from the colony in 1899 under suspicion of working "the blackest of Oriental magic" on Harris.[1] Arai returned to Japan, where he opened a hermitage of his own in suburban Tokyo, becoming spiritual instructor to a dedicated group of students that included Tanaka Shōzō, founder of Japan's first environmental movement.[2] Ray P. Clarke, of Lay, Clarke and Co., likewise lost Harris's favor in 1900 due to his "low animal quality" and habit of associating with "horseracers and a low class of people."[3] Clarke died a year later when a bale of hay fell on him at Fountaingrove, giving Nagasawa full control of the colony's winemaking.[4] The women of the colony died one by one: Alice Parting in 1898, Eusardia Nicholas in 1903, Celia Requa in 1906, Margaret Parting in 1911, and Jane Lee Waring Harris in 1916.[5] Nagasawa felt the weight of their absence. "Now I am the only one of that group," Nagasawa lamented to Edwin Markham in 1921. "I have gone through many trials and tribulations; at times I had become almost in despair in continuing to carry on the duty assigned for me by our Beloved Father."[6]

One ongoing trial involved dealing with his new nemesis Robert M. Hart, who with his wife Mary had been named potential inheritors of Fountaingrove in the "queer terms" of Jane Lee Waring Harris's land transfer in 1900. Robert and Mary had met at Fountaingrove in the 1880s, fallen in love, and Harris had permitted them to marry. During Jane's last years, she lived with the Harts in San Diego, and in her will, she left her cash savings of $130,000 to Mary Hart. This upset Nagasawa; he disliked Robert, believing him to be racially prejudiced, and, because most of the $130,000 had come from the Fountaingrove winery, he thought the money should have gone back into the business. With prohibition looming, the Harts relinquished any potential interest in Fountaingrove in 1919; in exchange, Nagasawa agreed to not challenge their inheritance of the $130,000.[7]

Unholy Sensations. Joshua Paddison, Oxford University Press. © Oxford University Press 2025.
DOI: 10.1093/oso/9780197775325.003.0013

In the 1920s, Hart again angered Nagasawa when Hart became involved in "one cult society after another," including the Mazdaznan Society, and tried to pitch Harris's biography to a Hollywood film studio.[8] Aghast, Nagasawa informed Hart that this notion was "a height of folly and at least in bad taste," insisting that Harris would "always shun publicity regarding our life, which is too sacred for ordinary mind to understand."[9] Hart replied that, of course, "the intimate, sacred knowledge breathed out to his little family circle by our Father" would not be included in a movie, but "there is plenty of uplift, cheer, instruction that *can* be given *now*."[10] One cannot help but wonder what a 1920s Hollywood movie about Harris would have been like, but ultimately nothing came of Hart's plans.

The two men's relationship turned truly antagonistic in 1930 when Hart sued Nagasawa for control of Fountaingrove, claiming that his 1919 relinquishment had been coerced. The California legislature had passed several racist Alien Land Laws barring Japanese immigrants from owning land in the state, and Hart hoped those laws would help him seize title from Nagasawa.[11] To embarrass Nagasawa, Hart announced that he was willing to reveal "intimate details of the religious cult founded by Harris" during the trial, but Nagasawa's lawyers managed to keep all discussion of "cult practices" out of the testimony.[12] Nagasawa won the case, but Hart appealed to the California Supreme Court.[13] His lawyer's brief played on anti-Japanese stereotypes, emphasizing that Nagasawa was "a Japanese, a subject of the Emperor of Japan, an ineligible alien" who had used "cunning and quiet methods to obtain a stranglehold upon 1,895 acres of agricultural land in this state."[14] However, Nagasawa surprisingly triumphed again, helped by the fact that the "queer terms" transfer and Hart's relinquishment had occurred before the state's most restrictive Alien Land Laws had been passed in 1920 and 1923.[15]

Nagasawa's elite samurai family background, education, and proximity to Harris had always made him unusual among Japanese immigrants in Sonoma County, and he continued to occupy a uniquely privileged status. Among Japanese Americans in California, his wealth was rivaled only by a few other highly successful landowners such as George Shima, the "potato king" of the San Joaquin Delta, and Kiyoshi Hirasaki, the "garlic king" of Gilroy.[16] Nagasawa had served, with Shima, on the Japanese Commission for the Panama Pacific Exhibition of 1914 and also as one of seven wine judges there.[17] Locals often referred to Nagasawa as the "Baron of Fountaingrove." During Prohibition, he drew on his wine reserves to host lavish dinners for visiting Japanese dignitaries and businessmen as well as American luminaries such as Edwin Markham, Jack London, Thomas Edison, and Luther Burbank.[18] He spoke English with a Scottish accent, a residue of time spent as a student in Aberdeen, accentuating his air of European lordliness.[19]

As had been the case when Harris ran Fountaingrove, Nagasawa's success as a winemaker—and grape juice producer during Prohibition—endeared him to Santa Rosa's business community. In a 1924 interview with sociologist Robert E. Park, who was conducting research for Stanford University's Survey of Race Relations, Nagasawa reported that "in spite of the prejudice against the Japanese in other parts of California, he is living on the best of terms with his neighbors."[20] California's Japanese American newspapers celebrated Nagasawa's successes, calling him the "widely known Japanese prince and pioneer" and "one of the two wealthiest Japanese on the Pacific Coast."[21]

Nagasawa seldom discussed the Brotherhood of the New Life, presenting himself as a respectable entrepreneur. However, his correspondence with Markham and surviving members of the Brotherhood showed that he remained a lifelong student of Harris's writings.[22] Robert E. Park noted that Nagasawa displayed multiple pictures of Harris in Aestivossa and "spoke with the greatest reverence of Mr. Harris's life and his mystical religious and communistic doctrines."[23] Similarly, Nagasawa told an interviewer from the *Japanese American News,* a Japanese-language newspaper in San Francisco, "Harris taught me that my body is a palace for the Lord, and I believe this." He never married and seems to have continued to practice divine respiration and celibacy.[24]

This meant that Nagasawa would have no children to pass Fountaingrove lands to after his death. By the 1930s, several of Nagasawa's relatives lived at Fountaingrove, including his nephew Tomoki Ijichi, Tomoki's wife Hiro, and their son Kosuke and daughter Amy, both of whom had been born at Fountaingrove. According to family lore, after the passage of the first Alien Land Law in 1913, Nagasawa had sent his nephew Tomoki to Japan "to find a bride," return with her, and produce American-born children who could inherit Fountaingrove.[25] Nagasawa had a particular fondness for young Kosuke, and in 1931, he carved off seventy-three acres of the Fountaingrove lands and gifted them to the boy, then age fourteen, as a token of his "love and affection."[26]

In early 1934, Nagasawa's health began to fail, and he sought a buyer for the remainder of the Fountaingrove property. The land had passed back and forth from Harris to several colonists to Jane Lee Waring Harris and eventually to Nagasawa, never having been offered for sale to the public, so their

Kanaye Nagasawa with his relatives, including his nephew Tomoki Ijichi, Tomoki's wife Hiro, and their children Kosuke and Amy; courtesy Gaye LeBaron Collection, Special Collections, Sonoma State University Library.

value was unknown but estimated to be at least $500,000. Over the years, the town of Santa Rosa had expanded northward toward Fountaingrove, making it less remote and the lands more and more valuable. Kosuke and Amy Ijichi were still minors, so Nagasawa sought to sell the property and give the proceeds to his relatives, which was allowed under state law. However, on March 1, 1934, Nagasawa died before any sale could occur. According to the Ijichis, he gathered them together the night before and whispered, "The transition is near now . . . and it shall be beautiful."[27]

California law banned Japanese immigrants from serving as executors, so Nagasawa had put his white lawyer Wallace Ware in charge of his estate. The two men had a long history. Ware's father, Allison Ware, had been in the Knights Templar with Harris and served as Fountaingrove's lawyer for many years, and Wallace had represented Nagasawa in his legal struggles against Robert M. Hart.[28] Nagasawa's will dictated that his land, buildings, and possessions—including Harris's library, resplendent furnishings, and artworks—should be liquidated and the proceeds distributed to Tomoki, Hiro, and Kosuke Ijichi and his other nephews Eikichi Sasaki and Kiichi Isonaga, all of whom lived at Fountaingrove.[29]

As he had grown in wealth, Nagasawa had received unusually positive treatment from the media and the legal system, but this treatment did not extend to his family members after his death. Wallace Ware immediately angered them by naming himself and his brothers as pallbearers at the funeral rather than Nagasawa's Japanese relatives.[30] Ware sold off a few parcels of the Fountaingrove lands, including one to the Santa Rosa Chamber of Commerce, before selling the bulk of Fountaingrove, including all its buildings and the winery, to a white couple named Errol and Glendolyn MacBoyle for only $90,000.[31] The Great Depression drove down the value of Nagasawa's estate, but this was still a shockingly small amount considering Harris had paid about $50,000 for the undeveloped land in the nineteenth century. After paying off Nagasawa's Prohibition era loans and taking for himself a $25,000 fee plus thousands more in expenses, Ware ended up distributing only about $3,500 total to Nagasawa's five relatives. Kosuke Ijichi unhappily made an additional $5,000 when Ware, acting as trustee because Kosuke was still under eighteen, sold off the seventy-three acres Nagasawa had given him in 1931 to the MacBoyles as part of the larger Fountaingrove real estate deal, without Kosuke's consent.[32] To add insult to injury, Ware rudely evicted Nagasawa's family from Fountaingrove, giving them only twenty-four hours to pack their bags.[33]

A few years later, Japan's attack on Pearl Harbor unleashed a virulent anti-Japanese hostility that had simmered in California for decades. Executive Order 9066 authorized the forced removal of people of Japanese heritage living on the West Coast, including Nagasawa's relatives. The now-widowed Hiro Ijichi, her children Kosuke and Amy, Eikichi Sasaki, and Kiichi Isonaga were all forced into concentration camps, first an assembly center in Stockton and then the Rohwer Relocation Center in Arkansas.[34] Kosuke had just started college at the University of California, Davis; Amy was still in high school. The War Relocation Authority's bookkeeping system designated the Ijichi family number 26277. Camp newspapers show that they, like other internees, strove to make the best of a traumatic situation. At Stockton, Kosuke oversaw a horseshoes contest and taught first aid; at Rohwer, he helped organize a "Kite Day" contest and served as treasurer of the Red Cross unit.[35] Throughout these difficulties, Hiro instructed her son to carry himself with pride, reminding him throughout his life, "Remember, you are Samurai."[36]

Epilogue

The Land Has Been Waiting

After the death of Kanaye Nagasawa, the Fountaingrove lands in Santa Rosa skyrocketed in value while they were stripped, bit by bit, of their history. Erroll MacBoyle, who had made a fortune as the owner of a gold mine in Grass Valley, promised to restore the "early-day glamour and reputation" of the Fountaingrove wine label, but he had so little knowledge of the history of the lands he owned that he incorrectly listed 1873 as the winery's start.[1] In 1948, the MacBoyles auctioned off the "Fabulous Treasures of Fountaingrove": hundreds of Thomas Lake Harris's "Victorian furnishings, paintings, works of art, and library," along with a six hundred-year-old "antique Oriental sword" purchased in Japan by Nagasawa.[2] Erroll MacBoyle died a year later, and his widow, Glendolyn, married a German-born industrialist and financier named Siegfried Bechhold whose Armored Tank Corporation had developed the Sherman tank during World War II. Siegfried ripped out the vines Nagasawa had planted and turned Fountaingrove into a cattle ranch boasting "quality Herefords, polled and horned."[3]

After Siegfried's death in 1956, Glendolyn's lawyers seized control of Fountaingrove, naming her "legally incompetent to manage her business affairs," and sold the lands to ranchers named Robert and Mary Ellen Walter for $450,000.[4] The Walters tore down the once-grand Aestivossa manor house in 1969 and the Familistery soon after. The Commandery had been razed decades earlier. By this point, the only remaining structure from the nineteenth century was a round barn Nagasawa had constructed in 1899.

The Walters turned over forty-five acres to the city of Santa Rosa, sold two hundred acres to Hewlett-Packard's Microwave Division, and sold the rest of Fountaingrove in 1979 to a real estate development group called Teachers Management & Investment (TMI) Corporation for a whopping $9.6 million.[5] TMI then subdivided the land, constructing a hotel, golf course, country club, and office complexes, selling off the remainder to developers who built hundreds of private suburban homes.[6] A massive

Unholy Sensations. Joshua Paddison, Oxford University Press. © Oxford University Press 2025.
DOI: 10.1093/oso/9780197775325.003.0014

fire in 2017 destroyed Nagasawa's round barn along with many houses and offices in the area, but rebuilding commenced immediately.[7] Today, the total value of what was once Fountaingrove's lands is incalculable but surely in the billions.

A strange sort of collective misremembering happened in Santa Rosa during this process. The notoriety that surrounded Harris during his life-time and that lingered for decades after his death faded over time. Locals largely forgot Fountaingrove's scandalous history as a "cult," despite the best efforts of longtime *Santa Rosa Press Democrat* columnist Gaye LeBaron, who wrote numerous articles excavating that history.[8] Beginning in the 1970s, the name Fountaingrove, with its connotations of water, wine, trees, and natural spaces, proliferated in Santa Rosa, from the Fountaingrove Parkway, built for Hewlett-Packard, to the Fountaingrove country club, Fountaingrove Executive Center, Fountaingrove Lodge, Fountaingrove Deli, and Fountaingrove Dentistry. Similarly, the memory of Harris lives on in the form of Thomas Lake Harris Drive, paved in the 1980s as development expanded into the former Fountaingrove lands.

In the 1980s, the Greenwich Development Company, which built more than eighty "lush homesites" in the area, made strategic misuse of Fountaingrove's history in its marketing campaign. In newspaper advertisements and a glossy brochure for potential homebuyers, Greenwich used the slogan, "Since 1875, the land has been waiting." The brochure featured a selection of colorized, historic photographs of Harris, described in the brochure as a "philosopher and visionary." The brochure emphasized Harris's wealth and elegance, suggesting homebuyers could share his lifestyle: "This was a community designed for the good life. Just as Fountaingrove is today."[9] Similarly, the Fountaingrove country club, when telling "Our Story," described Harris as merely a "prolific author, delving deeply into religious and social concepts."[10] Harris's elaborate theology had been scrubbed away into blandness, turning him into an emblem of feel-good concepts like "utopia" and "harmony." Needless to say, there was no mention of counterparts, communal bathing, secret abortions, or forced intergenerational sex, which had dominated headlines in the 1890s.

Nagasawa's biography also proved useful to city leaders and developers. Greenwich Development Company's brochure sported a cover that depicted Fountaingrove's hills in brushstrokes that resembled Japanese calligraphy. The brochure played up Nagasawa's "brilliant" life and career, giving their development project an air of Orientalist exoticism. The Fountaingrove country club similarly employed "Japanese-style" architecture and decor as a "tribute" to Nagasawa's memory.[11] Meanwhile, Santa Rosa's civic leaders seized on Nagasawa as an appealing way to demonstrate the city's racial diversity and Asian American heritage. They installed a bronze bust of Nagasawa in City Hall in 1985 and later named a public park in the former Fountaingrove lands after him.[12]

Even President Ronald Reagan made use of Nagasawa. In a 1983 speech before the Japanese legislature, Reagan cited Nagasawa's life story as one of the "many miracles hard-working Japanese have brought to our shores." Reagan said Nagasawa "came to California to learn and stayed to enrich our lives. Both our countries owe much to this Japanese warrior-turned-businessman."[13] Cast as an American success story, Nagasawa had become an exemplar of the model minority myth, a way of denying the violence of xenophobia and racism in the United States.[14] The actual story of how racist laws and the machinations of a white lawyer robbed Nagasawa's intended heirs of a fortune had no place in this narrative. The Ijichi family

Real estate brochure, Greenwich Development Company, 1985; courtesy Gaye LeBaron Collection, Special Collections, Sonoma State University Library.

never forgot, of course. When Kosuke and Amy Ijichi would occasionally return to Santa Rosa as adults, he would tell his sister, "This could have been all yours."[15]

This erasure of Fountaingrove's history was far from complete. Some people still recognized Harris as a progenitor of the cult leader, especially during the cult scare of the 1970s when media sources, secular anti-cult experts, and Christian counter-cult activists declared a war on cults.[16] After the tragedy at Jonestown, Guyana, when more than nine hundred members of the Peoples Temple died in 1978, observers compared Jim Jones to Harris. One biographer of Jones pointed out that he "almost duplicated some techniques of Thomas Lake Harris," such as calling himself "Father" and separating children from their parents. Like Harris, Jones had moved his multiethnic community to northern California—in Jones's case, to Redwood Valley in Mendocino County—to prepare for the coming apocalypse, and like Harris, Jones communicated with unseen spirits who guided and provided him with spiritual authority.[17] Writers also compared Harris to another notorious California cult leader—Charles Manson, whose bearded visage and cockeyed gaze resembled the *San Francisco Call*'s full-page illustration of Harris from 1901, and in later years to Branch Davidian leader David Koresh and NXIVM founder Keith Raniere.[18]

So many aspects of recent cult scares resemble the Chevaillier-Harris scandal. The language of "mesmerism" and "hypnotism" became replaced, during the Cold War, with talk of "brainwashing" and "programming," but modern cult leaders stood accused of the same thing Chevaillier said Harris had done: using the power of one's mind to take control of other people's finances and bodies, exposing Americans' troubling lack of mental fortitude.[19] Just as Chevaillier had made headlines with talk of nonnormative, nonconsensual sexual practices going on at Fountaingrove, latter-day anti-cult activists lingered on details of supposed sexual deviance in cults, especially concerning the "corruption" of white girls and women, as in the Children of God, Manson's "free love sex cult," the Branch Davidians, the Fundamentalist Church of Jesus Christ of Latter-day Saints, NXIVM, and a "sex cult" at Sarah Lawrence College.[20]

Just as media reports during the Chevaillier scandal portrayed Harris and his followers in racialized terms, so too did popular portrayals emphasize the blackness and "foreignness" of many later groups called cults, including the Peoples Temple, MOVE in Philadelphia, the Rajneesh movement in Oregon, and Sun Myung Moon's Unification Church.[21] Just as religious groups outside the Christian mainstream attacked Harris to help maintain their own respectability, some groups more recently labeled as cults turned against other groups. To give two examples from 1978, the International Society of Krishna Consciousness sent a booklet to media outlets requesting not to be "lumped in" with America's many dangerous cults, and a Unification Church official told the press, "There is absolutely no comparison between Rev. Moon and a lunatic like Jim Jones."[22] Finally, the association between California and cult activity established in the Harris scandal would be a long-lasting one, to the point that *Vanity Fair* magazine asked, "What Is It About California and Cults?" in 2020, reiterating many earlier considerations of the topic.[23]

In a final echo of Chevaillier's lecture in Santa Rosa in February 1892, the modern anti-cult movement came to town in October 1980 in the form of a conference on "Cults and Mind Control" at Santa Rosa Junior College. Columnist Gaye LeBaron and two instructors at the junior college, Don Emblen and Harvey Hansen, gave talks about Harris, declared the "grand-daddy" of California cult leaders. Like Robert M. Hart before him, Hansen had unsuccessfully tried to get a Hollywood movie made about Harris; Hansen's unproduced screenplay focused on the Chevaillier scandal, including an invented scene where Harris carries a hypnotized Chevaillier to bed.[24] Speakers drew a connection from Fountaingrove to Peoples Temple, which had attracted a few people from Sonoma County, and the Unification Church, Hare Krishnas, and Synanon, all of which had chapters near Santa Rosa as of 1980.

Margaret Thaler Singer, a U.C. Berkeley psychologist and leading anti-cult expert who had helped popularize the idea that cult leaders "brainwashed" their followers, gave the keynote address at the Santa Rosa conference. She estimated that up to three million Americans—roughly one out of every seventy-five—were involved in cults. Her comments about how cult leaders operated could have been taken directly from the Chevaillier scandal. Singer said that young people, "foreign students," and "refugees" were especially likely to succumb to a cult, but anyone who was "vulnerable" could fall prey. Inside a cult, "there's a new language," Singer said. "Sexuality is controlled." Families are separated. A new member is told, "the group will be his family," with the cult leader as father. Cult leaders focus on people's breathing, she said, to better manipulate them to "abandon their will and consciousness." Days are filled with chores and manual labor, nights with "long, repetitive lectures couched in hypnotic metaphors."[25]

Like Chevaillier before her, Singer believed that she was saving people's lives through her anti-cult campaign. And there was no end to the work: after giving her keynote in Santa Rosa, Singer rushed to the airport to fly to London to testify as a cult expert in a trial involving the Unification Church. The so-called Moonies had sued a London newspaper, the *Daily Mail*, for libel after it published an article saying that the Church's California branch "brainwashed" members and broke up families while its leader Sun Myung Moon lived in "opulent luxury." Singer's anti-cult testimony proved a turning point in the trial, the longest and costliest libel suit in English history up to that point, helping the *Daily Mail* to triumph. "His followers believe he is the new Messiah," said the judge when delivering the verdict, going on to suggest that the Unification Church's tax-exempt status as a religion should be revoked.[26] He knew a cult when he saw one.

Today, more than forty-five years after the Santa Rosa "Cults and Mind Control" conference and more than 130 years after the Chevaillier-Harris scandal, public interest in cults remains strong. A steady stream of documentary television series, tell-all books, true crime podcasts, and media reports serve up salacious stories of manipulative (usually male) leaders and brainwashed (usually female) followers.[27] The fact that the leaders of some of these groups clearly engaged in abusive behavior, including the sexual abuse of women and children, only seems to confirm the need for constant scrutiny of movements outside the religious mainstream. All religious leaders who coerce others or abuse their power need to be held accountable, including Thomas Lake Harris. However, as religion scholar Megan Goodwin has pointed out, "our nation's sexual abuse problem is enormous and endemic," yet public outcry about abuse within minority religions is in "staggering disproportion" to their size and influence.[28]

From the Fountaingrove scandal onward, the category of the cult has operated as a way of demonizing certain groups as dangerous in terms of religion, race, gender, and sexuality. The category was created and sustained by newspapers chasing readers, activists striving to "rescue" victims, ministers condemning "false" religions, authorities protecting what they consider public morality, and members of minority religions hoping to avoid being labeled a cult themselves. The modern concept of the cult began in the early 1890s, grew in power throughout the early twentieth century, erupted into a public "crisis" in the 1970s, and shows no sign of diminishing in the twenty-first century. Lurking on the perilous margins of religion, sex, gender, race, and nation, cults continue to frighten and fascinate us in equal measure.

Notes

Introduction
Secrets of the Sonoma Eden Unveiled

1. *San Francisco Chronicle*, February 17, 1892: 5; *San Francisco Call*, February 17, 1892: 8; *San Francisco Evening Bulletin*, February 17, 1892: 1; *Los Angeles Times*, February 17, 1892: 4; *San Francisco Examiner*, February 18, 1892: 9.
2. Hugh G. Urban, *New Age, Neopagan, and New Religious Movements: Alternative Spirituality in Contemporary America* (Berkeley: University of California Press, 2015), 8; Timothy Miller, "Are the Cult Wars Over? And If So, Who Won?," in *"Cult Wars" in Historical Perspective: New and Minority Religions*, ed. Eugene V. Gallagher (New York: Routledge, 2017), 33–42; Amanda Montell, *Cultish: The Language of Fanaticism* (New York: Harper Wave, 2021), 29–30.
3. E.g., *Chicago Inter Ocean*, April 26, 1884: 3; *Baltimore Sun*, June 10, 1884: 5; *London Pall Mall Gazette*, May 25, 1889: 7; *Philadelphia Times*, September 14, 1889: 3.
4. Richard Kent Evans, *MOVE: An American Religion* (New York: Oxford University Press, 2020), 195.
5. For overviews, see W. Michael Ashcraft, "A History of the Study of New Religious Movements," *Nova Religio: The Journal of Alternative and Emergent Religions* 9 (2005): 93–105; and Aled Thomas and Edward Graham-Hyde, eds., *"Cult" Rhetoric in the 21st Century: Deconstructing the Study of New Religious Movements* (New York: Bloomsbury, 2024).
6. One exception is Philip Jenkins, *Mystics and Messiahs: Cults and New Religions in American History* (New York: Oxford University Press, 2000), 46–50.
7. For previous, briefer treatments of the Chevaillier-Harris scandal, see Herbert W. Schneider and George Lawton, *A Prophet and a Pilgrim: Being the Incredible History of Thomas Lake Harris and Laurence Oliphant* (New York: Columbia University Press, 1942), 465–70, 534–58; Gaye LeBaron, "Serpent in Eden: The Final Utopia of Thomas Lake Harris and What Happened There," *Markham Review* 4 (Feb. 1969): 14–24; Robert V. Hine, *California's Utopian Colonies* (Berkeley: University of California Press, 1983), 30–32; Arthur Versluis, "Sexual Mysticisms in Nineteenth Century America: John Humphrey Noyes, Thomas Lake Harris, and Alice Bunker Stockham," in *Hidden Intercourse: Eros and Sexuality in the History of Western Esotericism*, ed. Wouter J. Hanegraaff and Jeffrey J. Kripal (Leiden: Brill, 2008), 341; and Adam Morris, *American Messiahs: False Prophets of a Damned Nation* (New York: Liveright, 2019), 126–32.
8. W. Paul Reeve, *Religion of a Different Color: Race and the Mormon Struggle for Whiteness* (New York: Oxford University Press, 2015); Peter Coviello, *Make Yourselves Gods: Mormons and the Unfinished Business of American Secularism* (Chicago: University of Chicago Press, 2019); K. Mohrman, *Exceptionally Queer: Mormon Peculiarity and U.S. Nationalism* (Minneapolis: University of Minnesota Press, 2022).
9. On "heathen," see Joshua Paddison, *American Heathens: Religion, Race, and Reconstruction in California* (Berkeley: University of California Press, 2012); and Kathryn Gin Lum, *Heathen: Religion and Race in American History* (Cambridge, MA: Harvard University Press, 2022). On the religio-racial dimensions of "cult," see Judith Weisenfeld, *New World A-Coming: Black Religion and Racial Identity During the Great Migration* (New York: New York University Press, 2016); and Emily Suzanne Clark and Brad Stoddard, eds., *Race and New Religious Movements in the USA: A Documentary Reader* (London: Bloomsbury Academic, 2019).
10. Sally L. Kitch, *Chaste Liberation: Celibacy and Female Cultural Status* (Urbana: University of Illinois Press, 1989); Kara M. French, *Against Sex: Identities of Sexual Restraint in Early America* (Chapel Hill: University of North Carolina Press, 2021).
11. Megan Goodwin, "Sex and New Religions," in *The Oxford Handbook of New Religious Movements*, vol. 2, ed. James R. Lewis and Inga Tøllefsen (New York: Oxford University Press, 2016), 303; Megan Goodwin, *Abusing Religion: Literary Persecution, Sex Scandals, and American Minority Religions* (New Brunswick, NJ: Rutgers University Press, 2020).

12. Lawrence Foster, *Religion and Sexuality: The Shakers, the Mormons, and the Oneida Community* (Champaign: University of Illinois Press, 1984); Lawrence Foster, *Women, Family, and Utopia: Communal Experiments of the Shakers, the Oneida Community, and the Mormons* (Syracuse: Syracuse University Press, 1992); Paul E. Johnson and Sean Wilentz, *The Kingdom of Matthias: A Story of Sex and Salvation in 19th-Century America* (New York: Oxford University Press, 1994); Sarah Barringer Gordon, *The Mormon Question: Polygamy and Constitutional Conflict in Nineteenth-Century America* (Chapel Hill: University of North Carolina Press, 2002); Paul B. Moyer, *The Public Universal Friend: Jemima Wilkinson and Religious Enthusiasm in Revolutionary America* (Ithaca, NY: Cornell University Press, 2015); French, *Against Sex*.

13. Catherine Wessinger, ed., *Women's Leadership in Marginal Religions: Explorations Outside the Mainstream* (Urbana: University of Illinois Press, 1993); Susan J. Palmer, *Moon Sisters, Krishna Mothers, Rajneesh Lovers: Women's Roles in New Religions* (Syracuse: Syracuse University Press, 1994); Pamela Vance, *Women in New Religions* (New York: New York University Press, 2015); Inga Bårdsen Tøllefsen and Christian Giudice, eds., *Female Leaders in New Religious Movements* (New York: Palgrave Macmillan, 2017).

14. Pamela Haag, *Consent: Sexual Rights and the Transformation of American Liberalism* (Ithaca, NY: Cornell University Press, 1999).

15. Jessica R. Pliley, *Policing Sexuality: The Mann Act and the Making of the FBI* (Cambridge, MA: Harvard University Press, 2014), 9–31.

16. Carey McWilliams, *Southern California: An Island on the Land* (New York: Duell, Sloan & Pearce, 1946), 249.

17. Sandra Sizer Frankiel, *California's Spiritual Frontiers: Religious Alternatives in Anglo-Protestantism, 1850–1910* (Berkeley: University of California Press, 1988); John K. Simmons and Brian Wilson, *Competing Visions of Paradise: The California Experience of 19th Century American Sectarianism* (Santa Barbara: Fithian Press, 1993); Laurie F. Maffly-Kipp, *Religion and Society in Frontier California* (New Haven, CT: Yale University Press, 1994).

18. Edward Leo Lyman, "The Rise and Decline of Mormon San Bernardino," *Brigham Young University Studies* 29 (1989): 43–63.

19. *Banner of Light*, June 30, 1866: 3; Robert J. Chandler, "In the Van: Spiritualists as Catalysts for the California Women's Suffrage Movement," *California History* 73 (1994): 188–201; Molly McGarry, *Ghosts of Futures Past: Spiritualism and the Cultural Politics of Nineteenth-Century America* (Berkeley: University of California Press, 2008).

20. *Sacramento Daily Union*, September 28, 1886; *Los Angeles Daily Herald*, May 20, 1888: 3; *San Francisco Daily Alta California*, June 4, 1888: 2; *San Jose Daily Mercury*, October 15, 1888: 3; *Harmony* 1, no. 1 (1888); *San Francisco Daily Alta California*, June 11, 1889: 5; Rolf Swenson, "Pilgrims at the Golden Gate: Christian Scientists on the Pacific Coast, 1880–1915," *Pacific Historical Review* 72 (2003): 229–63; Frankiel, *California's Spiritual Frontiers*, 68–78.

21. *Los Angeles Star*, October 27, 1855: 2; William B. Rice, *William Money: A Southern California Savant* (Los Angeles: Dawson's Book Shop, 1943).

22. Laurie Maffly-Kipp, "Engaging Habits and Besotted Idolatry: Viewing Chinese Religions in the American West," in *Race, Religion, Region: Landscapes of Encounter in the American West*, ed. Fay Botham and Sara M. Patterson (Tucson: University of Arizona Press, 2006), 60–88; Paddison, *American Heathens*.

23. *Buddhist Ray* 1, no. 1 (Jan. 1888); *San Francisco Call*, September 28, 1891, 8; *Los Angeles Herald*, May 9, 1892: 8; *San Francisco Call*, December 16, 1894: 11; Thomas A. Tweed, *The American Encounter with Buddhism, 1844–1912: Victorian Culture and the Limits of Dissent* (Bloomington: Indiana University Press, 1992), 31–32.

24. Frederick Jackson Turner, "The Significance of the Frontier in American History," in *Annual Report of the American Historical Association for the Year 1893* (Washington, D.C.: Government Printing Office, 1894), 200.

25. On California as a racial, sexual, and gender frontier, see Susan Lee Johnson, *Roaring Camp: The Social World of the California Gold Rush* (New York: W. W. Norton, 2000); Nan Alamilla Boyd, *Wide-Open Town: A History of Queer San Francisco to 1965* (Berkeley: University of California Press, 2005); Nayan Shah, *Stranger Intimacy: Contesting Race, Sexuality and the Law in the North American West* (Berkeley: University of California Press, 2012); Lawrence Culver, *The Frontier of Leisure: Southern California and the Shaping of Modern America* (New York: Oxford University Press, 2012); Stacey L. Smith, *Freedom's Frontier: California and the Struggle over Unfree Labor, Emancipation, and Reconstruction* (Chapel Hill: University of North Carolina Press, 2013); Clare Sears, *Arresting Dress: Cross-Dressing, Law, and Fascination in*

Nineteenth-Century San Francisco (Durham, NC: Duke University Press, 2015); Christopher Herbert, *Gold Rush Manliness: Race and Gender on the Pacific Slope* (Seattle: University of Washington Press, 2018); and Amy Sueyoshi, *Discriminating Sex: White Leisure and the Making of the American "Oriental"* (Champaign: University of Illinois Press, 2018).

26. Christopher B. Daly, *Covering America: A Narrative History of a Nation's Journalism* (Amherst: University of Massachusetts Press, 2012), 123, 130–31; Dennis Brian, *Pulitzer: A Life* (New York: John Wiley & Sons, 2001), 2; Lisa Duggan, *Sapphic Slashers: Sex, Violence, and American Modernity* (Durham, NC: Duke University Press, 2000); Michael Ayers Trotti, *The Body in the Reservoir: Murder and Sensationalism in the South* (Chapel Hill: University of North Carolina Press, 2008); Gretchen Soderlund, *Sex Trafficking, Scandal, and the Transformation of Journalism, 1885–1917* (Chicago: University of Chicago Press, 2013).

27. Ari Adut, *On Scandal: Moral Disturbances in Society, Politics, and Art* (New York: Cambridge University Press, 2008).

28. Bruce Michelson, *Printer's Devil: Mark Twain and the American Publishing Revolution* (Berkeley: University of California Press, 2004); Tom Culbertson, "The Golden Age of American Political Cartoons," *Journal of the Gilded Age and Progressive Era* 7 (2008): 276–95; Vanessa Meikle Schulman, "'Making the Magazine': Visuality, Managerial Capitalism, and the Mass Production of Periodicals, 1865–1890," *American Periodicals* 22 (2012): 1–28.

29. Catherine L. Albanese, *A Republic of Mind and Spirit: A Cultural History of Metaphysical Religion in America* (New Haven, CT: Yale University Press, 2007); Catherine L. Albanese, *The Delight Makers: Anglo-American Metaphysical Religion and the Pursuit of Happiness* (Chicago: University of Chicago Press, 2023).

30. David G. Bromley, Anson D. Shupe Jr., and J. C. Ventimiglia, "Atrocity Tales, the Unification Church, and the Social Construction of Evil," *Journal of Communication* 29, no. 3 (1979): 42–53; James T. Richardson, "Peoples Temple and Jonestown: A Corrective Comparison and Critique," *Journal for the Scientific Study of Religion* 19 (1980): 239–55; James R. Lewis, "Apostates and the Legitimation of Repression: Some Historical and Empirical Perspectives on the Cult Controversy," *Sociological Analysis* 49 (1989): 386–96; Michelle Mueller, "Escaping the Perils of Sensationalist Television Reduction: A&E Networks' *Escaping Polygamy* as a Reality TV Atrocity Tale," *Nova Religio: The Journal of Alternative and Emergent Religions* 22 (2019): 60–83.

31. Elizabeth Elbourne, "Introduction: Key Themes and Perspectives," in *Sex, Power, and Slavery*, ed. Gwyn Campbell and Elizabeth Elbourne (Athens: Ohio University Press, 2014), 8.

32. A. W. Manning to John Whitehead, March 19, 1913, A. W. Manning File, Center for Swedenborgian Studies Library and Archives, Berkeley.

33. Susan J. Palmer, "NXIVM and #MeToo," *Nova Religio: The Journal of Alternative and Emergent Religions* 24 (2021): 104–12; Tom McCarthy, "The Called, the Chosen, and the Tempted: Psychologists, the Church, and the Scandal," *American Catholic Studies* 125 (2014): 1–49; Robert J. Orsi, *History and Presence* (Cambridge, MA: Harvard University Press, 2016), 215–48. See also the Religion and Sexual Abuse Project, founded 2019, https://www.religionandsexualabuseproject.org.

34. Katherine Pratt Ewing, "Religion, Spirituality, and the Sexual Scandal," *The Immanent Frame* (blog), August 2, 2010, https://tif.ssrc.org/2010/08/02/religion-spirituality-sexual-scandal/.

Chapter 1

1. Thomas Lake Harris, *Brotherhood of the New Life: Its Fact, Law, Method and Purpose* (Santa Rosa: Fountaingrove Press, 1891).

2. Thomas Lake Harris, *An Epic of the Starry Heaven* (New York: Partridge & Brittan, 1854), 204–7.

3. Harris, *An Epic of the Starry Heaven*, vii, xv, xvi, 208–10; S. B. Brittan, ed., *The Spiritual Telegraph*, library ed. (New York: Partridge & Brittan, 1854), 293–98.

4. Andrew Jackson Davis, *The Principles of Nature, Her Divine Relations, and a Voice to Mankind* (Boston: Colby & Rich, 1847); S. C. Hewitt, *Messages from the Superior State, Communicated from John Murray through John M. Spear* (Boston: Bela Marsh, 1853); Nathan Francis White, *Voices from Spirit-Land* (New York: Partridge & Brittan, 1854); E. C. Henck, *Spirit Voices: Odes, Dictated by Spirits of the Second Sphere* (Philadelphia: G. D. Henck, 1855). On spiritualism generally, see R. Laurence Moore, *In Search of White Crows: Spiritualism, Parapsychology, and American Culture* (New York: Oxford University Press, 1977); Ann Braude, *Radical Spirits: Spiritualism and Women's Rights in Nineteenth-Century America* (Bloomington: Indiana University Press, 1989); Bret E. Carroll, *Spiritualism in Antebellum America* (Bloomington: Indiana University Press, 1997); Ann Taves, *Fits, Trances, and*

Visions: Experiencing Religion and Explaining Experience from Wesley to James (Princeton, NJ: Princeton University Press, 1999), 166–206; Robert S. Cox, *Body and Soul: A Sympathetic History of American Spiritualism* (Charlottesville: University of Virginia Press, 2003); John B. Buescher, *The Other Side of Salvation: Spiritualism and the Nineteenth-Century Religious Experience* (Boston: Skinner House Books, 2004); Catherine L. Albanese, *A Republic of Mind and Spirit: A Cultural History of Metaphysical Religion in America* (New Haven, CT: Yale University Press, 2007); Molly McGarry, *Ghosts of Futures Past: Spiritualism and the Cultural Politics of Nineteenth-Century America* (Berkeley: University of California Press, 2008); Emily Suzanne Clark, *A Luminous Brotherhood: Afro-Creole Spiritualism in Nineteenth-Century New Orleans* (Chapel Hill: University of North Carolina Press, 2016); Simone Natale, *Supernatural Entertainments: Victorian Spiritualism and the Rise of Modern Media Culture* (University Park: Penn State University, 2016); and Erik R. Seeman, *Speaking with the Dead in Early America* (Philadelphia: University of Pennsylvania Press, 2019).

5. Elisha Harrington, *The Utica Directory* (Utica, NY: Dauby and Maynard, 1829), 68; Elisha Harrington, *The Utica Directory* (Utica, NY: E. A. Maynard, 1832), 46; Richard McCully, *The Brotherhood of the New Life and Thomas Lake Harris* (Glasgow: John Thomson, 1893), 1–20; Arthur A. Cuthbert, *The Life and World-Work of Thomas Lake Harris, Written from Direct Personal Knowledge* (Glasgow: C. W. Pearce, 1908), 86; Thomas Lake Harris, "An Autobiographic Letter from T. L. Harris," 1896, reel 7, item 55, in Jack T. Ericson, ed., *Thomas Lake Harris and the Brotherhood of the New Life: Books, Pamphlets, Serials and Manuscripts, 1854–1942*, microfilm (New York: New York Times, 1974).

6. Whitney Cross, *The Burned-Over District: The Social and Intellectual History of Enthusiastic Religion in Western New York, 1800–1850* (New York: Harper & Row, 1950), 63–64; Mary P. Ryan, "A Woman's Awakening: Evangelical Religion and the Families of Utica, New York, 1800–1840," *American Quarterly* 30 (1978): 602–23; Barry Hankins, *The Second Great Awakening and the Transcendentalists* (Westport, CT: Greenwood Press, 2004), 45, 88–89.

7. Jane Lee Waring Harris, diary, July 12, 1903, reel 14, item 314, in Ericson, *Thomas Lake Harris.*

8. McCully, *The Brotherhood of the New Life*, 21–22; *New York Universalist Union*, November 11, 1843: 827–29.

9. Cross, *The Burned-Over District*, 43–44; Braude, *Radical Spirits*, 46–48; Ann Lee Bressler, *The Universalist Movement in America, 1770–1880* (New York: Oxford University Press, 2001), 56–58; John Benedict Buescher, *The Remarkable Life of John Murray Spear: Agitator for the Spirit Land* (Notre Dame, IN: University of Notre Dame Press, 2006), 14–15; Albanese, *A Republic of Mind and Spirit*, 150–60.

10. *New York Aurora*, March 19, 1842; Richard B. Stott, *Workers in the Metropolis: Class, Ethnicity, and Youth in Antebellum New York City* (Ithaca, NY: Cornell University Press, 2019); Daniel S. Levy, *Manhattan Phoenix: The Great Fire of 1835 and the Emergence of Modern New York* (New York: Oxford University Press, 2022). Whitman and Harris probably never met, but Whitman would later become an admirer of Harris's poetry; see David S. Reynolds, *Walt Whitman's America: A Cultural Biography* (New York: Alfred A. Knopf, 1995), 264–71.

11. *Utica Evangelical Magazine and Gospel Advocate*, October 18, 1844: 334.

12. *Boston Universalist Miscellany*, 3 (April 1846): 404; *Boston Trumpet and Universalist Magazine*, September 12, 1846: 49–50; Robert Darnton, *Mesmerism and the End of the Enlightenment in France* (Cambridge, MA: Harvard University Press, 1986).

13. John Bovee Dods, *Six Lectures on the Philosophy of Mesmerism* (New York: Fowlers and Wells, 1847), 71; *Boston Trumpet and Universalist Magazine*, August 8, 1846: 30; September 12, 1846: 50; *Boston Universalist Quarterly and General Review*, October 1847: 372; Robert C. Fuller, *Mesmerism and the American Cure of Souls* (Philadelphia: University of Pennsylvania Press, 1982); Bressler, *The Universalist Movement in America*, 102–7; Fred Nadis, *Wonder Shows: Performing Science, Magic, and Religion in America* (New Brunswick, NJ: Rutgers University Press, 2005), 87–91; David Schmit, "Re-Visioning Antebellum American Psychology: The Dissemination of Mesmerism, 1836–1854," *History of Psychology* 8 (2005): 403–34; Martin Willis, *Mesmerists, Monsters, and Machines: Science Fiction and the Cultures of Science in the Nineteenth Century* (Kent, OH: Kent State University Press, 2006); Emily Ogden, *Credulity: A Cultural History of U.S. Mesmerism* (Chicago: University of Chicago Press, 2018).

14. Harris, "An Autobiographic Letter from T. L. Harris," 5–6; Brittan, *The Spiritual Telegraph*, 403; Braude, *Radical Spirits*, 51–52.

15. Andrew Jackson Davis, *The Magic Staff: An Autobiography* (New York: J. S. Brown & Co., 1857), 342; *New York Univercoelum and Spiritual Philosopher*, December 11, 1847: 25.

16. Andrew Jackson Davis, *The Great Harmonia*, vol. 1 (Boston: Benjamin B. Mussey & Co., 1850), 6, 9; Andrew Jackson Davis, *The Philosophy of Spiritual Intercourse* (New York: Fowlers and Wells, 1851), 26; Andrew Jackson Davis, *The Present Age and Inner Life* (New York: Partridge & Brittan, 1853), 24; Braude, *Radical Spirits*, 33–35; Carroll, *Spiritualism in Antebellum America*, 16–21; Cox, *Body and Soul*, 7–10; Albanese, *A Republic of Mind and Spirit*, 206–20.

17. *New York Daily Tribune*, May 23, 1844: 4; *Utica Evangelical Magazine and Gospel Advocate*, January 12, 1844: 16; *Philadelphia Ladies' Garland and Family Wreath*, October 1845: 77.

18. *New York Univercoelum and Spiritual Philosopher*, September 23, 1848: 267; October 14, 1848: 311.

19. *New York American People's Journal of Science, Literature, and Art*, January 1, 1850: 31; Moore, *In Search of White Crows*, 73, 77–78; Albanese, *A Republic of Mind and Spirit*, 265–66.

20. Abel C. Thomas, *A Century of Universalism in Philadelphia and New York* (Philadelphia: J. Fagan and Son, 1872), 314; *Boston Trumpet and Universalist Magazine*, February 12, 1848: 138; Braude, *Radical Spirits*, 46–48; Bressler, *The Universalist Movement in America*, 108–20; Buescher, *The Other Side of Salvation*, 56–58; Albanese, *A Republic of Mind and Spirit*, 150–60.

21. *Boston Trumpet and Universalist Magazine*, February 12, 1848: 138; Harris, "An Autobiographic Letter from T. L. Harris," 5–6; *New York Univercoelum and Spiritual Philosopher*, November 25, 1848: 401–2; *Utica Evangelical Magazine and Gospel Advocate*, March 31, 1848: 102.

22. Carl J. Guarneri, *The Utopian Alternative: Fourierism in America* (New York: Cornell University Press, 1991), 157–58, 352; Nicholas V. Riasanovsky, *The Teaching of Charles Fourier* (Berkeley: University of California Press, 2020).

23. *Cleveland Herald*, February 22, 1848: 3; *New York Univercoelum and Spiritual Philosopher*, April 15, 1848: 312; April 29, 1848: 345–46; *Utica Evangelical Magazine and Gospel Advocate*, March 31, 1848: 102; John Humphrey Noyes, *History of American Socialisms* (Philadelphia: J. B. Lippincott, 1870), 366–76; Frank Podmore, *Modern Spiritualism: A History and a Criticism*, vol. 1 (London: Methuen & Co., 1902), 175; James M. Morris, "Communes and Cooperatives: Cincinnati's Early Experiments in Social Reform," *Cincinnati Historical Society Bulletin* 33 (Spring 1975): 56–80; John C. Spurlock, *Free Love: Marriage and Middle-Class Radicalism in America, 1825–1860* (New York: New York University Press, 1988), 89–90; Catherine M. Rokicky, *Creating a Perfect World: Religious and Secular Utopias in Nineteenth-Century Ohio* (Athens: Ohio University Press, 2002), 131.

24. *New York Univercoelum and Spiritual Philosopher*, September 30, 1848: 282; December 23, 1848: 49–51; *Boston Christian Register*, November 24, 1848: 1; James Parton, *The Life of Horace Greeley* (New York: Mason Brothers, 1855), 426–27; Robert C. Williams, *Horace Greeley: Champion of American Freedom* (New York: New York University Press, 2006), 194.

25. *New York Univercoelum and Spiritual Philosopher*, September 30, 1848: 280; Davis, *The Magic Staff*, 395, 407; Catherine L. Albanese, "On the Matter of Spirit: Andrew Jackson Davis and the Marriage of God and Nature," *Journal of the American Academy of Religion* 60 (1992): 9; Catherine L. Albanese, *The Delight Makers: Anglo-American Metaphysical Religion and the Pursuit of Happiness* (Chicago: University of Chicago Press, 2023), 158–59.

26. Davis, *The Magic Staff*, 409–10; Spurlock, *Free Love*, 92–97; Braude, *Radical Spirits*, 127–36; McGarry, *Ghosts of Futures Past*, 95–100; Thomas Lake Harris, *Lecture on Spiritual Manifestations, Past, Present, and Future* (Boston: George C. Rand, 1853), 15.

27. *Auburn Wisconsin Chief*, January 22, 1850: 3; February 5, 1850: 4; E. W. Capron, *Modern Spiritualism: Its Facts and Fanaticisms* (Boston: Bela Marsh, 1855), 111; Emma Hardinge, *Modern American Spiritualism: A Twenty Years' Record of the Communion Between Earth and the World of Spirits* (New York: self-published, 1870), 58; Eliza Ann Benedict et al., *Spiritual Exposition of the Prophetic Scriptures of the New Testament* (Auburn, NY: E. H. Baxter and E. A. Benedict, 1850).

28. *New York Tribune*, January 29, 1851: 6; James Leander Scott, *A Journal of a Missionary Tour Through Pennsylvania, Ohio, Indiana, Illinois, Iowa, Wiskonsin, and Michigan* (Providence, RI: self-published, 1843); Ethan Wilcox, "Cookey Hill," in *Three Papers Delivered Before the Westerly Historical Society of Westerly, Rhode Island* (Westerly, RI: Utter Company, 1915), 19; *New York National Magazine*, October 1852: 353, 356.

29. *Schenectady Cabinet*, January 20, 1852: 3; Capron, *Modern Spiritualism*, 119–20; Noyes, *History of American Socialisms*, 569.

30. *Mountain Cove Journal and Spiritual Harbinger*, August 19, 1852: 5; *Fayette Observer*, November 2, 1852: 2; *Southern Literary Messenger*, July 1853: 392; *Auburn Wisconsin Chief*, August 10, 1852: 2; *Belmont Chronicle*, January 28, 1853: 1; Carroll, *Spiritualism in Antebellum America*, 85.

31. *New Orleans Times-Picayune*, July 31, 1852: 2; August 5, 1852: 1; *Mountain Cove Journal and Spiritual Harbinger*, February 10, 1853: 75.

32. *New York Tribune*, May 7, 1851: 7; *New York Spiritual Telegraph*, October 16, 1852: 4; *New York Journal of Progress*, June 11, 1853: 107; Capron, *Modern Spiritualism*, 128–31; Paul E. Johnson and Sean Wilenz, *The Kingdom of Matthias: A Story of Sex and Salvation in 19th-Century America* (New York: Oxford University Press, 1994).

33. *Mountain Cove Journal and Spiritual Harbinger*, January 13, 1853: 67; April 7, 1853: 91; June 16, 1853: 106; September 1, 1853: 128; September 29, 1853: 135; Harris, *Lecture on Spiritual Manifestations*, 13, 17–19.

34. *New York Spiritual Telegraph*, October 16, 1852: 4; July 2, 1853: 2; Capron, *Modern Spiritualism*, 131; *Chicago Religio-Philosophical Journal*, July 12, 1890: 105.

35. Hardinge, *Modern American Spiritualism*, 59, 207–13; D. D. Howe, *Lights and Shadows of Spiritualism* (London: Virtue & Co., 1877), 197–202; Maria Monk, *The Awful Disclosures of Maria Monk* (New York: Howe & Bates, 1836). On antebellum anti-Catholicism, see Ray Allen Billington, *The Protestant Crusade, 1800–1860* (New York: Macmillan, 1938); Jenny Franchot, *Roads to Rome: The Antebellum Protestant Encounter with Catholicism* (Berkeley: University of California Press, 1994); Sandra Frink, "Women, the Family, and the Fate of the Nation in American Anti-Catholic Narratives, 1830–1860," *Journal of the History of Sexuality* 18 (2009): 237–64; and Cassandra L. Yacovassi, *Escaped Nuns: True Womanhood and the Campaign Against Convents in Antebellum America* (New York: Oxford University Press, 2018).

36. Taves, *Fits, Trances, and Visions*, 165; McGarry, *Ghosts of Futures Past*, 56–57; Robert Wuthnow, *American Misfits and the Making of Middle-Class Respectability* (Princeton, NJ: Princeton University Press, 2017), 101–34; Bret E. Carroll, "Spiritualism and Community in Antebellum America: The Mountain Cove Episode," *Communal Societies* 12 (1992): 20–39; Carroll, *Spiritualism in Antebellum America*, 166–76; Buescher, *The Other Side of Salvation*, 79–80; Albanese, *A Republic of Mind and Spirit*, 268–70.

37. J. L. Scott, *Scenes from Beyond the Grave: Trance of Marietta Davis* (Dayton, OH: S. Deuel, 1855); Brittan, *The Spiritual Telegraph*, 293; *New York Times*, February 19, 1855: 3; Harris, *An Epic of the Starry Heaven*; Thomas Lake Harris, *A Lyric of the Morning Land* (New York: Partridge & Brittan, 1854); Thomas Lake Harris, *A Lyric of the Golden Age* (New York: Partridge & Brittan, 1856).

38. See also William L. Davis, "The Book of Mormon and the Limits of Naturalistic Criteria: Comparing Joseph Smith and Andrew Jackson Davis," *Dialogue* 53 (2020): 73–103.

39. Capron, *Modern Spiritualism*, 199; Harris, *An Epic of the Starry Heaven*, i–xiv, 202, 208–10; Harris, *A Lyric of the Morning Land*, 255–56; Harris, *A Lyric of the Golden Age*, xvi, xxvi–xxvii; Buescher, *The Other Side of Salvation*, 71–72.

40. Harris, *A Lyric of the Golden Age*, xxxi–xxxii; Braude, *Radical Spirits*, 30; McAllister, "The Poetic Vision of Thomas Lake Harris," 71.

41. Harris, *A Lyric of the Morning Land*, 56, 208, 244, 246.

42. Harris, *A Lyric of the Morning Land*, 48–49.

43. Harris, *A Lyric of the Golden Age*, 4; Brittan, *The Spiritual Telegraph*, 405; Herbert W. Schneider and George Lawton, *A Prophet and a Pilgrim: Being the Incredible History of Thomas Lake Harris and Laurence Oliphant* (New York: Columbia University Press, 1942), 20; Melissa Daggett, *Spiritualism in Nineteenth-Century New Orleans: The Life and Times of Henry Louis Rey* (Lexington: University Press of Kentucky, 2017), 25.

44. Thomas Lake Harris, "Some Ways of the Evil Woman," n.d., reel 8, item 203; Thomas Lake Harris, "The Annunciation of the Son of Man," 1875, reel 12, item 260, both in Ericson, *Thomas Lake Harris*; William Alfred Hinds, *American Communities* (Oneida, NY: Office of the American Socialist, 1878), 146.

45. Kara M. French, *Against Sex: Identities of Sexual Restraint in Early America* (Chapel Hill: University of North Carolina Press, 2021), 3–4.

46. Thomas Lake Harris, *Veritas: A Word Song* (Glasgow: C. W. Pearce & Co., 1910), 2; Thomas Lake Harris, *The Marriage of Heaven and Earth* (Glasgow: C. W. Pearce & Co., 1903), 234.

47. Thomas Lake Harris, "Marriage and Divorce," *The Herald of Light* 2, no. 2 (June 1858): 69, 72.

48. Emanuel Swedenborg, *The Delights of Wisdom Pertaining to Conjugial Love* (New York: American Swedenborg Printing and Publishing Society, 1892); Carroll, *Spiritualism in Antebellum America*, 16–34; Leigh Eric Schmidt, *Hearing Things: Religion, Illusion, and the American Enlightenment* (Cambridge, MA: Harvard University Press, 2000), 199–245; Cox, *Body and Soul*, 12–16; Cathy Gutierrez, "Bodies and Sex in Spiritualist Heavens," in *Hidden Intercourse: Eros and Sexuality in the History of Western Esotericism*, ed. Wouter J. Hanegraaff and Jeffrey J. Kripal (New York: Fordham University Press, 2008), 309–32.

49. Thomas Lake Harris to George Bush, November 10, 1853, box 1, item 36, George Bush Papers, 1830–1859, William L. Clements Library, University of Michigan.

50. Ralph Waldo Emerson, "Swedenborg; or, the Mystic," in his *Representative Men* (Boston: Phillips, Sampson and Company, 1850); George Bush, "Revelations of A. J. Davis," in *Mesmer and Swedenborg* (New York: John Allen, 1847), 159–206; George Bush and B. F. Barrett, *Davis' Revelations Revealed* (New York: John Allen, 1847); Carroll, *Spiritualism in Antebellum America*, 26; Seeman, *Speaking with the Dead in Early America*, 165–70.

51. B. F. Barrett, *Rev. B. F. Barrett's Review of Rev. T. L. Harris' Lectures on "Spiritual Philosophy"* (Cincinnati: Cincinnati *Daily Times*, 1848), 11; Schneider and Lawton, *A Prophet and a Pilgrim*, 36–37.

52. *The Herald of Light* 2, no. 2 (June 1858): 90, 98.

53. Thomas Lake Harris, *Arcana of Christianity*, vol. 1, part 1 (New York: New Church Publishing Association, 1858), 423, 432.

54. *Springfield Republican*, August 28, 1858.

55. *New Jerusalem Magazine*, August 1857: 111–12.

56. *The Swedenborgian* 1, no. 1 (January 1858): 63.

57. *The Herald of Light*, May 1859: 47.

58. *The Herald of Light*, July 1859: 168.

59. Harris, *Brotherhood of the New Life*, 14.

Chapter 2

1. Alzire A. Chevaillier, "The New Republic," *Problem of Life and International Journal of Truth* 3 no. 6 (June 1891): 293–94.

2. Thomas Lake Harris, *The Great Republic: A Poem of the Sun* (New York: Brotherhood of the New Life, 1867), 73–74; Ruth Le Prade, "The Angel of the Jails," 1942, p. 260, box 25, Poets Garden Records, Special Collections Library, University of Southern California.

3. *Annual Report of the School Committee of the City of Boston* (Boston: Alfred Mudge & Son, 1868), 61; Wendy J. Deichman Edwards and Carolyn De Swarte Gifford, eds., *Gender and the Social Gospel* (Urbana: University of Illinois Press, 2003); Christopher H. Evans, *The Social Gospel in American Religion: A History* (New York: New York University Press, 2017).

4. Alzire A. Chevaillier, "The Brotherhood of Man," *International Magazine of Christian Science* 3 no. 11 (May 1889): 388.

5. F. B. Sanborn, ed., *Proceedings of the Eighth Annual Conference of Charities and Corrections* (Boston: Conference of Charities, 1881), 319; R. Rudy Higgens-Evenson, *The Price of Progress: Public Services, Taxation, and the American Corporate State, 1877 to 1929* (Baltimore, MD: Johns Hopkins University Press, 2003), 34.

6. Alzire A. Chevaillier to Henry Wadsworth Longfellow, February 25, 1879, item 1089, Letters to Henry Wadsworth Longfellow, 1807–1882, Houghton Library, Harvard University; Alzire A. Chevaillier to John Davis Long, December 11, 1879, folder 6, box 5, John Davis Long Papers, Massachusetts Historical Society, Boston.

7. Alzire A. Chevaillier to Mary Baker Eddy, n.d. [ca. March 1885], folder 388, Incoming Correspondence of Mary Baker Eddy, Mary Baker Eddy Library, Boston; *Washington Post*, June 23, 1882: 1; Charles E. Rosenberg, *The Trial of the Assassin Guiteau: Psychiatry and the Law in the Gilded Age* (Chicago: University of Chicago Press, 1995), 229; Candace Millard, *Destiny of the Republic: A Tale of Madness, Medicine and the Murder of a President* (New York: Doubleday, 2011), 279–81; James C. Clarke, *The Murder of James A. Garfield: The President's Last Days and the Trial and Execution of His Assassin* (New York: McFarland, 1993), 141; Susan Wels, *An Assassin in Utopia: The True Story of a Nineteenth-Century Sex Cult and a President's Murder* (New York: Pegasus Books, 2023), 194–96.

8. Benjamin F. Butler, *Argument Before the Tewksbury Investigation Committee* (Boston: Democratic Central Committee, 1883), 37; Richard Harmond, "The 'Beast' in Boston: Benjamin F. Butler as Governor of Massachusetts," *Journal of American History* 55 (1968):

273; David Wagner, *Ordinary People: In and Out of Poverty in the Gilded Age* (Boulder, CO: Paradigm, 2007), 34.

9. *Springfield Republican*, October 8, 1883: 8.

10. *U.S. and Canada, Passenger and Immigration Lists Index, 1500s–1900s* (Provo: Ancestry.com Operations, Inc, 2010).

11. Frost Thorn and Charles Chevaillier to Amos Clark, petition 21584712; 1847 Census, Nacogdoches County, p. 20; Records of the District Court, Nacogdoches County Courthouse, Nacogdoches, Texas.

12. John Clark, *Records of the Descendants of Hugh Clark: Of Watertown, Mass. 1640–1866* (Boston: self-published, 1866).

13. *Manual of the Public Schools of the City of Boston* (Boston: Municipal Printing Office, 1880), 40.

14. Benjamin R. Tucker, "The Life of Benjamin R. Tucker," 1928, box 8, Benjamin R. Tucker Papers, Rare Books and Manuscript Division, New York Public Library.

15. *Marshall Messenger*, December 26, 1919: 3.

16. Folder 16, box 13, Poets Garden Records, Special Collections Library, University of Southern California.

17. "Rough notes dictated to Ruth Le Prade by Faith Chevaillier," n.d., folder 18, box 13, Poets Garden Records, Special Collections Library, University of Southern California.

18. Peter D. Williams, *Religion, Art, and Money: Episcopalians and American Culture from the Civil War to the Great Depression* (Chapel Hill: University of North Carolina Press, 2016), 30, 49–50; Gillis J. Harp, *Brahmin Prophet: Phillips Brooks and the Path of Liberal Protestantism* (New York: Rowman & Littlefield, 2003), 130–34.

19. Le Prade, "The Angel of the Jails," 1942, box 25, Poets Garden Records, Special Collections Library, University of Southern California.

20. *International Magazine of Truth*, 6, no. 12 (Sept. 15, 1890): 468–69.

21. Alzire A. Chevaillier to Mary Baker Eddy, ca. March 1885, folder 388, Incoming Correspondence of Mary Baker Eddy, Mary Baker Eddy Library, Boston.

22. F. G. Gosling, *Before Freud: Neurasthenia and the American Medical Community, 1870–1910* (Urbana: University of Illinois Press, 1987); Eric Caplan, *Mind Games: American Culture and the Birth of Psychotherapy* (Berkeley: University of California Press, 1998), 37–42; Beryl Satter, *Each Mind a Kingdom: American Women, Sexual Purity, and the New Thought Movement, 1875–1920* (Berkeley: University of California Press, 1999), 52–55.

23. Mary Baker Eddy, "Notices for the Massachusetts Metaphysical College," 1882, A10214, Mary Baker Eddy Library, Boston.

24. Mary Baker Eddy, *Historical Sketch of Metaphysical Healing* (Boston: Massachusetts Metaphysical College, 1885), 8, 11.

25. Alzire A. Chevaillier to Mary Baker Eddy, April 7, 1885, folder 388, Incoming Correspondence of Mary Baker Eddy; Christian Scientist Association, meeting minutes with list of members, April 1, 1885, EOR11, Mary Baker Eddy Library, Boston.

26. Stephen Gottschalk, *The Emergence of Christian Science in American Religious Life* (Berkeley: University of California Press, 1973), xvii; Rennie B. Schoepflin, *Christian Science on Trial: Religious Healing in America* (Baltimore, MD: Johns Hopkins University Press, 2003), 45–46; Amy B. Voorhees, *A New Christian Identity: Christian Science Origins and Experience in American Culture* (Chapel Hill: University of North Carolina Press, 2021).

27. Rosemary R. Hicks, "Religion and Remedies Reunited: Rethinking Christian Science," *Journal of Feminist Studies in Religion* 20 (Fall 2004): 41, 47; Schoepflin, *Christian Science on Trial*; Satter, *Each Mind a Kingdom*, 66–68; Voorhees, *A New Christian Identity*, 139–60.

28. Alzire A. Chevaillier to Christian Science Board of Directors, June 29, 1932, folder 12, box 8, Reminiscences of Mary Baker Eddy, Mary Baker Eddy Library, Boston.

29. Alzire A. Chevaillier to Mary Baker Eddy, April 7, 1885, folder 388, Incoming Correspondence of Mary Baker Eddy, Mary Baker Eddy Library, Boston.

30. Alzire A. Chevaillier to Mary Baker Eddy, n.d. [ca. March 1885], folder 388, Incoming Correspondence of Mary Baker Eddy, Mary Baker Eddy Library, Boston.

31. Ann Braude, "The Perils of Passivity: Women's Leadership in Spiritualism and Christian Science," in *Women's Leadership in Marginal Religions: Explorations Outside the Mainstream*, ed. Catherine Wessinger (Urbana: University of Illinois Press, 1993), 60–61.

32. Alzire A. Chevaillier to Mary Baker Eddy, November 4, 1885, folder 388, Incoming Correspondence of Mary Baker Eddy, Mary Baker Eddy Library, Boston.

33. Alzire A. Chevaillier to Septimus J. Hanna, March 30, 1900, folder 388, Incoming Correspondence of Mary Baker Eddy, Mary Baker Eddy Library, Boston.

34. Robert Peel, *Mary Baker Eddy: The Years of Trial* (New York: Holt, Rinehart and Winston, 1971), 173; Madeleine B. Stern, ed., "Introduction," *Louisa May Alcott: Signature of Reform* (Boston: Northeastern University Press, 2002), 6.

35. Gottschalk, *The Emergence of Christian Science*, 101, 116; Satter, *Each Mind a Kingdom;* Schoepflin, *Christian Science on Trial*; Gail M. Harley, *Emma Curtis Hopkins: Forgotten Founder of New Thought* (Syracuse: Syracuse University Press, 2002); Catherine L. Albanese, *The Delight Makers: Anglo-American Metaphysical Religion and the Pursuit of Happiness* (Chicago: University of Chicago Press, 2023), 245–65.

36. Satter, *Each Mind a Kingdom*, 4.

37. Alzire A. Chevaillier to Edward Bellamy, 1889, item 163, Edward Bellamy Correspondence, 1850–1898, Harvard University Library.

38. Alzire A. Chevaillier, "Practical Demonstration," *International Journal of Christian Science* 3, no. 4 (Oct. 1888): 143–44.

39. Alzire A. Chevaillier, "Death," *International Magazine of Christian Science*, 3 no. 6 (Dec. 1888), 194–99.

40. Alzire A. Chevaillier, "The Prayer of Thanksgiving Versus the Prayer of Supplication," *International Magazine of Christian Science* 3, no. 7 (Jan. 1889): 232.

41. Alzire A. Chevaillier to Mary Baker Eddy, May 3, 1889, folder 388, Incoming Correspondence of Mary Baker Eddy, Mary Baker Eddy Library, Boston.

42. Andrew Ventimiglia, *Copyrighting God: Ownership of the Sacred in American Religion* (Cambridge: Cambridge University Press, 2019), 199.

43. Eddy, *Historical Sketch*; "Perverted Metaphysics Versus Theology of Christian Science," *Christian Science Journal* 3 no. 11 (1886): 197.

44. Gottschalk, *The Emergence of Christian Science*, 114; Schoepflin, *Christian Science on Trial*, 28, 144.

45. Mary Baker Eddy to Julia A. D. Adams, July 6, 1887, Mary Baker Eddy Library, Boston.

46. Mary Baker Eddy to Hannah A. Larminie, 1888, folder 388, Mary Baker Eddy Library, Boston.

47. *Boston Globe*, April 30, 1888: 3; Schoepflin, *Christian Science on Trial*, 82–84.

48. Alzire A. Chevaillier, "The Brotherhood of Man," *International Magazine of Christian Science* 3, no. 11 (May 1889): 393–94.

49. Arthur Lipow, *Authoritarian Socialism in America: Edward Bellamy and the Nationalist Movement* (Berkeley: University of California Press, 1982), 122–24; Lyman Tower Sargent, "Edward Bellamy's Boston in 2000 from 1888 to 1897: The Evolution of Bellamy's Future Boston from *Looking Backward* Through *Equality*," *Utopian Studies* 27 (2016): 169; Catherine Tumber, *American Feminism and the Birth of New Age Spirituality: Searching for the Higher Self, 1875–1915* (Lanham, MD: Rowman & Littlefield, 2002), 71.

50. Chevaillier, "The Brotherhood of Man," 390.

51. "Special Notice," *International Magazine of Christian Science* 3, no. 10 (April 1889).

52. J. Herbie DiFonzo, *Beneath the Fault Line: The Popular and Legal Culture of Divorce in Twentieth-Century America* (Charlottesville: University Press of Virginia, 1997), 55; J. Herbie DiFonzo, "Addicted to Fault: Why Divorce Reform Has Lagged in New York," *Pace Law Review* 27 (Summer 2007): 559–603.

53. *Chicago Daily Tribune*, July 8, 1889: 4.

54. ""Statement of A. and Mary Bently Worthington," "An Open Letter," *International Magazine of Christian Science* 4, no. 1 (July 1889): 10–31.

55. *New York Sun*, June 4, 1889: 5.

56. John C. Spurlock, *Free Love: Marriage and Middle-Class Radicalism in America, 1825–1860* (New York: New York University Press, 1988); John D'Emilio and Estelle B. Freedman, *Intimate Matters: A History of Sexuality in America*, 3rd ed. (Chicago: University of Chicago Press, 2012), 112–16; Ann Braude, *Radical Spirits: Spiritualism and Women's Rights in Nineteenth-Century America*, 2nd ed. (Bloomington: Indiana University Press, 2001), 127–36; Carol Faulkner, *Unfaithful: Love, Adultery, and Marriage Reform in Nineteenth-Century America* (Philadelphia: University of Pennsylvania Press, 2019); Ana Stevenson, *The Woman as Slave in Nineteenth-Century American Social Movements* (New York: Palgrave Macmillan, 2019); Holly Jackson, *American Radicals: How Nineteenth-Century Protest Shaped the Nation* (New York: Crown, 2019), 123–57.

57. Joanne E. Passet, *Sex Radicals and the Quest for Women's Equality* (Urbana: University of Illinois Press, 2003); Barbara Goldsmith, *Other Powers: The Age of Suffrage, Spiritualism, and the Scandalous Victoria Woodhull* (New York: Alfred A. Knopf, 1998); Helen Lefkowitz Horowitz, *Rereading Sex: Battles over Sexual Knowledge and Suppression in Nineteenth-Century America* (New York: Alfred A. Knopf, 2002), 342–85; D'Emilio and Freedman, *Intimate Matters*, 156–67; Amanda Frisken, *Victoria Woodhull's Sexual Revolution: Political Theater and the Popular Press in Nineteenth-Century America* (Philadelphia: University of Pennsylvania Press, 2004), 40–41; Molly McGarry, *Ghosts of Futures Past: Spiritualism and the Cultural Politics of Nineteenth-Century America* (Berkeley: University of California Press, 2008), 94–101.

58. Alex Owen, *The Darkened Room: Women, Power, and Spiritualism in Late Victorian England* (Chicago: University of Chicago Press, 1989), 37–38; P. C. Kemeny. *The New England Watch and Ward Society* (New York: Oxford University Press, 2019), 99–101.

59. Mary Baker Eddy, "Wedlock," *Miscellaneous Writings, 1883–1896* (Boston: First Church of Christ, Scientist, 1896), 288; Peel, *Mary Baker Eddy*, 14; Satter, *Each Mind a Kingdom*, 69, 76–77.

60. Mary Baker Eddy, *Science and Health* (Boston: Christian Science Publishing Co., 1875), 314–15; Gottschalk, *The Emergence of Christian Science*, 241–42.

61. Lynn (MA) Transcript, October 14, 1876; quoted in Cindy Peyser Safronoff, *Crossing Swords: Mary Baker Eddy vs. Victoria Claflin Woodhull and the Battle for the Soul of Marriage* (Seattle: This One Thing, 2015).

62. Mary Baker Eddy, "Conjugal Rights," *Christian Science Journal* 7, no. 3 (June 1889): 109–13; "Separation of Truth and Error," *Christian Science Journal* 7, no. 4 (July 1889): 188–90.

63. Mary Baker Eddy to John F. Linscott and Ellen Brown Linscott, May 10, 1889, L04118, Mary Baker Eddy Library, Boston.

64. Alzire A. Chevaillier, "Judge Not," *International Journal of Christian Science* 4, no. 1 (July 1889): 1–3.

65. *International Journal of Christian Science* 4, no. 3 (Sept. 1889): 122; *New York Sun*, July 7, 1889: 14

66. *Bismark Tribune*, February 8, 1889; *New York Sun*, July 28, 1889: 13; *New York Sun*, July 31, 1889: 2; *Turner Country Herald*, August 8, 1889: 2; *Wichita Daily Eagle*, August 15, 1889: 9.

67. *Chicago Daily Tribune*, July 29, 1889: 5;; *International Journal of Christian Science* 4, no. 2 (Aug. 1889): 78.

68. *New York Sun*, July 29, 1889: 4; *International Magazine of Truth* 5, no. 1 (Oct. 15, 1889): 24.

69. *New York Times*, September 26, 1889: 4; John Hosking, *A Christchurch Quack Exposed* (Christchurch: H. J. Weeks, 1893); Stevan Eldred-Grigg, *Pleasures of the Flesh: Sex and Drugs in Colonial New Zealand, 1840–1915* (Wellington: Reed Books, 1984), 129–36; Marc Demarest, "Olcott's Gilded Theosopher: A Short Life of Samuel Oakley Crawford," *Theosophical History* 16 (July-October 2012). https://theohistory.org/issue-archive/volume-xvi/vol-xvi-no-3-4/.

70. *Chicago Daily Tribune*, August 5, 1889: 8; *Los Angeles Times*, August 18, 1889: 9.

71. *New York Sun*, July 29, 1889: 4; *Wilmington Evening Journal*, July 31, 1889: 4.

72. *Forth Worth Daily Gazette*, September 21, 1889: 4.

73. *Chicago Daily Tribune*, August 25, 1889: 10.

74. *New York Evening World*, September 2, 1889: 4.

75. *Wichita Eagle*, September 8, 1889: 4; *Chicago Daily Tribune*, July 29, 1889: 4.

76. Schoepflin, *Christian Science on Trial*, 106–9; Ventimiglia, *Copyrighting God*, 127–38; Voorhees, *A New Christian Identity*, 167–86.

77. *International Magazine of Truth* 5, no. 1 (Oct.15, 1889): 24.

78. *International Magazine of Truth* 5, no. 1 (Oct.15, 1889): 29.

79. *International Magazine of Truth* 5, no. 1 (Oct. 15, 1889): 1.

80. Peel, *Mary Baker Eddy*, 262.

81. *International Magazine of Truth* 5, no. 1 (Oct. 15, 1889): 30–31; 6, no. 5 (Feb. 15, 1890): 188; 6, no. 8 (May 15, 1890): 302–3; 6, no. 12 (Sept. 15, 1890): 464–68.

82. *New Orleans Daily Picayune*, July 13, 1890: 10.

83. *New York Times*, August 6, 1890: 8; *New York World*, September 13, 1890: 1; *New York World*, September 22, 1890: 1; *New York Times*, December 11, 1890: 3; Benjamin Loren Hartley, *Evangelicals at a Crossroads: Revivalism and Social Reform in Boston, 1860–1910* (Durham, NH: University of New Hampshire Press, 2011), 86–88.

84. Alzire A. Chevaillier, "Constitutional Liberty," *Boston Arena* 1, no. 4 (Mar. 1890): 432–40; Alzire A. Chevaillier, "White Child Slavery," *Boston Arena* 1, no. 5 (Apr. 1890): 598–601;

Kimberly A. Hamlin, *Free Thinker: Sex, Suffrage, and the Extraordinary Life of Helen Hamilton Gardener* (New York: W. W. Norton, 2020), 136.

85. *International Magazine of Truth* 6, no. 3 (Dec. 15, 1889): 117; *International Magazine of Truth* 6, no. 12 (Sept. 15, 1890): 1.

86. *International Magazine of Truth* 6, no. 12 (Sept. 15, 1890): 463.

87. Eddy, *Science and Health*, 237; Braude, *Radical Spirits*, 186–89.

88. W. J. Colville, *Inspirational Lectures and Impromptu Poems* (London: J. Burns, 1884), xii; McGarry, *Ghosts of Future Past*, 166–69.

89. *Honolulu Daily Bulletin*, August 7, 1886: 3.

90. *Sacramento Daily Union*, September 28, 1886; *Los Angeles Daily Herald*, May 20, 1888: 3; *San Francisco Daily Alta California*, June 4, 1888: 2; *San Francisco Daily Alta California*, June 11, 1889: 5.

91. *Problem of Life* 1, no. 1 (Jan. 1890): 12–13, 17.

92. Susan Goodier and Karen Pastorello, *Women Will Vote: Winning Suffrage in New York State* (Ithaca, NY: Cornell University Press, 2017), 19–22; Johanna Neuman, *Gilded Suffragists: The New York Socialites who Fought for Women's Right to Vote* (New York: New York University Press, 2017).

93. "The Copy of *Science and Health* Owned by Susan B. Anthony," 2011, marybakereddylibrary.org.

94. Elizabeth Cady Stanton to Benjamin F. and Sara Francis Underwood, April 5, 1887, in *The Selected Papers of Elizabeth Cady Stanton and Susan B. Anthony*, vol. 5, ed. Ann D. Gordon (New Brunswick, NJ: Rutgers University Press, 2009), 20; the friend in question was Henrietta Frances Lord.

95. Sue Davis, *The Political Thought of Elizabeth Cady Stanton: Women's Rights and the American Political Traditions* (New York: New York University Press, 2008), 178–95; Grace Ferrell, *Lillie Devereux Blake: Retracing a Life Erased* (Amherst: University of Massachusetts Press, 2002), 164–65; Kathi Kern, *Mrs. Stanton's Bible* (Ithaca, NY: Cornell University Press, 2001), 60–61, 116–21, 142–48; Pamela E. Klassen, *Spirits of Protestantism: Medicine, Healing, and Liberal Christianity* (Berkeley: University of California Press, 2011), 72–77.

96. Alzire A. Chevaillier, *Woman's Place in the Great Reform Movements of This Age* (New York: Unity Publishing Company, 1891).

97. Edward Bellamy, "Women and Nationalism," *The New Nation*, March 28, 1891: 139.

98. *Problem of Life and International Magazine of Truth*, May 1891: 248.

99. Marie Sinclair Caithness to Alzire A. Chevaillier, May 21, 1891, Poets Garden Records, Special Collections Library, University of Southern California; *Oakland Enquirer*, October 21, 1891: 8.

100. *The International Magazine of Christian Science* 3, no. 1 (July 1888) 3 no. 2 (Aug. 1888): 45; 3, no. 12 (June 1889): 430.

101. Edward Bellamy, "The New Republic," *The New Nation*, March 21, 1891: 123.

102. *Chicago New Church Independent*, July 1892: 337.

103. *Chicago New Church Independent*, July 1892: 335.

104. *Problem of Life and International Magazine of Truth*, May 1891: 255, 262.

Chapter 3

1. *Belfast News-Letter*, June 22, 1891: 4; *Seattle Post-Intelligencer*, June 12, 1891: 4.

2. Margaret Oliphant, "Laurence Oliphant," *Blackwood's Edinburgh Magazine*, February 1889: 280–96.

3. Vineta Colby and Robert Alan Colby, *The Equivocal Virtue: Mrs. Oliphant and the Victorian Literary Market Place* (New York: Archon Books, 1966), 183–84.

4. Margaret Oliphant, *Memoir of the Life of Laurence Oliphant and of Alice Oliphant, His Wife*, 2 vols. (London: William Blackwood and Sons, 1891).

5. Oliphant, *Memoir of the Life of Laurence Oliphant*, vol. 1, 185, 197, 206, 208, 314.

6. Margaret Oliphant, *The Autobiography of Margaret Oliphant: The Complete Text* (London: Oxford University Press, 1990), 41, 128; Oliphant, *Memoir of the Life of Laurence Oliphant*, vol. 2, 12; Elisabeth Jay, *Mrs. Oliphant: "A Fiction to Herself"* (Oxford: Clarendon Press, 1995), 140–49; Alison Milbank, "Margaret Oliphant (1828–97): Opening Doors of Interpretation," in *Anglican Women Novelists: From Charlotte Brontë to P. D. James*, ed. Judith Maltby and Alison Shell (New York: T&T Clark, 2019), 45–58.

7. *London Times*, May 26, 1859: 5; *Marylebone Mercury*, April 14, 1860.

8. *Yorkshire Spiritual Telegraph*, January 24, 1857: 126; Janet Oppenheim, *The Other World: Spiritualism and Psychical Research in England, 1850–1914* (Cambridge: Cambridge University Press, 1985), 7–12; Alex Owen, *The Darkened Room: Women, Power, and Spiritualism in Late Victorian England* (Philadelphia: University of Pennsylvania Press, 1990), 19–25.

9. Thomas Lake Harris, "Editorial Correspondence," *Herald of Light*, July 1859: 191.

10. William Howitt, *History of the Supernatural*, vol. 2 (London: Longman, Green, 1863), 208; Alfred J. Gabay, *The Covert Enlightenment: Eighteenth Century Counterculture and Its Aftermath* (West Chester, PA: Swedenborg Foundation, 2005), 235.

11. J. Ewing Richie, "Laurence Oliphant's 'Prophet,'" *London Literary World*, June 5, 1891: 537.

12. Thomas Lake Harris, "Editorial Correspondence," *Herald of Light*, December 1859: 115.

13. Thomas Lake Harris, *Modern Spiritualism: Its Truth and Errors* (London: W. White, 1860).

14. Thomas Lake Harris, *The Song of Satan: A Series of Poems, Originating with a Society of Infernal Spirits, and Received During Temptation-Combats* (New York: New Church Publishing Association, 1859).

15. *London Morning Advertiser*, January 16, 1860: 5.

16. *Boston Banner of Light*, April 7, 1860: 8; *Appleton (Wisconsin) Motor*, March 1, 1860; *Springfield Republican*, February 18, 1860: 4; *New York Times*, February 25, 1860: 4.

17. *London Spiritual Magazine*, February 1860: 90; March 1860: 104.

18. *London Spiritual Magazine*, April 1860: 150; May 1860: 198–99.

19. *Boston Banner of Light*, March 24, 1860: 6.

20. *New York Spiritual Telegraph and Fireside Preacher*, February 18, 1860: 510–11.

21. Clement John Wilkinson, *James John Garth Wilkinson: A Memoir of His Life* (London: Kegan Paul, Trench, Trübner & Co., 1911), 102.

22. W. Woodman, "Spiritualism: What Is It? What Are Its Pretensions?," *Intellectual Repository for the New Church*, May–October, 1860; Edward Brotherton, *Spiritualism, Swedenborg, and the New Church: An Examination of Claims* (London: W. White, 1860), 2; *Intellectual Repository for the New Church*, February 1, 1861: 73–82.

23. *Circular to the Members and Friends of the Swedenborg Society* (London: Swedenborg Society, 1861), 47; "How Jem Mace Became a Pillar of the Swedenborg Church," *London Reasoner*, December 16, 1860: 402; Richard Lines, *A History of the Swedenborg Society, 1810–2010* (London: South Vale Press, 2012), 56–59.

24. *New Jerusalem Magazine*, July 1860: 11, 30–31; Woodbury M. Fernald, *A New Age for the New Church* (Boston: Cowles and Company, 1860), 69.

25. *New Jerusalem Magazine*, May 1861: 604.

26. *Circular to the Members and Friends of the Swedenborg Society*, 53.

27. "Experiences of a Sister in the New Life," 1881, in Herbert W. Schneider and George Lawton, *A Prophet and a Pilgrim: Being the Incredible History of Thomas Lake Harris and Laurence Oliphant* (New York: Columbia University Press, 1942), 518.

28. Wilkinson, *James John Garth Wilkinson*, 103; Edward Maitland, ed., *Anna Kingsford: Her Life, Letters, Diary, and Work*, vol. 1 (London: George Redway, 1896), 284.

29. Tanya Cheadle, *Sexual Progressives: Reimagining Intimacy in Scotland, 1880–1914* (Manchester: Manchester University Press, 2020), 82–84; Oliphant, *Memoir of the Life of Laurence Oliphant*, vol. 2, 2–3, 23.

30. Justin McCarthy, *The Comet of a Season* (London: Chatto & Windus, 1890), 64–65.

31. Emily Lawless to Margaret Oliphant, May 25, 1891, quoted in Jay, *Mrs. Oliphant*, 144.

32. Oliphant, *Memoir of the Life of Laurence Oliphant*, vol. 2, 5–6.

33. Thomas Lake Harris, *The Millennial Age: Twelve Discourses on the Spiritual and Social Aspects of the Times* (London: W. White, 1860), 235–36, 239.

34. Emanuel Swedenborg, *The Spiritual Diary of Emanuel Swedenborg*, trans. George Bush and John H. Smithson, vol. 3 (London: James Speirs, 1883), 22–23.

35. Brotherton, *Spiritualism, Swedenborg, and the New Church*, 54–55.

36. Thomas Lake Harris, *Arcana of Christianity*, vol. 3 (New York: Brotherhood of the New Life, 1867), 33, 207, 226.

37. Cheadle, *Sexual Progressives*, 82–84.

38. *The Herald of Light*, November 1861: 12, 48.

39. *Boston Liberator*, April 24, 1846: 66; July 22, 1855: 116; *Rochester North Star*, January 26, 1850: 4.

40. Arthur A. Cuthbert, *The Life and World-Work of Thomas Lake Harris, Written from Direct and Personal Knowledge* (Glasgow: C. W. Pearce, 1908), 18.

41. *The Herald of Light*, November 1861: 12.
42. Harris, *Arcana of Christianity*, vol. 3, 234.
43. Cuthbert, *The Life and World-Work*, 189.
44. Thomas Lake Harris to Samuel Leavitt, February 8, 1871, reel 8, item 235, in Jack T. Ericson, ed., *Thomas Lake Harris and the Brotherhood of the New Life: Books, Pamphlets, Serials and Manuscripts, 1854–1942*, microfilm (New York: New York Times, 1974).
45. "Extracts from Old Letters of the Brotherhood of the New Life," in Schneider and Lawton, *A Prophet and a Pilgrim*, 168, 172, 175–76; Harris, *Arcana of Christianity*, vol. 3, 174; Jane Lee Waring to Mrs. P. and Miss N., March 18, 1883, Thomas Lake Harris Correspondence, Syracuse University Library.
46. Cuthbert, *The Life and World-Work*, 190–91.
47. Oliphant, *Memoir of the Life of Laurence Oliphant*, vol. 2, 14–20; Laurence Oliphant, *Episodes in a Life of Adventure: Or, Moss from a Rolling Stone* (London: William Blackwood and Sons, 1887), 418–19.
48. *London Spiritual Magazine*, June 1, 1869: 285.
49. *London Spiritual Magazine*, March 1, 1867: 101; May 1, 1867: 219; January 1, 1868: 4.
50. Cuthbert, *The Life and World-Work*, 189.
51. Oliphant, *Memoir of the Life of Laurence Oliphant*, vol. 2, 21.
52. *Newcastle Journal*, February 15, 1869: 2; *London Spiritual Magazine*, April 1, 1869: 181.
53. *New York Sun*, April 30, 1869: 2; *New York Tribune*, September 9, 1869: 2.
54. Oliphant, *Memoir of the Life of Laurence Oliphant*, vol. 2, 23–26, 30–31.
55. James Gregory, *Reformers, Patrons, and Philanthropists: The Cowper-Temples and High Politics in Victorian England* (London: I. B. Tauris, 2009), 112–18.
56. Laurence Oliphant to William Cowper, 1867, Harris-Oliphant Papers, Columbia University.
57. Laurence Oliphant to Georgina Cowper, October 26, 1867, Harris-Oliphant Papers, Columbia University.
58. Fannie Brownell, "Recollections of the Life and Work of Thomas Lake Harris," *Azoth: The Occult Magazine of America*, January 1920: 22.
59. Oliphant, *Memoir of the Life of Laurence Oliphant*, vol. 2, 36.
60. Rosamond Dale Owen, *My Perilous Life in Palestine* (New York: G. Allen & Unwin Limited, 1928), 23.
61. Schneider and Lawton, *Prophet and Pilgrim*, 114; Anne Taylor, *Laurence Oliphant, 1829–1888* (New York: Oxford University Press, 1982), 126; Jeffrey D. Lavoie, *Laurence Oliphant (1829–1888) and the Household: The Christian Mystical Teachings of a Nineteenth Century Religious Leader* (New York: Palgrave Macmillan, 2021), 11–12.
62. Laurence Oliphant to William Cowper, December 29, 1867, Harris-Oliphant Papers, Columbia University.
63. William Alfred Hinds, *American Communities* (Oneida, NY: Office of the American Socialist, 1878), 143–46.
64. Thomas Lake Harris, *Brotherhood of the New Life: Its Fact, Law, Method, and Purpose* (Santa Rosa: Fountaingrove Press, 1891), 4.
65. *International Psychic Gazette*, July 1916: 312.
66. Laurence Oliphant to Georgina Cowper, July 18, 1869, Harris-Oliphant Papers, Columbia University.
67. Oliphant, *Memoir of the Life of Laurence Oliphant*, vol. 2, 45.
68. "Experiences of a Sister in the New Life," 514–24.
69. Oliphant, *Memoir of the Life of Laurence Oliphant*, vol 2, 201.
70. *International Psychic Gazette*, August 1916, 345.
71. Oliphant, *Memoir of the Life of Laurence Oliphant*, vol 2, 28, 64–65.
72. *Exeter Flying Post*, March 16, 1870: 8.
73. Laurence Oliphant, *Piccadilly: A Fragment of Contemporary Biography* (London: William Blackwood and Sons, 1870).
74. *London Pall Mall Gazette*, July 17, 1871: 8; Harris and Jane Lee Waring visited Laurence in Paris in 1871; see Schneider and Lawton, *A Prophet and a Pilgrim*, 205.
75. Laurence Oliphant to Thomas Robinson, *Manchester Recipient* 3 (1871): 328, quoted in Richard McCully, *The Brotherhood of the New Life and Thomas Lake Harris* (Glasgow: John Thompson, 1893), 88.
76. Oliphant, *Memoir of the Life of Laurence Oliphant*, vol. 2, 92.
77. *Falkirk Herald*, March 28, 1872: 3.

78. Oliphant, *Memoir of the Life of Laurence Oliphant*, vol 2, 101, 104.

79. Oliphant, *Memoir of the Life of Laurence Oliphant*, vol 2, 86–89, 202.

80. Oliphant, *Memoir of the Life of Laurence Oliphant*, vol. 2, 109–15.

81. *London Morning Advertiser*, June 14, 1872: 7; Taylor, *Laurence Oliphant*, 172.

82. Owen, *My Perilous Life in Palestine*, 23.

83. Alice Oliphant to Georgina Cowper-Temple, December 6, 1872, Harris-Oliphant Papers, Columbia University.

84. *Bedfordshire Times and Independent*, April 5, 1873: 7.

85. Oliphant, *Memoir of the Life of Laurence Oliphant*, vol. 2, 137, 143.

86. Alice Oliphant to Georgina Cowper-Temple, July 6, 1876, Harris-Oliphant Papers, Columbia University.

87. Thomas Lake Harris, "Localities: March of Events," n.d., Harris-Oliphant Papers, Columbia University.

88. *San Francisco Daily Alta California*, February 24, 1875: 1; *Sonoma Democrat*, July 31, 1875: 5; *Santa Rosa Daily Democrat*, November 23, 1875: 3; Deed book 49, p. 637, Sonoma County Records, Santa Rosa.

89. *Pacific Rural Press*, February 14, 1880: 109; Thomas Pinney, *A History of Wine in America: From the Beginnings to Prohibition* (Berkeley: University of California Press, 1989), 334.

90. Kevin Starr, *Americans and the California Dream, 1850–1915* (New York: Oxford University Press, 1973); Sandra Sizer Frankiel, *California's Spiritual Frontiers: Religious Alternatives in Anglo-Protestantism, 1850–1910* (Berkeley: University of California Press, 1988); Laurie F. Maffly-Kipp, *Religion and Society in Frontier California* (New Haven, CT: Yale University Press, 1994).

91. *San Francisco Golden Gate*, August 29, 1885: 4.

92. Simone Cinotto, *Soft Soil, Black Grapes: The Birth of Italian Winemaking in California* (New York: New York University Press, 2012), 75–81; Julia Ornelas-Higdon, *The Grapes of Conquest: Race, Labor, and the Industrialization of California Wine, 1769–1920* (Lincoln: University of Nebraska Press, 2023), 86–93.

93. Schneider and Lawton, *A Prophet and a Pilgrim*, 301

94. Harris, *Arcana of Christianity*, vol. 3, 47.

95. "Experiences of a Sister in the New Life," 519.

96. Laurence Oliphant to William Cowper-Temple, January 10, 1877, Harris-Oliphant Papers, Columbia University.

97. Oliphant, *Memoir of the Life of Laurence Oliphant*, vol. 2, 164, 159.

98. Schneider and Lawton, *A Prophet and a Pilgrim*, 277–79.

99. Gregory, *Reformers, Patrons, and Philanthropists*, 112, 212.

100. Laurence Oliphant to William Cowper-Temple, June 30, 1877, Harris-Oliphant Papers, Columbia University.

101. Laurence Oliphant, *The Land of Gilead, with Excursions in the Lebanon* (London: William Blackwood and Sons, 1880).

102. Oliphant, *Memoir of the Life of Laurence Oliphant*, vol. 2, 165–66, 189.

103. Maitland, *Anna Kingsford*, vol. 1, 32, 277–83; Edward Maitland, ed., *Clothed with the Sun: Being the Illuminations of Anna (Bonus) Kingsford* (New York: Frank F. Lovell & Company, 1889), 293–94; Owen, *The Place of Enchantment*, 98–101.

104. *London Spiritualist and Journal of Psychological Science*, October 22, 1880: 197.

105. McCully, *The Brotherhood of the New Life*, 156.

106. Oliphant, *Memoir of the Life of Laurence Oliphant*, vol. 2, 119.

107. Owen, *My Perilous Life in Palestine*, 28–29.

108. Oliphant, *Memoir of the Life of Laurence Oliphant*, vol. 2, 159–60, *Independent Calistogian*, January 9, 1878: 3.

109. *Independent Calistogian*, October 6, 1880: 3.

110. Oliphant, *Memoir of the Life of Laurence Oliphant*, vol. 2, 194.

111. Oliphant, *Memoir of the Life of Laurence Oliphant*, vol. 2, 201.

112. Owen, *My Perilous Life in Palestine*, 30; *North British Daily Mail*, June 20, 1881: 5.

113. McCully, *The Brotherhood of the New Life*, 156; *Marin Journal*, October 27, 1881: 3; Cloverdale Cemetery, Cloverdale, California.

114. Owen, *My Perilous Life in Palestine*, 29–30; Oliphant, *Memoir of the Life of Laurence Oliphant*, vol. 2, 210.

115. Schneider and Lawton, *A Prophet and a Pilgrim*, 342–44; *Sacramento Daily Record-Union*, February 2, 1883: 3.
116. Schneider and Lawton, *A Prophet and a Pilgrim*, 325–27, 346–55.
117. Oliphant, *Memoir of the Life of Laurence Oliphant*, vol. 2, 217, 169.
118. Shalom Goldman, *Zeal for Zion: Christians, Jews, and the Idea of the Promised Land* (Chapel Hill: University of North Carolina Press, 2009), 42–87; Norma Claire Moruzzi, "Strange Bedfellows: The Question of Lawrence Oliphant's Christian Zionism," *Modern Judaism* 26 (2006): 55–73.
119. Oliphant, *Memoir of the Life of Laurence Oliphant*, vol. 2, 253–54.
120. Laurence Oliphant and Alice Oliphant, *Sympneumata: Or, Evolutionary Forces Now Active in Man* (London: William Blackwood and Sons, 1885), 81, 182; Julie Chajes, "Alice and Laurence Oliphant's Divine Androgyne and 'The Woman Question,'" *Journal of the American Academy of Religion* 84 (2016): 498–529.
121. Oliphant, *Memoir of the Life of Laurence Oliphant*, vol. 2, 281; *The Scotsman*, April 4, 1885: 8; *Aberdeen Free Press*, May 2, 1885; *Glasgow Herald*, September 20, 1886: 8.
122. Oliphant, *Memoir of the Life of Laurence Oliphant*, vol. 2, 315.
123. *Nottingham Evening Post*, January 21, 1886: 4; Oliphant, *Memoir of the Life of Laurence Oliphant*, vol. 2, 307, 210.
124. Laurence Oliphant, *Scientific Religion: Or, the Higher Possibilities of Life and Practice Through the Operation of Natural Forces* (London: William Blackwood and Sons, 1888)
125. Oliphant, *Memoir of the Life of Laurence Oliphant*, vol. 2, 316.
126. Owen, *My Perilous Life in Palestine*, 15.
127. Taylor, *Laurence Oliphant*, 245; Oliphant, *Memoir of the Life of Laurence Oliphant*, vol. 2, 360-61.
128. *London Light*, September 8, 1888: 442; February 15, 1902: 76.
129. *London Daily News*, December 24, 1888: 6; *Newcastle Daily Chronicle*, December 24, 1888: 4; *London Globe*, December 24, 1888: 1; *London Spectator*, December 29, 1888: 1846–47; *London Athenaeum*, December 28, 1888: 884. An exception to this trend was *London Pall Mall Gazette*, December 24, 1888: 7.
130. *Yorkshire Evening Post*, June 2, 1891: 1.

Chapter 4

1. Mitziko Sawada, *Tokyo Life, New York Dreams: Urban Japanese Visions of America, 1890–1924* (Berkeley: University of California Press, 1996), 190. For consistency, I have rendered all Japanese names in U.S. fashion (given name preceding surname), following Nagasawa's and Arai's own usage.
2. *San Francisco Chronicle*, December 27, 1891: 1.
3. *San Francisco Daily Alta California*, February 24, 1875: 1.
4. *Sonoma Democrat*, August 9, 1884: 1; *San Francisco Chronicle*, January 1, 1892: 18.
5. The $50,820 includes his initial purchase in 1875; see Deed book 49, p. 637; Deed book 62, p. 51; Deed book 62, p. 315; Deed book 66, p. 597; Deed book 66, p. 599; Deed book 71, p. 73; Deed book 84, p. 530; Deed book 94, p. 582; Deed book 95 p. 234; Deed book 123, p. 108, Sonoma County Records, Santa Rosa.
6. *Sonoma County Journal*, August 14, 1857: 3; *Santa Rosa Democrat*, October 31, 1889: 3.
7. *An Illustrated History of Sonoma County* (Chicago: Lewis Publishing Company, 1889), 366.
8. *San Francisco Chronicle*, June 11, 1891: 7.
9. *Sonoma Democrat*, November 27, 1875: 5.
10. *An Illustrated History of Sonoma County*, 367.
11. *San Francisco Chronicle*, December 13, 1891: 10; December 27, 1891: 1.
12. *An Illustrated History of Sonoma County*, 366.
13. *Fountaingrove Wine News*, May 1889: 1, in *Wayward Tendrils* 7, no. 2 (1997); *Sonoma Democrat*, January 2, 1892: 18.
14. Arthur A. Cuthbert, *The Life and World-Work of Thomas Lake Harris, Written from Direct and Personal Knowledge* (Glasgow: C. W. Pearce, 1908), 193–94.
15. Thomas Lake Harris to Samuel Swan, n.d., in Herbert W. Schneider and George Lawton, *A Prophet and a Pilgrim: Being the Incredible History of Thomas Lake Harris and Laurence Oliphant* (New York: Columbia University Press, 1942), 474.
16. William Oxley, *Modern Messiahs and Wonder Workers* (London: Trubner & Co., 1889), 68.

17. Gaye LeBaron, *The Japanese "Baron" of Fountaingrove* (Santa Rosa: Santa Rosa Junior College, 1976); Paul Akiria Kadota and Terry Earl Jones, *Kanaye Nagasawa: A Biography of a Satsuma Student* (Kagoshima, Japan: Kagoshima Prefectural Junior College, 1990); Andrew Cobbing, *The Satsuma Students in Britain: Japan's Early Search for the "Essence of the West"* (Richmond, Surrey: Curzon Press, 2000); John E. Van Sant, *Pacific Pioneers: Japanese Journeys to America and Hawaii, 1850–80* (Urbana: University of Illinois Press, 2000), 79–96; Benjamin C. Duke, *The History of Modern Japanese Education: Constructing the National School System, 1872–1890* (Brunswick, NJ: Rutgers University Press, 2008), 28–40.

18. *Dublin Evening Mail*, June 26, 1865: 4; *Bedford Times and Independent*, August 5, 1865: 5.

19. *Aberdeen Press and Journal*, June 27, 1866: 4; June 26, 1867: 1; *Banffshire Journal and General Advertiser*, June 25, 1867: 1; Alexander McKay, *Scottish Samurai: Thomas Blake Glover, 1838–1911* (Edinburgh: Canongate Books, 2012).

20. *Edinburgh Evening News*, October 27, 1884: 4; Alexander Shewan, *Spirat Adhuc Amor: The Record of the Gym (Chanonry House School)* (Aberdeen: Rosemount Press, 1923), 29, 156–71.

21. Laurence Oliphant, *Episodes in a Life of Adventure* (London: William Blackwood and Sons, 1887), 157–60.

22. *London Express*, September 17, 1866: 2; *Carlisle Journal*, January 29, 1867: 1.

23. John Bright, *The Diaries of John Bright* (New York: William Morrow, 1931), 305.

24. Cobbing, *The Satsuma Students in Britain*; Van Sant, *Pacific Pioneers*, 83–85.

25. Laurence Oliphant to Georgina Cowper, September 1867, Harris-Oliphant Papers, Columbia University.

26. Laurence Oliphant to William Cowper, September 29, 1867, Harris-Oliphant Papers, Columbia University.

27. *New York Sun*, April 30, 1869: 2.

28. Bright, *The Diaries of John Bright*, 306.

29. Laurence Oliphant to Georgina Cowper, November 6, 1868, Harris-Oliphant Papers, Columbia University.

30. Laurence Oliphant to William Cowper, September 29, 1867, Harris-Oliphant Papers, Columbia University.

31. Ivan Parker Hall, *Mori Arinori* (Cambridge, MA: Harvard University Press, 1973), 44.

32. Kanaye Nagasawa to Robert Hart, August 17, 1925, reel 13, item 304, in Jack T. Ericson, ed., *Thomas Lake Harris and the Brotherhood of the New Life: Books, Pamphlets, Serials and Manuscripts, 1854–1942*, microfilm (New York: New York Times, 1974).

33. Thomas Lake Harris, "The Bridal Word," n.d., p. 213, box 6, Harris-Oliphant Papers, Columbia University.

34. Thomas Lake Harris to C. M. Berridge, January 25, 1884, in Schneider and Lawton, *A Prophet and a Pilgrim*, 426.

35. Thomas Lake Harris, "A Prophecy of Japan," n.d., p. 3, folder 23, box 21, Harris-Oliphant Papers, Columbia University.

36. *The Ten-Year Book of Cornell University*, vol. 4 (Ithaca, NY: Cornell University, 1908), 397.

37. Cuthbert, *The Life and World-Work of Thomas Lake Harris*, 45; *International Psychic Gazette*, August 1916: 345.

38. Kanaye Nagasawa, diary, 1871, "Fountaingrove—Kanaye Nagasawa Diaries" folder, Gaye LeBaron Collection, Special Collections, Sonoma State University Library.

39. Mori Arinori to Kanaye Nagasawa, April 8, 1871, reel 8, item 235, in Ericson, *Thomas Lake Harris*; Van Sant, *Pacific Pioneers*, 88; Duke, *The History of Modern Japanese Education*, 39–40.

40. Hall, *Mori Arinori*; Chinami Oka, "Arai Ōsui and the Transnational Reimagination of Civilization in the Late Nineteenth-Century United States," *Historical Journal* 66 (2023): 101–21; Chinami Oka, *Reopening the Opening of Japan: Transnational Approaches to Modern Japan and the Wider World* (New York: Brill, 2023), 300–23.

41. Kanaye Nagasawa to Edwin Markham, March 14, 1921, reel 13, item 304, in Ericson, *Thomas Lake Harris*.

42. *Sonoma Democrat*, January 10, 1891: 2.

43. *Santa Rosa Press Democrat*, October 14, 1878: 3; on anti-Chinese racism and the California wine industry, see Julia Ornelas-Higdon, *The Grapes of Conquest: Race, Labor, and the Industrialization of California Wine, 1769–1920* (Lincoln: University of Nebraska Press, 2023), 131–69.

44. Sawada, *Tokyo Life, New York Dreams*, 13–16.

45. *Sonoma Democrat*, January 10, 1891: 3.

46. *San Francisco Chronicle*, June 11, 1891: 7; December 13, 1891: 10.
47. *San Francisco Chronicle*, December 27, 1891: 1.
48. *San Francisco Chronicle*, December 13, 1891: 10.
49. *San Francisco Chronicle*, December 13, 1891: 10.
50. *New York Tribune*, May 20, 1891: 7.
51. *New York Evening World*, September 24, 1890: 1.
52. *New York Tribune*, May 20, 1891: 7.
53. Alzire A. Chevaillier, "Sincerity and Tolerance," *Problem of Life and International Magazine of Truth*, June 1891: 303.
54. *New York Times*, June 7, 1891: 8.
55. *Los Angeles Times*, June 8, 1891: 1; *Sacramento Daily Union*, June 8, 1891: 1; *San Francisco Call*, June 8, 1891: 1; *Boston Daily Advertiser*, June 8, 1891: 1.
56. *Springfield Republican*, June 12, 1891: 3.
57. *New York Times*, June 14, 1891: 10.
58. *San Francisco Chronicle*, June 11, 1891: 7.
59. *Boston Herald*, June 27, 1891: 8.
60. Alexander V. G. Allen, *Life and Letters of Phillips Brooks*, vol. 3 (New York: E. P. Dutton, 1900), 438.
61. *New York Times*, June 7, 1891: 19; *New York Tribune*, June 7, 1891: 14; *New York Sun*, June 27, 1891: 7.
62. *San Francisco Chronicle*, June 21, 1891: 4. Like the February 10, 1885, article discussed in chapter 5, this was likely planted by Alfred W. Manning.
63. *New York Tribune*, June 22, 1891: 2.
64. *San Bernardino Kaleidoscope*, June 20, 1891: 1.
65. *Glasgow Herald*, May 22, 1891: 4; *London Evening Standard*, May 28, 1891: 3; *Birmingham Daily Mail*, May 29, 1891: 2.
66. *London Evening Standard*, May 30: 5; June 4, 1891: 3.
67. Thomas Lake Harris, *Brotherhood of the New Life: Its Fact, Law, Method, and Purpose* (Santa Rosa: Fountaingrove Press, 1891); *Sonoma Democrat*, August 22, 1891: 1.
68. *New York Sun*, July 6, 1891: 4.
69. Thomas Lake Harris, "A Letter from T. L. Harris," *Chicago Religio-Philosophical Journal*, July 4, 1891: 84. Alzire Chevaillier was an admirer of the *Religio-Philosophical Journal*; see her letter, November 8, 1890: 384.
70. John C. Bundy to Thomas Lake Harris, July 7, 1891, John C. Bundy Papers, folder 26, box 2, Kislak Center for Special Collections, University of Pennsylvania.
71. John C. Bundy to Marius C. C. Church, July 2, 1891, John C. Bundy Papers, folder 18, box 1, Kislak Center for Special Collections, University of Pennsylvania.
72. Jane Lee Waring, letter, July 2, 1891, Thomas Lake Harris Correspondence, Syracuse University Library.
73. *San Francisco Chronicle*, December 13, 1891: 10.
74. Thomas Lake Harris, *Lyra Triumphalis: People Songs: Ballads and Marches* (Santa Rosa: Fountaingrove Press, 1891), 23.

Chapter 5

1. *San Francisco Pacific Rural Press*, May 18, 1889: 1.
2. *San Francisco Chronicle*, December 13, 1891: 10.
3. *San Francisco Chronicle*, December 13, 1891: 10.
4. Thomas Lake Harris, *Brotherhood of the New Life: Its Fact, Law, Method, and Purpose* (Santa Rosa: Fountaingrove Press, 1891); Thomas Lake Harris, *Lyra Triumphalis: People Songs: Ballads and Marches* (Santa Rosa: Fountaingrove Press, 1891); Thomas Lake Harris, *God's Breath in Man and in Humane Society* (Santa Rosa: Fountaingrove Press, 1891).
5. Harris, *God's Breath in Man*, 9, 27, 34.
6. Alzire A. Chevaillier, "Editorial Notes," *Problem of Life and International Magazine of Truth*, September/October 1891: 394.
7. *Omaha World-Herald*, October 20, 1891: 4; *Atchison (Kansas) Champion*, November 3, 1891: 2; *Derby Mercury*, December 16, 1891: 8.
8. *London Pall Mall Gazette*, September 8, 1891: 1–2; Janet Oppenheim, *The Other World: Spiritualism and Psychical Research in England, 1850–1914* (Cambridge: Cambridge University

Press, 1985), 33–34; Stewart J. Brown, *W. T. Stead: Nonconformist and Newspaper Prophet* (New York: Oxford University Press, 2019).

9. *London St. James's Gazette*, August 28, 1891: 4.
10. Harris, *Brotherhood of the New Life*, 18.
11. *London Light*, June 20, 1891: 295; *London Medium and Daybreak*, October 2, 1891: 631; November 6, 1891: 716.
12. *Chicago Progressive Thinker*, October 31, 1891: 2.
13. *London Light*, June 27, 1891: 306; August 1, 1891: 367.
14. *Chicago Religio-Philosophical Journal*, August 15, 1891: 183; August 29, 1891: 209.
15. Alex Owen, *The Place of Enchantment: British Occultism and the Culture of the Modern* (Chicago: University of Chicago Press, 2004), 29–36.
16. See, e.g., *London Pall Mall Gazette*, September 4, 1891: 1; September 8, 1891: 2; September 16, 1891: 3; November 28, 1891: 3.
17. Thomas Lake Harris, *Wisdom of the Adepts: Esoteric Science in Human History* (Santa Rosa: Fountaingrove Press, 1884), vi; H. P. Blavatsky, *Isis Unveiled: A Master-Key to the Mysteries of Ancient and Modern Science and Theology* (New York: J. W. Bouton, 1877); H. P. Blavatsky, *The Secret Doctrine: The Synthesis of Science, Religion, and Philosophy* (London: Theosophical Publishing Company, 1888), viii.
18. Margaret Oliphant, *Memoir of the Life of Laurence Oliphant and of Alice Oliphant, His Wife*, vol. 2 (London: William Blackwood and Sons, 1891), 269; Laurence Oliphant, "The Sisters of Thibet," *Nineteenth Century*, November 1884: 715–30.
19. *London Lucifer*, July 1889: 440; July 1890: 381.
20. *London Lucifer*, September 15, 1891: 62, November 15, 1891: 177–81.
21. *Birmingham Daily Gazette*, November 28, 1891; *London Pall Mall Gazette*, November 28, 1891: 4.
22. *New York Herald-Tribune*, January 10, 1892: 17.
23. John [Pulsford?], letter to Jane Lee Waring, November 29, 1891, reel 13, item 302, in Jack T. Ericson, ed., *Thomas Lake Harris and the Brotherhood of the New Life: Books, Pamphlets, Serials and Manuscripts, 1854–1942*, microfilm (New York: New York Times, 1974).
24. *Problem of Life and International Magazine of Truth*, November 1891: 438, 454; *Napa Journal*, October 1, 1891: 3; *Oakland Enquirer*, October 21, 1891: 8.
25. *Santa Rosa Daily Democrat*, September 13, 1891: 1.
26. Chevaillier, "Editorial Notes," 395; see also her dispatch to *Kansas City Unity*, September 1891: 5.
27. *San Francisco Chronicle*, December 13, 1891: 10.
28. *San Francisco Chronicle*, December 13, 1891: 10; December 27, 1891: 1; Alzire A. Chevaillier, "Laurence Oliphant and the Primate," *International Magazine of Truth*, January 1892: 7, reel 14, item 319, in Ericson, *Thomas Lake Harris*.
29. *San Francisco Chronicle*, December 13, 1891: 10; December 27, 1891: 1; Chevaillier, "Laurence Oliphant and the Primate," 3, in Ericson, *Thomas Lake Harris*.
30. *Chicago New Church Independent*, July 1892: 337.
31. Chevaillier, "Editorial Notes," 395.
32. Bailey Millard, *History of the San Francisco Bay Region* (Chicago: American Historical Society, 1924), 328; *California Farmer and Journal of Useful Sciences*, March 4, 1875: 1; John W. Brown Jr. and James Boyd, *History of San Bernardino and Riverside Counties*, vol. 2 (Chicago: Western Historical Association, 1922), 929–30; *San Francisco City Directory* (San Francisco: R. L. Polk, 1890), 91.
33. John Martin, ed., *Diary of the Mission, Spiritual and Earthly, by the Late James Johnston* (Liverpool: self published, 1881); *New Church Jerusalem*, April 1882: 213; A. W. Manning to John Whitehead, March 19, 1913, A. W. Manning File, Center for Swedenborgian Studies Library and Archives, Berkeley; Herbert W. Schneider and George Lawton, *A Prophet and a Pilgrim: Being the Incredible History of Thomas Lake Harris and Laurence Oliphant* (New York: Columbia University Press, 1942), 462–64. On James Johnston, see Erik R. Seeman, *Speaking to the Dead in Early America* (Philadelphia: University of Pennsylvania Press, 2019), 167.
34. Some of Manning's Swedenborgian correspondents conducted their own inquiries into Harris; these included J. M. Shepherd, Thomas Nelmes, James Barr, and a Mr. Alsop.
35. *San Francisco Chronicle*, February 10, 1885: 5.
36. John B. Ellis, *Free Love and Its Votaries; or, American Socialism Unmasked* (New York: United States Publishing Company, 1870); Carol Faulkner, *Unfaithful: Love, Adultery, and Marriage*

Reform in Nineteenth-Century America (Philadelphia: University of Pennsylvania Press, 2019), 136–39.

37. Sarah Barringer Gordon, *The Mormon Question: Polygamy and Constitutional Conflict in Nineteenth-Century America* (Chapel Hill: University of North Carolina Press, 2002).

38. Laurence Oliphant, to [William?] Cowper, January 3, 1869, Harris-Oliphant Papers, Columbia University.

39. Deed book 94, p. 464, Sonoma County Records, Santa Rosa.

40. A follow-up article in the *Chronicle* claimed that the first report had caused widespread disillusionment at Fountaingrove, causing it to be to be "broken up"; see *San Francisco Chronicle*, March 10, 1885: 5.

41. Schneider and Lawton, *Prophet and Pilgrim*, 425.

42. *Chicago New Church Independent*, July 1885: 335.

43. *Chicago Religio-Philosophical Journal*, June 21, 1890: 52.

44. Alzire A. Chevaillier, "An Open Letter to William Dean Howells," *California Illustrated World*, February 1892, reel 14, item 320, in Ericson, *Thomas Lake Harris*; Chevaillier, "Laurence Oliphant and the Primate," 6.

45. *San Francisco Chronicle*, December 27, 1891: 1.

46. Chevaillier, "Laurence Oliphant and the Primate," 3.

47. Alzire A. Chevaillier, "The Dangers of Occult Science," *Problem of Life and International Magazine of Truth*, November 1891: 142.

48. Arthur A. Cuthbert to Jane Lee Waring, November 22, 1891, reel 13, item 302, in Ericson, *Thomas Lake Harris*.

49. Barna Csuros, "The Poet and the Seer," *Markham Review* 4 (February 1969): 4; Louis Filler, *The Unknown Edwin Markham: His Mystery and Its Significance* (Yellow Springs, OH: Antioch Press, 1966), 42–46.

50. Kanaye Nagasawa to Edwin Markham, November 29, 1891, reel 8, item 235, in Ericson, *Thomas Lake Harris*.

Chapter 6

1. *San Francisco Chronicle*, December 13, 1891: 10.

2. *San Francisco Pioneer*, February 12, 1870: 2.

3. *Daily Alta California*, January 7, 1870: 1; *San Jose Mercury News*, January 26, 1870: 2; *San Francisco Chronicle*, June 2, 1872; Philip J. Ethington, *The Public City: The Political Construction of Urban Life in San Francisco, 1850–1900* (New York: Cambridge University Press, 1994), 215; Gayle Gullett, *Becoming Citizens: The Emergence and Development of the California Women's Movement, 1880–1911* (Urbana: University of Illinois Press, 2000), 15; Ann Braude, *Radical Spirits: Spiritualism and Women's Rights in Nineteenth-Century America* (Bloomington: Indiana University Press, 1989), 194.

4. *Minutes of the Annual Convention of the Women's Christian Temperance Union of California*, 1888, 49; Donald G. Cooper, "The California Suffrage Campaign of 1896: Its Origin, Strategies, Defeat," *Southern California Quarterly* 71 (1989): 311–25; Rebecca J. Mead, *How the Vote Was Won: Woman Suffrage in the Western United States, 1868–1914* (New York: New York University Press, 2004), 18–25; Joshua Paddison, "'Woman Is Everywhere the Purifier': The Politics of Temperance, 1878–1900," in *California Women and Politics: From the Gold Rush to the Great Depression*, ed. Robert W. Cherny, Mary Ann Irwin, and Ann Marie Wilson (Lincoln: University of Nebraska Press, 2011), 70–71.

5. Mrs. T. B. H. Stenhouse, *Tell It All: The Story of a Life's Experience in Mormonism* (Hartford, CT: A. D. Worthington & Co., 1872), viii–xiii.

6. *Chicago Times*, August 11, 1873; Ann Eliza Young, *Wife No. 19: Or, A Story of a Life in Bondage* (Hartford, CT: Dustin, Gilman & Co., 1876), 11.

7. Gray Brechin, *Imperial San Francisco: Urban Power, Earthly Ruin* (Berkeley: University of California Press, 2006), 173–78; Christopher B. Daly, *Covering America: A Narrative History of a Nation's Journalism* (Amherst: University of Massachusetts Press, 2012), 123, 130–31; Dennis Brian, *Pulitzer: A Life* (New York: John Wiley & Sons, 2001).

8. Carole Haber, *The Trials of Laura Fair: Sex, Murder, and Insanity in the Victorian West* (Chapel Hill: University of North Carolina Press, 2013); Lynn M. Hudson, "'Strong Animal Passions' in the Gilded Age: Race, Sex, and a Senator on Trial," *Journal of the History of Sexuality* 9 (2000): 62–84.

9. Susan Lee Johnson, *Roaring Camp: The Social World of the California Gold Rush* (New York: W. W. Norton, 2000); Nan Alamilla Boyd, *Wide-Open Town: A History of Queer San Francisco*

to 1965 (Berkeley: University of California Press, 2005); Clare Sears, *Arresting Dress: Cross-Dressing, Law, and Fascination in Nineteenth-Century San Francisco* (Durham, NC: Duke University Press, 2015).

10. Amy Sueyoshi, *Discriminating Sex: White Leisure and the Making of the American "Oriental"* (Champaign: University of Illinois Press, 2018), 32.

11. Altina L. Waller, *Reverend Beecher and Mrs. Tilton: Sex and Class in Victorian America* (Amherst: University of Massachusetts Press, 1982); Glenn Wallach, "'A Depraved Taste for Publicity': The Press and Private Life in the Gilded Age," *American Studies* 39 (1998): 31–57; Barbara Goldsmith, *Other Powers: The Age of Suffrage, Spiritualism, and the Scandalous Victoria Woodhull* (New York: Alfred A. Knopf, 1998); Richard Wightman Fox, *Trials of Intimacy: Love and Loss in the Beecher-Tilton Scandal* (Chicago: University of Chicago Press, 1999).

12. *New York Times*, January 11, 1891: 2; Edward M. Brown, "Neurology and Spiritualism in the 1870s," *Bulletin of the History of Medicine* 57 (1983): 563–77.

13. *San Francisco Chronicle*, December 17, 1891: 3; January 4, 1892: 3.

14. *San Francisco Call*, July 13, 1890: 6.

15. *Sacramento Daily Union*, April 3, 1890: 2; May 4, 1890: 2; June 12, 1890: 2; *Santa Rosa Daily Democrat*, September 30, 1891: 1; *San Francisco Evening Bulletin*, December 15, 1891: 1. On broader cultural concerns about hypnosis in the transatlantic world, see Andreas-Holger Maehle, "History of Hypnotism in Europe and the Significance of Place," *Notes and Records: The Royal Society Journal of the History of Science* 71 (2017): 119–23; Alan Gauld, *A History of Hypnotism* (Cambridge: Cambridge University Press, 1992); Alison Winter, *Mesmerized: Powers of Mind in Victorian Britain* (Chicago: University of Chicago Press, 1998); D. Pick, *Svengali's Web: The Alien Enchanter in Modern Culture* (New Haven, CT: Yale University Press, 2000); Fred Nadis, *Wonder Shows: Performing Science, Magic, and Religion in America* (New Brunswick, NJ: Rutgers University Press, 2005), 97–112; W. Hughes, *That Devil's Trick: Hypnotism and the Victorian Popular Imagination* (Manchester: Manchester University Press, 2015); and Emily Ogden, *Credulity: A Cultural History of US Mesmerism* (Chicago: University of Chicago Press, 2018).

16. On the origins and historiography of "brainwashing," see Benjamin Zablocki, "Towards a Demystified and Disinterested Scientific Theory of Brainwashing," in *Misunderstanding Cults: Searching for Objectivity in a Controversial Field*, ed. Benjamin Zablocki and Thomas Robbins (Toronto: University of Toronto Press, 2001), 159–214; and Elizabeth Aileen Young, "The Use of the 'Brainwashing' Theory by the Anti-Cult Movement in the United States of America, Pre-1996," *Zeitschrift für junge Religionswissenschaft* 7 (2012): 5–19.

17. Rebecca L. Davis, *Public Confessions: The Religious Conversions that Changed American Politics* (Chapel Hill: University of North Carolina Press, 2021), 90.

18. *San Francisco Chronicle*, December 20, 1891: 4.

19. *San Francisco Chronicle*, December 13, 1891: 10.

20. Barbara Young Welke, *Law and the Borders of Belonging in the Long Nineteenth Century United States* (New York: Cambridge University Press, 2010).

21. Peggy Pascoe, *Relations of Rescue: The Search for Female Moral Authority in the American West, 1874–1939* (New York: Oxford University Press, 1990), 150–51; John D'Emilio and Estelle B. Freedman, *Intimate Matters: A History of Sexuality in America*, 3rd ed. (Chicago: University of Chicago Press, 2012), 179–80; Sharon R. Ullman, *Sex Seen: The Emergence of Modern Sexuality in America* (Berkeley: University of California Press, 1997), 151.

22. D'Emilio and Freedman, *Intimate Matters*, 208–15; Grace Peña Delgado, "Border Control and Sexual Policing: White Slavery and Prostitution Along the U.S.-Mexico Borderlands, 1903–1910," *Western Historical Quarterly* 43 (2012): 157–78; Alex Smolak, "White Slavery, Whorehouse Riots, Venereal Disease, and Saving Women: Historical Context of Prostitution Interventions and Harm Reduction in New York City During the Progressive Era," *Social Work in Public Health* 28 (2013): 496–508; Jessica R. Pliley, *Policing Sexuality: The Mann Act and the Making of the FBI* (Cambridge, MA: Harvard University Press, 2014), 9–31; Jessica R. Pliley, "From White Slavery to Anti-Prostitution, the Long View: Law, Policy, and Sex Trafficking," in *Human Bondage and Abolition: New Histories of Past and Present Slaveries*, ed. Elizabeth Swanson and James Brewer Stewart (Cambridge: Cambridge University Press, 2018), 190–218.

23. *San Francisco Call*, March 20, 1891: 2; October 22, 1893: 13; November 29, 1893: 2.

24. Gretchen Soderlund, *Sex Trafficking, Scandal, and the Transformation of Journalism, 1885–1917* (Chicago: University of Chicago Press, 2013).

25. *San Francisco Chronicle*, December 27, 1891: 1.
26. *San Francisco Chronicle*, December 25, 1891: 7; December 13, 1891: 10.
27. *San Francisco Chronicle*, December 27, 1891: 1.
28. Dennis M. Ogawa, *From Japs to Japanese: An Evolution of Japanese-American Stereotypes* (Berkeley: McCutchan, 1971); Masao Miyoshi, *As We Saw Them: The First Japanese Embassy to the United States (1860)* (Berkeley: University of California Press, 1979); Sheila K. Johnson, *The Japanese Through American Eyes* (Stanford, CA: Stanford University Press, 1988); Robert A. Rosenstone, *Mirror in the Shrine: American Encounters with Meiji Japan* (Cambridge, MA: Harvard University Press, 1988); Joseph M. Henning, *Outposts of Civilization: Race, Religion, and the Formative Years of American-Japanese Relations* (New York: New York University Press, 2000).
29. Evelyn Nakano Glenn, *Issei, Nisei, War Bride: Three Generations of Japanese American Women in Domestic Service* (Philadelphia: Temple University Press, 1986), 22–31; Ronald Takaki, *A Different Mirror: A History of Multicultural America* (Boston: Little, Brown, 1993), 246–47; Eiichiro Azuma, *Between Two Empires: Race, History, and Transnationalism in Japanese America* (New York: Oxford University Press, 2005), 17–33; Jennifer L. Hochschild and Brenna Marea Powell, "Racial Reorganization and the United States Census, 1850–1930: Mulattoes, Half-Breeds, Mixed Parentage, Hindoos, and the Mexican Race," *Studies in American Political Development* 22 (2008): 59–96.
30. *San Francisco Call*, June 15, 1892: 8.
31. Takaki, *A Different Mirror*, 45; Tomás Almaguer, *Racial Fault Lines: The Historical Origins of White Supremacy in California* (Berkeley: University of California Press, 1994), 184–86.
32. *Sacramento Daily Record-Union*, July 7, 1892: 3; Roger Daniels, *The Politics of Prejudice: The Anti-Japanese Movement in California and the Struggle for Japanese Exclusion* (Berkeley: University of California Press, 1962); Almaguer, *Racial Fault Lines*, 183–204. On the earlier but still ongoing anti-Chinese movement, see Stuart Creighton Miller, *Unwelcome Immigrant: The American Image of the Chinese, 1785–1885* (Berkeley: University of California Press, 1969); Alexander Saxton, *The Indispensable Enemy: Labor and the Anti-Chinese Movement in California* (Berkeley: University of California Press, 1971); Ronald T. Takaki, *Iron Cages: Race and Culture in Nineteenth-Century America* (New York: Alfred A. Knopf, 1979); Robert G. Lee, *Orientals: Asian Americans in Popular Culture* (Philadelphia: Temple University Press, 1999); John Kuo Wei Tchen, *New York Before Chinatown: Orientalism and the Shaping of American Culture, 1776–1882* (Baltimore, MD: Johns Hopkins University Press, 1999); Najia Aarim-Heriot, *Chinese Immigrants, African Americans, and Racial Anxiety in the United States, 1848–82* (Urbana: University of Illinois Press, 2003); Helen Heran Jun, *Race for Citizenship: Black Orientalism and Asian Uplift from Pre-Emancipation to Neoliberal America* (New York: New York University Press, 2011), 15–32; and Joshua Paddison, *American Heathens: Religion, Race, and Reconstruction in California* (Berkeley: University of California Press, 2012).
33. *San Francisco Morning Call*, March 21, 1891: 1, March 22, 1902: 6; *Los Angeles Herald*, March 24, 1896: 2, June 19, 1898: 11; *Sacramento Record-Union*, October 18, 1899: 6.
34. *San Francisco Daily Alta California*, September 6, 1885; *Trip Through Japan* (San Francisco: Deakin Bros. & Co., 1886); Chelsea Foxwell, "Crossings and Dislocations: Toshio Aoki (1854–1912), a Japanese Artist in California," *Nineteenth-Century Art Worldwide* 11 (2012), http://www.19thc-artworldwide.org/autumn12/foxwell-toshio-aoki-a-japanese-artist-in-california.
35. John MacKenzie, *Orientalism: History, Theory, and the Arts* (Manchester: Manchester University Press, 1995), 124; Mari Yoshihara, *Embracing the East: White Women and American Orientalism* (New York: Oxford University Press, 2003); Carmen Birkle, "Orientalisms in 'Fin-de-Siècle' America," *Amerikastudien/American Studies* 51 (2006): 323–42; Josephine Lee, *The Japan of Pure Invention: Gilbert and Sullivan's The Mikado* (Minneapolis: University of Minnesota Press, 2010).
36. Orientalist-minded white women of the era used male Asian "native informants" in similar fashion; see Yoshihara, *Embracing the East*, 194.
37. Ala Alryyes, ed., *A Muslim American Slave: The Life of Omar Ibn Said* (Madison: University of Wisconsin Press, 2011), 32.
38. Chevaillier was born in 1850; Nagasawa in 1852; Arai in 1857.
39. *San Francisco Chronicle*, December 25, 1891: 7.
40. John E. Van Sant, *Pacific Pioneers: Japanese Journeys to America and Hawaii, 1850–80* (Urbana: University of Illinois Press, 2000), 90.

41. Lee, *Orientals*, 88, 97–105; Jennifer Ting, "Bachelor Society: Deviant Heterosexuality and Asian American Historiography," in *Privileging Positions: The Sites of Asian American Studies*, ed. Gary Y. Okihiro et al. (Pullman: Washington State University Press, 1995), 271–80; Henry Yu, "Mixing Bodies and Cultures: The Meaning of America's Fascination with Sex Between 'Orientals' and 'Whites,'" in *Sex, Love, Race: Crossing Boundaries in North American History*, ed. Martha Hodes (New York: New York University Press, 1999), 444–63; Karen J. Leong, "'A Distinct and Antagonistic Race': Constructions of Chinese Manhood in the Exclusionist Debates," in *Across the Great Divide: Cultures of Manhood in the American West*, ed. Matthew Basso, Laura McCall, and Dee Garceau (New York: Routledge, 2001), 131–48; Shah, *Stranger Intimacy*, 77–104; Mary Ting Yi Lui, *The Chinatown Trunk Mystery: Murder, Miscegenation, and Other Dangerous Encounters in Turn-of-the-Century New York City* (Princeton, NJ: Princeton University Press, 2005).

42. See, e.g., *San Francisco Call*, March 24, 1909: 2, June 20, 1910: 12; September 23, 1910: 8.

43. Examples include *Harper's Weekly*, June 12, 1869: 384; *San Francisco Thistleton's Illustrated Jolly Giant*, November 18, 1876: 333; and *San Francisco Wasp*, November 18, 1876: 138.

44. Theodore H. Hittell, ed., *Supplement to the Codes and Statutes of the State of California*, vol. 3 (San Francisco: A. L. Bancroft and Company, 1880), 209; Peggy Pascoe, *What Comes Naturally: Miscegenation Law and the Making of Race in America* (New York: Oxford University Press, 2009), 87–89; Sueyoshi, *Discriminating Sex*, 33–44.

45. Lui, *The Chinatown Trunk Mystery*, 111–42.

46. George Henry Preble, *The Opening of Japan: A Diary of Discovery in the Far East, 1853–1856* (Norman: University of Oklahoma Press, 1962), 181.

47. Joseph Rogala, *A Collector's Guide to Books on Japan in English* (Richmond, Surrey: Japan Library, 2001), 82.

48. Henning, *Outposts of Civilization*, 23–24.

49. *San Francisco Call*, September 22, 1898: 5, April 6, 1899: 2; Scott Clark, *Japan: A View from the Bath* (Honolulu: University of Hawai'i Press, 1994), 33–35.

50. *San Francisco Chronicle*, December 25, 1891: 7.

51. *San Francisco Chronicle*, December 13, 1891: 10; N. K. Rutter, "Sybaris—Legend and Reality," *Greece & Rome* 17 (1970): 168–76.

52. *San Francisco Chronicle*, December 13, 1891: 10; Mary Roberts, *Intimate Outsiders: The Harem in Ottoman and Orientalist Art and Travel Literature* (Durham, NC: Duke University Press, 2007), 90.

53. Robert Battistini, "Glimpses of the Other Before Orientalism: The Muslim World in Early American Periodicals, 1785–1800," *Early American Studies* 8 (2010): 446–74; Jennifer Graber, "Beyond Prophecy: Native Visionaries in American Religious Studies," *American Religion* 2 (2020): 53–54.

54. Terry L. Givens, *The Viper on the Hearth: Mormons, Myths, and the Construction of Heresy* (New York: Oxford University Press, 1997), 121–52; Martha M. Ertman, "Race Treason: The Untold Story of America's Ban on Polygamy," *Columbia Journal of Gender and Law* 19 (2010): 287–366; Richard V. Francaviglia, *Go East Young Man: Imagining the American West as the Orient* (Logan: Utah State University Press, 2011), 87–125; J. Spencer Fluhman, *"A Peculiar People": Anti-Mormonism and the Making of Religion in Nineteenth-Century America* (Chapel Hill: University of North Carolina Press, 2012), 110–17; W. Paul Reeve, *Religion of a Different Color: Race and the Mormon Struggle for Whiteness* (New York: Oxford University Press, 2015); Peter Coviello, *Make Yourselves Gods: Mormons and the Unfinished Business of American Secularism* (Chicago: University of Chicago Press, 2019); K. Mohrman, *Exceptionally Queer: Mormon Peculiarity and U.S. Nationalism* (Minneapolis: University of Minnesota Press, 2022).

55. These include *New York World*, December 13, 1891: 7; *New York Tribune*, December 13, 1891: 4; *Chicago Daily Tribune*, December 13, 1891: 3; *Wheeling Register*, December 15, 1891: 1; and *Galveston Daily News*, December 17, 1891: 3.

56. These include *London Mercury*, December 12, 1891: 13; *London St. James Gazette*, December 14, 1891: 11; *London Pall Mall Gazette*, December 14, 1891: 6; *Manchester Courier and Lancashire General Advertiser*, December 19, 1891: 17; and *London Weekly Dispatch*, December 20, 1891: 1.

57. *Harrisburg Patriot*, December 14, 1891: 4; *Springfield Republican*, December 20, 1891: 4.

58. *London Pall Mall Gazette*, September 4, 1891: 1; two other early references to Fountaingrove as a "cult" are *London Pall Mall Gazette*, September 8, 1891: 1; and *Pittsburgh Dispatch*, October 16, 1891: 4.

59. *Harrisburg Patriot*, December 14, 1891: 4.

60. *San Francisco Chronicle*, January 4, 1892: 7.
61. *New York Times*, January 10, 1892: 4.
62. *Springfield Republican*, December 20, 1891: 4.
63. *San Francisco Chronicle*, December 20, 1891: 4.
64. *San Francisco Chronicle*, December 13, 1891: 10.

Chapter 7

1. James W. Cassedy, "The Flamboyant Colonel Waring: An Anti-Contagionist Holds the American Stage in the Age of Pasteur and Koch," *Bulletin of the History of Medicine* 36 (1962): 163–74; Marvin V. Melosi, *Garbage in the Cities: Refuse Reform and the Environment* (Pittsburgh: University of Pittsburg Press, 2005), 42–52.
2. *San Francisco Chronicle*, December 27, 1891: 1.
3. Jane Lee Waring to George E. Waring Jr., December18, 1891, reel 8, item 235, in Jack T. Ericson, ed., *Thomas Lake Harris and the Brotherhood of the New Life: Books, Pamphlets, Serials and Manuscripts, 1854–1942*, microfilm (New York: New York Times, 1974).
4. Lynn M. Hudson, "'Strong Animal Passions' in the Gilded Age: Race, Sex, and a Senator on Trial," *Journal of the History of Sexuality* 9 (2000): 62–84; Carole Haber, *The Trials of Laura Fair: Sex, Murder, and Insanity in the Victorian West* (Chapel Hill: University of North Carolina Press, 2013), 210–11; *San Francisco Chronicle*, February 14, 1892: 24.
5. Unidentified to Jane Lee Waring, December 19, 1891, reel 8, item 235, in Ericson, *Thomas Lake Harris*.
6. Edwin Miller Wheelock to Jane Lee Harris, December 24, 1891, binder 1, folder 1, V. Valta Parma Collection, Hamilton College Library.
7. *Glasgow Citizen*, December 29, 1891; *London Lucifer*, January 15, 1892: 423–24.
8. *London Echo*, February 12, 1892, reel 14, item 320, in Ericson, *Thomas Lake Harris*.
9. "Letter from a Distinguished English Authoress," January 15, 1892, from "Mimeograph No. 15," in Herbert W. Schneider and George Lawton, *A Prophet and a Pilgrim: Being the Incredible History of Thomas Lake Harris and Laurence Oliphant* (New York: Columbia University Press, 1942), 550.
10. "A Letter from Mr. Samuel Clark," January 16, 1892, from "Mimeograph No. 11," reel 13, item 302, in Ericson, *Thomas Lake Harris*.
11. "Mimeograph 8½," January 1892, reel 8, item 235, Ericson, *Thomas Lake Harris* microfilm.
12. "Letter from Thomas Lake Harris," January 18, 1892, from "Mimeograph No. 9," reel 8, item 235, Ericson, ed., *Thomas Lake Harris*.
13. Julia Bush, *Women Against the Vote: Female Anti-Suffragism in Britain* (New York: Oxford University Press, 2007); Susan Goodier, *No Votes for Women: The New York State Anti-Suffrage Movement* (Champaign: University of Illinois Press, 2013), 17–18.
14. Eleanor Webley to George Lawton, January 16, 1930, reel 13, item 308, in Ericson, *Thomas Lake Harris*.
15. *San Francisco Chronicle*, January 14, 1892: 12.
16. See, e.g., *Lincoln Evening News*, January 9, 1892: 4; *Topeka Daily Capitol*, January 19, 1892: 7; and *Kalamazoo Gazette*, February 13, 1892: 7.
17. *The Problem of Life*, January 1892.
18. *The Problem of Life*, February 1892: 65–67; Jane Lee Waring to Arthur A. Cuthbert, February 4, 1892, box 1, folder 5, V. Valta Parma Collection, Hamilton College Library.
19. Alzire A. Chevaillier, "Laurence Oliphant and the Primate," *International Magazine of Truth*, January 1892, reel 14, item 319, in Ericson, *Thomas Lake Harris*.
20. "A Statement by George E. Waring Jr.," February 5, 1892, from "Mimeograph No. 17," in Schneider and Lawton, *A Prophet and a Pilgrim*, 551; *Philadelphia Times*, March 6, 1892: 4.
21. William Dean Howells, "Editor's Study," *Harper's New Monthly Magazine*, October 1891: 800–3.
22. William Dean Howells, "Editor's Study," *Harper's New Monthly Magazine*, February 1892: 480–81.
23. William Dean Howells to George E. Waring Jr., February 17, 1892, box 2, Papers of William Dean Howells, University of Virginia Library.
24. Howard A. Wilson, "William Dean Howells's Unpublished Letters about the Haymarket Affair," *Journal of the Illinois State Historical Society* 56 (1963): 5–19; Timothy L. Parrish, "Haymarket and *Hazard*: The Lonely Politics of William Dean Howells," *Journal of American Culture* 17 (1994): 23–31; Jesse W. Schwartz, "'Dynamite Talk': William Dean Howells, Racial Socialism, and a Legal Theory of Literary Complicity," *Nineteenth-Century Literature* 73 (2019): 522–50.

25. Alzire A. Chevaillier, "An Open Letter to Mr. William Dean Howells," *California Illustrated World*, February 1892, reel 14, item 320, in Ericson, *Thomas Lake Harris*.

26. Schneider and Lawton, *A Prophet and a Pilgrim*, 466. Adam Morris, in his recent treatment, simply says that "there was no corroborating evidence for Chevaillier's claims"; *American Messiahs: False Prophets of a Damned Nation* (New York: Liveright, 2019), 127.

27. A. W. Manning to John Whitehead, March 19, 1913, Center for Swedenborgian Studies Library and Archives, Berkeley.

28. A. W. Manning to William H. Alden, March 21, 1920, in Schneider and Lawton, *A Prophet and a Pilgrim*, 463.

29. M. J. Nolan, "Paraphrenia," *British Journal of Psychiatry*, April 1922: 159–61; John Benedict Buescher, "The Mental Mechanism of Dr. Sivartha," 2021, 83–86, http://iapsop.com.

30. William Alfred Hinds, *American Communities* (Oneida, NY: Office of the American Socialist, 1878), 146.

31. Ray Strachey, ed., *Religious Fanaticism: Extracts from the Papers of Hannah Whitall Smith* (London: Faber & Gwyer Limited, 1928), 217–18, 234.

32. *The Ladies' Repository*, September 1872: 238; *Harper's Weekly*, March 2, 1872: 169; *Brooklyn Union*, December 10, 1874: 4; Lois A. Boyd, "Shall Women Speak?: Confrontation in the Church, 1876," *Journal of Presbyterian History* 56 (1978): 281–94; Edward Blum, "'Paul Has Been Forgotten': Women, Gender, and Revivalism during the Gilded Age," *Journal of the Gilded Age and Progressive Era* 3 (2004): 247–70.

33. Theodore Ledyard Cuyler, *Recollections of a Long Life: An Autobiography* (New York: Baker & Taylor Co., 1902), 249; Mrs. Harlan Cleveland, "Sarah Frances Smiley: An Impression," *American Church Monthly* 4 (July 1919): 984–97.

34. Strachey, ed., *Religious Fanaticism*, 167, 177–78; Barbara Strachey, *Remarkable Relations: The Story of the Pearsall Smith Women* (New York: Universe Books, 1982), 39; Brett Malcolm Grainger, *Church in the Wild: Evangelicals in Antebellum America* (Cambridge, MA: Harvard University Press, 2019), 139–57.

35. Strachey, *Religious Fanaticism*, 234–37.

36. Schneider and Lawton, *A Prophet and a Pilgrim*, 149, 213.

37. *Fredonia Censor*, July 24, 1912, in Schneider and Lawton, *A Prophet and a Pilgrim*, 222.

38. Mary S. Emerson, *Among the Chosen* (New York: Holt, 1884), 31–33, 177, 203–6.

39. "Experiences of a Sister in the New Life," 1881, in Schneider and Lawton, *A Prophet and a Pilgrim*, 511, 519, 531.

40. Charles Hunter to his sister Mary, December 1, 1881, Thomas Lake Harris Correspondence, Syracuse University Library.

41. *San Francisco Chronicle*, December 13, 1891: 10.

42. "Experiences of a Sister in the New Life," 530.

43. Thomas Lake Harris, *Arcana of Christianity*, vol. 3 (New York: Brotherhood of the New Life, 1867), 207.

44. *International Psychic Gazette*, September 1916: 367.

45. Thomas Lake Harris, *Brotherhood of the New Life: Its Fact, Law, Method and Purpose* (Santa Rosa: Fountaingrove Press, 1891), 6.

46. Schneider and Lawton, *A Prophet and a Pilgrim*, 222, 483.

47. Strachey, *Religious Fanaticism*, 221–23; Schneider and Lawton, *A Prophet and a Pilgrim*, 376, 405, 415; Anne Taylor, *Laurence Oliphant, 1829–1888* (New York: Oxford University Press, 1982), 248–56; Bart Casey, *The Double Life of Laurence Oliphant: Victorian Pilgrim and Prophet* (New York: Post Hill Press, 2015), 250–53; Jeffrey D. Lavoie, *Laurence Oliphant (1829–1888) and The Household: The Christian Mystical Teachings of a Nineteenth Century Religious Leader* (New York: Palgrave Macmillan, 2021), 65–72.

48. John D. Wrathall, "Provenance as Text: Reading the Silences Around Sexuality in Manuscript Collections," *Journal of American History* 79 (1992): 165–78; Anjali Arondekar, "Without a Trace: Sexuality and the Colonial Archive," *Journal of the History of Sexuality* 14 (2005): 10–27.

Chapter 8

1. "Mysticism and Harris: Secrets of the Sonoma Eden Unveiled," February 10, 1892, Poets Garden Records, Special Collections Library, University of Southern California.

2. *Washington Post*, February 5, 1892: 1; *New York Herald-Tribune* February 5, 1892: 1; *Sydney Evening News*, February 6, 1892: 1.

3. *Manchester Courier*, February 6, 1892: 7; *Twentieth Century Magazine*, n.d. [February 1892], reel 14, item 320, in Jack T. Ericson, ed., *Thomas Lake Harris and the Brotherhood of the New*

Life: Books, Pamphlets, Serials and Manuscripts, 1854–1942, microfilm (New York: New York Times, 1974).

4. *San Francisco Wave*, February 13, 1892: 8.
5. *San Francisco Chronicle*, February 5, 1892: 10; February 15, 1892: 10.
6. Jane Lee Waring to J. Duncan, February 2, 1892, Thomas Lake Harris Correspondence, Syracuse University Library.
7. Jane Lee Waring to Arthur A. Cuthbert, February 4, 1892, box 1, folder 5, V. Valta Parma Collection, Hamilton College Library.
8. Thomas Lake Harris to John S. Weller, February 11, 1892, reel 9, item 238, in Ericson, *Thomas Lake Harris.*
9. *Chicago New Church Independent*, February 1892: 88–90, 94.
10. Jane Lee Waring to Miss [unknown], February 1892, reel 9, item 238, in Ericson, *Thomas Lake Harris.*
11. The term "cognitive dissonance" was coined by sociologists studying an apocalyptic UFO "cult"; see Leon Festinger, Henry W. Riecken, and Stanley Schachter, *When Prophecy Fails: A Social and Psychological Study of a Modern Group that Predicted the Destruction of the World* (Minneapolis: University of Minnesota Press, 1956).
12. *San Francisco Examiner*, February 18, 1892: 9.
13. *San Francisco Call*, February 17, 1892: 8; *San Francisco Chronicle*, February 17, 1892: 5.
14. Ellen Carol Dubois and Linda Gordon, "Seeking Ecstasy on the Battlefield: Danger and Pleasure in Nineteenth-Century Feminist Sexual Thought," *Feminist Studies* 9 (1983): 7–25; Sara Moslener, *Virgin Nation: Sexual Purity and American Adolescence* (New York: Oxford University Press, 2015).
15. Sandra Sizer Frankiel, *California's Spiritual Frontiers: Religious Alternatives in Anglo-Protestantism, 1850–1910* (Berkeley: University of California Press, 1988), 140.
16. *San Francisco New Church Pacific*, January 1892: 214.
17. *San Francisco New Californian: A Theosophic Journal*, February 1892: 287–88.
18. *The Path*, February 1892: 346–47.
19. *London Lucifer*, January 1892: 425.
20. *The Problem of Life and International Magazine of Truth*, June 1891: 299–300.
21. *Chicago Progressive Thinker*, December 26, 1891: 6.
22. *The Problem of Life* 1, no. 1 (January 1890): 41; Molly McGarry, *Ghosts of Futures Past: Spiritualism and the Cultural Politics of Nineteenth-Century America* (Berkeley: University of California Press, 2008), 60–63.
23. *Chicago Religio-Philosophical Journal*, January 2, 1892: 512.
24. *San Francisco Morning Call*, February 16, 1892: 4; February 17, 1892: 8; *San Francisco Chronicle*, February 17, 1892: 5; *San Francisco Evening Bulletin*, February 17, 1892: 1; *Los Angeles Times*, January 17, 1892: 4;
25. *San Francisco Morning Call*, February 16, 1892: 4.
26. Lawrence Sasso to S. C. Chevaillier, February 1892, folder 4, box 12, Poets Garden Records, Special Collections Library, University of Southern California.
27. *Santa Rosa Daily Republican*, February 18, 1892: 4; February 19, 1892: 4.
28. *Sonoma Democrat*, January 30, 1892: 1.
29. *Sonoma Democrat*, February 20, 1892: 1.
30. *Sonoma Democrat*, August 22, 1891: 1.
31. Thomas Lake Harris to Thomas Larkin Thompson, undated [February 1892], reel 13, item 302, in Ericson, *Thomas Lake Harris.*
32. Philip J. Ethington, *The Public City: The Political Construction of Urban Life in San Francisco, 1850–1900* (Cambridge: Cambridge University Press, 1994).
33. *Santa Rosa Daily Democrat*, January 1892: 10.
34. *San Francisco Chronicle*, February 12, 1892: 10; *San Francisco Call*, February 13, 1892: 8.
35. *San Francisco Chronicle*, February 23, 1892: 2; *Santa Rosa Daily Republican*, February 22, 1892: 4.
36. *Sonoma Democrat*, February 27, 1892: 1.
37. *Sonoma Democrat*, September 2, 1882: 3; June 2, 1883: 2; October 10, 1885: 1.
38. J. Avery Shepherd to Thomas Lake Harris, February 18, 1892, reel 13, item 302, in Ericson, *Thomas Lake Harris.*
39. Thomas Lake Harris to C. H. Thompson, February 18, 1892, in Schneider and Lawton, *A Prophet and a Pilgrim*, 549.

40. Sarah and Alzire Chevaillier, "A Card," March 3, 1892, reel 14, item 320, in Ericson, *Thomas Lake Harris.*
41. *Harrisburg Patriot,* December 14, 1891, 4.
42. *San Francisco Examiner,* February 18, 1892: 9.
43. Cyrus Teed, *The Illumination of Koresh: Marvelous Experience of the Great Alchemist Thirty Years Ago, at Utica, N.Y.* (Chicago: Guiding Star Publishing House, n.d.); Howard D. Fine, "The Koreshan Unity: The Chicago Years of a Utopian Community," *Journal of the Illinois State Historical Society* 68 (1975): 213–27.
44. *Chicago Flaming Sword,* July 11, 1891: 4.
45. Sally L. Kitch, *Chaste Liberation: Celibacy and Female Cultural Status* (Urbana: University of Illinois Press, 1989), 59–60, 94–96.
46. Cyrus Teed to Abiel W. K. Andrews, March 20, 1885, folder 22, box 226, Koreshan Unity Collection, State Archives of Florida.
47. *New York Times,* August 10, 1884: 1.
48. Adam Morris, *American Messiahs: False Prophets of a Damned Nation* (New York: Liveright, 2019), 157–59.
49. *Chicago Daily Tribune,* April 10, 1887: 6; *Daily Alta California,* February 15, 1891: 4.
50. John Cleves Symmes, "No. 1. Circular" (St. Louis: n.p., 1818); Brad Whitsel, "Walter Siegmeister's Inner-Earth Utopia," *Utopian Studies* 12 (2001): 82–102; Gillen D'Arcy Wood, *Land of Wondrous Cold: The Race to Discover Antarctica and Unlock the Secrets of Its Ice* (Princeton, NJ: Princeton University Press, 2020), 34–39.
51. *Chicago Daily Tribune,* July 20, 1890: 26.
52. *Cincinnati Enquirer,* July 16, 1890: 6; *Spokane Falls Review,* July 7, 1890: 11.
53. *Chicago Daily Tribune,* August 3, 1890: 26.
54. *San Francisco Call,* August 10, 1891: 7.
55. George Chauncey, "Long-Haired Men and Short-Haired Women: Building a Gay World in the Heart of Bohemia," in *Greenwich Village: Culture and Counterculture,* ed. Rick Beard and Leslie Cohen Berlowitz (New Brunswick, NJ: Rutgers University Press, 1993), 151–64; Arnaldo Testi, "The Gender of Reform Politics: Theodore Roosevelt and the Culture of Masculinity," *Journal of American History* 81 (1995): 1526; Adam Rome, "Political Hermaphrodites: Gender and Environmental Reform in Progressive America," *Environmental History* 11 (2006): 450.
56. *Chicago Flaming Sword,* February 7, 1891: 2.
57. *Chicago Daily Tribune,* August 7, 1891: 8.
58. J. C. Branner, "Memoir of James E. Mills," *Bulletin of the Geological Society of America* 14 (Mar. 31, 1904): 513.
59. *San Francisco Examiner,* December 20, 1891: 8; December 26, 1891: 3.
60. *San Francisco Chronicle,* October 16, 1891: 8; October 27, 1891: 12.
61. *Terre Haute Saturday Evening Mail,* September 19, 1891: 7; *San Francisco Examiner,* February 18, 1892: 3; *San Francisco Call,* February 17, 1892: 7.
62. *Los Angeles Times,* October 27, 1891: 1; *Austin Daily Statesman,* August 8, 1891: 1; *Oakland Tribune,* March 16, 1892: 6.
63. *Chicago Flaming Sword,* January 2, 1892: 1.
64. *Chicago Flaming Sword,* January 30, 1892: 2.
65. *Chicago Flaming Sword,* January 30, 1892: 3.
66. *San Francisco Call,* February 17, 1892: 7.
67. *Chicago Flaming Sword,* January 30, 1892: 2.
68. *Chicago Flaming Sword,* February 6, 1892: 1–2.
69. *Chicago Daily Tribune,* February 25, 1892: 2.
70. *San Francisco Call,* February 17, 1892: 7.
71. *Chicago Daily Tribune,* October 29, 1891: 3; *Shenandoah Evening Herald,* February 26, 1892: 2; *Los Angeles Times,* April 18, 1892: 10.
72. *San Francisco Chronicle,* February 26, 1892: 5.
73. *Los Angeles Times,* June 15, 1891: 3.

Chapter 9

1. *San Francisco Examiner,* March 4, 1892: 1; *London Pall Mall Gazette,* March 30, 1892: 3.
2. *Louisville Courier-Journal,* March 4, 1892: 1.
3. *The Two Worlds: A Journal Devoted to Spiritualism, Occult Science, Ethics, Religion, and Reform,* April 1, 1892: 168

4. *San Francisco Call*, March 4, 1892: 8; *Los Angeles Times*, March 4, 1892: 4; *Sacramento Record-Union*, March 4, 1892: 1.

5. *San Francisco Chronicle*, March 4, 1892: 1.

6. Stephanie Coontz, *Marriage, a History: From Obedience to Intimacy, or How Love Conquered Marriage* (New York: Viking, 2005); Rebecca L. Davis, *More Perfect Unions: The American Search for Marital Bliss* (Cambridge, MA: Harvard University Press, 2010), 17–23; Clare Virginia Eby, *Until Choice Do Us Part: Marriage Reform in the Progressive Era* (Chicago: University of Chicago Press, 2014), 26–32; Nicholas J. Syrett, *American Child Bride: A History of Minors and Marriage in the United States* (Chapel Hill: University of North Carolina Press, 2016), 127–29.

7. Bonnie L. Ford, "Women, Marriage, and Divorce in California, 1849–1872," *California Legal History* 16 (2021): 3032.

8. *San Francisco Examiner*, December 21, 1891: 3.

9. *Feather River Bulletin*, March 28, 1895: 2; Charlotte K. Goldbert, "The Schemes of the Adventuresses: The Abolition and Revival of Common-Law Marriage," *William and Mary Journal of Race, Gender, and Social Justice* 13 (2006–2007): 483–538.

10. *Oakland Tribune*, March 4, 1892: 4.

11. *San Francisco Call*, September 3, 1892: 8.

12. Jane Lee Waring Harris to Richard McCully, March 17, 1892, V. Valta Parma Collection, Hamilton College Library.

13. Jane Lee Waring Harris to Arthur A. Cuthbert, March 29, 1892, V. Valta Parma Collection, Hamilton College Library.

14. Thomas Lake Harris to Richard McCully, March 18, 1892, in *The Brotherhood of the New Life and Thomas Lake Harris*, ed. Richard McCully (Glasgow: John Thomson, 1893), 384–85.

15. Deed book 137, p. 196; Deed book 137, p. 199; Sonoma County Records, Santa Rosa.

16. Deed book 147, p. 271, Sonoma County Records, Santa Rosa.

17. Jane Lee Waring Harris to Kanaye Nagasawa, May 5, 1892, V. Valta Parma Collection, Hamilton College Library.

18. Jane Lee Waring Harris to Arthur A. Cuthbert, March 22, 1892, V. Valta Parma Collection, Hamilton College Library.

19. Jane Lee Waring Harris to Arthur A. Cuthbert, April 24, 1892, V. Valta Parma Collection, Hamilton College Library.

20. Waring Harris to Nagasawa, May 5, 1892.

21. Waring Harris to Cuthbert, March 22, 1892.

22. *Sonoma Democrat*, March 5, 1892: 5.

23. Letter sheet, March 1892, Poets Garden Records, Special Collections Library, University of Southern California.

24. *Chicago New Church Independent*, March 1892, 132–34.

25. *Chicago New Church Independent*, March 1892, 133.

26. Thomas Lake Harris, *The Lord: The Two-in-One, Declared, Manifested, and Glorified* (Brocton, NY: Brotherhood of the New Life, 1876).

27. *Chicago New Church Independent*, March 1892, 136–37; Wayne Alvord, "T. L. Nugent, Texas Populist," *Southwestern Historical Quarterly* 57 (1953): 65–81.

28. *Boston Globe*, April 22, 1892: 10.

29. Alzire A. Chevaillier to Septimus J. Hanna, March 30, 1900, Incoming Correspondence File, Mary Baker Eddy Library, Boston.

30. Margaret Oliphant, "Preface to the New Edition," *Memoir of the Life of Laurence Oliphant, and of Alice Oliphant, His Wife*, rev. ed. (London: Blackwood and Sons, 1892), v–vii.

31. *San Francisco Examiner*, March 16, 1892: 5.

32. *Chicago Tribune*, March 16, 1892: 3; March 21, 1892: 3.

33. *Chicago Tribune*, May 1, 1892: 2.

34. *Chicago Tribune*, May 16, 1892: 1; Lyn Millner, *The Allure of Immortality: An American Cult, a Florida Swamp, and a Renegade Prophet* (Gainesville: University Press of Florida, 2023), 121–22.

35. *Chicago Tribune*, May 15, 1892: 1; May 18, 1892: 3.

36. *San Francisco Chronicle*, April 24, 1892: 11; *Buffalo Courier*, February 27, 1892: 4; May 20, 1892: 4; *New York Urn*, March 25, 1892: 1.

37. *San Francisco Argonaut*, May 23, 1892: 1; June 20, 1892: 3.

38. *Indianapolis Journal*, June 5, 1891: 4; *Pittsburgh Dispatch*, May 13, 1889: 1.

39. *Chicago Tribune*, March 5, 1892: 1; May 8, 1892: 25; May 29, 1892: 33.

40. *Detroit Free Press*, March 29, 1892: 8; *Louisville Courier-Journal*, June 18, 1892: 4; Julieanna Frost, "The Rise and Fall of Prince Michael Mills and the Detroit Jezreelites," *American Communal Societies Quarterly* 8 (2014): 146–62.
41. Reprinted in *Pratt (Kansas) Republican*, April 28, 1892: 4.
42. *Chicago Figaro*, May 28, 1892: 219.
43. *Boston Globe*, December 9, 1891: 10
44. *Chicago Tribune*, March 6, 1892: 12.
45. *Chicago Tribune*, May 8, 1892: 25; *Louisville Courier-Journal*, June 18, 1892: 4.
46. Allan Peterkin, *One Thousand Beards: A Cultural History of Facial Hair* (Vancouver: Arsenal Pulp Press, 2001), 86–96; Christopher Oldstone-Moore, *Of Beards and Men: The Revealing History of Facial Hair* (Chicago: University of Chicago Press, 2016), 190, 212–19.
47. *San Francisco Chronicle*, June 11, 1891: 7; December 13, 1891: 10; *New York Sun*, July 6, 1891: 4; *St. Louis Dispatch*, October 11, 1891: 1; *Exeter Daily Gazette*, August 23, 1892: 6.
48. *San Francisco Chronicle*, December 13, 1891: 10.
49. *San Francisco Examiner*, November 17, 1891: 3.
50. *Salt Lake City Daily Tribune*, October 28, 1890: 2; *Chicago Tribune*, October 28, 1890: 1; Amanda Frisken, *Graphic News: How Sensational Images Transformed Nineteenth-Century Journalism* (Champaign: University of Illinois Press, 2020), 85–122.
51. Jennifer Graber, "Beyond Prophecy: Native Visionaries in American Religious Studies," *American Religion* 2 (2020): 53–54.
52. *Chicago Progressive Thinker*, June 25, 1892: 4.
53. Reprinted in *New York Evangelist*, September 3, 1891: 3.
54. James H. Deering, ed., *The Penal Code of California, Enacted in 1872; as Amended up to and Including 1903* (San Francisco: Bancroft-Whitney Co., 1903), 119, 123-24, 560.
55. *San Francisco Chronicle*, June 3, 1892: 3.
56. *Sonoma Democrat*, June 4, 1892: 5.
57. *Santa Rosa Daily Republican*, June 3, 1892: 4.
58. *San Francisco Chronicle*, June 4, 1892: 6.
59. Jane Lee Waring Harris to Arthur A. Cuthbert, June 5, 1892; June 6, 1892, V. Valta Parma Collection, Hamilton College Library.
60. "Extract from letters from Mrs. Harris to friends at Fountaingrove," June 1892, Thomas Lake Harris Correspondence, Syracuse University Library.
61. *Enterprise (Kansas) Integral Co-Operator*, March 3, 1892: 7.
62. "Extract from letters from Mrs. Harris."
63. María del Carmen Collado, "Entrepreneurs and Their Businesses During the Mexican Revolution," *Business History Review* 86 (2012): 719–74; Jason Ruiz, *Americans in the Treasure House: Travel to Porfirian Mexico and the Cultural Politics of Empire* (Austin: University of Texas Press, 2014); Kelly Lytle Hernández, *Bad Mexicans: Race, Empire, and Revolution in the Borderlands* (New York: W. W. Norton, 2022), 33–39.
64. Thomas Lake Harris to Arthur A. Cuthbert, November 8, 1892, V. Valta Parma Collection, Hamilton College Library.
65. Thomas Lake Harris to Arthur A. Cuthbert, November 14, 1892, V. Valta Parma Collection, Hamilton College Library.
66. Jane Lee Waring Harris to Arthur A. Cuthbert, November 28, 1892, V. Valta Parma Collection, Hamilton College Library.
67. Thomas Lake Harris to Arthur A. Cuthbert, n.d. [fall 1892], V. Valta Parma Collection, Hamilton College Library.
68. *San Francisco Call*, September 3, 1892: 8.
69. *Petaluma Imprint*, January 4, 1893.
70. Kimberly A. Hamlin, *Free Thinker: Sex, Suffrage, and the Extraordinary Life of Helen Hamilton Gardner* (New York: W. W. Norton, 2020), 130.
71. *Chicago New Church Independent*, July 1892: 301–2.
72. *Chicago New Church Independent*, July 1892: 304.
73. *Petaluma Imprint*, January 4, 1893.
74. *Chicago New Church Independent*, July 1892: 338.
75. *San Francisco Call*, January 4, 1893: 8.
76. *Chicago New Church Independent*, July 1892: 340.

Chapter 10

1. *Oakland Tribune*, May 28, 1891: 5; *San Francisco Chronicle*, January 5, 1896: 17; Herbert W. Schneider and George Lawton, *A Prophet and a Pilgrim: Being the Incredible History of Thomas Lake Harris and Laurence Oliphant* (New York: Columbia University Press, 1942), 483.
2. *Sonoma County Coroner's Inquests, 1852–1898* (Santa Rosa: Sonoma County Genealogical Society, 1991), 36; *San Francisco Chronicle*, January 4, 1896: 3.
3. *San Francisco Call*, February 14, 1896: 4.
4. *San Francisco Call*, September 3, 1892: 8; *New York Sun*, January 6, 1896: 9.
5. *San Francisco Examiner*, October 21, 1893: 14.
6. *San Francisco Chronicle*, January 4, 1896: 3; January 5, 1896: 17–18; January 6, 1896: 3; *Los Angeles Times*, January 5, 1896: 3; *San Francisco Examiner*, January 12, 1896: 27.
7. *San Francisco Chronicle*, January 5, 1896: 17–18; February 16, 1896: 24.
8. Carol K. Coburn and Martha Smith, *Spirited Lives: How Nuns Shaped Catholic Culture and American Life, 1836–1920* (Chapel Hill: University of North Carolina Press, 1999), 287.
9. *San Francisco Chronicle*, February 14, 1896: 1–2.
10. *San Francisco Examiner*, January 12, 1896: 27; *San Francisco Chronicle*, February 14, 1896: 1–2; *San Francisco Call*, February 15, 1896: 3.
11. *San Francisco Chronicle*, January 6, 1896: 3.
12. *San Francisco Chronicle*, January 5, 1896: 17–18.
13. *San Francisco Chronicle*, February 16, 1896: 24.
14. *San Francisco Chronicle*, February 15, 1896: 6; *San Francisco Call*, February 14, 1896: 4.
15. Jane Lee Waring Harris, diary, July 30, 1904; September 4, 1904; July 5, 1906, in Schneider and Lawton, *A Prophet and a Pilgrim*, 485.
16. Thomas Lake Harris to Arthur A. Cuthbert, July 3, 1893, in Schneider and Lawton, *A Prophet and a Pilgrim*, 478.
17. Thomas Lake Harris to Kanaye Nagasawa, January 23, 1897, V. Valta Parma Collection, Hamilton College Library, New York.
18. "Extracts from letters from Mrs. Harris," April 14, 1896, Thomas Lake Harris Correspondence, Syracuse University Library.
19. Jane Lee Waring Harris, diary, October 16, 1896, in Schneider and Lawton, *A Prophet and a Pilgrim*, 494.
20. *San Francisco Examiner*, September 20, 1896: 27; Thomas Lake Harris, "An Autobiographical Letter," January 7, 1896, 12, reel 7, item 55, in Jack T. Ericson, ed., *Thomas Lake Harris and the Brotherhood of the New Life: Books, Pamphlets, Serials and Manuscripts, 1854–1942*, microfilm (New York: New York Times, 1974).

Chapter 11

1. Jane Lee Waring Harris, to the Brotherhood of the New Life, March 29, 1906, in Herbert W. Schneider and George Lawton, *A Prophet and a Pilgrim: Being the Incredible History of Thomas Lake Harris and Laurence Oliphant* (New York: Columbia University Press, 1942), 502.
2. Arthur A. Cuthbert to the Brotherhood of the New Life, April 8, 1906; Jane Lee Waring Harris to William T. Stead, June 4, 1906, V. Valta Parma Collection, Hamilton College Library.
3. Two exceptions were *Santa Rosa Republican*, May 23, 1906: 2; and *Petaluma Daily Morning Courier*, May 23, 1906: 2.
4. Santa Rosa Commandery No. 14, Knights Templar, "Tribute to Sir Thomas Lake Harris," 1906, reel 9, item 242, in Jack T. Ericson, ed., *Thomas Lake Harris and the Brotherhood of the New Life: Books, Pamphlets, Serials and Manuscripts, 1854–1942*, microfilm (New York: New York Times, 1974).
5. *Harper's Weekly*, July 21, 1906: 1015.
6. Thomas Lake Harris, *The Triumph of Life* (Glasgow: C. W. Pearce & Co., 1903), 1–4; Thomas Lake Harris, *The Song of Theos* (Glasgow, C. W. Pearce & Co., 1903).
7. Jane Lee Waring Harris to Lady Alena, August 10, 1896, "Fountaingrove—Edwin Markham" folder, Gaye LeBaron Collection, Special Collections, Sonoma State University Library.
8. Jane Lee Waring Harris, diary, August 19, 1899, in Schneider and Lawton, *A Prophet and a Pilgrim*, 497.
9. Ray Strachey, ed., *Religious Fanaticism: Extracts from the Papers of Hannah Whitall Smith* (London: Faber & Gwyer, 1928), 237–38.

10. *San Francisco Call*, December 18, 1900: 5; Deed book 192, p. 204, Sonoma County Records, Santa Rosa. Officially the lands were sold for $40,000, but the colonists never paid.
11. *San Francisco Philosophical Journal*, January 19, 1901: 4.
12. *New York Sun*, December 25, 1900: 7.
13. *San Francisco Call*, April 10, 1895: 2; October 10, 1897: 18; *Belfast News-Letter*, May 2, 1896: 4; *Petaluma Daily Morning Courier*, November 29, 1898: 4.
14. *San Francisco Call*, May 19, 1901: 5.
15. On Koreshanity as a "cult," see *Pittsburgh Daily Post*, August 26, 1895: 3; on spiritualism, see *Seattle Post-Intelligencer*, February 3, 1895: 7; *New York Sun*, December 27, 1895: 5; *San Francisco Call*, May 27, 1896: 10; on Christian Science, see *San Francisco Call*, December 14, 1891: 1; *Coconino Weekly Sun*, November 21: 1895, 6; *Copper Country Evening News*, May 6, 1896: 1; on Theosophy, see *Indianapolis Journal*, March 9, 1891: 4; *Spokane Review*, August 15, 1891: 4; *York (Pennsylvania) Daily*, July 25, 1893: 2; *Madison Daily Leader*, March 2, 1894: 4; on Mormons, see *Calgary Weekly Herald*, August 6, 1890: 2; *London Pall Mall Gazette*, June 16, 1893: 11; *Minneapolis Journal*, October 30, 1899: 4.
16. *Raleigh Christian Advocate*, January 17, 1894: 1; Lafcadio Hearn, *Glimpses of Unfamiliar Japan*, vol. 2 (Boston: Houghton, Mifflin, 1894), 385; *Baptist Missionary Review* 4 (1898): 404; L. Austine Waddell, *The Buddhism of Tibet* (London: Luzac & Co., 1899); *Tacoma News Tribune*, March 7, 1891: 8; *Literary Digest*, December 11, 1897: 983; Philip Jenkins, *Mystics and Messiahs: Cults and New Religions in American History* (New York: Oxford University Press, 2000), 48–49.
17. As part of being labeled a cult, Christian Science was "heathenized"; see Pamela E. Klassen, *Spirits of Protestantism: Medicine, Healing, and Liberal Christianity* (Berkeley: University of California Press, 2011), 79–80.
18. A. H. Barrington, *The Anti-Christian Cults* (Milwaukee: Young Churchman Co., 1898), 5, 9.
19. George Hamilton Combs, *Some Latter-Day Religions* (Chicago: Fleming H. Revell Company, 1899); John Elward Brown, *In the Cult Kingdom* (Siloam Springs, AR: International Federation Publishing Company, 1918); Gaius Glenn Atkins, *Modern Religious Cults and Movements* (New York: Fleming H. Revell Company, 1923); Charles W. Ferguson, *A Confusion of Tongues* (Garden City, NY: Doubleday, 1928); J. K. Van Baalen, *The Chaos of Cults* (Grand Rapids: William B. Eerdmans, 1938).
20. *Los Angeles Evening Post-Record*, March 10, 1903: 2; *San Francisco Chronicle*, June 4, 1905: 25; *Los Angeles Herald*, August 11, 1907: 36; *San Francisco Call*, March 10, 1908: 5; February 9, 1909, 1; July 21, 1912: 45.
21. *Oakland Tribune*, February 7, 1909: 33.
22. *San Francisco Chronicle*, July 12, 1908: 22.
23. *Fresno Morning Republican*, August 7, 1906: 8; *San Francisco Examiner*, September 20, 1909: 1, 3; *Los Angeles Times*, July 16, 1906: 13.
24. The "silk underwear cult" was Mazdaznan; see *Stockton Evening Record*, December 5, 1918: 5.
25. Michael Williams, "Pan in California," *Catholic World*, April 1919: 20, 22.
26. *San Francisco Call*, October 28, 1895: 4; May 21, 1896: 13; *New York World*, June 27, 1897: 22; *San Francisco Examiner*, December 14, 1910: 1.

Chapter 12

1. *Boston Evening Transcript*, January 30, 1893: 5.
2. Quoted in Ruth Le Prade, "The Angel of the Jails," 1942, p. 371, box 25, Poets Garden Records, Special Collections Library, University of Southern California.
3. Le Prade, "The Angel of the Jails," 373.
4. Alzire A. Chevaillier to Gustave Percival Wicksell, December 11, 1893, reel 13, item 302, in Jack T. Ericson, ed., *Thomas Lake Harris and the Brotherhood of the New Life: Books, Pamphlets, Serials and Manuscripts, 1854–1942*, microfilm (New York: New York Times, 1974).
5. Alzire A. Chevaillier, "Address Before the American Railway Union Men of Los Angeles," July 11, 1894, folder 7, box 13, Poets Garden Records, Special Collections Library, University of Southern California.
6. *Los Angeles Evening Express*, October 23, 1900: 7; October 25, 1900: 5.
7. Beryl Satter, *Each Mind a Kingdom: American Women, Sexual Purity, and the New Thought Movement, 1875–1920* (Berkeley: University of California Press, 1999); Catherine L. Albanese, *The Delight Makers: Anglo-American Metaphysical Religion and the Pursuit of Happiness* (Chicago: University of Chicago Press, 2023), 243–85.

8. *Los Angeles Times*, July 14, 1925: 25.
9. *Los Angeles Master Mind*, August 1914: 180; Alzire A. Chevaillier to Septimus J. Hanna, March 30, 1900, Incoming Correspondence File, Mary Baker Eddy Library, Boston.
10. Satter, *Each Mind a Kingdom*, 7, 225–27.
11. Chevaillier to Hanna, March 30, 1900.
12. *Marshall (Texas) Evening Messenger*, April 18, 1904: 4.
13. Alzire A. Chevaillier to Ellen Browning Scripps, July 21, 1904, folder 75, drawer 1, Ellen Browning Scripps Collection, Correspondence, Scripps College.
14. Alzire A. Chevaillier to Ellen Browning Scripps, July 23, 1904, folder 75, drawer 1, Ellen Browning Scripps Collection, Correspondence, Scripps College.
15. Alice B. Stockham, *Karezza: Ethics of Marriage* (Chicago: Alice B. Stockham & Co., 1896), 23–24.
16. Marsha Silberman, "The Perfect Storm: Late Nineteenth-Century Chicago Sex Radicals: Moses Harman, Ida Craddock, Alice Stockham, and the Comstock Obscenity Laws," *Journal of the Illinois State Historical Society* 102 (2009): 324–67.
17. *San Francisco Chronicle*, February 17, 1892: 5.
18. Joanne E. Passet, *Sex Radicals and the Quest for Women's Equality* (Urbana: University of Illinois Press, 2003), 135–51; Leigh Eric Schmidt, *Heaven's Bride: The Unprintable Life of Ida C. Craddock, American Mystic, Scholar, Sexologist, Martyr, and Madwoman* (New York: Basic Books, 2010).
19. Chevaillier to Browning Scripps, July 23, 1904.
20. *McClure's*, December 1906: 212.
21. *Oakland Tribune*, December 10, 1906: 3; *Christian Science Journal*, January 1907: 631.
22. Mary Baker Eddy, *Science and Health* (Boston: Christian Science Publishing Co., 1875), 144.
23. Alzire A. Chevaillier to Caroline M. Severance, February 24, 1905, folder 10, box 15, Caroline M. Severance Papers, Huntington Library, Los Angeles.
24. *Los Angeles Herald*, April 13, 1908: 3; *Los Angeles Times*, November 28, 1916: 11; December 20, 1916: 19; *Los Angeles Evening Express*, January 31, 1917: 9; January 22, 1918: 15.
25. *Los Angeles Evening Post-Record*, January 13, 1927: 2; *Los Angeles Times*, July 4, 1927: 18.
26. *Los Angeles Times*, December 10, 1916: 17.
27. Kelly Lytle Hernández, *City of Inmates: Conquest, Rebellion, and the Rise of Human Caging in Los Angeles, 1771–1965* (Chapel Hill: University of North Carolina Press, 2017), 2, 62.
28. *Los Angeles Times*, January 6, 1930: 22; November 20, 1932: B6; April 27, 1935: A1.
29. Alzire A. Chevaillier to Ruth St. Denis, June 18, 1931, Personal Correspondence, Ruth St. Denis Letters, Jerome Robbins Dance Division, New York Public Library.
30. Faith Chevaillier, "International Hymn of Love and Peace," 1928, folder 6, box 42, Poets Garden Records, Special Collections Library, University of Southern California.
31. Edwin Markham, *California the Wonderful* (New York: Hearst's International Library Co., 1914), 341; Barna Csuros, "The Poet and the Seer," *Markham Review* 4 (Feb. 1969): 1–5.
32. Alzire A. Chevaillier, "Notes About My Humble Life Work," ca. 1932, Poets Garden Records, Special Collections Library, University of Southern California.
33. Le Prade, "The Angel of the Jails," 330.
34. Le Prade, "The Angle of the Jails," 355–57.
35. *San Francisco Call*, May 23, 1897: 25; *Los Angeles Times*, January 3, 1925: 20; Bailey Millard, *History of San Francisco Bay Region*, vol. 1 (Chicago: American Historical Society, 1924), 164.
36. Philip Jenkins, *Mystics and Messiahs: Cults and New Religions in American History* (New York: Oxford University Press, 2000), 43–44; Paul Eli Ivey, *Radiance from Halcyon: A Utopian Experiment in Religion and Science* (Minneapolis: University of Minnesota Press, 2013), 27.
37. *Los Angeles Times Sunday Magazine*, June 16, 1935: 15.

Chapter 13

1. Jane Lee Waring Harris to Edwin Markham, February 26, 1899, "Fountaingrove—Edwin Markham" folder, Gaye LeBaron Collection, Special Collections, Sonoma State University Library.
2. Ōsui Arai to Kanaye Nagasawa, July 7, 1899; Ōsui Arai to Edwin Markham, May 5, 1902, "Fountaingrove—Edwin Markham" folder, Gaye LeBaron Collection, Special Collections, Sonoma State University Library; Chinami Oka, "Arai Ōsui and the Transnational Reimagination of Civilization in the Late Nineteenth-Century United States," *Historical Journal*

66 (2023): 101–21; Chinami Oka, *Reopening the Opening of Japan: Transnational Approaches to Modern Japan and the Wider World* (New York: Brill, 2023), 300–23.

3. Herbert W. Schneider and George Lawton, *A Prophet and a Pilgrim: Being the Incredible History of Thomas Lake Harris and Laurence Oliphant* (New York: Columbia University Press, 1942), 488.

4. *Petaluma Argus-Courier*, June 14, 1901: 1.

5. *Santa Rosa Republican*, August 10, 1906: 4; May 9, 1911: 8; *Petaluma Daily Morning Courier*, November 15, 1898: 3; August 31, 1916: 6.

6. Kanaye Nagasawa to Edwin Markham, March 14, 1921, reel 9, item 304, in Jack T. Ericson, ed., *Thomas Lake Harris and the Brotherhood of the New Life: Books, Pamphlets, Serials and Manuscripts, 1854–1942*, microfilm (New York: New York Times, 1974).

7. Official records book 370, p. 234, Sonoma County Records, Santa Rosa; Paul Akiria Kadota and Terry Earl Jones, *Kanaye Nagasawa: A Biography of a Satsuma Student* (Kagoshima, Japan: Kagoshima Prefectural Junior College, 1990), 150–52.

8. Eleanor Webley to George Lawton, January 16, 1930, reel 13, item 308; Robert M. Hart to Kanaye Nagasawa, August 1925, reel 13, item 304, in Ericson, *Thomas Lake Harris*.

9. Kanaye Nagasawa to Robert M. Hart, August 17, 1925, reel 13, item 304, in Ericson, *Thomas Lake Harris*.

10. Robert M. Hart to Kanaye Nagasawa, August 27, 1925, reel 13, item 306, in Ericson, *Thomas Lake Harris*.

11. *Santa Rosa Press Democrat*, September 23, 1930: 1; Yuji Ichioka, *The Issei: The World of the First Generation Japanese Immigrants* (New York: Free Press, 1988), 153–56; Ronald Takaki, *Strangers from a Different Shore: A History of Asian Americans* (New York: Penguin Books, 1989), 203–8.

12. *Santa Rosa Press Democrat*, February 25, 1931: 2; February 26, 1931: 7.

13. *Santa Rosa Press Democrat*, September 17, 1931: 6.

14. Appellant's Reply Brief, Hart vs. Nagasawa, 1933, California Supreme Court, Sac. No. 4647, pp. 66, 77.

15. Hart v. Nagasawa, California Supreme Court, 24 P.2d 815 (Cal. 1933).

16. Roger Daniels, *The Politics of Prejudice* (Berkeley: University of California Press, 1962), 10; Don and Nadine Hata, "George Shima: 'The Potato King of California,'" *Journal of the West* 25 (1986): 55–63; Elliott Robert Barkan, *From All Points: America's Immigrant West, 1870s–1952* (Bloomington: Indiana University Press, 2007), 290.

17. *Oakland Tribune*, June 25, 1914: 9; *Sonoma West Times and News*, May 15, 1915: 2.

18. *Long Beach Press Telegram*, March 22, 1915, 2; Kadota and Jones, *Kanaye Nagasawa*, 153.

19. Idwall Jones, *Vines in the Sun* (New York: William Morrow, 1949), 132.

20. "Kanaye Nagasawa Life History," July 18, 1924, document 145, box 26, Survey of Race Relations, Hoover Institute Library, Stanford University; Eckard Toy, "Whose Frontier?: The Survey of Race Relations on the Pacific Coast in the 1920s," *Oregon Historical Quarterly* 107 (2006): 36–63.

21. *Los Angeles Japan-California Daily News*, August 27, 1933: 8; March 19, 1934: 8.

22. Kanaye Nagasawa to Edwin Markham, March 14, 1921; September 5, 1925, reel 13, item 304, in Ericson, *Thomas Lake Harris*.

23. "Kanaye Nagasawa Life History."

24. Thomas Lockley, "Nagasawa Kanaye: The Spiritual Life of California's Japanese Wine Pioneer," 桜文論叢 97 (2018): 22–23.

25. *Santa Rosa Press Democrat*, May 21, 1984: 15.

26. Official Records book 300, p. 353, Sonoma County Records, Santa Rosa.

27. *Santa Rosa Press Democrat*, May 16, 1931: 1; March 6, 1934: 3; Kadota and Jones, *Kanaye Nagasawa*, 158.

28. *History of Sonoma County, California*, vol. 2 (Chicago: S. J. Clarke Publishing Co., 1926), 702.

29. *Santa Rosa Press Democrat*, March 6, 1934: 3.

30. *Santa Rosa Press Democrat*, March 2, 1934: 2; Kadota and Jones, *Kanaye Nagasawa*, 159.

31. Deed book 418, pp. 217–218; Deed book 419, pp. 196–197; Official Records book, 392, p. 476; Deed book 422, p. 86, Sonoma County Records, Santa Rosa.

32. Deed book 422 p. 85, Sonoma County Records, Santa Rosa.

33. *Santa Rosa Press Democrat*, November 7, 1985: 29.

34. Japanese-American Internee Data File, 1942–1946, National Archives, Washington D.C.

35. *Stockton El Joaquin*, July 1, 1942; August 5, 1942: 5; *Rohwer Outpost*, March 27, 1943: 1; Nat R. Griswold, "Rohwer: From Final Report: Historical Statistical-Functional Report of Community

Activities Section," p. 24, 1945, Japanese American Relocation Digital Archive, Bancroft Library, University of California, Berkeley.

36. Gaye LeBaron and Bart Casey, *The Wonder Seekers of Fountaingrove* (Santa Rosa: Historia II Publication, 2018), 177.

Epilogue

1. *Santa Rosa Press Democrat*, June 27, 1937: 58.
2. *San Francisco Examiner*, April 3, 1948: 9; *The Fabulous Treasures of Fountaingrove* (San Francisco: Butterfield & Butterfield, 1948), "Fountaingrove—General" folder, Gaye LeBaron Collection, Special Collections, Sonoma State University Library.
3. *Santa Rosa Press Democrat*, January 4, 1953: 29; Fountaingrove Ranch letterhead, "Fountaingrove—History 1" folder, Gaye LeBaron Collection, Special Collections, Sonoma State University Library.
4. *Santa Rosa Press Democrat*, January 17, 1957: 5.
5. *Santa Rosa Press Democrat*, December 5, 1978: 20; Deed book 2707, p. 104; Deed book 2835, p. 718; Deed book 2724, p. 951; Deed book 3537, p. 557, Sonoma County Records, Santa Rosa.
6. *Santa Rosa Press Democrat*, June 26, 2006: B1, B3.
7. *Sacramento Bee*, October 11, 2017: A9; Lizzie Johnson, *Paradise: One Town's Struggle to Survive an American Wildfire* (New York: Crown, 2021), 400.
8. See the Gaye LeBaron Collection, Special Collections, Sonoma State University Library.
9. *Santa Rosa Press Democrat*, November 10, 1985: 16; May 2, 2007; Greenwich Development Company, brochure for Southridge and Firridge, 1985, "Fountaingrove—General 3" folder, Gaye LeBaron Collection, Special Collections, Sonoma State University Library.
10. "Our Story," Fountaingrove Club website, accessed June 2024, https://www.thefountaingroveclub.com/our-story.
11. *Santa Rosa Press Democrat*, October 15, 1986: 9.
12. *Santa Rosa Press Democrat*, November 5, 1985: 3.
13. Ronald Reagan, "Address Before the Japanese Diet in Tokyo," November 11, 1983, *Public Papers of the Presidents of the United States: Ronald Reagan, 1983*, vol. 2 (Washington, D.C.: Government Printing Office, 1985), 1574.
14. Robert G. Lee, *Orientals: Asian Americans in Popular Culture* (Philadelphia: Temple University Press, 1999), 145–61; Ellen Wu, *The Color of Success: Asian Americans and the Origins of the Model Minority* (Princeton, NJ: Princeton University Press, 2014).
15. Debra A. Klein, "The Grape King from Shogun Japan," *Daily Beast*, April 3, 2014, https://www.thedailybeast.com/the-grape-king-from-shogun-japan.
16. David G. Bromley and Anson D. Shupe, *Strange Gods: The Great American Cult Scare* (Boston: Beacon Press, 1981); Sean McCloud, *Making the American Religious Fringe: Exotics, Subversives, and Journalists, 1955–1993* (Chapel Hill: University of North Carolina Press, 2004).
17. Tim Reiterman, *Raven: The Untold Story of the Rev. Jim Jones and His People* (New York: E. P. Dutton, 1982); Adam Morris, *American Messiahs: False Prophets of a Damned Nation* (New York: Liveright, 2019), 292–301.
18. Robert V. Hine, *California's Utopian Colonies*, rev. ed. (Berkeley: University of California Press, 1983), xii; *New York Newsday*, March 14, 1993: 32; Susan J. Palmer, "NXIVM and #MeToo," *Nova Religio: The Journal of Alternative and Emergent Religions* 24 (2021): 107.
19. Susan L. Carruthers, *Cold War Captives: Imprisonment, Escape, and Brainwashing* (Berkeley: University of California Press, 2009); Matthew W. Dunne, *Cold War State of Mind: Brainwashing and Postwar American Society* (Amherst: University of Massachusetts Press; 2013); Joel E. Dimsdale, *Dark Persuasion: A History of Brainwashing from Pavlov to Social Media* (New Haven, CT: Yale University Press, 2021); Rebecca L. Davis, *Public Confessions: The Religious Conversions that Changed American Politics* (Chapel Hill: University of North Carolina Press, 2021), 90.
20. Susan Jean Palmer, *Moon Sisters, Krishna Mothers, Rajneesh Lovers: Women's Roles in New Religions* (Syracuse: Syracuse University Press, 1994); William Sims Bainbridge, *The Endtime Family: Children of God* (Albany: SUNY Press, 2002); Stuart A. Wright and James T. Richardson, "The Fundamentalist Latter Day Saints After the Texas State Raid: Assessing a Post-Raid Movement Trajectory," *Nova Religio: The Journal of Alternative and Emergent Religions* 17 (2014): 83–97; Laura Vance, *Women in New Religions* (New York: New York University Press, 2015); Megan Goodwin, *Abusing Religion: Literary Persecution, Sex Scandals, and American*

Minority Religions (New Brunswick, NJ: Rutgers University Press, 2020); Sarah Berman, *Don't Call It a Cult: The Shocking Story of Keith Raniere and the Women of NXIVM* (Lebanon, NH: Steerforth Press, 2021); *Stolen Youth: Inside the Cult at Sarah Lawrence*, Zachary Heinzerling, dir., Hulu, 2023.

21. Rebecca Moore, *Peoples Temple and Jonestown in the Twenty-First Century* (Cambridge: Cambridge University Press, 2022); Richard Ken Evans, *MOVE: An American Religion* (New York: Oxford University Press, 2020); Carl Abbott, "Revisiting Rajneeshpuram: Oregon's Largest Utopian Community as Western History," *Oregon Historical Quarterly* 116 (2015): 414–47; Emily Suzanne Clark and Brad Stoddard, eds., *Race and New Religious Movements in the U.S.A.: A Documentary Reader* (London: Bloomsbury Academic, 2019).

22. McCloud, *Making the American Religious Fringe*, 163; *Chicago Tribune*, November 23, 1978: 5.

23. Such considerations include Carey McWilliams, "The Cults of California," *Atlantic Monthly*, March 1946; *New York Times*, November 30, 1978: A18; *Chicago Tribune*, November 23, 1978: 1, 5; *Los Angeles Times*, November 27, 1978: C7; and Jane Borden, "What Is It About California and Cults?," *Vanity Fair*, September 3, 2020, https://www.vanityfair.com/hollywood/2020/09/california-cults-nxivm-the-vow.

24. *Petaluma Argus-Courier*, May 1, 1963: 2; *Santa Rosa Oak Leaf*, October 1980: 1; Harvey J. Hansen, "The Mystery of Fountain Grove?," 1976, "Fountaingrove—History 1" folder, Gaye LeBaron Collection, Special Collections, Sonoma State University Library.

25. *Santa Rosa Press Democrat*, September 28, 1980: 15; October 5, 1980: 15; *Mattoon (Ill.) Journal Gazette*, December 16, 1978: 3.

26. *London Daily Telegraph*, March 10, 1981: 10; April 1, 1981: 3; *Berkeley Gazette*, April 1, 1981: 1.

27. Aled Thomas and Edward Graham-Hyde, eds., *"Cult" Rhetoric in the 21st Century: Deconstructing the Study of New Religious Movements* (New York: Bloomsbury, 2024).

28. Goodwin, *Abusing Religion*, 1–2.

Acknowledgments

I first learned about Thomas Lake Harris, Alzire Chevaillier, and the Fountaingrove scandal in the pages of Robert V. Hine's book *California's Utopian Colonies*, which I read while in graduate school at UCLA. I was hunting for a topic for Stephen Aron's American West research seminar, and Hine's treatment, while brief, grabbed me. Many years later, this book is the final result of that grabbing. My thanks go to Steve Aron for his guidance over those years. A special thank you goes to Barbara Loomis, who introduced me to Paul E. Johnson and Sean Wilentz's *The Kingdom of Matthias*, another inspiration for this book.

Primary sources related to Harris and the Brotherhood of the New Life are scattered in several different repositories, and I owe an enormous debt to the archivists who helped me access those materials. After Harris's death, his widow Jane Lee Waring Harris turned the bulk of his unpublished writings over to Edwin Markham with the idea that he would organize and edit them into an anthology for public consumption, a project Markham never completed. Most of those manuscripts are now at Wagner College; my thanks go to Lisa Holland for her help accessing them. Another large collection of Harris-related materials is at Columbia University, much of which was compiled by Herbert W. Schneider and George Lawton during research for their book *A Prophet and a Pilgrim*; my thanks go to Kevin Schlottmann at Columbia for his willingness to keep looking for items I was certain they owned! A third collection, correspondence gifted to collector V. Valta Parma by Charles Pearce's widow Isabella, is at Hamilton College; a huge thank you goes to Christian Goodwillie and Mark Tillson for the friendly assistance they gave me when I visited Hamilton. A fourth collection, compiled by Santa Rosa journalist Gaye LeBaron, is at Sonoma State University; my thanks to Julie Dinkins (and to Gaye!) for help using it.

I am also grateful to the many archivists and librarians at other institutions who helped me find crucial primary sources for this book. These include the ones I personally visited—University of Southern California Special Collections, Special Collections Research Center at Syracuse University, Huntington Library, Center for Swedenborgian Studies, Urbana University

Library, Sonoma County History and Genealogy Library, Sonoma County Recorder's Office, Museum of Sonoma County, Bancroft Library at U.C. Berkeley, and Stanford University's Hoover Institute Library—as well as others with which I corresponded, including New York Public Library for the Performing Arts, Boston University Library, Harvard University Library, Yale University Library, University of Michigan Library, Massachusetts Historical Society, Scripps College Library, Indiana State University Special Collections, Asbury Seminary Library, Swedenborgian Library at Bryn Athyn College, Santa Rosa Junior College Library, State Archives of Florida, East Texas Research Center, Mohonk Mountain House, Haverford College Quaker & Special Collections, University of Pennsylvania's Kislak Center, University of Virginia Special Collections, and the indispensable International Association for the Preservation of Spiritualist and Occult Periodicals. The Mary Baker Eddy Library in Boston graciously supported my research with a summer fellowship that allowed me to visit. I also received funding for this book from the American Council of Learned Societies, Loyola Marymount University's American Cultures program (shout out to my student researcher extraordinaire, Michael Zwick!), Indiana University, Wittenberg University, and Department of History and Faculty Senate at Texas State University.

So many friends, colleagues, and fellow travelers kindly read and offered feedback on portions of this book (all errors remain my own, of course). These include my Young Scholars of American Religion cohort (everyone in the group but especially Quincy Newell, Jeff Wilson, and Ann Braude) and my fellow members of Southern Methodist University's Religion in the North American West Symposium, especially Brandi Denison and Brett Hendrickson and my summer 2022 writing group, Carleigh Beriont, Tom Bremer, and Lynne Gerber. At Texas State University, many colleagues offered feedback on chapter drafts; special thanks go to Jessica Pliley, Anadelia Romo, Joseph Laycock, Joaquín Rivaya-Martínez, Shannon Duffy, Dwonna Goldstone, Peter Dedek, Natasha Mikles, and Caroline Ritter. Others who graciously offered feedback or research help include Jennifer Graber, Kathryn Gin Lum, James Bennett, James T. Campbell, Jane Yamashiro, Ian Wilson, Tanya Cheadle, Valerie Matsumoto, Amy Sueyoshi, Andrew Leong, Seth Jacobowitz, Brandon Bayne, Judith Weisenfeld, and my fellow panelists at meetings of the American Academy of Religion, Western History Association, Organization of American Historians, American Studies Association, and Pacific Coast Branch of the American Historical

Association. I'd also like to thank Theodore Calderara and Zara Cannon-Mohammed at Oxford University Press for their support and editorial guidance, as well as anonymous reviewers for Oxford and the *Journal of the Gilded Age and Progressive Era*.

The final thank you goes to my wife, Geneva Gano, who read the entire manuscript and entertained countless conversations about Fountaingrove over the years. This book simply would not exist without her encouragement, insights, and love.

Index